516.2 Hi

W9-BVZ-209

The high school geometry tutor

- 809 1341

# WHAT THIS BOOK IS FOR

For as long as geometry has been taught in high schools, students have found this subject difficult to understand and learn. Despite the publication of hundreds of textbooks in this field, each one intended to provide an improvement over previous textbooks, students continue to remain perplexed, and the subject is often taken in class only to meet school/departmental requirements for a selected course of study.

In a study of the problem, REA found the following basic reasons underlying students' difficulties with geometry taught in schools:

(a) No systematic rules of analysis have been developed which students may follow in a step-by-step manner to solve the usual problems encountered. This results from the fact that the numerous different conditions and principles which may be involved in a problem, lead to many possible different methods of solution. To prescribe a set of rules to be followed for each of the possible variations, would involve an enormous number of rules and steps to be searched through by students, and this task would perhaps be more burdensome than solving the problem directly with some accompanying trial and error to find the correct solution route.

(b) Textbooks currently available will usually explain a given principle in a few pages written by a professional who has an insight in the subject matter that is not shared by students. The explanations are often written in an abstract manner which leaves the students confused as to the application of the principle. The explanations given are not sufficiently detailed and extensive to make the student aware of the wide range of applications and different aspects of the principle being studied. The numerous possible variations of principles and their applications are usually not discussed, and it is left for the students to discover these for themselves while doing the exercises. Accordingly, the average student is expected to rediscover that which has been long known and practiced, but not

iii

NEWARK PUBLIC LIBRARY
NEWARK, OHIO 43055-5054

published or explained extensively.

(c) The examples usually following the explanation of a topic are too few in number and too simple to enable the student to obtain a thorough grasp of the principles involved. The explanations do not provide sufficient basis to enable a student to solve problems that may be subsequently assigned for homework or given on examinations.

The examples are presented in abbreviated form which leaves out much material between steps, and requires that students derive the omitted material themselves. As a result, students find the examples difficult to understand--contrary to the purpose of the examples.

Examples are, furthermore, often worded in a confusing manner. They do not state the problem and then present the solution. Instead, they pass through a general discussion, never revealing what is to be solved for.

Examples, also, do not always include diagrams/graphs, wherever appropriate, and students do not obtain the training to draw diagrams or graphs to simplify and organize their thinking.

(d) Students can learn the subject only by doing the exercises themselves and reviewing them in class, to obtain experience in applying the principles with their different ramifications.

In doing the exercises by themselves, students find that they are required to devote considerably more time to geometry than to other subjects of comparable credits, because they are uncertain with regard to the selection and application of the theorems and principles involved. It is also often necessary for students to discover those "tricks" not revealed in their texts (or review books), that make it possible to solve problems easily. Students must usually resort to methods of trial-and-error to discover these "tricks", and as a result they find that they may sometimes spend several hours in solving a single problem.

(e) When reviewing the exercises in classrooms, instructors usually request students to take turns in writing solutions on

NEWARK PUBLIC LIBRARY
NEWARK, OHIO 43055 50-t

the boards and explaining them to the class. Students often find it difficult to explain in a manner that holds the interest of the class, and enables the class to follow the material written on the boards. The remaining students seated in the class are, furthermore, too occupied with copying the material from the boards, to listen to the oral explanations and concentrate on the methods of solution.

This book is intended to aid students in geometry in overcoming the difficulties described, by supplying detailed illustrations of the solution methods which are usually not apparent to students. The solution methods are illustrated by problems selected from those that are most often assigned for class work and given on examinations. The problems are arranged in order of complexity to enable students to learn and understand a particular topic by reviewing the problems in sequence. The problems are illustrated with detailed step-by-step explanations, to save the students the large amount of time that is often needed to fill in the gaps that are usually found between steps of illustrations in textbooks or review/outline books.

The staff of REA considers geometry a subject that is best learned by allowing students to view the methods of analysis and solution techniques themselves. This approach to learning the subject matter is similar to that practiced in various scientific laboratories, particularly in the medical fields.

In using this book, students may review and study the illustrated problems at their own pace; they are not limited to the time allowed for explaining problems on the board in class.

When students want to look up a particular type of problem and solution, they can readily locate it in the book by referring to the index which has been extensively prepared. It is also possible to locate a particular type of problem by glancing at just the material within the boxed portions. To facilitate rapid scanning of the problems, each problem has a heavy border around it. Furthermore, each problem is identified with a number immediately above the problem at the right-hand margin.

To obtain maximum benefit from the book, students should familiarize themselves with the section titled "How to Use this Book," located in the front of the volume.

To meet the objectives of this book, staff members of REA have selected problems commonly encountered in assignments and examinations, and have solved each problem meticulously to illustrate the steps that are particularly difficult for students to comprehend. Special gratitude is expressed to them for their efforts in this area, as well as to the numerous contributors who devoted their time to this book.

Gratitude is also expressed to the many persons involved in typing the manuscript--with its endless changes--and to the REA art staff, who prepared the numerous detailed illustrations and created the book's layout.

The difficult task of coordinating the efforts of all contributors was carried out by Carl Fuchs. His conscientious work deserves much appreciation. He also trained and supervised art and production personnel in the preparation of the book for printing.

Finally, special thanks are due Helen Kaufmann for her unique talent in rendering those difficult borderline decisions and for her constructive suggestions related to the design and organization of the book.

Max Fogiel, Ph.D.
Program Director

# HOW TO USE THIS BOOK

This book can be an invaluable aid to students in geometry as a supplement to their textbooks. The book is subdivided into 11 chapters, each dealing with a separate topic. The subject matter is developed beginning with lines and angles and extending through analytic (coordinate) and solid geometry. Sections on constructions, coordinate conversions, polygons, surface areas and volumes are included.

# HOW TO LEARN AND UNDERSTAND A TOPIC THOROUGHLY

1. Refer to your class text and read the section pertaining to the topic. You should become acquainted with the principles discussed there. These principles, however, may not be immediately clear to you.

2. Then locate the topic you are looking for by referring to the "Table of Contents" in the front of this book.

3. Turn to the page in which the topic begins and review the problems under each topic, in the order given. For each topic, the problems are arranged in order of complexity, from the simplest to the most difficult. Some problems may appear similar to others, but each problem has been selected to illustrate a different point or solution method.

To learn and understand a topic thoroughly and retain its contents, it will be necessary for students to review the problems several times. Repeated review is essential in order to gain experience in recognizing the principles that should be applied and in selecting the best solution technique.

# HOW TO FIND A PARTICULAR PROBLEM

To locate one or more problems related to particular subject matter, refer to the index. In using the index, be certain to note that the numbers given there refer to problem numbers, not to page numbers. This arrangement is intended to facilitate finding a problem more rapidly, since two or more problems may appear on a page.

It is the aim of this book to serve as a personal tutor to students by providing exceptionally detailed explanations to the problems that are typically found on exams.

If a particular type of problem cannot be found readily, it is recommended that the student refer to the Table of Contents and then turn to the chapter which is applicable to the problem being sought. By scanning or glancing at the material that is boxed, it will be possible to find problems related to the one being sought, without consuming considerable time. After the problems have been located, the solutions can be reviewed and studied in detail. For the purpose of locating problems rapidly, you should acquaint yourself with the organization of the book as found in the Table of Contents.

In preparing for an exam, it is useful to find the topics to be covered on the exam in the Table of Contents, and then review the problems under those topics several times. This should equip the student with information needed for the exam.

# CONTENTS

# SUMMARY OF ESSENTIAL GEOMETRIC THEOREMS & PROPERTIES

## AXIOMS

A quantity is equal to itself (reflexive law).

If two quantities are equal to the same quantity, they are equal to each other.

If a & b are any quantities, and a = b, then b = a (symmetric law).

The whole is equal to the sum of its parts.

If equal quantities are added to equal quantities, the sums are equal quantities.

If equal quantities are subtracted from equal quantities, the differences are equal quantities.

If equal quantities are multiplied by equal quantities, the products are equal quantities.

If equal quantities are divided by equal quantities (not 0), the quotients are equal quantities.

## LINES

Two points determine one and only one line.

Let A & B be two points on a line. The set of points on the line between A & B and including A & B is called the line segment AB.

A line which divides a line segment into two segments with equal measure is called a bisector of the line segment. The intersection of the two is called the midpoint of the line segment.

A line segment has only one midpoint.

If three or more points lie on the same line, they are said to be collinear.

Two lines are perpendicular if, and only if, they meet and form equal adjacent angles.

The perpendicular to a line through a point not on the line is unique.

The distance from a point to a line is the measure of the perpendicular segment drawn from the point to the line.

A perpendicular bisector of a line segment is a line that bisects and is perpendicular to the given line segment.

# ANGLES

An angle is the union of two rays with a common endpoint. The common endpoint is called the vertex of the angle.

An angle bisector is a ray that divides an angle into two angles that have equal measure.

A right angle is an angle whose measure is 90°.

All right angles are equal.

A straight angle is an angle whose sides form a line. The measure of a straight angle is 180°.

All straight angles are equal.

An acute angle is an angle whose measure is larger than 0° but less than 90°.

An obtuse angle is an angle whose measure is greater than 90° but less than 180°.

Two angles whose sum is 180° are called supplementary angles. Each angle is called the supplement of the other.

Supplements of the same or equal angles are themselves equal.

Two angles whose sum is 90° are called complementary angles. Each angle is called the complement of the other.

Complements of the same or equal angles are themselves equal.

Two angles are called adjacent angles if, and only if, they have a common vertex and a common side lying between them.

A pair of nonadjacent angles formed by two intersecting lines is called a pair of vertical angles.

Vertical angles are equal.

If two lines are cut by a transversal, nonadjacent angles on opposite sides of the transversal but on the interior of the two lines are called alternate interior angles.

If two lines are cut by a transversal, nonadjacent angles on opposite sides of the transversal and on the exterior of the two lines are called alternate exterior angles.

If two lines are cut by a transversal, angles on the same side of the transversal and in corresponding positions with respect to the lines are called corresponding angles.

# TRIANGLES

A triangle is a closed three-sides figure.

The points of intersection of the sides of a triangle are called the vertices of the triangle.

A right triangle is a triangle with one right angle.

The side opposite the right angle in a right triangle is called the hypotenuse of the right triangle. The other two sides are called arms or legs of the right triangle.

An equilateral triangle is a triangle all of whose sides are of equal measure.

An isosceles triangle is a triangle that has at least two sides of equal measure. The third side is called the base of the triangle.

A scalene triangle is a triangle that has no pair of sides with equal measure.

The perimeter of a triangle is the sum of the measures of the sides of a triangle.

If one of the sides of a triangle is extended, the angle formed which is adjacent to an angle of the triangle is called an exterior angle.

An exterior angle of a triangle is equal to the sum of the nonadjacent interior angles.

Two triangles are congruent if, and only if, all of their corresponding parts are equal. ($\cong$)

If the hypotenuse and an acute angle of one right triangle are equal, respectively, to the hypotenuse and an acute angle of a second right triangle, the triangles are congruent.

If three sides of one triangle are equal, respectively, to three sides of a second triangle, the triangles are congruent. (SSS = SSS)

If two sides and the included angle of one triangle are equal, respectively, to two sides and the included angle of a second triangle, the triangles are congruent. (SAS = SAS)

If two angles and the included side of one triangle are equal, respectively, to two angles and the included side of a second triangle, the triangles are congruent. (ASA = ASA)

If two angles and any side of one triangle are equal, respectively, to two angles and any side of a second triangle, the triangles are congruent. (AAS = AAS)

The sum of the measures of the interior angles of a triangle is 180°.

If two angles of one triangle are equal respectively to two angles of a second triangle, their third angles are equal.

The acute angles of a right triangle are complementary.

A triangle can have at most one right or obtuse angle.

An acute triangle is a triangle with all acute angles.

An obtuse triangle is a triangle with one obtuse angle.

If the hypotenuse and an arm of one right triangle are equal, respectively, to the hypotenuse and an arm of a second right triangle, the right triangles are congruent.

The perpendicular bisector of the base of an isosceles triangle passes through the vertex.

The bisector of the vertex angle of an isosceles triangle is the perpendicular bisector of the base of the triangle.

If a triangle has two equal angles, then the sides opposite those angles are equal.

If two sides of a triangle are equal, then the angles opposite those sides are equal.

In a right triangle, the square of the hypotenuse is equal to the sum of the squares of the other two sides.

If a triangle has sides of length a, b, and c and $c^2 = a^2 + b^2$, then the triangle is a right triangle.

In a 30°-60° right triangle, the hypotenuse is twice the length of the side opposite the 30° angle. The side opposite the 60° angle is equal to the length of the side opposite the 30° angle multiplied by $\sqrt{3}$.

In an isosceles 45° right triangle, the hypotenuse is equal to the length of one of its arms multiplied by $\sqrt{2}$.

A line segment that connects the midpoints of two sides of a triangle is parallel to the third side and half as long.

A median of a triangle is a line segment drawn from one vertex of a triangle to the midpoint of the opposite side.

The medians of a triangle meet in a point.

An altitude of a triangle is a line segment drawn from one vertex of the triangle perpendicular to the opposite side, or if necessary, to an extension of the opposite side.

The altitudes of a triangle meet in a point.

The perpendicular bisectors of the sides of a triangle meet at a point which is equally distant from the vertices of the triangle.

The angle bisectors of a triangle meet in a point which is equidistant from the sides of the triangle.

The point of intersection of the medians of a triangle is 2/3 of the way from the vertex to the midpoint of the opposite side.

# PARALLELISM

**PARALLEL LINES:**

Two lines are called parallel lines if, and only if, they are in the same plane and do not intersect.

Parallel lines are always the same distance apart.

Two lines are parallel if they are both perpendicular to a third line.

Given a line $\ell$ and a point P not on line $\ell$, there is only one line through point P that is parallel to line $\ell$.

If two lines are cut by a transversal so that alternate interior angles are equal, the lines are parallel.

If two parallel lines are cut by a transversal, all pairs of alternate interior angles are equal.

If two lines are cut by a transversal so that corresponding angles are equal, the lines are parallel.

If two parallel lines are cut by a transversal, each pair of corresponding angles is equal.

If two lines are cut by a transversal so that two interior angles on the same side of the transversal are supplementary, the lines are parallel.

If two parallel lines are cut by a transversal, pairs of interior angles on the same side of the transversal are supplementary.

If a line is perpendicular to one of two parallel lines, it is perpendicular to the other also.

If two lines are cut by a transversal so that alternate interior angles are not equal, the lines are not parallel.

If two lines are cut by a transversal so that corresponding angles are not equal, the lines are not parallel.

If two lines are cut by a transversal so that two interior angles on the same side of the transversal are not supplementary, the lines are not parallel.

If two nonparallel lines are cut by a transversal, the pairs of alternate interior angles are not equal.

## PARALLELOGRAM:

A parallelogram is a quadrilateral whose opposite sides are parallel. ($\square$)

Opposite sides of a parallelogram are equal.

Nonconsecutive angles of a parallelogram are equal.

Consecutive angles of a parallelogram are supplementary.

A diagonal of a parallelogram divides the parallelogram into two congruent triangles.

The diagonals of a parallelogram bisect each other.

If both pairs of opposite sides of a quadrilateral are equal, then the quadrilateral is a parallelogram.

If two opposite sides of a quadrilateral are both parallel and equal, the quadrilateral is a parallelogram.

If the diagonals of a quadrilateral bisect each other, then the quadrilateral is a parallelogram.

## RHOMBUS:

A rhombus is a parallelogram with two adjacent sides equal.

All sides of a rhombus are equal.

The diagonals of a rhombus are perpendicular to each other.

If the diagonals of a parallelogram are perpendicular, the parallelogram is a rhombus.

The diagonals of a rhombus bisect the angles of the rhombus.

A square is a rhombus with a right angle.

### RECTANGLE:

A rectangle is a parallelogram with one right angle.

All angles of a rectangle are right angles.

The diagonals of a rectangle are equal.

If the diagonals of a parallelogram are equal, the parallelogram is a rectangle.

### TRAPEZOID:

A trapezoid is a quadrilateral with two and only two sides parallel. The parallel sides are called bases.

An isosceles trapezoid is a trapezoid whose nonparallel sides are equal. A pair of angles including one of the parallel sides is called a pair of base angles.

The base angles of an isosceles trapezoid are equal.

If a line joins the midpoints of two sides of a triangle, that line is parallel to and equal to one-half of the third side.

The median of a trapezoid is parallel to the bases and equal to one-half their sum.

The median of a trapezoid is the line joining the midpoints of the non-parallel sides.

If three or more parallel lines cut off equal segments on one transversal, they cut off equal segments on all transversals.

## AREAS

The area of a rectangle is given by the formula $A = bh$ where b is the length of the base and h is the height of the rectangle.

The area of a triangle is given by the formula $A = 1/2\ bh$ where b is the length of a base and h is the corresponding height of the triangle.

The area of a parallelogram is given by the formula A = bh where b is the length of a base and h is the corresponding height of the parallelogram. The side to which an altitude is drawn is called a base. The length of an altitude is called a height.

The area of a rhombus is equal to one-half the product of its diagonals.

The area of a trapezoid is given by the formula A = 1/2 h(b + b') where h is the height and b and b' are the lengths of the bases of the trapezoid.

The area of a circle is given by the formula A =$\pi r^2$ where $\pi$ is approximately 3. 14 and r is the radius of the circle.

Any two congruent figures have the same area.

## RATIOS, PROPORTIONS, SIMILARITY

A ratio is the comparison of two numbers by their indicated quotient. A ratio is a fraction, with denominators not equal to zero.

A proportion is a statement that two ratios are equal.

In the proportion a/b = c/d the numbers a & d are called the extremes of the proportion, and the numbers b & c are called the means of the proportion. The single term, d, is called the fourth proportional.

In a proportion, the product of the means is equal to the product of the extremes. (If a/b = c/d, then ad = bc. )

A proportion may be written by inversion. (If a/b = c/d, then b/a = d/c. )

The means may be interchanged in any proportion. (If a/b = c/d, then a/c = b/d. )

The extremes may be interchanged in any proportion. (If a/b = c/d, then d/b = c/a. )

A proportion may be written by addition. (If $\frac{a}{b} = \frac{c}{d}$, then $\frac{a+b}{b} = \frac{c+d}{d}$. )

A proportion may be written by subtraction. (If $\frac{a}{b} = \frac{c}{d}$, then $\frac{a-b}{b} = \frac{c-d}{d}$. )

If three terms of one proportion are equal, respectively, to three terms of a second proportion, the fourth terms are equal. Thus, if $\frac{a}{b} = \frac{c}{d} = \frac{e}{f}$, then $\frac{a+c+e}{b+d+f} = \frac{a}{b}$.

A line parallel to one side of a triangle divides the other two sides proportionally.

If a line divides two sides of a triangle proportionally, it is parallel to the third side.

The bisector of one angle of a triangle divides the opposite side in the same ratio as the other two sides.

All congruent triangles are similar.

Two triangles similar to the same triangle are similar to each other.

If two triangles have one angle of one equal to one angle of the other and the respective sides including these angles are in proportion, the triangles are similar.

If three sides of one triangle are in proportion to the three corresponding sides of a second triangle, the triangles are similar.

Two triangles are similar if, and only if, two angles of one triangle are equal to two angles of the other triangle.

The altitude on the hypotenuse of a right triangle is the mean proportional between the segments of the hypotenuse.

Two polygons are similar if, and only if, all pairs of corresponding angles are equal and all pairs of corresponding sides are in proportion.

# CIRCLES

A circle is a set of points in the same plane equidistant from a fixed point called its center. A line segment drawn from the center of the circle to one of the points on the circle is called a radius of the circle.

The length of a diameter is twice the length of a radius.

A portion of a circle is called an arc of the circle.

In a circle, parallel lines intercept equal arcs.

The circumference of a circle is the distance about a circle. The circumference of a circle is given by the formula, $C = 2\pi r$ where r is the radius of the circle.

Two circles are congruent if, and only if, their radii or diameters are equal.

A semicircle is an arc of a circle whose endpoints lie on the extremities of a diameter of the circle.

An arc greater than a semicircle is called a major arc.

An arc less than a semicircle is called a minor arc.

An angle whose vertex is at the center of a circle and whose sides are radii is called a central angle.

The number of degrees in the arc intercepted by a central angle is equal to the number of degrees in the central angle. This number is called the measure of the arc.

A sector of a circle is the set of points between two radii and their intercepted arc.

The line passing through the centers of two circles is called the line of centers.

A line that intersects a circle in two points is called a secant.

A line segment joining two points on a circle is called a chord of the circle.

A chord that passes through the center of the circle is called a diameter of the circle.

An angle whose vertex is on the circle and whose sides are chords of the circle is called an inscribed angle.

The measure of an inscribed angle is equal to one-half the measure of its intercepted arc.

An angle formed by a tangent and a chord is equal to one-half the measure of the intercepted arc.

If two chords intersect within a circle, each angle formed is equal to one-half the sum of its intercepted arc and the intercepted arc of its vertical angle.

An angle formed by the intersection of two secants outside a circle is equal to one-half the difference of its intercepted arcs.

An angle formed by the intersection of a tangent and a secant outside a circle is equal to one-half the difference of the intercepted arcs.

A line drawn from the center of a circle perpendicular to a chord bisects the chord and its arc.

A line drawn from the center of a circle to the midpoint of a chord is perpendicular to the chord.

The perpendicular bisector of a chord passes through the center of the circle.

In the same circle or congruent circles equal chords have equal arcs.

In the same circle or congruent circles equal arcs have equal chords.

In the same circle or congruent circles, equal chords are equidistant from the center.

In the same circle or congruent circles, chords equidistant from the center are equal.

If two chords intersect within a circle, the product of the segments of one chord is equal to the product of the segments of the other chord.

If two circles intersect in two points, their line of centers is the perpendicular bisector of their common chord.

A line that has one and only one point of intersection with a circle is called a tangent to the circle. Their common point is called a point of tangency.

If two tangents are drawn to a circle from a point outside the circle, the tangents are of equal measure.

A line drawn from a center of a circle to a point of tangency is perpendicular to the tangent passing through the point of tangency. Also, if a line is perpendicular to a radius at its intersection with its circle, the line is tangent to the circle.

If two circles are tangent either internally or externally, the point of tangency and the centers of the circles are collinear.

If a secant and a tangent are drawn to a circle, the measure of the tangent is the mean proportional between the secant and its external segment.

If two secants are drawn to a circle from a point outside the circle, the products of the secants and their external segments are equal.

The opposite angles of an inscribed quadrilateral are supplementary.

If a parallelogram is inscribed within a circle, it is a rectangle.

## POLYGONS

A polygon is a convex figure with the same number of sides as angles.

A quadrilateral is a polygon with four sides.

An equilateral polygon is a polygon all of whose sides are of equal measure.

An equiangular polygon is a polygon all of whose angles are of equal measure.

A regular polygon is a polygon that is both equilateral and equiangular.

A circle can be inscribed in any regular polygon.

A circle can be circumscribed about any regular polygon.

The center of a circle that is circumscribed about a regular polygon is the center of the circle that is inscribed within the regular polygon.

If a circle is divided into n equal arcs, the chords of the arcs will form a regular polygon. (n>2)

If a circle is divides into n equal arcs and tangents are drawn to the circle at the endpoints of these arcs, the figure formed by the tangents will be a regular polygon. (n>2)

An apothem of a regular polygon bisects its respective side.

The radius of a regular polygon is a line segment drawn from the center of the polygon to one of its vertices.

A central angle of a regular polygon is the angle formed by radii drawn to two consecutive vertices.

A central angle of a regular polygon is given by the formula, $x = \frac{2}{n} \cdot 180°$, where n is the number of sides of the polygon.

The area of a regular polygon is equal to the product of one-half its apothem and its perimeter.

The sum of the interior angles of a polygon is given by the formula $S = (n - 2) \cdot 180°$, where n is the number of sides of the polygon.

The measure of an interior angle, a, of a regular polygon is given by the formula: $a = \frac{(n - 2) \cdot 180°}{n}$ where n is the number of sides of of the polygon.

The sum of the exterior angles of a polygon is always 360°.

The area of a sector of a circle divided by the area of the circle is equal to the measure of its central angle divided by 360°.

## INEQUALITIES

If the same quantity is added to both sides of an inequality, the sums are unequal and in the same order. (If $a<b$, then $a + c<b + c$.)

If equal quantities are added to unequal quantities, the sums are unequal and in the same order. (If $a< b$ and $c = d$, then $a + c<b + d$.)

If unequal quantities are subtracted from equal quantities, the differences are unequal and in the opposite order. (If $a < b$ and $c = d$, then $c - a > d - b$.)

If both sides of an inequality are multiplied by a positive number, the products are unequal and in the same order. (If $a < b$ and $c$ is a positive number, then $ac < bc$.)

If both sides of an inequality are multiplied by a negative number, the products are unequal in the opposite order. (If $a < b$ and $c$ is a negative number, then $ac > bc$.)

The relation "$<$" is transitive. (If $a < b$ and $b < c$, then $a < c$.)

If unequal quantities are added to unequal quantities of the same order, the sums are unequal quantities and in the same order. (If $a < b$ and $c < d$, then $a + c < b + d$.)

In a triangle an exterior angle is greater than either nonadjacent interior angle.

If two sides of a triangle are unequal, the angles opposite these sides are unequal in the same order.

If two angles of a triangle are unequal, the sides opposite these angles are unequal in the same order.

If two sides of one triangle are equal to two sides of a second triangle and the included angle of the first is greater than the included angle of the second, then the third side of the first triangle is greater than the third side of the second.

If two sides of one triangle are equal to two sides of a second triangle and the third side of the first is greater than the third side of the second, then the angle opposite the third side of the first triangle is greater than the angle opposite the third side of the second.

In the same circle or in equal circles, the greater of two central angles will intercept the greater arc.

In the same circle or in equal circles, the greater of two arcs will be intercepted by the greater of the central angles.

In the same circle or equal circles, the greater of two chords intercepts the greater minor arc.

In the same circle or equal circles, the greater of two minor arcs has the greater chord.

If two unequal chords form an inscribed angle within a circle, the shorter chord is the farther from the center of the circle.

# LOCUS

A circle is the locus of points at a given distance from a fixed point, called its center, and all in the same plane.

The locus of points whose coordinates satisfy a given linear equation is a straight line.

The locus of the vertex of the right angle of a right triangle with a fixed hypotenuse is a circle with the hypotenuse as diameter.

The locus of all points equidistant from the sides of an angle is the angle bisector.

The locus of all points equidistant from two points is the perpendicular bisector of the segment joining the two points.

The locus of a point at a given distance from a given line is a pair of lines, one on each side of the given line, parallel to the given line and at the given distance from it.

# COORDINATE GEOMETRY

Directed distance of a horizontal line segment from one point to a second is the x -coordinate of the second minus the x-coordinate of the first.

Directed distance of a vertical line segment from one point to a second is the y-coordinate of the second minus the y-coordinate of the first.

The slope, m, of a nonvertical line segment determined by points $P(x_1, y_1)$ and $Q(x_2, y_2)$ is given by $m = \dfrac{y_2 - y_1}{x_2 - x_1}$.

On a nonvertical line, all segments of the line have the same slope.

Two nonvertical lines are perpendicular if, and only if, their slopes are negative reciprocals.

Two nonvertical lines are parallel if, and only if, they have the same slope. Vertical lines are parallel.

A linear equation is any equation which can be written in the form of $Ax + By + C = 0$.

# CHAPTER 1

# METHODS OF PROOF

## DEDUCTIVE REASONING

How may the following three statements be arranged so that the first two will make it possible to deduce the third?
(a) An eagle has feathers. (b) All birds have feathers.
(c) An eagle is a bird.

Solution:  An arrangement of statements that would allow you to deduce the third one from the preceeding two is called a syllogism. A syllogism has three parts.

The first part is a general statement concerning a whole group. This is called the major premise.

The second part is a specific statement which indicates that a certain individual is a member of that group. This is called the minor premise.

The third and final part of a syllogism is a statement to the effect that the general statement concerning the group also applies to the individual. This statement is called a deduction.

The technique of employing a syllogism to arrive at a conclusion is called deductive reasoning. This technique will be used in this problem.

Statement (b) "All birds have feathers" is the major premise since it assigns a general characteristic to the whole group, in this case birds.

Statement (c) "An eagle is a bird" links the eagle to the larger group mentioned in the major premise and, therefore, (c) is the minor premise.

Statement (a) "An eagle has feathers" assigns the general trait, feathers, to the individual, eagles, and, thus, qualifies as the deduction.

Therefore, the order of the statements that allows you to deduce the third from the first two is (b), (c), (a).

● **PROBLEM 1-2**

All residents of this state who are registered voters are 18 years of age or older. If John is a resident of this state, by valid reasoning which of the following can we conclude: (a) If John is 18 or over, he is a registered voter; (b) If John is a registered voter, he is 18 or over. (c) If John is not a registered voter, he is not 18 or over.

<u>Solution</u>: To find the logically correct statement, we find which of the choices forms a valid syllogism with the given statement. The given statement "All residents of this state who are registered voters are 18 years of age or older" is the major premise, because it attributes a characteristic ("being 18 or older") to a general group ("residents of this state who are registered voters"). A minor premise links a particular example, John, to the general group. Note that there are two conditions to being a member of the group: a member must (1) be a resident of the state; and (2) be a registered voter. Therefore, any valid minor premise must include both conditions.

One condition of the minor premise is common to all the choices and therefore written in the front - "If John is a resident of this state". The second condition of the minor premise is different in each choice.

For choice (a), the minor premise is "John is a resident of this state and John is 18 or over". This is not enough to make John a resident of the state who is a registered voter. Thus, John is not linked to the group and choice (a) is not valid reasoning. Thinking about this in another way, it is definitely possible that apathetic John is over 18, and a resident of the state; and yet John may not have bothered to register.

For choice (b), the minor premise is "John is a resident of this state and John is a registered voter." This is enough to qualify John as a member of the group. Thus, the quality of the group can be linked with John in the conclusion - John is 18 or over. This is, indeed, the conclusion of (b). Thus choice (b) leads to valid reasoning.

For choice (c), the minor premise is "John is a resident of this state and John is not a registered voter." This is not enough to make John a member of the general group. The reasoning is invalid. It is possible for an apathetic 50 year old citizen not to register to vote.

2

# LOGIC

Identify the hypothesis and conclusion in the statement, "The median to the base of an isosceles triangle is perpendicular to the base."

**Solution:** The statement dealt with in this problem is a "simple" sentence, as opposed to the "if-then" type of statement. In general, if a statement is written as a simple sentence, then the subject of the sentence is the hypothesis, and the predicate is the conclusion.

In this example, the phrase "The median to the base of an isosceles triangle" is the subject of the sentence and, consequently, the hypothesis is "a line segment is the median to the base of an isosceles triangle." The phrase "is perpendicular to the base" is the predicate and, therefore, the conclusion is "the line is perpendicular to the base."

State whether the condition in the hypothesis is: both necessary and sufficient, necessary but not sufficient, not necessary but sufficient, neither necessary nor sufficient. (a) If a man is sick, he is a patient in a hospital. (b) If a man is a senator, he is a member of Congress. (c) If a figure is a square, then the figure is a quadrilateral.

**Solution:** A necessary condition is a fact or set of facts which must be given in the hypothesis of a conditional statement to make it possible to deduce the conclusion.

A sufficient condition is a fact or set of facts which, when given in the hypothesis, supplies enough information to make it possible to deduce the conclusion.

If a condition is necessary, it is essential that the fact be given in the hypothesis to have any chance of deducing the conclusion. A necessary condition will not always be enough to allow one to arrive at a conclusion by formal logic. On the other hand, a sufficient condition, when given, will always lead to a logical deduction of a certain conclusion.

(a) In this statement the hypothesis is "a man is sick," the conclusion is "he is a patient in a hospital." Certainly, if a man is a patient in a hospital, he must be sick. Therefore, it is at least necessary that he be sick before he can be in the hospital.

3

However, it is not sufficient that he be merely sick as the sole prerequisite for being in the hospital because one has many ways of being sick and not ending up in the hospital.

We conclude then that the hypothesis is necessary but not sufficient to deduce the stated conclusion.

In this part we showed the converse of that statement to be true which is a standard way to decide if the hypothesis is necessary. To prove sufficiency we must prove that the statement is true.

(b) The hypothesis is "the man is a senator," while the conclusion is "he is a member of Congress."

The converse is "If he is a member of Congress, he is a senator." This is false, because members of the House of Representatives are members of Congress but certainly not senators. Therefore, in the original statement, the hypothesis is not necessary because the conclusion can be reached under much different hypothetical conditions, i.e. if the hypothesis were "he is a member of the House of Representatives."

The statement is true and this lets us conclude that the hypothesis is sufficient for the conclusion. Once a person is a senator he is automatically a member of Congress.

Therefore, the hypothesis is not necessary but sufficient for the stated conclusion.

(c) In this statement, the hypothesis is "a figure is a square" and the conclusion is "the figure is a quadrilateral."

The statement is true since every square is a four sided polygon and every four sided polygon is a quadrilateral. Thus, the hypothetical condition is sufficient.

The converse is "if the figure is a quadrilateral, then the figure is a square." This is false since the figure could also be a rectangle or trapezoid. Since the converse is false the hypothesis of the original statement is not necessary.

The hypothesis is sufficient but not necessary.

# DIRECT PROOF

● PROBLEM 1-5

In the figure shown, the measure of ⅄ DAC equals the measure of ⅄ ECA and the measure of ⅄1 equals the measure of ⅄2. Show that the measure of ⅄3 equals the measure of ⅄4.

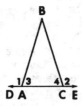

Solution: This proof will require the subtraction postulate, which states that if equal quantities are subtracted
from equal quantities, the differences are equal.

GIVEN: ∡ DAC ≅ ∡ ECA, ∡1 ≅ ∡2

PROVE: ∡3 ≅ ∡4

| STATEMENTS | REASONS |
|---|---|
| 1. m∡DAC = m∡ECA<br>   m∡1 = m∡2 | 1. Given. |
| 2. m∡DAC - m∡1 = m∡ECA - m∡2 | 2. Subtraction Postulate. |
| 3. m∡3 = m∡4 | 3. Substitution Postulate. |

● **PROBLEM 1-6**

Every line in a proof requires justification. In the proof
below the reasons have been omitted. Give the reasons.

GIVEN:    ∡1 ≅ ∡2; ∡3 ≅ ∡4
PROVE:    ∡H ≅ ∡F

| STATEMENTS | REASONS |
|---|---|
| 1. ∡1 ≅ ∡2; ∡3 ≅ ∡4 | 1. |
| 2. m∡1 + m∡3 = m∡2 + m∡4 | 2. |
| 3. m∡1 + m∡3 + m∡F = 180 | 3. |
| and m∡2 + m∡4 + m∡H = 180 | |
| 4. m∡1 + m∡3 + m∡F = m∡2 + m∡4 + m∡H | 4. |
| 5. m∡F = m∡H | 5. |

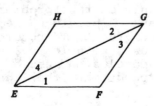

5

**Solution:** For any statement, several reasons may be possible. In steps 2, 3 and 4, below, alternative reasons are given. Any one will do. Even for a given reason, there may be a choice between citing or writing out the theorem. Generally, the shorter the reason, the better. Postulates and famous theorems can be named; however, theorems that are less well known should be written out.

The reasons for the proof in this question are:

(1) Given.

(2) The Angle Addition Postulate or the Addition Property of Equality; if a = b and c = d, then a + c = b + d.

(3) The measures of the interior angles of a triangle sum to 180° degrees or the interior angles of a triangle form a linear pair.

(4) Transitivity Postulate or Substitition Postulate or if a = b and b = c, then a = c.

(5) Subtraction Property of Equality.


# INDIRECT PROOF

● **PROBLEM 1-7**

Prove, by indirect method, that if two angles are not congruent, then they are not both right angles.

**Solution:** Indirect proofs involve considering two possible outcomes, the result we would like to prove and its negative, and then showing, under the given hypothesis, that a contradiction of prior known theorems, postulates, or definitions is reached when the negative is assumed.

In this case the outcomes can be that the two angles are not right angles or that the two angles are right angles. Assume the negative of what we want to prove - that the two angles are right angles.

The given hypothesis in this problem is that the two angles are not congruent. A previous theorem states that all right angles are congruent. Therefore, the conclusion we have assumed true leads to a logical contradiction. As such, the alternative conclusion must be true. Therefore, if two angles are not congruent, then they are not both right angles.

# INDUCTIVE REASONING

> Prove by mathematical induction
> $$1^2 + 2^2 + 3^2 + \ldots + n^2 = \frac{1}{6}n(n+1)(2n+1).$$

<u>Solution:</u> Mathematical induction is a method of proof. The steps are:
(1) The verification of the proposed formula or theorem for the smallest value of n. It is desirable, but not necessary, to verify it for several values of n.
(2) The proof that if the proposed formula or theorem is true for n = k, some positive integer, it is true also for n = k+1. That is, if the proposition is true for any particular value of n, it must be true for the next larger value of n.
(3) A conclusion that the proposed formula holds true for all values of n.

<u>Proof:</u>  Step 1.  Verify:

For  n = 1:  $1^2 = \frac{1}{6}(1)(1+1)[2(1)+1] = \frac{1}{6}(1)(2)(3) = \frac{1}{6}(6) = 1$

$$1 = 1$$

For  n = 2:  $1^2 + 2^2 = \frac{1}{6}(2)(2+1)[2(2)+1] = \frac{1}{6}(2)(3)(5) = \frac{1}{6}(6)(5)$

$$1 + 4 = (1)(5)$$

$$5 = 5$$

For  n = 3:  $1^2 + 2^2 + 3^2 = \frac{1}{6}(3)(3+1)[2(3)+1]$

$$1 + 4 + 9 = \frac{1}{6}(3)(4)(7) = \frac{1}{6}(12)(7) = 14$$

$$14 = 14$$

Step 2.  Let  k  represent any particular value of  n.  For n = k, the formula becomes

$$1^2 + 2^2 + 3^2 + \ldots + k^2 = \frac{1}{6}k(k+1)(2k+1). \qquad (A)$$

For  n = k+1, the formula is

$$1^2 + 2^2 + 3^2 + \ldots + k^2 + (k+1)^2 = \frac{1}{6}(k+1)[(k+1) + 1][2(k+1) + 1]$$

$$= \frac{1}{6}(k+1)(k+2)(2k+3). \qquad (B)$$

We must show that if the formula is true for  n = k, then it must be true for  n = k+1.  In other words, we must show that (B) follows from (A). The left side of (A) can be converted into the left side of (B) by merely adding $(k+1)^2$.  All that remains to be demonstrated is that when $(k+1)^2$ is added to the right side of (A), the result is the right side of (B).

$$1^2 + 2^2 + \ldots + k^2 + (k+1)^2 = \frac{1}{6}k(k+1)(2k+1) + (k+1)^2$$

Factor out  (k+1):

$$1^2 + 2^2 + 3^2 + \ldots + k^2 + (k+1)^2 = (k+1)\left[\frac{1}{6}k(2k+1) + (k+1)\right]$$

$$= (k+1)\left[\frac{k(2k+1)}{6} + \frac{(k+1)6}{6}\right]$$

$$= (k+1)\frac{2k^2 + k + 6k + 6}{6}$$

$$= \frac{(k+1)(2k^2 + 7k + 6)}{6}$$

$$= \frac{1}{6}(k+1)(k+2)(2k+3),$$

since $\qquad 2k^2 + 7k + 6 = (k+2)(2k+3).$

Thus, we have shown that if we add $(k+1)^2$ to both sides of the equation for $n = k$, then we obtain the equation or formula for $n = k+1$. We have thus established that if (A) is true, then (B) must be true; that is, if the formula is true for $n = k$, then it must be true for $n = k+1$. In other words, we have proved that if the proposition is true for a certain positive integer $k$, then it is also true for the next greater integer $k+1$.

Step 3. The proposition is true for $n = 1,2,3$ (Step 1). Since it is true for $n = 3$, it is true for $n = 4$ (Step 2, where $k = 3$ and $k+1 = 4$). Since it is true for $n = 4$, it is true for $n = 5$, and so on, for all positive integers $n$.

● **PROBLEM 1-9**

Prove by mathematical induction that

$$1 + 7 + 13 + \ldots + (6n - 5) = n(3n - 2).$$

Solution: (1) The proposed formula is true for $n = 1$, since $1 = 1(3 - 2)$.

(2) Assume the formula to be true for $n = k$, a positive integer; that is, assume

(A) $\qquad 1 + 7 + 13 + \ldots + (6k - 5) = k(3k - 2).$

Under this assumption we wish to show that

(B) $\qquad 1 + 7 + 13 + \ldots + (6k - 5) + (6k + 1) = (k+1)(3k+1).$

When $(6k+1)$ is added to both members of (A), we have on the right

$$k(3k-2) + (6k+1) = 3k^2 + 4k + 1 = (k+1)(3k+1);$$

hence, if the formula is true for $n = k$ it is true for $n = k + 1$.

(3) Since the formula is true for $n = k = 1$ (Step 1), it is true for $n = k + 1 = 2$; being true for $n = k = 2$ it is true for $n = k + 1 = 3$; and so on, for every positive integral value of $n$.

8

# CHAPTER 2

# BASIC ELEMENTS

## LINES

Using the accompanying three-dimensional model, determine whether each of the following sets is collinear and/or coplanar: {A,F,D}, {P,A,F}, {A,B,C,E}, and {A,F,D,E}.

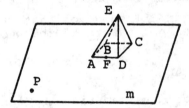

**Solution**: A set of points is collinear if there exists a straight line that contains every point in the set. A set of points is coplanar if there exists a plane that contains every point in the set.

Each point in the set {A,F,D} lie on the line $\overleftrightarrow{AD}$. Therefore, the set is collinear. Furthermore, points on the same line automatically lie on the same plane. Thus, the set of points {A,F,D} is both collinear and coplanar.

Each point in the set {P,A,F} is contained in plane m and, as such, points P, A, and F are coplanar. However, point P does not lie on the line determined by F and P, $\overleftrightarrow{FP}$; and, hence, the points are not collinear.

{A,B,C,E} are neither collinear nor coplanar. Point E does not lie on the plane determined by points A, B, and C (plane m) - thus the set cannot be coplanar. Points E and

C do not lie on the line determined by points A and B - thus the set cannot be collinear.

The set of points {A,F,D,E} is not collinear. Although F lies on the line determined by points A and D, point E does not. Therefore, the set is noncollinear. To determine whether or not the set is coplanar, consider the plane that contains points A, E, and D. Therefore, the set is coplanar if point F lies on this plane.

Since points A and D are contained in this new plane, the line determined by these points, $\overleftrightarrow{AD}$, and every point on the line lies on the new plane. Since F is a point on $\overleftrightarrow{AD}$, point F lies on the new plane. Therefore, points A,F, D, and E are coplanar.

● **PROBLEM 2-2**

---

Find point C between A and B in the figure below such that $\overline{AC} \cong \overline{CB}$.

---

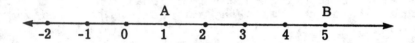

**Solution**: We must determine point C in such a way that $\overline{AC} \cong \overline{CB}$, or AC = CB. We are first given that C is between A and B. Therefore, since the measure of the whole is equal to the sum of the measure of its parts:

(I)    AC + CB = AB

Using these two facts, we can find the length of AC. From that we can find C.

First, since AC = CB, we substitute AC for CB in equation (I)

(II)   AC + AC = AB

(III)   2(AC) = AB

Dividing by 2 we have

(IV)       AC = ½ AB

To find AC, we must know AB. We can find AB from the coordinates of A and B. They are 1 and 5, respectively. Accordingly,

(V)        AB = |5 - 1|

(VI)       AB = 4

We substitute 4 for AB in equation (IV)

(VII)        $AC = \frac{1}{2}(4)$

(VIII)       $AC = 2$.

Therefore, C is 2 units from A. Since C is between A and B, the coordinate of C must be 3.

# ANGLES

● **PROBLEM 2-3**

In the following quadrilateral, find the angles from vertices A and B that are subtended by side $\overline{CD}$.

Solution:  To do this problem, we first must define "subtend." Consider a point X and a line segment $\overline{YZ}$.  Now, draw rays from the point through the endpoints of the segment (see figure.) There are two ways of defining the relation between the angle ∢YXZ and segment $\overline{YZ}$.  The angle ∢YXZ "intercepts" segment $\overline{YZ}$. From another point of view, the segment $\overline{YZ}$ "subtends" ∢YXZ.

In this problem, we are given that $\overline{DC}$ is the segment. We are asked first to consider A as the outside point, and then B.  If A is the outside point, and $\overline{CD}$ is the segment, then $\overline{CD}$ subtends ∢DAC.  If B is the outside point, and $\overline{CD}$ is the segment, then $\overline{CD}$ subtends ∢DBC.

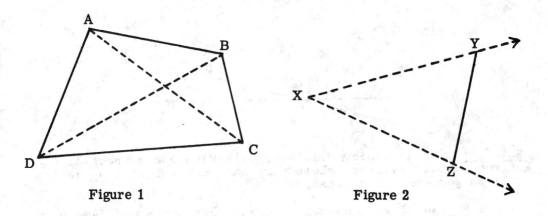

Figure 1                          Figure 2

● **PROBLEM 2-4**

In the figure, we are given $\overleftrightarrow{AB}$ and triangle ABC. We are told that the measure of ∢1 is five times the measure of ∢2. Determine the measures of ∢1 and ∢2.

11

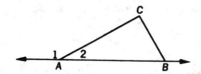

**Solution:** Since ∡1 and ∡2 are adjacent angles whose non-common sides lie on a straight line, they are, by definition, supplementary. As supplements, their measures must sum to 180°.

If we let x = the measure of ∡2
then,        5x = the measure of ∡1.

To determine the respective angle measures, set x + 5x = 180 and solve for x. 6x = 180. Therefore, x = 30 and 5x = 150.

Therefore, the measure of ∡1 = 150 and the measure of ∡2 = 30.


# PERPENDICULARITY

● **PROBLEM 2-5**

We are given straight lines $\overrightarrow{AB}$ and $\overrightarrow{CD}$ intersecting at point P. $\overrightarrow{PR} \perp \overrightarrow{AB}$ and the measure of ∡APD is 170. Find the measures of ∡1, ∡2, ∡3, and ∡4.

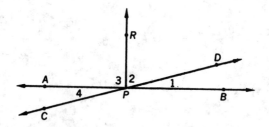

**Solution:** This problem will involve making use of several of the properties of supplementary and vertical angles, as well as perpendicular lines.

∡APD and ∡1 are adjacent angles whose non-common sides lie on a straight line, $\overrightarrow{AB}$. Therefore, they are supplements and their measures sum to 180°.

m∡APD + m∡1 = 180.

We know m∡APD = 170. Therefore, by substitution, 170 + m∡1 = 180. This implies m∡1 = 10.

∡1 and ∡4 are vertical angles because they are formed

by the intersection of two straight lines, $\overleftrightarrow{CD}$ and $\overleftrightarrow{AB}$, and
their sides form two pairs of opposite rays. As vertical
angles, they are, by theorem, of equal measure. Since m∡1
= 10, then m∡4 = 10.

Since $\overleftrightarrow{PR} \perp \overleftrightarrow{AB}$, at their intersection the angles formed
must be right angles. Therefore, ∡3 is a right angle and
its measure is 90. m∡3 = 90.

The figure shows us that ∡APD is composed of ∡3 and ∡2.
Since the measure of the whole must be equal to the sum of
the measures of its parts, m∡APD = m∡3 + m∡2. We know the
m∡APD = 170 and m∡3 = 90, therefore, by substitution, we
can solve for m∡2, our last unknown.

$$170 = 90 + m∡2$$

$$80 = m∡2$$

Therefore, m∡1 = 10,          m∡2 = 80

m∡3 = 90,          m∡4 = 10.

● **PROBLEM 2-6**

Show that the shortest segment joining a line with an
external point is the perpendicular segment from the point
to the line.

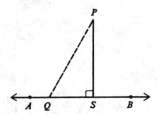

**Solution:** To prove the statement, choose any other line
segment joining the point and the line; and show that it
must be of greater length than the perpendicular. Note
that the new segment, the perpendicular, and the given line
form a right triangle with the right angle opposite the new
segment. Since the right angle is the largest angle of the
triangle, the side opposite it, the new segment, must be
greater than either of the other sides. In particular, the
new segment is longer than the perpendicular. Since the new
segment was any possible segment, the perpendicular is thus
shown to be shorter than any other segment.

GIVEN: $\overleftrightarrow{AB}$ with the external point P; $\overline{PS} \perp \overleftrightarrow{AB}$; $\overline{PQ}$ is
any segment from P to $\overleftrightarrow{AB}$ other than the perpen-
dicular from P to $\overleftrightarrow{AB}$.

13

PROVE: PS < PQ

| STATEMENT | REASONS |
|---|---|
| 1. $\overleftrightarrow{AB}$ with the external point P; $\overleftrightarrow{PS} \perp \overleftrightarrow{AB}$ | 1. Given |
| 2. ∢ PSA is a right angle | 2. Perpendicular lines form right angles. |
| 3. Select any point Q on $\overleftrightarrow{AB}$ | 3. Point Uniqueness Postulate. |
| 4. ∢ PQS is acute | 4. If a triangle has one right angle, then its other two angles must be acute. |
| 5. m ∢ PQS < m ∢ PSA | 5. Definition of an acute angle. |
| 6. PS < PQ | 6. If two angles of a triangle are not congruent, then the sides opposite those angles are not congruent, the longer side being opposite the angle with the greater measure. |

# CHAPTER 3

# CONGRUENCE

## TRIANGLES

● PROBLEM 3-1

In △ ABC, m ⦦ C = 125° and m ⦦ B = 35°. As drawn in the figure, which is the shortest side of the triangle?

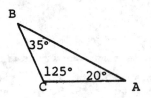

<u>Solution</u>: When the angles of a triangle are of unequal measure, the sides are, correspondingly, of unequal length - that is, the shortest side will be opposite the smallest angle.

Since the sum of the measures of the angles of a triangle is 180°, and since m ⦦ B = 35° and m ⦦ C = 125°, the m ⦦ A = 180° - (35°+125°) = 180° - 160° = 20°. Therefore, the side opposite < A will be the shortest. $\overline{BC}$ is this side.

Therefore, $\overline{BC}$ is the shortest side of △ ABC.

● PROBLEM 3-2

Given:   m ⦦ A = m ⦦ B.   AD = BE .
Prove:   m ⦦ CDE = m ⦦ CED.

<u>Solution</u>: This proof will revolve around the theorem stating that two angles of a triangle are of equal measure if and only if the sides opposite them are of equal length.

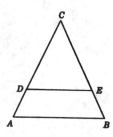

| Statements | Reasons |
|---|---|
| 1. m ∡ A = m ∡ B | 1. Given |
| 2. CA = CB | 2. If a triangle has two angles of equal measure, then the sides opposite those angles are equal in length. |
| 3. CB = CE + BE<br>   CA = CD + AD | 3. The measure of the whole is equal to the sum of the measures of its parts. |
| 4. CD + AD = CE + BE | 4. A quantity may be substituted for its equal. |
| 5. AD = BE | 5. Given |
| 6. CD = CE | 6. If equal quantities are subtracted from equal quantities, the differences are equal quantities. |
| 7. m ∡ CDE = m ∡ CED | 7. If two sides of a triangle are equal, then the angles opposite those sides are equal. |

● **PROBLEM 3-3**

As seen in the accompanying diagram, ΔABC is constructed in such a way that the measure of ∡ A equals 9x, m ∡ B equals 3x - 6, and m ∡ C equals 11x + 2, x being some unknown. Show that ΔABC is a right triangle.

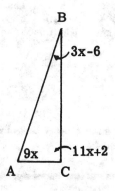

Solution: A triangle is a right triangle if one of its angles is a right angle. The best way to determine the "rightness" of this tri-angle would be to sum the measures of all its angles, set this sum equal to 180°, and solve for the unknown x. If the measure of one angle

turns out to be 90°, then it is a right angle and the triangle is a
right triangle.  The algebra is as follows:

$$m \angle A + m \angle B + m \angle C = 180$$
$$9x + 3x - 6 + 11x + 2 = 180$$
$$23x - 4 = 180$$
$$23x = 184$$
$$x = 8$$

Therefore,

$\angle$ A   measures   (9)(8)  or  72
$\angle$ B   measures   (3)(8) - 6  or  18

and

$\angle$ C   measures   (11)(8) + 2  or  90

Therefore, since $\angle$ C measures 90°, ΔABC is a right triangle.

● **PROBLEM 3-4**

The length of the median drawn to the hypotenuse of a right triangle
is 12 inches.  Find the length of the hypotenuse.  (See figure).

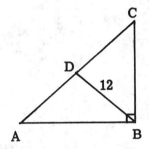

**Solution:** A theorem tells us that the length of the median to the
hypotenuse of a right triangle is equal to one-half the length of the
hypotenuse.  We must identify the median, the hypotenuse, their respective lengths, and substitute them according to the rule cited,
and to solve for any unknowns.

$\overline{AC}$ is the hypotenuse, $\overline{BD}$ the median of length 12", and the
length of $\overline{AC}$ is unknown.  By applying the above theorem we know,

(1).   BD = ½AC  and, by, substitution

(2).   12" = ½AC  which implies that  AC = 24" .

Therefore, the length of hypotenuse $\overline{AC}$ is 24 in.

● **PROBLEM 3-5**

Prove that an equilateral triangle has three equal angles.

**Solution:**   Draw equilateral ΔABC.

Hence, the problem can be restated as:

Given: equilateral ΔABC

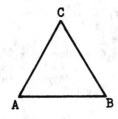

Prove: m⊬A = m⊬B = m⊬C.

| STATEMENTS | REASONS |
|---|---|
| 1. equilateral △ABC | 1. Given. |
| 2. AC ≅ BC ≅ AB | 2. Definition of an equilateral triangle. |
| 3. ⊬A ≅ ⊬B <br> ⊬A ≅ ⊬C <br> ⊬B ≅ ⊬C | 3. If two sides of a triangle are congruent, then the angles opposite those sides are congruent. |
| 4. ⊬A ≅ ⊬B ≅ ⊬C | 4. Transitive Property of Congruence. |

# PARALLEL LINES

● **PROBLEM 3-6**

Given: ⊬ 2 is supplementary to ⊬ 3 .
Prove: $\ell_1 \parallel \ell_2$ .

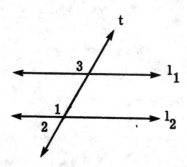

**Solution:** Given two lines intercepted by a transversal, if a pair of corresponding angles are congruent, then the two lines are parallel. In this problem, we will show that since ⊬ 1 and ⊬ 2 are supplementary and ⊬ 2 and ⊬ 3 are supplementary, ⊬ 1 and ⊬ 3 are congruent. Since corresponding angles ⊬ 1 and ⊬ 3 are congruent, it follows $\ell_1 \parallel \ell_2$

| Statement | Reason |
|---|---|
| 1. $\measuredangle$ 2 is supplementary to $\measuredangle$ 3 | 1. Given |
| 2. $\measuredangle$ 1 is supplementary to $\measuredangle$ 2 | 2. Two angles that form a linear pair are supplementary. |
| 3. $\measuredangle$ 1 $\cong$ $\measuredangle$ 3 | 3. Angles supplementary to the same angle are congruent. |
| 4. $\ell_1 \parallel \ell_2$ | 4. Given two lines intercepted by a transversal, if a pair of corresponding angles are congruent, then the two lines are parallel. |

● **PROBLEM 3-7**

If line $\overleftrightarrow{AB}$ is parallel to line $\overleftrightarrow{CD}$ and line $\overleftrightarrow{EF}$ is parallel to line $\overleftrightarrow{GH}$, prove that m $\measuredangle$ 1 = m $\measuredangle$ 2.

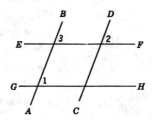

**Solution**: To show $\measuredangle$ 1 $\cong$ $\measuredangle$ 2, we relate both to $\measuredangle$ 3. Because $\overline{EF} \parallel \overline{GH}$, corresponding angles 1 and 3 are congruent. Since $\overline{AB} \parallel \overline{CD}$, corresponding angles 3 and 2 are congruent. Because both $\measuredangle$ 1 and $\measuredangle$ 2 are congruent to the same angle, it follows that $\measuredangle$ 1 $\cong$ $\measuredangle$ 2.

| Statements | Reasons |
|---|---|
| 1. $\overleftrightarrow{EF} \parallel \overleftrightarrow{GH}$ | 1. Given |
| 2. m $\measuredangle$ 1 = m $\measuredangle$ 3 | 2. If two parallel lines are cut by a transversal, corresponding angles are of equal measure. |
| 3. $\overleftrightarrow{AB} \parallel \overleftrightarrow{CD}$ | 3. Given |
| 4. m $\measuredangle$ 2 = m $\measuredangle$ 3 | 4. If two parallel lines are cut by a transversal, corresponding angles are equal in measure. |
| 5. m $\measuredangle$ 1 = m $\measuredangle$ 2 | 5. If two quantities are equal to the same quantity, they are equal to each other. |

As shown in the accompanying figure, if $\overline{BD}$ bisects ∡ ABC and $\overline{BC} \cong \overline{CD}$, prove formally that $\overleftrightarrow{CD} \parallel \overleftrightarrow{BA}$ .

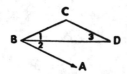

Solution: If two lines are cut by a transversal which form a pair of alternate interior angles that are congruent, then the two lines are parallel. The transversal of lines $\overleftrightarrow{CD}$ and $\overleftrightarrow{BA}$ is $\overleftrightarrow{BD}$, and ∡ 2 and ∡ 3 are alternate interior angles of this transversal. Our task is to prove ∡ 2 ≅ ∡ 3. From the above theorem, it then follows that $\overleftrightarrow{BA} \parallel \overleftrightarrow{CD}$.

| Statement | Reason |
|---|---|
| 1. $\overline{BC} \cong \overline{CD}$ | 1. Given |
| 2. ∡ 3 ≅ ∡ 1 | 2. If two sides of a triangle are congruent, the angles opposite these sides are congruent. |
| 3. ∡ 1 ≅ ∡ 2 | 3. An angle bisector divides the angle into two congruent angles. |
| 4. ∡ 3 ≅ ∡ 2 | 4. Transitive property of congruence. |
| 5. $\overleftrightarrow{CD} \parallel \overleftrightarrow{BA}$ | 5. If two lines are cut by a transversal which forms a pair of congruent alternate interior angles, then the two lines are parallel. |

● PROBLEM 3-9

Given: Δ ABC is isosceles with base $\overline{AB}$ .

∡ A ≅ ∡ 1

Prove: AB ∥ ED .

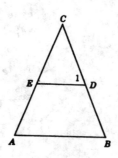

**Solution:** To show two lines parallel, it is sufficient to show that a pair of corresponding angles are congruent. Here, we use the fact that $\Delta$ ACB is isosceles to show $\not{\times}$ A $\cong$ $\not{\times}$ B. Combining this with the given, $\not{\times}$ 1 $\cong$ $\not{\times}$ A, we obtain $\not{\times}$ B$\cong$$\not{\times}$1. Since these are corresponding angles of $\overline{ED}$ and $\overline{AB}$, it follows that $\overline{ED} \parallel \overline{AB}$.

| Statements | Reasons |
|---|---|
| 1. $\Delta$ ABC is isosceles with base $\overline{AB}$ | 1. Given |
| 2. $\overline{AC} \cong \overline{BC}$ | 2. Definition of an isosceles triangle. |
| 3. $\not{\times}$ A $\cong$ $\not{\times}$ B | 3. If two sides of a triangle are congruent, then the angles opposite those sides are congruent. |
| 4. $\not{\times}$ A $\cong$ $\not{\times}$ 1 | 4. Given |
| 5. $\not{\times}$ B $\cong$ $\not{\times}$ 1 | 5. If two quantities are congruent to the same quantity, they are congruent to each other. |
| 6. $\overline{AB} \parallel \overline{ED}$ | 6. If two lines are cut by a transversal so that a pair of corresponding angles are congruent, the lines are parallel. |

● **PROBLEM** 3-10

Let $L_1$, $L_2$, and $L_3$ be lines in plane M. Prove that if $L_1 \parallel L_2$ and $L_3 \perp L_2$, then $L_3 \perp L_1$.

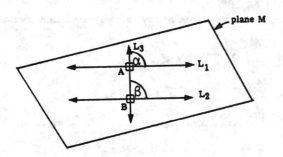

**Solution:** There are 2 cases to consider:

I) $L_3$ intersects $L_1$;

II) $L_3$ does not intersect $L_1$.

Each case is treated separately.

**Case I:** The figure shows the situation for this case. We shall use the fact that the consecutive interior angles of 2 parallel lines cut by a transversal are supplementary to prove that $m \sphericalangle \alpha = 90°$. (i.e., $L_3 \perp L_1$).

First note that $L_3$ acts as a transversal for parallel lines $L_1$ and $L_2$. Angles $\alpha$ and BAC are consecutive interior angles for $L_1$ and $L_2$, and are therefore supplementary. Hence, their measures must sum to $180°$, and we may write:

$$m \sphericalangle BAC + m \sphericalangle \alpha = 180° \qquad (1)$$

But, as the problem indicates, $\sphericalangle$ BAC is a right angle. Therefore,

$$m \sphericalangle BAC = 90° . \qquad (2)$$

Substituting (2) in (1) yields

$$m \sphericalangle \alpha + 90° = 180°$$

or

$$m \sphericalangle \alpha = 90° .$$

This implies that $L_3 \perp L_1$, as was to be shown.

<u>Case II</u>: In this situation, $L_3$ doesn't intersect $L_1$. But, if 2 lines don't intersect, they are parallel, i.e., $L_3 \parallel L_1$. However, we know (from the statement of the problem), that $L_1 \parallel L_2$. Coupling these 2 facts leads to the conclusion that $L_2 \parallel L_3$, which is contrary to the facts as given by the statement of the problem. Hence, this case need not be considered.

● **PROBLEM 3-11**

Prove the angle sum theorem: the sum of the measures of the angles of a triangle is $180°$.

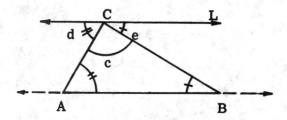

<u>Solution</u>: In the figure, L is constructed parallel to $\overline{AB}$ and it passes through C. Since $\overline{LC} \parallel \overline{AB}$, $\sphericalangle$ d $\cong \sphericalangle$ CAB because they are alternate interior angles. Similarly, $\sphericalangle$ e $\cong \sphericalangle$ CBA.

The sum of the angles of the triangle is

$$S = m \sphericalangle CAB + m \sphericalangle ACB + m \sphericalangle CBA .$$

Using the results found above,

$$S = m \sphericalangle d + m \sphericalangle ACB + m \sphericalangle e. \qquad (1)$$

But
$$m \angle d + m \angle e + m \angle c = 180°$$
since they sum to a straight angle (segment $\overline{CL}$).  Hence,
$$m \angle d + m \angle e = 180° - m \angle c .$$  (2)
Substituting (2) into (1),
$$S = 180° - m \angle c + m \angle ACB.$$
But, $\angle ACB = \angle c$.  Thus,
$$S = 180°.$$

● **PROBLEM 3-12**

Given:  △ ABE

$\overline{AB} \parallel \overline{CD}$

$\overline{CE} \cong \overline{DE}$

Prove:  AE = BE .

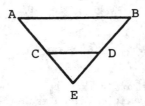

Solution:  If two angles of a triangle are congruent, then the two sides opposite them are congruent.  To show  AE = BE  in  △ABE, we show $\angle A \cong$ $\angle B$.  We prove this by the following steps: (1)  Since  CE = ED, $\angle$ DCE $\cong \angle$ CDE; (2)  Since  $\overline{AB} \parallel \overline{CD}$, the corresponding angles are congruent.  Thus,  $\angle A \cong \angle ECD$  and  $\angle B \cong \angle CDE$; (3)  Since  $\angle A$  and  $\angle B$  are congruent to congruent angles,  $\angle A \cong \angle B$.

| Statements | Reasons |
|---|---|
| 1. $\overline{CE} \cong \overline{DE}$ | 1. Given |
| 2. m $\angle$ ECD = m $\angle$ CDE | 2. If two sides of a triangle have equal .length, then the angles opposite those sides are of equal measure. |
| 3. $\overline{AB} \parallel \overline{CD}$ | 3. Given |
| 4. m $\angle$ ECD = m $\angle$ A | 4. If two parallel lines are cut by a transversal, the corresponding angles are of equal measure. |
| 5. m $\angle$ CDE = m $\angle$ A | 5. If two quantities are equal to the same quantity, they are equal to each other. |

23

6. m ∢ CDE = m ∢ B

    6. If two parallel lines are cut by a transversal, the corresponding angles are of equal measure.

7. m ∢ A = m ∢ B

    7. If two quantities are equal to the same quantity, they are equal to each other.

8. AE = BE

    8. If a triangle has two angles of equal measure, then the sides opposite those angles are of equal lengths.

### ● PROBLEM 3-13

Given: $\overline{AC}$ and $\overline{EB}$ bisect each other at D.

Prove: $\overline{AE} \parallel \overline{BC}$ .

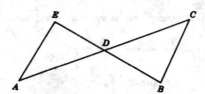

<u>Solution</u>: To show two lines are parallel, it is sufficient to show that a pair of alternate interior angles, such as ∢ A and ∢ C, are congruent.

We first prove ΔAED ≅ ΔCBD by the SAS postulate. Because corresponding parts of congruent triangles are congruent, ∢ A ≅ ∢ C, and thus the lines are parallel.

| <u>Statements</u> | <u>Reasons</u> |
|---|---|
| 1. $\overline{AC}$ and $\overline{EB}$ bisect each other at D. | 1. Given |
| 2. $\overline{ED} \cong \overline{BD}$<br>   $\overline{AD} \cong \overline{CD}$ | 2. Definition of bisector. |
| 3. ∢ EDA ≅ ∢ BDC | 3. Vertical angles are congruent. |
| 4. ΔEDA ≅ ΔBDC | 4. SAS ≅ SAS |
| 5. ∢ A ≅ ∢ C | 5. Corresponding parts of congruent triangles are congruent. |
| 6. $\overline{AE} \parallel \overline{BC}$ | 6. If two lines are cut by a transversal so that alternate interior angles are congruent, the lines are parallel. |

Prove that if both pairs of opposite sides of a quadrilateral are congruent, then they are also parallel.

Given: Quadrilateral ABCD; $\overline{AB} \cong \overline{CD}$; $\overline{AD} \cong \overline{BC}$

Prove: $\overline{AD} \parallel \overline{BC}$; $\overline{AB} \parallel \overline{CD}$

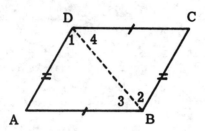

<u>Solution</u>: In the accompanying figure, the opposite sides of quadrilateral ABCD are congruent. Thus, $\overline{AB} \cong \overline{CD}$ and $\overline{AD} \cong \overline{BC}$. We must show $\overline{DC} \parallel \overline{AB}$ and $\overline{AD} \parallel \overline{BC}$.

To do this, we draw diagonal $\overline{DB}$. Remember that if alternate interior angles are congruent, the two lines are parallel. Thus, to show AB $\parallel$ CD, we prove $\angle 3 \cong \angle 4$. To show $\angle 3 \cong \angle 4$, we prove $\triangle ADB \cong \triangle CBD$ by the SSS Postulate. Thus, by corresponding parts, $\angle 3 \cong \angle 4$ and $\overline{AB} \parallel \overline{DC}$.

By corresponding parts, we can also say $\angle 1 \cong \angle 2$. Since $\angle 1$ and $\angle 2$ we alternate interior angles of $\overleftrightarrow{AD}$ and $\overleftrightarrow{BC}$, it follows that $\overline{AD} \parallel \overline{BC}$.

| <u>Statements</u> | <u>Reasons</u> |
|---|---|
| 1. Quadrilateral ABCD; $\overline{AB} \cong \overline{CD}$; $\overline{AD} \cong \overline{CD}$ | 1. Given. |
| 2. $\overline{DB} \cong \overline{DB}$ | 2. A segment is congruent to itself. |
| 3. $\triangle ADB \cong \triangle CBD$ | 3. The SSS Postulate. |
| 4. $\angle 1 \cong \angle 2$<br>$\angle 3 \cong \angle 4$ | 4. Corresponding angles of congruent triangles are congruent. |
| 5. $\overline{AD} \parallel \overline{BC}$, $\overline{AB} \parallel \overline{CD}$ | 5. If two coplanar lines are cut by a transversal such that the alternate interior angles are congruent, then the lines are parallel. |

We are given two triangles, ABC and EHD, as shown in the diagram, and the straight line segment AE . If AD ≅ EC, BC ≅ HD and BC ∥ HD, prove AB ∥ EH .

**Solution:** To prove $\overline{AB} \parallel \overline{EH}$, we first show that the alternate interior angles, ∢ BAC and ∢ HED, formed by transversal AE and segments $\overline{AB}$ and $\overline{EH}$, are congruent. Since a pair of congruent alternate interior angles are sufficient to prove two lines parallel, we may conclude that the $\overline{AB} \parallel \overline{EH}$.

To prove ∢ BAC and ∢ HED are congruent, we must first prove the triangles containing them, Δ's ABC and EHD, are congruent by the SAS ≅ SAS method.

| Statement | Reason |
|---|---|
| 1. $\overline{BC} \cong \overline{HD}$ | 1. Given |
| 2. $\overline{BC} \parallel \overline{HD}$ | 2. Given |
| 3. ∢ BCA ≅ ∢ HDE | 3. If two parallel lines are cut by a transversal, then alternate interior angles are congruent. |
| 4. $\overline{AE}$ is a line segment. | 4. Given |
| 5. $\overline{AD} \cong \overline{EC}$ | 5. Given |
| 6. $\overline{DC} \cong \overline{DC}$ | 6. Reflexive property of congruence. |
| 7. AD = EC; DC = DC | 7. Congruent segments are of equal lengths. |
| 8. AD + DC = EC + CD | 8. Addition Postulate |
| 9. AC = ED | 9. Point Betweenness Postulate. |
| 10. $\overline{AC} \cong \overline{ED}$ | 10. Segments of equal length are congruent. |
| 11. ΔABC ≅ ΔEHD | 11. SAS ≅ SAS |
| 12. ∢ BAC ≅ ∢ HED | 12. Corresponding parts of congruent triangles are congruent. |
| 13. $\overline{AB} \parallel \overline{EH}$ | 13. If two lines are cut by a transversal making a pair of alternate interior angles congruent, then the lines are parallel. |

● **PROBLEM 3-16**

In Figure 1, ∢ B measures 30°, $\overleftrightarrow{BQ} \parallel \overleftrightarrow{AP}$ and $\overleftrightarrow{BP} \parallel \overleftrightarrow{AC}$. Determine m ∢ 1, m ∢ 2, m ∢ 3, m ∢ 4, and m ∢ 5.

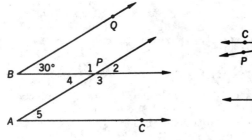

Figure 1                              Figure 2

<u>Solution</u>:  Prior to attacking the question at hand, we will establish
several important facts about angles formed by parallel lines cut by a
transversal. We will employ two characteristics about parallel lines:
(1)  Through a given external point, only one line can be drawn parallel
to a given line; and (2)  If <u>one</u> pair of alternate interior angles are
congruent, then the two lines must be parallel.  (See Figure 2).

The first fact we wish to show is that, given two parallel lines
$q_1$ and $q_2$ cut by transversal t, every pair of alternate interior
angles are congruent. We do this by indirect proof.  Suppose $q_1 \| q_2$
but alternate interior angles ⊀ 1 and ⊀ 2 are not congruent.
Draw $q_3$ through point B such that it forms ⊀ ABP so that ⊀ ABP ≅ ⊀ 2.
This leads to two contradictory lines of reasoning:

(A)  Because ⊀ ABP ≅ ⊀ 2 and ⊀ 1 is not ≅ ⊀ 2, it follows that
⊀ ABP is not ≅ ⊀ 1.  Since $q_3$ and $q_1$ make different angles with transversal t, lines $q_1$ and $q_3$ must be different lines.

(B)  Because alternate interior angles ⊀ ABP and ⊀ 2 are congruent,
(by assumption (2)) it follows that $q_3 \| q_2$.  Since both $q_3$ and $q_1$ are
lines parallel to $q_2$ and passing through external point B, (by assumption (1)) it follows that $q_1$ and $q_3$ are the same line.

Because the two lines of reasoning lead to different conclusions, our
original assumption - ⊀ 1 is not ≅ ⊀ 2 - must be false. We can thus conclude that if two parallel lines are cut by a transversal, <u>any</u> pair of
alternate interior angles are congruent.

Next we shall establish that if two parallel lines are cut by a transversal, each pair of corresponding angles are congruent. From the above
theorem, we know ⊀ 1 ≅ ⊀ 2. Since ⊀ 1 and ⊀ 3 are, by definition,
vertical angles, then ⊀ 1 ≅ ⊀ 3. Therefore, by transitivity, ⊀ 2 ≅ ⊀ 3
and we have the desired results.

Finally, we will prove that interior angles on the same side of the
transversal are supplementary.

Again, since alternate interior angles of parallel lines cut by a
transversal are congruent, we have ⊀ 1 ≅ ⊀ 2. Adjacent angles, whose
exterior sides are contained in a straight line, are supplementary.
Thus, their measures sum to 180°.  Therefore,

$$m \angle 1 + m \angle 4 = 180$$

$$m \angle 2 + m \angle 5 = 180 \ .$$

Since m ⊀ 1 = m ⊀ 2, the quantities can be interchanged to obtain the
following:
$$m \angle 2 + m \angle 4 = 180$$

$$m \angle 1 + m \angle 5 = 180 \ .$$

Angles 2 and 4, as well as ∡ 1 and ∡ 5, are interior angles on the same side of the transversal, and since their measures sum to 180°, they must be supplementary to each other. Therefore, we have established our third and final point.

Now we return to the original question. (See Figure 1.)

Since $\overleftrightarrow{BQ} \parallel \overleftrightarrow{AP}$ and ∡ B and ∡ 1 are interior angles on the same side of the transversal, by a theorem above, ∡ B and ∡ 1 are supplements, i.e. m ∡ B + m ∡ 1 = 180 . We are given m ∡ B = 30 . Therefore, by substitution, 30 + m ∡ 1 = 180, and m ∡ 1 = 150.

Angles B and 2 are corresponding angles formed by a transversal cutting parallel lines $\overleftrightarrow{BQ}$ and $\overleftrightarrow{AP}$. As such, m ∡ B = m ∡ 2. Therefore, m ∡ 2 = 30.

For the parallel lines $\overleftrightarrow{BP}$ and $\overleftrightarrow{AC}$ cut by transversal $\overleftrightarrow{AP}$, ∡ 5 and ∡ 2 are corresponding angles and, accordingly, are congruent. Therefore, m ∡ 5 = 30.

On the same set of parallel lines, ∡ 5 and ∡ 4 are alternate interior angles and, thus are congruent. Therefore, m ∡ 4 = 30.

The last angle we need to determine is ∡ 3. Angle 3 is on the same side of the transversal as ∡ 5 and on the interior of $\overleftrightarrow{BP} \parallel \overleftrightarrow{AC}$. Therefore, ∡ 3 is supplementary to ∡ 5. As such, m ∡ 3 + m ∡ 5 = 180. By substitution, m ∡ 3 + 30 = 180. Thus, m ∡ 3 = 150.

Collecting our results, we have: m ∡ 1 = 150, m ∡ 2 = 30, m ∡ 3 = 150, m ∡ 4 = 30, and m ∡ 5 = 30.

# ANGLE BISECTORS

● PROBLEM 3-17

Given:   DA bisects ∡ CAB.  DB bisects ∡ CBA.
         m ∡ 1 = m ∡ 2 .
Prove:   CA = CB.

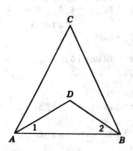

Solution: This proof will involve using the definition of angle bisector and the substitution and addition postulates to prove m ∡ CAB = m ∡ CBA. The desired results will be obtained recalling that the sides of a triangle opposite angles of equal measure are of equal length.

28

| Statements | Reasons |
|---|---|
| 1. DA bisects ∡ CAB<br>   DB bisects ∡ CBA | 1. Given |
| 2. m∡ CAD = m∡ 1<br>   m∡ CBD = m∡ 2 | 2. An angle bisector divides an angle into two angles of equal measure. |
| 3. m∡ = 1 = m∡ 2 | 3. Given |
| 4. m∡ CBD = m∡ 1 | 4. A quantity may be substituted for its equal. |
| 5. m∡ CAD = m∡ CBD | 5. If two quantities are equal to the same quantity, or equal quantities, then they are equal to each other. |
| 6. m∡ CAD + m∡ 1 =<br>   m∡ CBD + m∡ 2 | 6. If equal quantities are added to equal quantities, the sums are equal quantities. |
| 7. m∡ CAB = m∡ CAD + m∡ 1<br>   m∡ CBA = m∡ CBD + m∡ 2 | 7. The measure of the whole is equal to the sum of the measures of its parts. |
| 8. m∡ CAB = m∡ CBA | 8. If two quantities are equal to the same quantity, or equal quantities, then they're equal to each other. |
| 9. CA = CB | 9. If a triangle has two angles of equal measure then the sides opposite those angles are equal in length. |

● **PROBLEM 3-18**

Show that the angle bisectors of a triangle are concurrent at a point equidistant from the sides of the triangle.

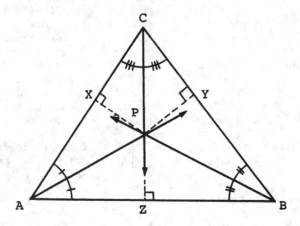

Solution:  The angle bisector of any angle is the set of points in the interior of the angle that are equidistant from the sides of the angle.

In △ABC, the intersection of the bisector of ∡ A and the bisector of ∡ B is a point P. Because P is on the bisector of ∡ A, the distance from P to AC equals the distance from P to AB . Because P is on the bisector of ∡ B, the distance from P to BC equals the distance from P to AB. By transitivity, the distance from P to $\overline{AC}$ equals the distance from P to $\overline{BC}$, i.e. P is equidistant from the sides of ∡ C. Therefore, point P, is also on the bisector of ∡ C, and the three bisectors are concurrent at a point equidistant from the sides of the triangle.

Given: The angle bisectors of ∆ABC .
Prove: The bisectors are concurrent at a point equidistant from the sides.

| Statements | Reasons |
|---|---|
| 1. The angle bisectors of ∆ABC | 1. Given |
| 2. Let P be the point of intersection of the bisectors of ∡A and ∡B. | 2. In a plane, two non-parallel, non-coincident lines intersect in a unique point. |
| 3. P is in the interior of ∡ A. <br> P is in the interior of ∡ B. | 3. All points (except for the vertex) of the angle bisector lie in the interior of the angle. |
| 4. P is in the interior of ∆ABC | 4. If a point is in the interior of two angles of a triangle, then it is in the interior of the triangle. |
| 5. Let X,Y, and Z be the points on sides $\overline{AC}$, $\overline{CB}$, and $\overline{AB}$ such that $\overline{PX} \perp \overline{AC}$, $\overline{PY} \perp \overline{CB}$, and $\overline{PZ} \perp \overline{AB}$ . | 5. From a given external point, only one line can be drawn perpendicular to a given line. |
| 6. PX, PY, and PZ are the distances from P to the sides | 6. The distance from an external point to a line is the length of the perpendicular segment from the point to the line. |
| 7. PX = PZ <br> PY = PZ | 7. All points on the angle bisector are equidistant from the sides of the angle. |
| 8. PX = PY | 8. Transitivity Postulate. |
| 9. P is in the interior of ∡ C. | 9. All points in the interior of a triangle are in the interior of each of the angles. |
| 10. P is on the angle bisector of ∡ C. | 10. All points in the interior of an angle that are equidistant from the sides of the angle are on the angle bisector. |
| 11. P is equidistant from the sides of ∆ABC. | 11. Follows from Steps 7 and 8. |
| 12. The angle bisectors are concurrent at a point equidistant from the sides. | 12. Lines are concurrent if their intersection consists of at least one point. Also, Step 11. |

# EXTERIOR ANGLES

● PROBLEM 3-19

In the figure, what can be said about ∡3 and ∡1? About ∡2 and ∡4? If m∡4 > m∡3, prove that m∡2 > m∡1.(See figure.)

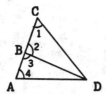

Solution: We use the Exterior Angle Theorem to find relationships between the given angles. This theorem states that an exterior angle of a triangle has greater measure than either of its remote interior angles. (An exterior angle of a triangle is any angle outside of the triangle which forms a linear pair with an angle of the triangle. A remote interior angle of a triangle is an angle of a triangle which does not form a linear pair with the given exterior angle in question.)

In the figure, ∡3 is an exterior angle of ΔBCD. ∡1 is a remote interior angle of the triangle, relative to angle 3. Hence, m∡3 > m∡1. Furthermore, ∡2 is an exterior angle of ΔBAD, and ∡4 is a remote interior angle of ΔBAD relative to ∡2. Hence, m∡2 > m∡4.

Given that m∡4 > m∡3, and using the conclusions drawn above, we may write the following string of inequalities:

$$m\angle 2 > m\angle 4$$
$$m\angle 4 > m\angle 3 \tag{1}$$
$$m\angle 3 > m\angle 1$$

Coupling the first two of these inequalities yields

$$m\angle 2 > m\angle 3 \quad \text{and} \quad m\angle 3 > m\angle 1.$$

Combining these 2 inequalities gives

$$m\angle 2 > m\angle 1.$$

● **PROBLEM 3-20**

Find the numerical measure of each of the angles of ΔABC if m∡A = 19x − 15, m∡C = 9x + 25, and m∡ABD = 26x + 20.

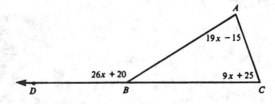

Solution: To find m∡A, m∡B and m∡C, we first solve for
∋  x can be solved for by using the Exterior Angle Theorem:
the measure of an exterior angle of the triangle equals the
sum of the remote interior angles. Therefore,

31

$$m\angle ABD = m\angle A + m\angle C$$

$$26x + 20 = (19x - 15) + (9x + 25) = 28x + 10$$

To isolate the variable x, we subtract 26x and 10 from both sides.

$$2x = 10 \qquad \text{or} \qquad x = 5.$$

Then $m\angle A = 19x - 15 = 19(5) - 15 = 80°$

$m\angle C = 9x + 25 = 9(5) + 25 = 70°$

Since, $\angle A$, $\angle B$, and $\angle C$ are angles of the same triangle,

$$m\angle A + m\angle B + m\angle C = 180°$$

or, $m\angle B = 180 - m\angle A - m\angle C = 180 - 80 - 70 = 30°$.

# CONGRUENT ANGLES

● **PROBLEM** 3-21

$\angle ABE$ is intersected by rays BD and BC in such a way that $\angle ABC \cong \angle DBE$. Prove that $\angle ABD \cong \angle CBE$.

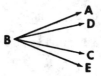

Solution: This proof will first employ the reflexive property of angles (An angle is congruent to itself) and then the Subtraction Postulate (Equal quantities subtracted from equal quantities yield equal quantities).

GIVEN: $\angle ABC \cong \angle DBE$

PROVE: $\angle ABD \cong \angle CBE$

| STATEMENTS | REASONS |
|---|---|
| 1. $\angle ABC \cong \angle DBE$ | 1. Given |
| 2. $\angle DBC \cong \angle DBC$ | 2. An angle is congruent to itself. |
| 3. $m\angle ABC = m\angle DBE$<br>$m\angle DBC = m\angle DBC$ | 3. Congruent angles have equal measures. |

| 4. m∡ABC−m∡DBC=m∡DBE−m∡DBC | 4. Subtraction Postulate. |
| 5. m∡ABD = m∡CBE | 5. Substitution Posulate. |
| 6. ∡ABD ≅ ∡CBE | 6. Angles of equal measure are congruent. |

● **PROBLEM** 3-22

In the figure shown, ΔABC is an isosceles triangle, such that $\overline{BA} \cong \overline{BC}$. Line segment $\overline{AD}$ bisects ∡BAC and $\overline{CD}$ bisects ∡BCA. Prove that ΔADC is an isosceles triangle.

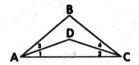

Solution: In order to prove ΔADC is isosceles, we must prove that 2 of its sides, $\overline{AD}$ and $\overline{CD}$, are congruent. To prove $\overline{AD} \cong \overline{CD}$ in ΔADC, we have to prove that the angles opposite $\overline{AD}$ and $\overline{CD}$, ∡1 and ∡2, are congruent.

| STATEMENT | REASON |
| --- | --- |
| 1. $\overline{BA} \cong \overline{BC}$ | 1. Given. |
| 2. ∡BAC ≅ ∡BCA  or m∡BAC = m∡BCA | 2. If two sides of a triangle are congruent, then the angles opposite them are congruent. |
| 3. $\overline{AD}$ bisects ∡BAC $\overline{CD}$ bisects ∡BCA | 3. Given. |
| 4. m∡1 = ½m∡BAC m∡2 = ½m∡BCA | 4. The bisector of an angle divides the angle into two angles whose measures are equal. |
| 5. m∡1 = m∡2 | 5. Halves of equal quantities are equal. |
| 6. ∡1 ≅ ∡2 | 6. If the measure of two angles are equal, then the angles are congruent. |
| 7. $\overline{CD} \cong \overline{AD}$ | 7. If two angles of a triangle are congruent, then the sides opposite these angles are congruent. |
| 8 ΔADC is an isosceles triangle | 8. If a triangle has two congruent sides, then it is an isosceles triangle. |

33

# CONGRUENT LINE SEGMENTS

Given isosceles triangle ABC with sides $\overline{AB} \cong \overline{AC}$, and the fact that $\overline{DB} \cong \overline{EC}$, prove that $\overline{AD} \cong \overline{AE}$.

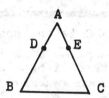

**Solution:** In this problem, we make use of the Subtraction Postulate as applied to congruency. The Subtraction Postulate states that when equal quantities are subtracted from equal quantities, the differences are equal.

| STATEMENT | REASON |
|---|---|
| 1. $\overline{AB} \cong \overline{AC}$ <br> $\overline{DB} \cong \overline{EC}$ | 1. Given. |
| 2. AB = AC <br> DB = EC | 2. Congruent segments are equal in length. |
| 3. AB - DB = AC - EC | 3. Subtraction Postulate. |
| 4. AD = AE | 4. Substitution Postulate. |
| 5. $\overline{AD} \cong \overline{AE}$ | 5. Segments of equal lengths are congruent. |

Lines have been drawn in rectangle ABCD from point A bisecting $\overline{CD}$, and from point C, bisecting $\overline{AB}$ (as in the figure). In a rectangle, opposite sides are of equal length. Therefore, $\overline{AB} \cong \overline{DC}$. Prove $\overline{AF} \cong \overline{EC}$.

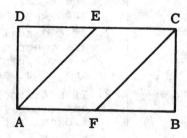

<u>Solution</u>: The Division Postulate states that congruent quantities divided by equal nonzero quantities result in quotients that are equal. This postulate will be employed in the following proof.

GIVEN: $\overline{AB} \cong \overline{DC}$; $\overline{AE}$ bisects $\overline{DC}$; $\overline{CF}$ bisects $\overline{AB}$

PROVE: $\overline{AF} \cong \overline{EC}$

| STATEMENT | REASON |
|---|---|
| 1. $\overline{AB} \cong \overline{DC}$; $\overline{AE}$ bisects $\overline{DC}$; $\overline{CF}$ bisects $\overline{AB}$ | 1. Given. |
| 2. EC = ½ DC<br>AF = ½ AB | 2. The bisector of a segment divides it into two congruent segments, **each of whose** measure is one half the measure of the original segment. |
| 3. EC = AF | 3. The Division Postulate. |
| 4. $\overline{AF} \cong \overline{EC}$ | 4. Line segments of equal length are congruent. |

# SIDE - ANGLE - SIDE POSTULATE

● **PROBLEM** 3-25

Given: $\overline{AD} \cong \overline{AC}$. $\overline{AB} \cong \overline{AE}$. Prove: ΔADB $\cong$ ΔACE.

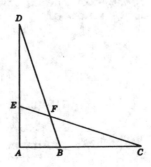

<u>Solution</u>: The fact that the relevant triangles overlap will aid us in completing this proof. We are given congruence between two pairs of corresponding sides. Furthermore the angle included between the sides is shared by the two triangles. By the SAS Postulate, the two triangles are congruent.

| STATEMENTS | REASONS |
|---|---|
| 1. $\overline{AD} \cong \overline{AC}$ | 1. Given. |
| 2. $\overline{AB} \cong \overline{AE}$ | 2. Given. |
| 3. $\angle A \cong \angle A$ | 3. Reflexive Property of Congruence; a quantity is congruent to itself. |
| 4. $\triangle ADB \cong \triangle ACE$ | 4. SAS $\cong$ SAS; if two sides and the included angle of one triangle are congruent, respectively, to two sides and the included angle of a second triangle, then the triangles are congruent. |

● **PROBLEM 3-26**

Given: $\triangle ABE$, $\overline{AE} \cong \overline{BE}$, $\overline{AC} \cong \overline{BD}$. Prove: $\angle 3 \cong \angle 4$.

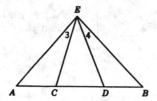

Solution: Angles 3 and 4 are corresponding parts of $\triangle$'s EAC and EBD. We can prove the required congruence, therefore, by showing $\triangle EAC \cong \triangle EBD$.

From the given information, we have congruence between two pairs of corresponding sides. We can use the fact that the angles opposite the congruent sides of a triangle are congruent to show congruence of the corresponding included angles. Hence, by the SAS posulate, we will have proved $\triangle EAC \cong \triangle EBD$.

| STATEMENTS | REASONS |
|---|---|
| 1. $\overline{AE} \cong \overline{BE}$ | 1. Given. |
| 2. $\angle A \cong \angle B$ | 2. If two sides of a triangle are congruent, then the angles opposite those sides are congruent. |
| 3. $\overline{AC} \cong \overline{BD}$ | 3. Given. |
| 4. $\triangle EAC \cong \triangle EBD$ | 4. SAS $\cong$ SAS |
| 5. $\angle 3 \cong \angle 4$ | 5. Corresponding parts of congruent triangles are congruent. |

In the figure, $\overline{SR}$ and $\overline{ST}$ are straight line segments. $\overline{SX} \cong \overline{SY}$ and $\overline{XR} \cong \overline{YT}$. Prove that $\triangle RSY \cong \triangle TSX$.

**Solution:** The triangles are overlapping in this problem because they share a common angle.

This proof will employ the S.A.S. Postulate for showing congruence between two triangles.

| STATEMENT | REASON |
|---|---|
| 1. $\overline{SX} \cong \overline{SY}$ | 1. Given. |
| 2. $\overline{XR} \cong \overline{YT}$ | 2. Given. |
| 3. SX = SY; XR = YT | 3. Congruent segments are of equal length. |
| 4. SX + XR = SY + YT   or   SR = ST | 4. Addition Postulate |
| 5. $\overline{SR} \cong \overline{ST}$ | 5. Segments of equal length are congruent. |
| 6. $\measuredangle S \cong \measuredangle S$ | 6. Reflexive Property of Congruence. |
| 7. $\triangle RSY \cong \triangle TSX$ | 7. S.A.S. $\cong$ S.A.S. |

$\overline{AD}$ is a straight line segment. Triangles AEB and DFC are drawn in such a way that $\measuredangle A \cong \measuredangle D$ and $\overline{AE} \cong \overline{DF}$. Additionally, it is given that $\overline{AC} \cong \overline{BD}$. Prove that $\triangle AEB \cong \triangle DFC$.

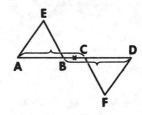

Solution:    Since we are given some information about two
sides and the included angle, it seems logical to use the
postulate which states that if two sides of a triangle and
the included angle are congruent to two sides and the included angle of another triangle, then the triangles are
congruent.

GIVEN: ⦨A ≅ ⦨D; $\overline{AE}$ ≅ $\overline{DF}$; $\overline{AC}$ ≅ $\overline{BD}$

Prove: △AEB ≅ △DFC

| STATEMENT | REASON |
|---|---|
| 1. $\overline{AE}$ ≅ $\overline{DF}$ | 1. Given. |
| 2. ⦨A ≅ ⦨D | 2. Given. |
| 3. $\overline{AD}$ is a straight line segment | 3. Given. |
| 4. $\overline{AC}$ ≅ $\overline{DB}$ | 4. Given. |
| 5. $\overline{BC}$ ≅ $\overline{BC}$ | 5. Reflexive property of congruence |
| 6. $\overline{AC}$ - $\overline{BC}$ ≅ $\overline{DB}$ - $\overline{BC}$ or $\overline{AB}$ ≅ $\overline{DC}$ | 6. If congruent segments are subtracted from congruent segments the differences are congruent segments. |
| 7. △AEB ≅ △DFC | 7. S.A.S. ≅ S.A.S. |

● **PROBLEM 3-29**

We are given quadrilateral LMNP with $\overline{LS}$ and $\overline{MR}$ drawn as
shown in the figure. If $\overline{LP}$ ⊥ $\overline{PN}$, $\overline{MN}$ ⊥ $\overline{PN}$, $\overline{LP}$ ≅ $\overline{MN}$ and
$\overline{PR}$ ≅ $\overline{NS}$, then prove that △LPS ≅ △MNR.

Solution:  Triangles LPS and MNR overlap in the sense that
$\overline{RS}$ is shared by both side PS of △LPS and side RN of △MNR.
This feature will aid us in proving the congruence required
by the problem.

| STATEMENT | REASON |
|---|---|
| 1. $\overline{LP}$ ≅ $\overline{MN}$ | 1. Given. |
| 2. $\overline{LP}$ ⊥ $\overline{PN}$  and  $\overline{MN}$ ⊥ $\overline{PN}$ | 2. Given. |

| | |
|---|---|
| 3. ⧽LPS and ⧽MNR are right angles | 3. Perpendicular lines intersect and form right angles. |
| 4. ⧽LPS ≅ ⧽MNR | 4. All right angles are congruent. |
| 5. $\overline{RS}$ ≅ $\overline{SR}$ | 5. Reflexive Property of Congruence. |
| 6. $\overline{PR}$ ≅ $\overline{NS}$ | 6. Given. |
| 7. RS = SR; PR = NS | 7. Congruent segments are of equal length. |
| 8. RS + PR = SR + NS or SP = NR | 8. Addition Postulate. |
| 9. $\overline{SP}$ ≅ $\overline{NR}$ | 9. Segments of equal length are congruent. |
| 10. △LPS ≅ △MNR | 10. SAS Postulate. |

● **PROBLEM 3-30**

Given: $\overline{DC}$ ≅ $\overline{AB}$. ⧽CDA ≅ ⧽BAD. Prove: $\overline{AC}$ ≅ $\overline{BD}$.

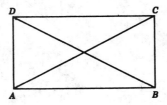

Solution: Noticing that $\overline{AC}$ and $\overline{BD}$ are corresponding parts of overlapping triangles CDA and BAD will assist us in completing this proof. We are given congruence between two corresponding parts and will use the fact that the triangles overlap to gain the third congruence.

| STATEMENTS | REASONS |
|---|---|
| 1. $\overline{DC}$ ≅ $\overline{AB}$ | 1. Given. |
| 2. ⧽CDA ≅ ⧽BAD | 2. Given. |
| 3. $\overline{DA}$ ≅ $\overline{DA}$ | 3. Reflexive Property of Congruence. |
| 4. △CDA ≅ △BAD | 4. SAS ≅ SAS. |
| 5. $\overline{AC}$ ≅ $\overline{BD}$ | 5. Corresponding parts of congruent triangles are congruent. |

39

In the figure, $\overline{AB} \cong \overline{AC}$ and $\overline{A'B} \cong \overline{A'C}$. Using the SAS Postulate prove that $\triangle AA'B \cong \triangle AA'C$.

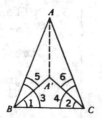

Solution: We shall use the fact that the base angles of an isosceles triangle are congruent to prove that $\angle 5 \cong \angle 6$ (see figure). Using this and the given facts we can then prove that $\triangle AA'B \cong \triangle AA'C$ by the S.A.S. Postulate.

Because $\overline{AB} \cong \overline{AC}$ and $\overline{A'B} \cong \overline{A'C}$, $\triangle ABC$ and $\triangle A'BC$ are both isosceles. Since the base angles of an isosceles triangle are congruent, we obtain (see figure)

$$\angle 1 \cong \angle 2 \tag{1}$$

$$\angle 3 \cong \angle 4 \tag{2}$$

Subtracting (1) from (2) yields

$$(\angle 3 - \angle 1) \cong (\angle 4 - \angle 2) \quad \text{or} \quad \angle 5 \cong \angle 6.$$

From the given facts, $\overline{AB} \cong \overline{AC}$ and $\overline{A'B} \cong \overline{A'C}$. Hence, by the S.A.S. Postulate, $\triangle AA'B \cong \triangle AA'C$.

Prove that any point on the perpendicular bisector of a line segment is equidistant from the endpoints of the segment.

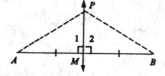

Solution: Let A and B be the endpoints and M the midpoint of the line segment. Let P be any point on the bisector. The distances from P to the endpoints are AP and BP.

AP and BP are corresponding sides of triangles $\triangle APM$ and $\triangle BPM$. We show $\triangle APM \cong \triangle BPM$ by the SAS Postulate and thus AP must equal BP. Since P is an arbitrary point on the bisector, then all points of the perpendicular bisector must be equidistant from the endpoints of the bisected segment.

GIVEN: P is any point on the perpendicular bisector of $\overline{AB}$; the bisector and $\overline{AB}$ intersect at point M.

PROVE: PA = PB

| STATEMENTS | REASONS |
|---|---|
| 1. P is any point on the perpendicular bisector of $\overline{AB}$. The bisector and $\overline{AB}$ intersect at M | 1. Given. |
| 2. $\overleftrightarrow{PM} \perp \overline{AB}$ | 2. The perpendicular bisector of a segment is the line perpendicular to the segment at its midpoint. |
| 3. $\measuredangle$ 1 and $\measuredangle$ 2 are right angles | 3. Perpendicular lines intersect at right angles. |
| 4. $\measuredangle$ 1 $\cong$ $\measuredangle$ 2 | 4. All right angles are congruent. |
| 5. M is the midpoint of $\overline{AB}$ | 5. Definition of perpendicular bisector. |
| 6. AM = MB | 6. The midpoint of a segment divides the segment into two equal segments. |
| 7. Draw the auxiliary segments $\overline{PA}$ and $\overline{PB}$. | 7. Any two distinct points determine a line (Line Postulate). |
| 8. $\overline{PM} \cong \overline{PM}$ | 8. Any segment is congruent to itself. |
| 9. $\triangle PAM \cong \triangle PBM$ | 9. The SAS Postulate. |
| 10. PA = PB | 10. Corresponding sides of congruent triangles are congruent. |

41

# ANGLE - SIDE - ANGLE POSTULATE

We are given, as shown in the figure, ΔACB and ΔADB and are told that straight line $\overleftrightarrow{AE}$ bisects ⊀CAD. Also given is ⊀CBE ≅ ⊀DBE. Prove ΔACB ≅ ΔADB.

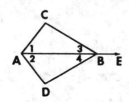

Solution: The most direct way to prove congruence in this case is to make use of the ASA Postulate. This postulate tells us that if two angles and the included side of one triangle are congruent, respectively, to two angles and the included side of another triangle, then the two triangles are congruent.

| STATEMENT | REASON |
|---|---|
| 1. $\overleftrightarrow{AE}$ bisects ⊀CAD | 1. Given. |
| 2. ⊀1 ≅ ⊀2 | 2. An angle bisector divides the angle into two congruent angles. |
| 3. $\overline{AB}$ ≅ $\overline{AB}$ | 3. Reflexivity of congruence. |
| 4. $\overleftrightarrow{AE}$ is a straight line | 4. Given. |
| 5. ⊀CBE ≅ ⊀DBE | 5. Given. |
| 6. ⊀3 is supplementary to ⊀CBE and ⊀4 is supplementary to ⊀DBE | 6. If the non-common sides of two adjacent angles lie on a straight line, then the angles are supplementary. |
| 7. ⊀3 ≅ ⊀4 | 7. Supplements of congruent angles are congruent. |
| 8. ΔACB ≅ ΔADB | 8. A.S.A. Postulate. |

Given: ΔABC. DC = EC. ⊀1 = ⊀2. Prove: $\overline{AC}$ ≅ $\overline{BC}$.

Solution: The segments in question, $\overline{AC}$ and $\overline{BC}$, are corresponding parts of overlapping Δ's CDB and CEA. The proof is set up using the ASA postulate to show ΔCDB ≅ ΔCEA.

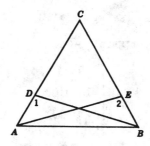

| STATEMENTS | REASONS |
|---|---|
| 1. ∢1 = ∢2 | 1. Given. |
| 2. ∢1 and ∢CDB are supplements ∢2 and ∢CEA are supplements | 2. Adjacent angles whose non-common sides form a straight line are supplements. |
| 3. ∢CDB = ∢CEA | 3. Supplements of equal angles are equal. |
| 4. ∢C = ∢C | 4. Reflexive law. |
| 5. $\overline{DC} \cong \overline{EC}$ | 5. Given. |
| 6. ΔCDB $\cong$ ΔCEA | 6. ASA $\cong$ ASA. |
| 7. $\overline{AC} \cong \overline{BC}$ | 7. Corresponding parts of congruent triangles are congruent. |

● **PROBLEM** 3-35

If ∢3 $\cong$ ∢4 and $\overline{QM}$ bisects ∢PQR, prove that M is the midpoint of $\overline{PR}$.

<u>Solution</u>: To show that M is the midpoint of $\overline{PR}$, we prove that M divides $\overline{PR}$ into two congruent segments - that is, $\overline{PM} \cong \overline{MR}$. If we prove ΔPQM $\cong$ ΔRQM, $\overline{PM} \cong \overline{MR}$ follows by corresponding parts.

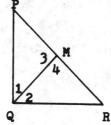

We prove ΔPQM $\cong$ ΔRQM by the ASA Postulate: (1) ∢1 $\cong$ ∢2 because $\overline{QM}$ bisects ∢PQR; (2) $\overline{QM} \cong \overline{QM}$; and (3) ∢3 $\cong$ ∢4 is given. We present our results in the formal, two column proof format..

43

GIVEN: ∡3 ≅ ∡4; $\overline{QM}$ bisects ∡PQR.

PROVE: M is the midpoint $\overline{PR}$.

| STATEMENTS | REASONS |
|---|---|
| 1. ∡3 ≅ ∡4; $\overline{QM}$ bisects ∡PQR | 1. Given. |
| 2. ∡1 ≅ ∡2 | 2. The angle bisector of an angle divides the angle into two congruent angles. |
| 3. $\overline{QM}$ ≅ $\overline{QM}$ | 3. Every segment is congruent to itself. |
| 4. ΔPQM ≅ ΔRQM | 4. ASA Postulate. |
| 5. $\overline{PM}$ ≅ $\overline{RM}$ | 5. Corresponding sides of congruent triangles are congruent. |
| 6. M is the midpoint of PR | 6. Definition of a midpoint. |

● **PROBLEM 3-36**

Given: ∡1 ≅ ∡2; ∡3 ≅ ∡4. Prove: RM = RN.

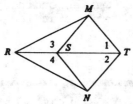

Solution: In most proofs, the necessary congruences are not always given. Frequently, to show two triangles congruent, we have to prove the congruence of corresponding parts by proving another set of triangles congruent. Here, we must show RM = RN or $\overline{RM}$ ≅ $\overline{RN}$. $\overline{RM}$ and $\overline{RN}$ are corresponding sides of ΔRMS and ΔRNS. In these triangles, we have that ∡3 ≅ ∡4 and $\overline{RS}$ ≅ $\overline{RS}$. To prove congruence, we must also show $\overline{MS}$ ≅ $\overline{NS}$. We can show $\overline{MS}$ ≅ $\overline{NS}$ by proving ΔMST ≅ ΔNST. Thus we (1) prove ΔMST ≅ ΔNST by the ASA Postulate; (2) show $\overline{MS}$ ≅ $\overline{NS}$ by corresponding parts; and (3) show ΔRMS ≅ ΔRNS by the SAS Postulate.

| STATEMENTS | REASONS |
|---|---|
| 1. ∡1 ≅ ∡2; ∡3 ≅ ∡4 | 1. Given. |
| 2. ∡MST and ∡3 are supplementary ∡NST and ∡4 are supplementary | 2. Two angles that form a linear pair are supplementary. |

44

| STATEMENT | REASON |
|---|---|
| 3. ⟩MST ≅ ⟩NST | 3. Angles supplementary to congruent angles are congruent. |
| 4. $\overline{ST} ≅ \overline{ST}$ | 4. A segment is congruent to itself. |
| 5. △SMT ≅ △SNT | 5. The ASA Postulate. |
| 6. $\overline{MS} ≅ \overline{NS}$ | 6. Corresponding sides of congruent triangles are congruent. |
| 7. $\overline{RS} ≅ \overline{RS}$ | 7. A segment is congruent to itself. |
| 8. △RMS ≅ △RNS | 8. The SAS Postulate. |
| 9. $\overline{RM} ≅ \overline{RN}$ | 9. Corresponding sides of congruent triangles are congruent. |
| 10. RM = RN | 10. Congruent segments are of the same length. |

● **PROBLEM 3-37**

Prove that the altitudes drawn to the legs of an isosceles triangle are congruent.

Solution: The accompanying figure shows an isosceles triangle ABC with $\overline{BA} ≅ \overline{BC}$, and altitudes $\overline{CD}$ and $\overline{AE}$. By the definition of altitudes, $\overline{CD} \perp \overline{AB}$ and $\overline{AE} \perp \overline{BC}$.

We must prove that $\overline{CD} ≅ \overline{AE}$. This can be done by proving △AEC ≅ △CDA and employing the corresponding parts rule of congruent triangles.

The congruent triangle postulate that can be best used in this problem is the one which states that two triangles are congruent if two angles and a side opposite one of the angles in one triangle are congruent to the corresponding parts of the other triangle. We shall refer to this rule as A.A.S. Postulate.

| STATEMENT | REASON |
|---|---|
| 1. In △ABC, $\overline{BA} ≅ \overline{BC}$ | 1. Given. |
| 2. ⟩BAC ≅ ⟩BCA | 2. If two sides of a triangle are congruent, the angles opposite these sides are congruent. |

45

| | |
|---|---|
| 3. $\overline{AE} \perp \overline{BC}$, $\overline{CD} \perp \overline{BA}$ | 3. Given. |
| 4. ⟩CDA and ⟩AEC are right angles | 4. When two perpendicular lines intersect, they form right angles. |
| 5. ⟩CDA $\cong$ ⟩AEC | 5. All right angles are congruent. |
| 6. $\overline{AC} \cong \overline{AC}$ | 6. Reflexive property of congruence. |
| 7. △ADC $\cong$ △CEA | 7. A.A.S. $\cong$ A.A.S. |
| 8. $\overline{CD} \cong \overline{AE}$ | 8. Corresponding parts of congruent triangles are congruent. |

# SIDE - SIDE - SIDE POSTULATE

● **PROBLEM 3-38**

Prove: the median drawn to the base of an isosceles triangle bisects the vertex angle.

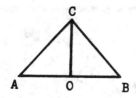

Solution: Draw isosceles △ABC with median $\overline{CO}$, as in the figure shown.

We are asked to prove ⟩ACO $\cong$ ⟩BCO. By proving △ACO $\cong$ △BCO, we can derive the desired result since the angles are corresponding angles of the two triangles.

Given: isosceles △ABC; median $\overline{CO}$

Prove: $\overline{CO}$ bisects ⟩C

| STATEMENTS | REASONS |
|---|---|
| 1. $\overline{CO}$ is a median | 1. Given. |
| 2. $\overline{AO} \cong \overline{BO}$ | 2. Definition of median. |
| 3. △ABC is isosceles | 3. Given. |
| 4. $\overline{AC} \cong \overline{BC}$ | 4. Definition of an isosceles triangle. |
| 5. $\overline{CO} \cong \overline{CO}$ | 5. Reflexive property. |

46

| 6. ΔAOC $\overset{\sim}{=}$ ΔBOC | 6. SSS $\overset{\sim}{=}$ SSS |
|---|---|
| 7. ⟩ACO $\overset{\sim}{=}$ ⟩BCO | 7. Corresponding parts of congruent triangles are congruent. |
| 8. $\overline{CO}$ bisects ⟩C | 8. A segment that divides an angle into two angles that have equal measure bisects that angle. |

● **PROBLEM 3-39**

Prove the median to the base of an isosceles triangle is perpendicular to the base. (In the figure, Δ ABC is isosceles, such that $\overline{CA} \overset{\sim}{=} \overline{CB}$, and $\overline{CM}$ is the median to base $\overline{AB}$. Prove $\overline{CM} \perp \overline{AB}$.)

Solution: Two methods can be used to solve this problem. The first method will utilize the theorem which states that two lines intersecting to form two congruent adjacent angles are perpendicular. The second method will employ the fact that two points each equdistant from the end-points of a line segment determine the perpendicular bisector of the line segment.

Method 1: This method involves proving ΔCMA $\overset{\sim}{=}$ ΔCMB, and by coresponding parts, showing that ⟩1 $\overset{\sim}{=}$ ⟩2. Since two adjacent angles are congruent, $\overline{CM} \perp \overline{AB}$. To prove ΔCMA $\overset{\sim}{=}$ ΔCMB, use the S.S.S. $\overset{\sim}{=}$ S.S.S. method.

| STATEMENT | REASON |
|---|---|
| 1. $\overline{CA} \overset{\sim}{=} \overline{CB}$ | 1. Given. |
| 2. $\overline{CM}$ is the median to base $\overline{AB}$ | 2. Given. |
| 3. $\overline{AM} \overset{\sim}{=} \overline{BM}$ | 3. A median in a triangle divides the side to which it is drawn into two congruent parts. |
| 4. $\overline{CM} \overset{\sim}{=} \overline{CM}$ | 4. Reflexive property of congruence. |
| 5. ΔCMA $\overset{\sim}{=}$ ΔCMB | 5. S.S.S. $\overset{\sim}{=}$ S.S.S. |
| 6. ⟩CMA $\overset{\sim}{=}$ ⟩CMB | 6. Corresponding parts of congruent triangles are congruent. |

| STATEMENT | REASON |
|---|---|
| 7. ∢CMA and ∢CMB are adjacent angles | 7. Two angles are adjacent if they have a common vertex and a common side but do not have common interior points. |
| 8. $\overline{CM} \perp \overline{AB}$ | 8. Two line segments are perpendicular if they intersect and form congruent adjacent angles. |

Method 2:  This method involves proving that point C and point M are both equidistant from the endpoints, A and B, of $\overline{AB}$. By the second theorem mentioned above, this will prove that $\overline{CM}$ is perpendicular to $\overline{AB}$.

| STATEMENT | REASON |
|---|---|
| 1. $\overline{CA} \cong \overline{CB}$ or C is equidistant from A and B | 1. Given. |
| 2. $\overline{CM}$ is a median | 2. Given |
| 3. $\overline{MA} \cong \overline{MB}$ or M is equidistant from A and B | 3. A median in a triangle divides the side to which it is drawn into two congruent parts. |
| 4. $\overline{CM} \perp \overline{AB}$ | 4. Two points, each equidistant from the endpoints of a line segment, determine the perpendicular bisector of the line segment. |

● PROBLEM 3-40

Let ABC be an equilateral triangle. Let D be the midpoint of $\overline{AB}$. Prove that $\triangle DCB \cong \triangle DCA$. What kind of triangle is $\triangle DCB$? What can be said about ∢ACD and ∢BCD? (See figure.)

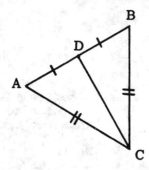

Solution:  We use the S.S.S. Postulate to prove that $\triangle DCB \cong \triangle DCA$. We know that D is the midpoint of $\overline{AB}$. Hence, $\overline{DA} \cong \overline{DB}$. Also, ABC is an equilateral triangle, thus $\overline{AC} \cong \overline{BC}$.

Lastly, $\overline{DC} \cong \overline{DC}$ by the reflexive property. By the S.S.S. Postulate $\triangle DCB \cong \triangle DCA$.

Since $\triangle DCB \cong \triangle DCA$,

then    m∡ADC $\cong$ m∡BDC.                                                    (1)

But, from the figure

m∡ADC + m∡BDC = 180°.                                                    (2)

Using (1) in (2) yields
m∡ADC = m∡BDC = 90°.

Hence, $\triangle DCB$ is a right triangle.

Again, because $\triangle DCB \cong \triangle DCA$,

∡ACD $\cong$ ∡BCD                                                    (3)

As shown above,

m∡ADC = 90°.                                                    (4)

Since $\triangle ABC$ is equilateral,

m∡DAC = 60°.                                                    (5)

By the angle sum theorem,

m∡DAC + m∡ACD + m∡ADC = 180°.                                                    (6)

Inserting (4) and (5) in (6) gives

m∡ACD = 30°.                                                    (7)

Hence, using (7) in (3)

m∡ACD = m∡BCD = 30°.

● **PROBLEM 3-41**

In triangle ABC, lines are drawn from points B and A to sides $\overline{AC}$ and $\overline{BC}$, respectively. As shown in the figure, two smaller triangles are formed. It is given that $\overline{CA} \cong \overline{CB}$, $\overline{CE} \cong \overline{CD}$, and $\overline{BE} \cong \overline{AD}$.

(a) Prove that ∡EAB $\cong$ ∡DBA; (b) Find the measure of ∡EAB, if it is represented by 5x - 8 and the measure of ∡DBA equals 3x + 12.

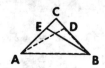

Separate the Triangles

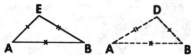

Solution:   (a) By proving that overlapping triangles EAB and DBA are congruent, and employing the theorem which states that corresponding parts of congruent triangles are congruent, we can show ⧸EAB ≅ ⧸DBA. Since most of the given information concerns sides of the triangles, the logical plan of attack is to prove congruence through the S.S.S. ≅ S.S.S. method.

| STATEMENT | REASON |
|---|---|
| 1. $\overline{BE} \cong \overline{AD}$ | 1. Given. |
| 2. $\overline{CA} \cong \overline{CB}$; $\overline{CE} \cong \overline{CD}$ | 2. Given. |
| 3. CA= CB; CE = CD | 3. Congruent segments are of equal measure. |
| 4. CA- CE = CB - CD | 4. Subtraction of equal quantities from equal quantities yields equals. |
| 5. EA = DB | 5. Substitution Postulate. Point Betweenness Postulate. |
| 6. $\overline{EA} \cong \overline{DB}$ | 6. Segments of equal length are congruent. |
| 7. $\overline{AB} \cong \overline{AB}$ | 7. Reflexive Property of Congruence. |
| 8. ΔEAB ≅ ΔDBA | 8. S.S.S. ≅ S.S.S. |
| 9. ⧸EAB ≅ ⧸DBA | 9. Corresponding parts of congruent triangles are congruent. |

(b) We proved in part (a) that ⧸EAB ≅ ⧸DBA. Thus, the measures of the two angles are equal, m⧸EAB = m⧸DBA. We have an algebraic representation for each measure and, by setting them equal to each other, we can solve for the unknown and substitute to determine the measure of ⧸EAB.

m⧸EAB = m⧸DBA

5x − 8 = 3x + 12

2x = 20

x = 10

m⧸EAB = 5(10) − 8 = 50 − 8 = 42.

Therefore, the measure of ⧸EAB is 42°.

Given: $\overline{QS}$ intersects $\overline{PR}$ at T such that RQ = RS and QT = ST.
Prove: $\overline{TP}$ bisects ⦠SPQ.

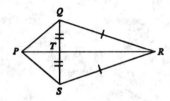

Solution:  $\overline{TP}$ bisects ⦠SPQ only if ⦠SPT ≅ ⦠QPT. Showing
ΔPTQ ≅ ΔPTS or ΔPQR ≅ ΔPSR would be sufficient to show
⦠SPT ≅ ⦠QPT. Consider ΔPQR and ΔPSR. $\overline{PR}$ ≅ $\overline{PR}$. $\overline{QR}$ ≅ $\overline{SR}$.
To show ΔPQR ≅ ΔPSR, we need one more congruence - either
a pair of sides or else ⦠QRT ≅ ⦠SRT.

   We can show ⦠QRT ≅ ⦠SRT by proving ΔQTR ≅ ΔSTR by the
SSS Postulate. Thus, ΔPQR ≅ ΔPSR by the SAS Postulate.
⦠QPT ≅ ⦠SPT by corresponding angles, and $\overline{TP}$ bisects ⦠QPS.

| STATEMENTS | REASONS |
|---|---|
| 1. $\overline{QS}$ intersects $\overline{PR}$ at T such that RQ=RS;QT=ST | 1. Given |
| 2. $\overline{QT}$ ≅ $\overline{ST}$  $\overline{RQ}$ ≅ $\overline{RS}$ | 2. Two segments of equal lengths are congruent. |
| 3. $\overline{TR}$ ≅ $\overline{TR}$ | 3. A segment is congruent to itself. |
| 4. ΔQTR ≅ ΔSTR | 4. The SSS Postulate. |
| 5. ⦠QRT ≅ ⦠SRT | 5. Corresponding parts of congruent triangles are congruent. |
| 6. $\overline{PR}$ ≅ $\overline{PR}$ | 6. A segment is congruent to itself. |
| 7. ΔPQR ≅ ΔPSR | 7. The SAS Postulate. |
| 8. ⦠QPR ≅ ⦠SPR | 8. Corresponding parts of congruent triangles are congruent. |
| 9. $\overline{TP}$ bisects ⦠SPQ | 9. If a segment divides an angle into two congruent angles, then the segment bisects the angle. |

# HYPOTENUSE-LEG POSTULATE

Quadrilateral ABCD is, as shown in the figure, cut by the line $\overline{AC}$. If $\overline{CB} \perp \overline{AB}$, $\overline{CD} \perp \overline{AD}$, and $\overline{BC} \cong \overline{DC}$. Prove that $\overline{AC}$ bisects ⦧BAD.

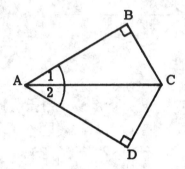

Solution: To prove $\overline{AC}$ is the bisector of ⦧BAD, it is necessary to prove ⦧1 $\cong$ ⦧2. This can be done by proving $\triangle ABC \cong \triangle ADC$ and then using the rule which assigns congruence to corresponding parts of congruent triangles in order to prove ⦧1 $\cong$ ⦧2.

The hypotenuse leg theorem is used in this proof. It states that two right triangles are congruent if the hypotenuse and the leg of one triangle are congruent to the corresponding parts of the other triangle. Notationally, it can be written hy. leg. $\cong$ hy. leg.

| STATEMENT | REASON |
|---|---|
| 1. $\overline{CB} \perp \overline{AB}$, $\overline{CD} \perp \overline{AD}$ | 1. Given |
| 2. ⦧ABC and ⦧ADC are right triangles | 2. When perpendicular lines intersect, they form right angles. |
| 3. $\triangle$'s ABC and ADC are right triangles | 3. A triangle which contains a right angle is a right triangle. |
| 4. $\overline{BC} \cong \overline{CD}$ | 4. Given. |
| 5. $\overline{AC} \cong \overline{AC}$ | 5. Reflexive property of congruence. |
| 6. $\triangle ABC \cong \triangle ADC$ | 6. Hy. leg $\cong$ Hy. leg. |

| 7. $\angle 1 \cong \angle 2$ | 7. Corresponding parts of congruent triangles are congruent. |
| 8. AC bisects $\angle$BAD | 8. A segment which divides an angle into two congruent angles bisects the angle. |

● **PROBLEM 3-44**

On diameter $\overline{AB}$ of semicircle O, two points C and D are located on opposite sides of the center O so that $\overline{AC} \cong \overline{BD}$. At C and D, perpendiculars are constructed from $\overline{AB}$ and extended to meet arc $\overset{\frown}{AB}$ at points E and F, respectively. Using the fact that all radii of a semicircle are congruent, prove $\overline{CE} \cong \overline{DF}$.

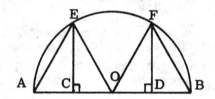

Solution: If we can prove $\triangle ECO \cong \triangle FDO$, then we will be able to conclude that $\overline{CE} \cong \overline{DF}$. Since the triangles include a right angle, they are right triangles and, as such, we can use the hypotenuse-leg theorem to prove congruence between them. Hypotenuse-leg is similar to the SSS Postulate because, when you know the hypotenuse and leg of a right triangle the third leg is uniquely determined by Pythagoras' Theorem.

| STATEMENT | REASON |
| --- | --- |
| 1. $\overline{EC} \perp \overline{AO}$ and $\overline{FD} \perp \overline{BO}$ | 1. Given |
| 2. $\angle$ECO and $\angle$FDO are right angles | 2. Perpendicular lines intersect to form right angles. |
| 3. $\triangle ECO$ and $\triangle FDO$ are right triangles | 3. A triangle which contains a right angle is a right triangle. |
| 4. $\overline{OA} \cong \overline{OB}$ | 4. Radii of the same circle are congruent. |
| 5. $\overline{AC} \cong \overline{BD}$ | 5. Given. |
| 6. OA - AC = OB - BD or OC = OD or $\overline{OC} \cong \overline{OD}$ | 6. Subtraction Property of Equality |
| 7. $\overline{OE} \cong \overline{OF}$ | 7. Same as reason 4. |

| | |
|---|---|
| 8. $\triangle ECO \cong \triangle FDO$ | 8. Two right triangles are congruent if the hypotenuse and leg of one triangle are congruent to the hypotenuse and leg of the second. |
| 9. $\overline{CE} \cong \overline{DF}$ | 9. Corresponding sides of congruent triangles are congruent. |

● **PROBLEM 3-45**

Given: DB and AC intersect at O. m∡1 = m∡2 = 90°. $\overline{CD} \cong \overline{CB}$.
Prove: $\overline{OD} \cong \overline{OB}$.

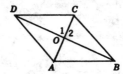

Solution: Since $\overline{OD}$ and $\overline{OB}$ are corresponding parts of right triangles COD and COB respectively, we can derive the required congruence by proving $\triangle COD \cong \triangle COB$. The hypotenuse leg theorem for congruence will be used.

| STATEMENTS | REASONS |
|---|---|
| 1. m∡1 = m∡2 = 90° | 1. Given. |
| 2. ∡1 and ∡2 are right angles | 2. A right angle has a measure of 90°. |
| 3. $\triangle COD$ and $\triangle COB$ are right triangles | 3. A right triangle is a triangle with one right angle. |
| 4. $\overline{CD} \cong \overline{CB}$ | 4. Given. |
| 5. $\overline{CO} \cong \overline{CO}$ | 5. Reflexive property of congruence. |
| 6. $\triangle COD \cong \triangle COB$ | 6. hy.leg $\cong$ hy. leg |
| 7. $\overline{OD} \cong \overline{OB}$ | 7. Corresponding parts of congruent triangles are congruent. |

● **PROBLEM 3-46**

Given: $\triangle ABC$ is isosceles with base $\overline{AB}$. $\overline{BD} \perp \overline{AC}$. $\overline{AE} \perp \overline{BC}$.
∡1 $\cong$ ∡2. Prove ∡3 $\cong$ ∡4.

Solution: In this problem, we must first notice that ∡3 and ∡4 are corresponding parts of rt.$\triangle$'s AEB and BDA, respectively. Hence, by proving $\triangle BDA \overset{\sim}{=} \triangle AEB$, we can deduce that $\angle 3 \overset{\sim}{=} \angle 4$. The hypotenuse leg theorem for congruence will be employed.

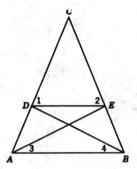

| STATEMENTS | REASONS |
|---|---|
| 1. $\overline{BD} \perp \overline{AC}$; $\overline{AE} \perp \overline{BC}$ | 1. Given. |
| 2. $\angle BDA$ and $\angle AEB$ are right angles | 2. Perpendicular lines meet to form right angles. |
| 3. $\triangle BDA$ and $\triangle AEB$ are right triangles | 3. A right triangle is a triangle with one right angle. |
| 4. $\triangle ABC$ is isosceles | 4. Given. |
| 5. $\overline{AC} \overset{\sim}{=} \overline{BC}$ | 5. Definition of an isosceles triangle. |
| 6. $AD + DC = AC$<br>$BE + EC = BC$ | 6. The whole is congruent to the sum of its parts. |
| 7. $AD + DC = BE + EC$ | 7. Addition Postulate. |
| 8. $\angle 1 \overset{\sim}{=} \angle 2$ | 8. Given. |
| 9. $\overline{DC} \overset{\sim}{=} \overline{EC}$ or $DC = EC$ | 9. If a triangle has two congruent angles, then the sides opposite those angles are congruent. |
| 10. $AD = BE$ | 10. If congruent quantities are subtracted from congruent quantities, then the differences are congruent quantities. (Steps 9 and 7). |
| 11. $AB = AB$ | 11. Reflexive law. |
| 12. $\triangle BDA \overset{\sim}{=} \triangle AEB$ | 12. hy. leg $\overset{\sim}{=}$ hy. leg. |
| 13. $\angle 3 = \angle 4$ | 13. Corresponding parts of congruent triangles are equal. |

# CHAPTER 4

# INEQUALITIES

## LINES AND ANGLES

We are given, as the figures show, ∢ ABC and ∢ DEF. m ∢ ABC > m ∢ DEF. If m ∢ ABG = m ∢ DEH, prove m ∢ GBC > m ∢ HEF.

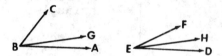

**Solution:** By realizing that when equal quantities are subtracted from unequal quantities, the differences are unequal in the same order, we can proceed directly to the proof.

Consult the diagram to clarify the steps of the proof.

| Statements | Reasons |
|---|---|
| 1. m ∢ ABC > m ∢ DEF | 1. Given |
| 2. m ∢ ABG = m ∢ DEH | 2. Given |
| 3. m ∢ ABC - m ∢ ABG > m ∢ DEF - m ∢ DEH  or  m ∢ GBC > m ∢ HEF | 3. If equal quantities are subtracted from unequal quantities, the differences are unequal in the same order. |

In the accompanying figure, unequal angles ABC and DEF are bisected by $\overleftrightarrow{BG}$ and $\overleftrightarrow{EH}$, respectively. If m ∢ ABC > m ∢ DEF, prove m ∢ ABG > m ∢ DEH.

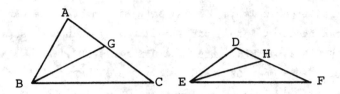

m∡ABC > m∡DEF

BG and EH bisect ∡ABC and ∡DEF respectively

<u>Solution</u>: The fact that unequal quantities remain unequal in the same order when they are divided by equal positive quantities will be employed in this proof. (Since we are dealing with an angle bisector, the specific form to be used will be that halves of unequal quantities are unequal in the same order.)

| Statements | Reasons |
|---|---|
| 1. m ⊰ ABC > m ⊰ DEF | 1. Given |
| 2. $\frac{m ⊰ ABC}{2} > \frac{m ⊰ DEF}{2}$ or <br> ½m ⊰ ABC > ½m ⊰ DEF | 2. Halves of unequal quantities are unequal in the same order. |
| 3. $\overleftrightarrow{BG}$ bisects ⊰ ABC <br> $\overleftrightarrow{EH}$ bisects ⊰ DEF | 3. Given |
| 4. m ⊰ ABG = ½m ⊰ ABC <br> m ⊰ DEH = ½m ⊰ DEF | 4. A bisector of an angle divides the angle into two congruent angles. |
| 5. m ⊰ ABG > m ⊰ DEH | 5. A quantity may be substituted for its equal in any inequality. (See steps (2) and (4).) |

**● PROBLEM 4-3**

Let ⊰ AOB and ⊰ COB be a linear pair and ⊰ MPN and ⊰ QPN be another linear pair. Prove that m ⊰ AOB > m ⊰ MPN if and only if m ⊰ QPN > m ⊰ COB.

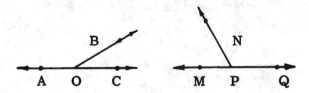

<u>Solution</u>: Two angles form a linear pair if they share a common ray, and if their second rays are directly opposite to each other. In the figure, ⊰ AOB and ⊰ COB are a linear pair. They share a common ray, $\overrightarrow{OB}$, and their second rays, $\overrightarrow{OA}$ and $\overrightarrow{OC}$, are directly opposite. Similarly, ⊰ MPN and ⊰ QPN are a linear pair.

Since the given theorem is an "if and only if" theorem, we can prove it by breaking it up into 2 parts and proving each part separately.

Part I: If $m \angle AOB > m \angle MPN$, then $m \angle QPN > m \angle COB$.

Part II: If $m \angle QPN > m \angle COB$, then $m \angle AOB > m \angle MPN$.

We proceed to prove Part I by noting that 2 angles which form a linear pair are supplementary. Since $\angle AOB$ and $\angle COB$ are a linear pair,

$$m \angle AOB + m \angle COB = 180° \qquad (1)$$

Because $\angle MPN$ and $\angle QPN$ form a linear pair,

$$m \angle MPN + m \angle QPN = 180° \qquad (2)$$

Equating (1) and (2) yields

$$m \angle MPN + m \angle QPN = m \angle AOB + m \angle COB$$

or

$$m \angle AOB - m \angle MPN = m \angle QPN - m \angle COB \qquad (3)$$

But, the hypothesis of Part I states that

$$m \angle AOB > m \angle MPN$$

or

$$m \angle AOB - m \angle MPN > 0 \qquad (4)$$

However, comparing (4) and (3) yields

$$m \angle QPN - m \angle COB > 0$$

or

$$m \angle QPN > m \angle COB$$

Therefore, Part I is proven. We next prove Part II.

Again, we use the fact that a linear pair of angles is supplementary. We can still use equations (1) and (2) above, because they are a statement of the fact that the angles shown in the figure are supplementary. Hence, equating (1) and (2) yields

$$m \angle MPN + m \angle QPN = m \angle AOB + m \angle COB$$

or

$$m \angle QPN - m \angle COB = m \angle AOB - m \angle MPN \qquad (5)$$

From the hypothesis of Part II,

$$m \angle QPN > m \angle COB$$

or

$$m \angle QPN - m \angle COB > 0 \qquad (6)$$

Comparing (6) and (5) yields

$$m \angle AOB - m \angle MPN > 0$$

or

$$m \angle AOB > m \angle MPN.$$

● **PROBLEM 4-4**

If D and E are the respective midpoints of sides $\overline{AB}$ and $\overline{AC}$ of $\triangle ABC$, and $AD < AE$, prove that $AB < AC$.

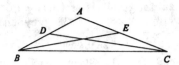

Solution: By the definition of midpoint, AB = 2(AD) and AC = 2(AE).
Since we are given AD < AE, then, by the multiplication postulate for
inequalities, AB < AC.

Given: Δ ABC with D and E as the respective midpoints of $\overline{AB}$
and $\overline{AC}$; AD < AE.

Prove: AB < AC

| Statements | Reasons |
|---|---|
| 1. Δ ABC, with D and E the respective midpoints of $\overline{AB}$ and $\overline{AC}$ ; AD < AE | 1. Given |
| 2. 2(AD) < 2(AE) | 2. For all real numbers a,m, and n, if m > n and a > 0, then am > an. (Multiplication Postulate for Inequality). |
| 3. AB = 2(AD); AC = 2(AE) | 3. Definition of midpoint. |
| 4. AB < AC | 4. Substitution Postulate. |

● **PROBLEM 4-5**

Given: ∢ 1 ≅ ∢ 2; ∢ 3 ≅ ∢ 4; $\overline{GD}$ ≅ $\overline{HD}$; EH = CG; $\overline{BHD}$; $\overline{EGHC}$; $\overline{APGD}$.
Prove: m ∢ 5 < m ∢ 6.

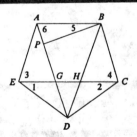

Solution: We can relate ∢ 5 and ∢ 6 as angles of Δ BAP or we
can relate them to a third angle not in Δ BAP. Too many parts of
Δ BAP are unknown for the first method to be useful to us. It is
difficult to see how we can show PB > AP and, therefore, m ∢ 6 > m ∢ 5.

Using the second method, we note the symmetry of the figure:
∢ 1 ≅ ∢ 2; ∢ 3 ≅ ∢ 4. It would seem reasonable that Δ ADB is isosceles. If this were so, then base angles ∢ 6 and ∢ ABD would be
congruent. Since m ∢ 5 < m ∢ ABD, m ∢ 5 < m ∢ 6.

We show Δ ADB is isosceles by showing AD = DB. Since AD =

AG + GD, DB = DH + HB, and it is given that GD = HD, we need only show
AG = BH. We do this by showing △ AEG ≅ △ BHC by the ASA Postulate.

| Statements | Reasons |
|---|---|
| 1. ∠ 1 ≅ ∠ 2; ∠ 3 ≅ ∠ 4; $\overline{GD}$ ≅ $\overline{HD}$; <br> EH = CG; $\overline{BHD}$; $\overline{EGHC}$; $\overline{APGD}$ | 1. Given. (We show △ AEG ≅ △ BHC by noting that ∠ 3 ≅ ∠ 4, $\overline{EG}$ ≅ $\overline{HC}$, and ∠ AGE ≅ ∠ BHC. In Step 2 to 4, we show ∠ AGE ≅ ∠ BHC.) |
| 2. ∠ HGD ≅ ∠ GHD | 2. The base angles of an isosceles triangle are congruent. |
| 3. ∠ AGE ≅ ∠ HGD; <br> ∠ BHC ≅ ∠ GHD | 3. The opposite angles formed by intersecting lines are congruent. (Vertical Angle Theorem.) |
| 4. ∠ AGE ≅ ∠ BHC | 4. Angles congruent to congruent angles are congruent. (We now show $\overline{EG}$ ≅ $\overline{HC}$ in Steps 5 to 8.) |
| 5. EH = EG + GH <br>  CG = CH + HG | 5. Point Betweenness Postulate. |
| 6. EG + GH = CH + HG | 6. Substitution Postulate. (Steps 5, 1). |
| 7. EG = HC | 7. Subtraction Postulate. |
| 8. $\overline{EG}$ ≅ $\overline{HC}$ | 8. Segments of equal length are congruent. |
| 9. △ AEG ≅ △ BCH | 9. The ASA Postulate. |
| 10. $\overline{AG}$ ≅ $\overline{BH}$ | 10. Corresponding parts of congruent triangles are congruent. |
| 11. AG = BH | 11. Congruent segments are of equal length. |
| 12. HD = GD | 12. Same reason as Step 11. |
| 13. AD = AG + GD <br>  BD = BH + HD | 13. Definition of "betweenness." |
| 14. AD = BD | 14. Substitution Postulate. |
| 15. ∠ 6 ≅ ∠ ABD | 15. The base angles of an isosceles triangle are congruent. |
| 16. m ∠ 5 < m ∠ ABD | 16. If point P is in the interior of ∠ ABD, then m ∠ ABP < m ∠ ABD. |
| 17. m ∠ 5 < m ∠ 6 | 17. If a = b and c < a, then c < b. |

# EXTERIOR ANGLE THEOREM

### ● PROBLEM 4-6

In isosceles triangle ABC, with $\overline{AC}$ ≅ $\overline{CB}$ base $\overline{AB}$ is extended
to D, and $\overline{CD}$ is drawn. Prove that CD > CA (see figure).

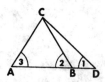

Solution: The cornerstone of this proof is a theorem
stating that the measure of an exterior angle of a tri-

angle is greater than the measure of either remote interior angle. It can be derived from the fact that both the measure of the exterior angle, and the sum of the measures of the non-adjacent interior angles, when added to the measure of the adjacent interior angle, will sum to 180°. Since the non-adjacent angles must have positive measure, the measure of the exterior angle must be greater than either one alone.

The required conclusion, CD > CA, will be reached by applying the theorem that if two angles of a triangle are unequal, the sides opposite these angles are unequal, and the greater side lies opposite the greater angle.

We will use the first theorem to show m∡3 > m∡1 and then, by the second theorem, conclude CD, opposite ∡3, is greater than CA, opposite ∡1.

| STATEMENT | REASON |
|---|---|
| 1. In △CBD, m∡2 > m∡1 | 1. The measure of an exterior angle of a triangle is greater than the measure of either non-adjacent interior angle. |
| 2. $\overline{AC} \cong \overline{CB}$ | 2. Given. |
| 3. ∡3 $\cong$ ∡2    or    m∡3 = m∡2 | 3. Base angles of an isosceles triangle are congruent. |
| 4. m∡3 > m∡1 | 4. A quantity may be substituted for its equal in any inequality. |
| 5. CD > CA | 5. If two angles of a triangle are unequal, then the sides opposite these angles are unequal, and the side of greater length lies opposite the angle of greater measure. |

● PROBLEM 4-7

Given: Quadrilateral ABCD and straight rays $\overrightarrow{ADF}$ and $\overrightarrow{ABE}$.
Prove: m∡EBC + m∡FDC > ½(m∡A + m∡C). (Hint: Draw $\overline{AC}$)

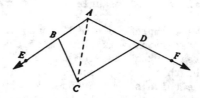

Solution: We have made use of the hint by drawing $\overline{AC}$ in the figure shown.

Notice, that m∢A = m∢BAC + m∢CAD and m∢C = m∢BCA + m∢ACD.

Since the measure of the whole is equal to the sum of the measures of its parts, we can substitute m∢A = m∢BAC + m∢CAD and m∢C = m∢BCA + m∢ACD in the equation to be proven. Hence, the equation becomes

m∢EBC + m∢FDC > ½(m∢BAC + m∢CAD + m∢BCA + m∢ACD).

We will be able to derive this form of the results using the Exterior Angle Theorem. Recall that the theorem tells us that the measure of an exterior angle of a triangle is greater than the measure of either remote interior angle.

Hence, in △ABC

m∢EBC > m∢BAC     and     m∢EBC > m∢BCA.

Similarly, in △DAC,

m∢FDC > m∢ACD     and     m∢FDC > m∢CAD.

We know that the sum of unequals are unequal in the same order. Accordingly,

2m∢EBC + 2m∢FDC > m∢BAC + m∢BCA + m∢ACD + m∢CAD.

Dividing by 2 and rearranging, we obtain

m∢EBC + m∢FDC > ½(m∢BAC + m∢CAD + m∢BCA + m∢ACD).

These are exactly the results we set out to obtain.


# TRIANGLE INEQUALITY THEOREM

● PROBLEM 4-8

If the lengths of two sides of a triangle are 10 and 14, the length of the third side may be which of the following: (a) 2 (b) 4 (c) 22 (d) 24?

Solution: By the Triangle Inequality Theorem, we know that the sum of the lengths of any two sides of a triangle must be greater than the length of the third.

Therefore, in this example, we can discover which of the lengths are possible answers by determining if the sum of the lengths of the two shortest sides is greater than the length of the longest side.

(a) 2 cannot be the third side, because 2 + 10 is not > 14.
(b) 4 cannot be the third side, because 4 + 10 is not > 14.
(c) 22 can be the third, because 10 + 14 > 22.
(d) 24 cannot be the third side, because 10 + 14 is not > 24.

Therefore, the third side may be 22.

Given: Point P is an interior point of Δ ABC.

Prove: AB + AC > BP + PC (Hint: extend $\overleftrightarrow{BP}$ so that it intersects $\overline{AC}$ at point N).

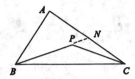

**Solution**: We are asked to prove an inequality involving the sides of triangles. Therefore, we apply the Triangle Inequality Theorem. This theorem states that the sum of the lengths of any two sides of a triangle is greater than the length of the third. We must now find triangles whose sides include AB, AC, BP, and PC. We use the hint and extend $\overleftrightarrow{BP}$ so that $\overleftrightarrow{BP}$ intersects $\overline{AC}$ at point N. Thus, we obtain Δ ABN and Δ PNC whose sides comprise all the lengths in question - plus an extra length PN. By the Triangle Inequality Theorem, we know in Δ ABN that AB + AN > BN or (since BN = BP + PN) that AB + AN > BP + PN. In Δ PNC, PN + NC > PC. Summing the two equations together, we obtain an inequality involving AB, AC, BP, and PC: AB + AN + NC + PN > BP + PC + PN. Combining AN + NC to obtain AC, and cancelling PN from both sides, we obtain the desired result: AB + AC > BP + PC.

| Statements | Reasons |
|---|---|
| 1. Point P is in the interior of Δ ABC | 1. Given |
| 2. $\overleftrightarrow{BP}$ intersects $\overline{AC}$ at point N | 2. Two noncoincident, nonparallel coplanar lines intersect at a point. |
| 3. AB + AN > BN<br>PN + NC > PC | 3. Triangle Inequality Theorem. |
| 4. BN = PN + PB<br>AC = AN + NC | 4. Point Betweenness Postulate. |
| 5. AB + AN + PN + NC > BN + PC | 5. Addition Postulate of Inequality. |
| 6. AB + AC + PN > PN + PB + PC | 6. Substitution Postulate. |
| 7. AB + AC > PB + PC | 7. If a > b, then a - c > b - c. |

# CHAPTER 5

# QUADRILATERIALS

## PARALLELOGRAMS

● **PROBLEM** 5-1

Prove that the diagonals of a parallelogram bisect each other.

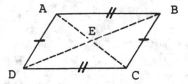

Solution: To prove that $\overline{AC}$ bisects $\overline{DB}$ (and vice versa) we must prove that $\overline{AE} \cong \overline{CE}$ and $\overline{DE} \cong \overline{BE}$. We shall do this by showing that $\triangle AED \cong \triangle CEB$ (see figure).

Because ABCD is a parallelogram, opposite sides $\overline{AD} \cong \overline{CB}$. Also, $\angle DAE \cong \angle BCE$ because they are alternate interior angles for the parallel segments $\overline{AD}$ and $\overline{CB}$ cut by transversal $\overline{AC}$. Lastly, $\angle AED \cong \angle CEB$, since they are vertical angles. By the AAS Postulate, $\triangle AED \cong \triangle CEB$. Hence, by corresponding parts, $\overline{AE} \cong \overline{CE}$ and $\overline{DE} \cong \overline{BE}$. From this, we conclude the diagonals of a parallellogram bisect each other.

● **PROBLEM** 5-2

Prove that a quadrilateral, in which one pair of opposite sides are both congruent and parallel, is a parallelogram.

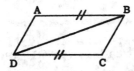

Solution:  In quadrilateral ABCD (as shown in the figure)
assume $\overline{AB} \cong \overline{CD}$ and $\overline{AB} \parallel \overline{CD}$. We shall prove that $\triangle DAB \cong \triangle BCD$
by the SAS Postulate. We will then know that $\overline{DA} \cong \overline{BC}$. Since
we already know that $\overline{AB} \cong \overline{CD}$, we will have shown that both
pairs of opposite sides of the quadrilateral are congruent,
implying that ABCD is a parallelogram.

As given, $\overline{AB} \cong \overline{CD}$. Furthermore, since $\overline{AB} \parallel \overline{CD}$, then
$\angle ABD \cong \angle CDB$. This follows because these angles are alternate
interior angles of parallel segments cut by a transversal.
Lastly, $\overline{DB}$ is shared by both triangles, therefore $\overline{DB} \cong \overline{DB}$.
By the SAS Postulate, $\triangle DAB \cong \triangle BCD$. This implies that $\overline{DA} \cong \overline{BC}$.
We have shown that both pairs of opposite sides of
quadrilateral ABCD are congruent. This implies that ABCD is
a parallelogram.

● **PROBLEM 5-3**

In parallelogram ABCD, if the measure of $\angle B$ exceeds the
measure of $\angle A$ by 50°, find the measure of $\angle B$.

Solution:  There is a theorem which states that the consecutive angles of a parallelogram are supplementary. This
fact, more generally stated, tells us that when a transversal cuts across parallel lines the interior angles on
the same side of the transversal are supplementary. In the
parallelogram shown, $\overline{AD} \parallel \overline{BC}$ and $\overline{AB}$ is a transversal.
Therefore, it follows that $\angle A$ and $\angle B$, being interior angles
on the same side of the transversal, are supplements and
their measures sum to 180°.

Hence, to find the measure of $\angle B$ (1) Let x = the
measure of $\angle A$. (2) Then, x + 50 = the measure of $\angle B$. It
follows then that

$$x + (x + 50) = 180$$

$$2x + 50 = 180$$

$$2x = 130$$

$$x = 65 \quad \text{and } x + 50 = 115.$$

Therefore, the measure of $\angle B$ is 115°.

65

Given: P, Q, R, and S are the respective midpoints of sides $\overline{AB}$, $\overline{BC}$, $\overline{CD}$, and $\overline{AD}$ of quadrilateral ABCD. Prove: Quadrilateral PQRS is a parallelogram.

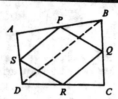

**Solution:** There are seven different ways to show that a quadrilateral is a parallelogram. We can prove that (1) both pairs of opposite sides are parallel, (2) both pairs of opposite sides are congruent, (3) one pair of opposite sides are both parallel and congruent, (4) the opposite angles are congruent, (5) the angles of one pair of opposite angles are congruent and the sides of a pair of opposite sides are parallel, (6) the angles of one pair of opposite angles and the sides of one pair of opposite sides are congruent, or (7) the diagonals bisect each other.

Here, it is not obvious at all how to proceed. There is nothing given about the quadrilateral with which we are concerned, neither parallelism nor congruence, that can help us.

By drawing diagonal $\overline{BD}$ of ABCD, we form triangles ABD and CBD. Since sides $\overline{SP}$ and $\overline{RQ}$ of PQRS join the midpoints of two sides of $\triangle$ABD and $\triangle$CBD respectively, they are the midlines of the triangles they lie in. According to several theorems on midlines, both $\overline{SP}$ and $\overline{RQ}$ are parallel to, and half as long as $\overline{BD}$, the side of the triangles not cross by them. By method (3), we will prove that quadrilateral PQRS is a parallelogram.

| STATEMENTS | REASONS |
|---|---|
| 1. P, Q, R, and S are the respective midpoints of sides $\overline{AB}$, $\overline{BC}$, $\overline{CD}$, and $\overline{AD}$ of quadrilateral ABCD. | 1. Given. |
| 2. $\overline{SP}$ is a midline of $\triangle$ABD. | 2. A midline of a triangle is the line segment joining the midpoints of two sides of the triangle. |
| 3. $\overline{SP}$ \|\| $\overline{DB}$ | 3. The midline of a triangle is parallel to the third side. |
| 4. SP = ½ DB | 4. The midline of a triangle is half as long as the third side of the triangle. |

| 5. $\overline{QR}$ is a midline of $\triangle CDB$ | 5. Definition of midline. |
|---|---|
| 6. $\overline{QR} \parallel \overline{DB}$ | 6. The midline of a triangle is parallel to the third side of the triangle. |
| 7. $QR = \frac{1}{2} DB$ | 7. The midline of a triangle is half as long as the third side of the triangle. |
| 8. $\overline{SP} \parallel \overline{QR}$ | 8. If each of two lines is parallel to a third line, then they are parallel to each other. |
| 9. $SP = QR$ | 9. Transitive property. |
| 10. Quadrilateral PQRS is a parallelogram. | 10. A quadrilateral is a parallelogram if two of its sides are both congruent and parallel. |

● PROBLEM 5-5

In triangle ABC (shown in the accompanying figure), D is the midpoint of $\overline{AC}$ and E is the midpoint of $\overline{CB}$. If $\overline{DE}$ is extended to F so that $\overline{DE} \cong \overline{EF}$ and $\overline{FB}$ is drawn, prove that ABFD is a parallelogram.

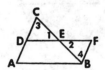

Solution: To prove that ABFD is a parallelogram it is necessary to show that one pair of its opposite sides are both congruent and parallel. The fact that alternate interior angles of parallel lines cut by a transversal are congruent will be used to prove two sides are parallel. To prove congruence of the same two sides, the corresponding parts rule for congruent triangles will be employed. To derive both of the properties, congruence between $\triangle$'s BEF and CED must be established.

| STATEMENT | REASON |
|---|---|
| 1. $\overline{CE} \cong \overline{BE}$ | 1. Given. (E is the midpoint of $\overline{CB}$.) |
| 2. $\overline{DE} \cong \overline{FE}$ | 2. Given. |
| 3. $\angle 1 = \angle 2$ | 3. If two angles are vertical angles, then they are congruent. |
| 4. $\triangle CED \cong \triangle BEF$ | 4. S.A.S. $\cong$ S.A.S. |

| | |
|---|---|
| 5. $\angle 3 \cong \angle 4$ | 5. Corresponding parts of congruent triangles are congruent. |
| 6. $\overline{FB} \parallel \overline{CA}$ or $\overline{FB} \parallel \overline{DA}$ | 6. If two lines are cut by a transversal making a pair of alternate interior angles congruent, then the lines are parallel. |
| 7. $\overline{FB} \cong \overline{DC}$ | 7. Same as reason 5. |
| 8. $\overline{DC} \cong \overline{DA}$ | 8. Given. (D midpoint of $\overline{CA}$.) |
| 9. $\overline{FB} \cong \overline{DA}$ | 9. Transitivity of congruence. |
| 10. ABFD is a parallelogram. | 10. A quadrilateral is a parallelogram if one pair of opposite sides are both congruent and parallel. |

# RHOMBI

● PROBLEM 5-6

If the diagonals of a parallelogram meet at right angles, prove that the parallelogram is a rhombus.

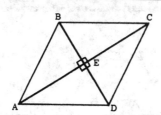

<u>Solution</u>: The accompanying figure shows parallelogram ABCD, whose diagonals ($\overline{BD}$ and $\overline{AC}$) meet at right angles. By definition, a rhombus is a quadrilateral, all of whose sides are congruent. Our strategy will be to use the properties of a parallelogram to show that $\overline{AB} \cong \overline{CD}$ and $\overline{BC} \cong \overline{DA}$. We shall then prove that $\triangle AEB \cong \triangle AED$, which implies that $\overline{AB} \cong \overline{AD}$. Coupling these facts will show that ABCD is a quadrilateral, all of whose sides are congruent. (i.e. a rhombus).

Since ABCD is a parallelogram, it is a quadrilateral. Furthermore, by the properties of paralellograms, opposite sides are congruent. That is

$$\overline{AB} \cong \overline{CD}$$

and $\overline{BC} \cong \overline{DA}$. (1)

Now, focus attention on △AEB and △AED. $\overline{BE} \cong \overline{DE}$, because the diagonals of a parallelogram bisect each other. ⟩BEA ≅ ⟩DEA, since both are right angles. Lastly, $\overline{AE} \cong \overline{AE}$, since it is common to both triangles. By the SAS (side angle side) Postulate, △AEB ≅ △AED.

Therefore, by corresponding parts

$$\overline{AB} \cong \overline{AD} \qquad\qquad (2)$$

Using (2) in (1) yields,

$$\overline{AB} \cong \overline{CD}$$

$$\overline{AB} \cong \overline{AD}$$

$$\overline{AD} \cong \overline{CB}$$

or   $\overline{AB} \cong \overline{CD} \cong \overline{AD} \cong \overline{CB}$

which shows that ABCD is a quadrilateral, all of whose sides are congruent. Hence, ABCD is a rhombus.

● **PROBLEM** 5-7

In the figure shown, $\overrightarrow{BF}$ bisects angle CBA. $\overline{DE} \parallel \overrightarrow{BA}$ and $\overline{GE} \parallel \overrightarrow{BC}$. Prove GEDB is a rhombus.

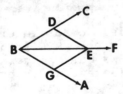

Solution: We want to show that GEDB is a parallelogram which has congruent adjacent sides, since this is, by definition, a rhombus.

We will prove that GEDB is a parallelogram, and then prove △BEG ≅ △BED in order to deduce that adjacent sides $\overline{GE}$ and $\overline{DE}$ are congruent.

| STATEMENT | REASON |
|---|---|
| 1. $\overline{DE} \parallel \overrightarrow{BA}$, $\overline{GE} \parallel \overrightarrow{BC}$ | 1. Given. |
| 2. GEDB is a parallelogram | 2. A quadrilateral in which all opposite sides are parallel is a parallelogram. |
| 3. $\overrightarrow{BF}$ is the angle bisector of ⟩CBA | 3. Given. |

69

| | |
|---|---|
| 4. ∢DBE ≅ ∢GBE | 4. An angle bisector divides the angle into two congruent angles. |
| 5. $\overline{BG}$ ≅ $\overline{DE}$ | 5. Opposite sides of a parallelogram are congruent. |
| 6. $\overline{BE}$ ≅ $\overline{BE}$ | 6. Reflexive Property of Congruence. |
| 7. ΔBEG ≅ ΔBED | 7. S.A.S. ≅ S.A.S. |
| 8. $\overline{GE}$ ≅ $\overline{DE}$ | 8. Corresponding sides of congruent triangles are congruent. |
| 9. GEDB is a rhombus | 9. A rhombus is a parallelogram with adjacent sides congruent. |

● **PROBLEM 5-8**

As drawn in the figure, ABCD is a parallelogram. The lengths of each side can be represented in the following algebraic manner:

$$AB = 2x + 1$$
$$DC = 3x - 11$$
$$AD = x + 13$$

Show that ABCD is a rhombus.

Solution: A rhombus is a quadrilateral in which all sides are congruent. Since ABCD is given to be a parallelogram we know it is a quadrilateral whose opposite sides are congruent. Therefore, to prove ABCD is a rhombus, it is sufficient to show that any two consecutive sides are congruent. (Any congruent sides are of equal length.)

In effect, we are given DC ≅ AB and want to show AD ≅ AB.

Set the length of $\overline{AB}$ equal to the length of $\overline{DC}$ and solve for x. Then, substitute back into the expressions for the length of $\overline{AB}$ and $\overline{AD}$ to determine whether they are equal.

$$DC = AB$$
$$3x - 11 = 2x + 1$$
$$3x - 2x = 1 + 11$$

$$x = 12.$$

Then, $AB = 2x + 1 = 2(12) + 1 = 25$

$$AD = x + 13 = 12 + 13 = 25.$$

Therefore, the length of $\overline{AB}$ = length of $\overline{AD}$ and $\overline{AB} \cong \overline{AD}$.

Therefore, ABCD is a rhombus because it is a quadrilateral (a parallelogram) in which two consecutive sides are congruent.

● **PROBLEM** 5-9

Given: $\overline{AN}$ is an angle bisector of $\triangle ABC$; $\overrightarrow{CNBH}$; $\overline{HA} \perp \overline{AN}$; $\overrightarrow{CAR}$; $\overrightarrow{HR} \parallel \overline{AB}$; $\overrightarrow{ABP}$; $\overrightarrow{HP} \parallel \overline{CA}$. Prove: quadrilateral APHR is a rhombus.

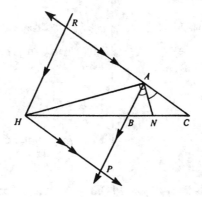

Solution: Aside from the various collinearities, we are given: (1) $\overrightarrow{HP} \parallel \overline{CA}$; $\overrightarrow{HR} \parallel \overline{AB}$; (2) $\overline{AN}$ is an angle bisector of $\triangle ABC$; and (3) $\overline{HA} \perp \overline{AN}$. From (1), we can show that quadrilateral APHR has both pairs of opposite sides parallel, and therefore APHR is a parallelogram.

Given that a figure is a parallelogram, we can show that it is a rhombus if we show that a diagonal of the parallelogram bisects an angle of the parallelogram. Most of the information we are given involves vertex A. Therefore, we prove the result by showing diagonal $\overline{AH}$ bisects ∢RAP or m∢RAH = m∢HAP; we set out finding expressions for m∢RAH and m∢HAP; and try to show them equal.

| STATEMENTS | REASONS |
|---|---|
| 1. $\overline{AN}$ is an angle bisector of $\triangle ABC$; $\overrightarrow{CNBH}$; $\overline{HA} \perp \overline{AN}$; $\overrightarrow{CAR}$; $\overrightarrow{HR} \parallel \overline{AB}$; $\overrightarrow{ABP}$; $\overrightarrow{HP} \parallel \overline{CA}$ | 1. Given. |

| Statements | Reasons |
|---|---|
| 2. $\overline{RA} \parallel \overline{HP}$; $\overline{HR} \parallel \overline{AP}$ | 2. Two segments each on separate parallel lines are parallel. |
| 3. $\square$ APHR is a parallelogram | 3. If both pairs of opposite sides of a quadrilateral are parallel, then the quadrilateral is a parallelogram. |
| 4. $\angle$HAN is a right angle or m$\angle$HAN = 90° | 4. Perpendicular lines intersect to form right angles. |
| 5. $\angle$HAB and $\angle$BAN are complementary | 5. Two angles that form a right angle are complementary. |
| 6. m$\angle$RAC = m$\angle$RAH + m$\angle$HAN + m$\angle$NAC | 6. Angle Sum Postulate. |
| 7. m$\angle$RAC = 180° | 7. The measure of a straight angle is 180°. |
| 8. 180° = m$\angle$RAH + 90° + m$\angle$NAC | 8. Substitution Postulate. |
| 9. 90° = m$\angle$RAH + m$\angle$NAC | 9. Subtraction Postulate. |
| 10. $\angle$RAH and $\angle$NAC are complementary | 10. Two angles whose measures sum to 90° are complementary angles. |
| 11. $\angle$NAC $\cong$ $\angle$BAN | 11. Definition of angle bisector. |
| 12. $\angle$RAH $\cong$ $\angle$HAB | 12. Angles complementary to congruent angles are congruent. |
| 13. $\overline{HA}$ bisects $\angle$RAP | 13. Definition of angle bisector. |
| 14. Quadrilateral APHR is a rhombus | 14. If the diagonal of a parallelogram bisects an angle of the parallelogram, then the parallelogram is a rhombus. |

# SQUARES

● PROBLEM 5-10

In the accompanying figure, △ABC is given to be an isosceles right triangle with $\angle$ABC a right angle and AB $\cong$ BC. Line segment $\overline{BD}$, which bisects $\overline{CA}$, is extended to E, so that $\overline{BD} \cong \overline{DE}$. Prove BAEC is a square.

Solution: A square is a rectangle in which two consecutive sides are congruent. This definition will provide the framework for the proof in this problem. We will prove that BAEC is a parallelogram that is specifically a rectangle with consecutive sides congruent, namely a square.

| STATEMENT | REASON |
|---|---|
| 1. $\overline{BD} \cong \overline{DE}$ and $\overline{AD} \cong \overline{DC}$ | 1. Given ($\overline{BD}$ bisect $\overline{CA}$) |
| 2. BAEC is a parallelogram | 2. If diagonals of a quadrilateral bisect each other, then the quadrilateral is a parallelogram. |
| 3. ⦟ABC is a right angle | 3. Given. |
| 4. BAEC is a rectangle | 4. A parallelogram, one of whose angles is a right angle, is a rectangle. |
| 5. $\overline{AB} \cong \overline{BC}$ | 5. Given. |
| 6. BAEC is a square | 6. If a rectangle has two congruent consecutive sides, then the rectangle is a square. |

## ● PROBLEM 5-11

Given: Square ABCD; P is any point of $\overline{AB}$, Q is any point on $\overline{AD}$, $\overline{CQ} \perp \overline{PD}$ at R. Prove $\overline{PD} \cong \overline{QC}$.

Solution: $\overline{PD}$ and $\overline{QC}$ are corresponding parts of $\triangle APD$ and $\triangle DQC$. It is then sufficient to show $\triangle APD$ and $\triangle DQC$ are congruent. We do this using the AAS Postulate.

| STATEMENTS | REASONS |
|---|---|
| 1. Square ABCD; P is any point of $\overline{AB}$ so that $\overline{APB}$; $\overline{CQ} \perp \overline{PD}$ at R; $\overline{AQD}$ | 1. Given. |

73

| | |
|---|---|
| 2. ∢DAP and ∢ADC are right angles. | 2. All angles of a square are right angles. |
| 3. ∢DAP ≅ ∢ADC | 3. All right angles are congruent. |
| 4. $\overline{AD}$ ≅ $\overline{DC}$ | 4. All sides of a square are congruent. |
| 5. ∢APD and ∢ADP are complementary | 5. The acute angles of a right triangle (△DAP) are complementary |
| 6. ∢DQR and ∢ADP are complementary | 6. The acute angles of a right triangle (△QDR) are complementary |
| 7. ∢APD ≅ ∢DQR | 7. Angles complementary to congruent angles are congruent. |
| 8. △APD ≅ △DQC | 8. The AAS Postulate. |
| 9. $\overline{PD}$ ≅ $\overline{QC}$ | 9. Corresponding parts of congruent triangles are congruent. |

● **PROBLEM 5-12**

In the accompanying figure, WXYZ is a square. It has been placed in such a way inside quadrilateral ABCD that when its sides are extended to the vertices of ABCD, $\overline{AW}$ ≅ $\overline{BX}$ ≅ $\overline{CY}$ ≅ $\overline{DZ}$. All segments shown are straight line segments. Show that ABCD is a square.

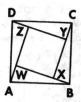

**Solution:** In this problem we will set out to show △'s AWB, BXC, CYD, and DZA are congruent. Then, by several applications of the fact that corresponding parts of congruent triangles are congruent, we will show that ABCD is a quadrilateral all of whose sides are congruent, and which contains a right angle (i.e., ABCD is a square).

| STATEMENT | REASON |
|---|---|
| 1. WXYZ is a square | 1. Given. |
| 2. $\overline{AW}$ ≅ $\overline{BX}$ ≅ $\overline{CY}$ ≅ $\overline{DZ}$ | 2. Given. |

| | |
|---|---|
| 3. $\overline{WZ} \cong \overline{XW} \cong \overline{YX} \cong \overline{ZY}$ | 3. All four sides of a square are congruent. |
| 4. $\overline{AW} + \overline{WZ} \cong \overline{BX} + \overline{XW}$ $\overline{CY} + \overline{YX} \cong \overline{DZ} + \overline{ZY}$ or $\overline{AZ} \cong \overline{BW} \cong \overline{CX} \cong \overline{DY}$ | 4. Congruent quantities added to congruent quantities result in congruent quantities. |
| 5. $\overline{DZ} \cong \overline{AW} \cong \overline{BX} \cong \overline{CY}$ | 5. Given. |
| 6. $\overleftrightarrow{BW}, \overleftrightarrow{CX}, \overleftrightarrow{DY}$ and $\overleftrightarrow{AZ}$ are straight lines | 6. Given. |
| 7. $\overline{BW} \perp \overline{AZ}, \overline{AZ} \perp \overline{DY},$ $\overline{DY} \perp \overline{CX}$ and $\overline{CX} \perp \overline{BW}$ | 7. The sides of a square meet to form right angles and are, therefore, perpendicular. |
| 8. $\angle AZD, \angle AWB, \angle CXB$ and $\angle CYD$ are right angles | 8. Perpendicular lines intersect to form right angles. |
| 9. $\angle AZD \cong \angle AWB \cong \angle CXB \cong \angle CYD$ | 9. All right angles are congruent. |
| 10. $\triangle AZD \cong \triangle BWA \cong \triangle CXB \cong \triangle DYC$ | 10. SAS $\cong$ SAS. |
| 11. $\overline{AD} \cong \overline{DC} \cong \overline{CB} \cong \overline{BA}$ | 11. Corresponding sides of congruent triangles are congruent. |
| 12. $\angle WAB$ is complementary to $\angle WBA$ | 12. The acute angles of right triangles are complementary. |
| 13. $\angle ZAD \cong \angle WBA$ | 13. Corresponding parts of congruent triangles are congruent. |
| 14. $\angle WAB$ is complementary to $\angle ZAD$ | 14. An angle congruent to a given angle's complement is complementary to that given angle. |
| 15. $m\angle WAB + m\angle ZAD = 90°$ | 15. The sum of the measures of two complements is 90°. |
| 16. $m\angle DAB = m\angle WAB + m\angle ZAD$ | 16. The measure of the whole is equal to the sum of the measures of its parts. |
| 17. $m\angle DAB = 90°$ | 17. Substitution Postulate. |
| 18. $\angle DAB$ is a right angle | 18. An angle that measures 90° is a right angle. |
| 19. ABCD is a square | 19. A quadrilateral that contains a right angle and all of whose sides are congruent is a square. |

# RECTANGLES

In parallelogram ABCD, as shown in the figure, $\overline{DE} \perp \overline{AB}$ and $\overline{BF} \perp \overline{DC}$. With this in mind, prove altitudes $\overline{DE} \cong \overline{BF}$.

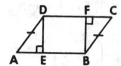

Solution:   To prove that $\overline{DE} \cong \overline{BF}$, the best approach would be to prove that the triangles, which have $\overline{DE}$ and $\overline{BF}$ as corresponding parts, are congruent. Therefore, we want to prove that $\triangle AED \cong \triangle CFB$. The method of proving congruence that is best for this problem is the one in which two triangles are shown to be congruent because two angles and the side opposite one angle in one triangle are congruent to the corresponding parts of another triangle. (A.A.S. $\cong$ A.A.S.)

Additionally, to prove the parts congruent it is essential to remember that opposite sides and angles in a parallelogram are congruent.

| STATEMENT | REASON |
|---|---|
| 1. ABCD is a parallelogram. | 1. Given. |
| 2. $\overline{AD} \cong \overline{CB}$ | 2. Opposite sides of a parallelogram are congruent. |
| 3. $\angle A \cong \angle C$ | 3. Opposite angles of a parallelogram are congruent. |
| 4. $\overline{DE} \perp \overline{AB}$ and $\overline{BF} \perp \overline{DC}$ | 4. Given. |
| 5. $\angle E$ and $\angle F$ are right angles. | 5. When perpendicular lines intersect they form right angles. |
| 6. $\angle E \cong \angle F$ | 6. All right angles are congruent. |
| 7. $\triangle AED \cong \triangle CFB$ | 7. a.a.s. $\cong$ a.a.s. |
| 8. $\overline{DE} \cong \overline{BF}$ | 8. Corresponding parts of congruent triangles are congruent. |

Prove that a rectangle is a parallelogram.

<u>Solution</u>:  A rectangle is a quadrilateral, all of whose angles measure 90°(see figure). We will show that ABCD is a parallelogram by analyzing the pairs of angles ABC and BCD, and DAB and ABC.

Since ⦨ABC, ⦨BCD, and ⦨DAB are all right angles,

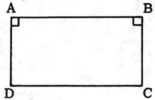

m⦨ABC = 90°                                                      (1)

m⦨BCD = 90°                                                      (2)

m⦨DAB = 90°                                                      (3)

Adding (1) and (2) shows that ⦨ABC and ⦨BCD are supplementary:

m⦨ABC + m⦨BCD = 180°.                                           (4)

Adding (1) and (3) shows that ⦨ABC and ⦨DAB are supplementary:

m⦨ABC + m⦨DAB = 180°.                                           (5)

Now, if the consecutive interior angles of 2 lines crossed by a transversal sum to 180°, then the 2 lines are parallel.

⦨ABC and ⦨BCD are consecutive interior angles of line segments $\overline{AB}$ and $\overline{DC}$. Also, ⦨ABC and ⦨DAB are consecutive interior angles of line segments $\overline{AD}$ and $\overline{BC}$. Using these facts, plus (4) and (5), we conclude that $\overline{AD} \parallel \overline{BC}$ and $\overline{AB} \parallel \overline{DC}$. By definition this means that ABCD, a rectangle, is a parallelogram.

In the figure shown, we are given rectangle ABCD.
(a) Prove  $\overline{AC} \cong \overline{BD}$. (b) Prove ΔAEB is isosceles.

77

<u>Solution</u>: (a) In this part, we are asked to prove that the diagonals $\overline{AC}$ and $\overline{BD}$ are congruent. Since the only given fact is that ABCD is a rectangle, we are proving that, in general, the diagonals of a rectangle are congruent.

We will do this by proving $\triangle ACB \cong \triangle BDA$, using the SAS Postulate.

| STATEMENT | REASON |
|---|---|
| 1. ABCD is a rectangle | 1. Given. |
| 2. $\overline{AD} \cong \overline{BC}$ | 2. Opposite sides of a rectangle are congruent. |
| 3. $\overline{AB} \cong \overline{BA}$ | 3. Reflexive Property of Congruence. |
| 4. ∡DAB and ∡CBA are right angles | 4. All angles of a rectangle are right angles. |
| 5. ∡DAB $\cong$ ∡CBA | 5. All right angles are congruent. |
| 6. $\triangle ACB \cong \triangle BDA$ | 6. SAS $\cong$ SAS |
| 7. $\overline{AC} \cong \overline{BD}$ | 7. Corresponding sides of congruent triangles are congruent. |

(b) To prove $\triangle AEB$ isosceles, we must prove that $\overline{AE} \cong \overline{EB}$. We can do this by showing that the angles opposite these sides are congruent.

| STATEMENT | REASON |
|---|---|
| 1. $\triangle ACB \cong \triangle BDA$ | 1. Results from part (a). |
| 2. ∡CAB $\cong$ ∡DBA | 2. Corresponding angles of congruent triangles are congruent. |
| 3. In $\triangle AEB$, $\overline{AE} \cong \overline{EB}$ | 3. In a triangle, if two angles are congruent, then the sides opposite those angles are congruent. |
| 4. $\triangle AEB$ is isosceles | 4. By definition, if a triangle has a pair of congruent sides, then it is isosceles. |

Prove that the bisectors of the angles of a rectangle enclose a square.

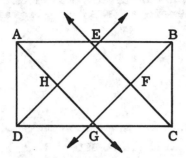

Solution: In the diagram, the angle bisectors of rectangle ABCD intersect at points E, F, G, and H. We must show that quadrilateral EFGH is a square. To do this we will show that (1) EFGH is a rectangle and (2) two adjacent sides of EFGH are congruent.

To show that EFGH is a rectangle, we show that it is a quadrilateral with four right angles. We will do this with several applications of the theorem stating that the angle sum of a triangle is 180°.

$\overline{AG}$ is an angle bisector of ⟩DAB. Since quadrilateral ABCD is a rectangle, then ⟩DAB is a right angle. Thus, ⟩DAH = ½(90°) = 45°. Similarly, $\overline{DE}$ is an angle bisector of ⟩ADC, and thus ⟩HDA = ½(90°) = 45°. In △HDA, m⟩AHD + m⟩HDA + m⟩DAH = 180°, or m⟩AHD = 180°- m⟩DAH - m⟩HDA = 180° - 45° - 45° = 90°. Because ⟩EHG and ⟩AHD are opposite angles, m⟩EHG = m⟩AHD = 90°. By similar reasoning, we can show m⟩EFG = 90°.

To show m⟩DEC is 90°, note that m⟩HDG = ½m⟩ADG = ½(90°) = 45°. Also, m⟩ECD = ½ m⟩BCD = ½(90°) = 45°. In △DEC, m⟩HDG + m⟩ECD + m⟩DEC = 180°. m⟩DEC = 180° - m⟩EDC - m⟩ECD = 180° - 45° - 45° = 90°. By analogous reasoning we can show m⟩AGB = 90°.

Since all four vertex angles are right angles, quadrilateral EFGH is a rectangle. The proof of the second part - that two adjacent sides of EFGH are congruent - follows:

(1) DE = EC:     Note m⟩EDC = m⟩ECD = 45°. Thus, △DEC is isosceles and DE = EC.

(2) △AHD ≅ △BFC:     m⟩DAH = m⟩CBF = 45°. m⟩ADH = m⟩BCF = 45°. Opposite sides of rectangle ABCD are congruent. Thus, $\overline{AD}$ ≅ $\overline{BC}$. By the ASA Postulate, △AHD ≅ △BFC.

(3) HD = FC:     Corresponding parts of congruent triangles are congruent and equal in length.

(4) DE - HD =
    EC - FC :     By the Subtraction Property of Equality.

(5) HE = EF:      Substitution Postulate.

   Thus, in rectangle EFGH, two adjacent sides HE and EF
are congruent. Therefore, EFGH is a square.


# TRAPEZOIDS

● PROBLEM 5-17

We are given parallelogram ABCD and straight line segment
$\overline{AE}$. (See the figure.) ⟩CBE $\cong$ ⟩CEB. Present a formal proof
to show AECD is an isosceles trapezoid.

Solution:  A trapezoid is a quadrilateral that has two and
only two sides parallel. It is isosceles if the two non-
parallel sides are congruent.

   In this problem, we will first prove AECD is a
trapezoid. Then, $\overline{DA}$ will be shown to be congruent to $\overline{CE}$
by first proving that both of the former are congruent to
the same segment and then applying the transitive property
of congruence.

| STATEMENT | REASON |
|---|---|
| 1. ABCD is a parallelogram | 1. Given. |
| 2. $\overline{DC}$ || $\overline{AB}$ (or $\overline{DC}$ || $\overline{AE}$) | 2. Opposite sides of a paral- lelogram are parallel. |
| 3. $\overline{DA}$ || $\overline{CB}$ | 3. Same as reason 2. |
| 4. $\overline{DA}$ ⊬ $\overline{CE}$ | 4. Through a point not on a given line only one line can be drawn parallel to that given line. |
| 5. AECD is a trapezpoid | 5. A trapezoid is a quadri- lateral that has two and only two sides parallel. |
| 6. $\overline{DA}$ $\cong$ $\overline{CB}$ | 6. A pair of opposite sides of a parallelogram are congruent, and statement 1. |

| 7. ∢CBE ≅ ∢CEB | 7. Given. |
|---|---|
| 8. $\overline{CB}$ ≅ $\overline{CE}$ | 8. If two angles of a triangle are congruent, then the sides opposite those angles are congruent. |
| 9. $\overline{DA}$ ≅ $\overline{CE}$ | 9. Transitive property of congruence. |
| 10. AECD is an isosceles trapezoid | 10. An isosceles trapezoid is a trapezoid whose non-parallel sides are congruent. |

● **PROBLEM** 5-18

The lengths of the bases of an isosceles trapezoid are 8 and 14, and each of the base angles measures 45°. Find the length of the altitude of the trapezoid.

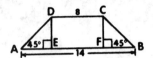

Solution: As can be seen in the figure, it is helpful to draw both altitudes $\overline{DE}$ and $\overline{CF}$. DCFE is a rectangle because $\overline{DC}$ || $\overline{AB}$ (given by the definition of a trapezoid), $\overline{DE}$ || $\overline{CF}$ (they are both ⊥ to the same line) and ∢E is a right angle ($\overline{DE}$ ⊥ $\overline{AB}$). Opposite sides of a rectangle are congruent. Therefore, DC = EF = 8.

ΔAED ≅ ΔBFC because ∢DEA ≅ ∢CFB (both are right angles).

∢DAE ≅ ∢CBF, and $\overline{DA}$ ≅ $\overline{BC}$.(The last two facts come from the definition of an isosceles trapezoid).Therefore, by corresponding parts, $\overline{AE}$ ≅ $\overline{BF}$. Then, AE = ½(AB - EF) and, substituting AE = ½(14 - 8) = ½(6) = 3.

In ΔAED, m∢E = 90 and m∢A = 45. By the angle sum postulate for triangles, m∢D = 45. Since ΔAED has two angles of equal measure, it must be an isosceles triangle. Therefore, AE = DE = 3.

Therefore, the length of the altitude of trapezoid ABCD is 3.

● **PROBLEM** 5-19

Prove that the line containing the median of a trapezoid bisects any altitude of the trapezoid.

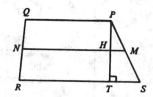

**Solution:** The median of a trapezoid is the line segment joining the midpoints of the nonparallel sides. Since the median is everywhere half way between the bases, it is everywhere equidistant from the two bases and, as such, is parallel to them. The nonparallel sides and any altitude of a trapezoid are all transversals of the parallel bases and median.

There is a theorem that states if three or more parallel lines intercept congruent segments on one transversal, then they intercept congruent segments on any other transversal. Since parallel lines $\overleftrightarrow{QP}$, $\overleftrightarrow{NM}$, and $\overleftrightarrow{RS}$ cut equal segments on $\overline{QR}$ and $\overline{PS}$, they cut $\overline{PT}$ equally.

Given: Trapezoid PQRS with altitude $\overline{PT}$ intersecting median $\overline{MN}$ at H.

Prove: $\overline{MN}$ bisects $\overline{PT}$.

| STATEMENTS | REASONS |
|---|---|
| 1. Trapezoid PQRS with altitude $\overline{PT}$ meeting median $\overline{MN}$ at H. | 1. Given. |
| 2. $\overline{MN} \parallel \overline{SR}$ | 2. The median of a trapezoid is parallel to the bases. |
| 3. M is the midpoint of $\overline{PS}$ | 3. Definition of the median of a triangle. |
| 4. $\overline{PM} \cong \overline{MS}$ | 4. Definition of the midpoint of a line segment. |
| 5. $\overline{PH} \cong \overline{HT}$ | 5. If three or more parallel lines intercept congruent segments on a transversal, then they intercept congruent segments on any other transversal. |
| 6. $\overline{MN}$ bisects $\overline{PT}$ | 6. Definition of bisection. |

# CHAPTER 6

# GEOMETRIC PROPORTIONS AND SIMILARITIES

## RATIO AND PROPORTIONS

**• PROBLEM 6-1**

Solve for the unknown, c, in the proportion 18 : 6 = c : 9.

Solution: A theorem tells us that, in a proportion, the product of the means is equal to the product of the extremes.

In this problem, 6 and c are the means and 18 and 9 are the extremes. Therefore,

$$6c = 18 \times 9$$

$$6c = 162$$

$$c = \frac{162}{6} = 27.$$

The answer c = 27 can be checked by substituting back into the original proportion.

$$18 : 6 = 27 : 9$$

$$3 : 1 = 3 : 1$$

Since the two ratios are equal, c = 27.

**• PROBLEM 6-2**

Line segments $\overline{AC}$ and $\overline{BD}$ intersect at E, as shown in the accompanying diagram. $\overline{AB}$ is parallel to $\overline{CD}$. (a) Prove that $\triangle ABE \sim \triangle CDE$ and (b) if DE = 10, BE = 15 and CE = 20, find AE.

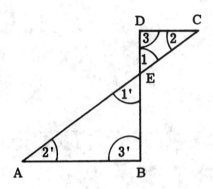

Solution: (a) For this proof, we will employ the theorem which tells us that two triangles are similar if two angles of one triangle are congruent to two corresponding angles of the other.

| STATEMENT | REASON |
|---|---|
| 1. $\overline{AC}$ and $\overline{BD}$ are straight line segments | 1. Given. |
| 2. $\angle 1$ and $\angle 1'$ are vertical angles | 2. Definition of vertical angles |
| 3. $\angle 1 \overset{\sim}{=} \angle 1'$ | 3. If two angles are vertical angles, then they are congruent. |
| 4. $\overline{AB} \parallel \overline{CD}$ | 4. Given. |
| 5. $\angle 2 \overset{\sim}{=} \angle 2'$ | 5. If parallel lines are cut by a transversal, then the alternate interior angles are congruent. |
| 6. $\triangle ABE \sim \triangle CDE$ | 6. A.A. Similarity Theorem. |

   (b) Corresponding sides of similar triangles must be proportional. Therefore, since DE corresponds to BE and CE corresponds to AE, the proportion DE : BE = CE : AE must hold. The lengths of all sides other than $\overline{AE}$ are known and can be substituted into the proportion, enabling us to calculate AE.

$$10 : 15 = 20 : AE$$

$$10 \, (AE) = 15 \cdot 20$$

$$AE = 30.$$

In the accompanying figure, the line segment, $\overline{KL}$, is drawn parallel to $\overline{ST}$, intersecting $\overline{RS}$ at K and $\overline{RT}$ at L in $\triangle RST$. If RK = 5, KS = 10, and RT = 18, then find RL.

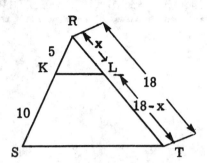

Solution: If a line is parallel to one side of a triangle, then it divides the other two sides proportionally. Since $\overline{KL} \parallel \overline{ST}$, $\overline{RT}$ and $\overline{RS}$ are divided proportionally.

Let x = RL. Then 18 − x = LT. Set up the proportion

$$\frac{RK}{KS} = \frac{RL}{LT}$$ and substitute to obtain

$$\frac{5}{10} = \frac{x}{18 - x}$$

or    10x = 90 − 5x

15x = 90

x = 6

Therefore, x = RL = 6.

Alternatively, instead of forming a ratio of upper to lower segment, we can form a ratio of the upper segment to the whole side.

We are given RT = 18, RS = 15, and RK = 5. If we let RL = x, the proportion becomes

$$\frac{RK}{RS} = \frac{RL}{RT}$$

$$\frac{5}{15} = \frac{x}{18}$$

15x = 90

x = 6.

It is seen, then, that the same solution can be arrived at in several ways.

# PROVING TRIANGLES SIMILAR

In the accompanying figure, triangle ABC is similar to triangle A'B'C', and AC corresponds to A'C'. (a) Find the ratio of similitude. (b) Find A'B' and B'C'.

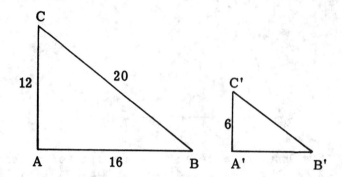

Solution: (a) The ratio of similitude of two similar polygons is defined as the ratio of the measures of any two corresponding sides. We are told AC corresponds to A'C'. Therefore,

Ratio of Similitude = $\frac{AC}{A'C'} = \frac{12}{6} = \frac{2}{1} = 2 : 1$.

(b) The ratio of similitude of ΔABC to ΔA'B'C' being 2 : 1 tells us that each side of ΔABC is twice as long as its corresponding part in ΔA'B'C'. Conversely, each side of ΔA'B'C' is ½ as long as its corresponding side in ΔABC.

(i)  A'B' = ½ (AB) = ½(16) = 8.

(ii)  B'C' = ½ (BC) = ½(20) = 10.

Let ABC be a triangle where D is a point on $\overline{AB}$, and E is a point on $\overline{AC}$. Prove that if $\overline{DE} \parallel \overline{BC}$, then AB/AD = BC/DE. (See figure.)

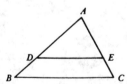

Solution: We will use the fact that $\overline{DE} \parallel \overline{BC}$ to prove that ΔADE ∿ ΔABC. We can then set up a proportion and show that AB/AD = BC/DE.

Since the corresponding angles of 2 parallel lines cut by a transversal are congruent, $\angle ADE \cong \angle ABC$ and $\angle AED \cong \angle ACB$. Furthermore, $\angle DAE \cong \angle BAC$. Therefore, by the A.A.A. (angle angle angle) Similarity Theorem, $\triangle ADE \sim \triangle ABC$. Hence, corresponding sides of the 2 triangles must be proportional, and we may write

$$\frac{AD}{AB} = \frac{AE}{AC} = \frac{DE}{BC} \qquad \text{or} \qquad \frac{AD}{AB} = \frac{DE}{BC} \, .$$

Taking reciprocals of both sides:

$$\frac{AB}{AD} = \frac{BC}{DE} \, .$$

● PROBLEM 6-6

(a) In $\triangle ABC$, if D is the midpoint of $\overline{AB}$, E is the midpoint of $\overline{AC}$, and F is the midpoint of $\overline{BC}$, then prove that $\overline{DE} \parallel \overline{BC}$, $\overline{EF} \parallel \overline{AB}$, and $\overline{DF} \parallel \overline{AC}$. (b) Prove that $\triangle DEF \sim \triangle CBA$.

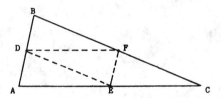

Solution: (a) The method is to show that $\triangle ADE \sim \triangle ABC$. We will then have $\angle ADE \cong \angle ABC$ and be able to conclude that $\overline{DE} \parallel \overline{BC}$. The same procedure is used for the pairs of triangles CFE and CBA, and BDF and BAC.

Focus attention on triangles ADE and ABC.

First, D and E are the midpoints of $\overline{BA}$ and $\overline{CA}$, respectively. Hence,

$$\frac{AD}{AB} = \frac{AE}{AC} = \frac{1}{2}$$

Also, $\angle DAE \cong \angle BAC$. Therefore, by the Side Angle Side (S.A.S.) Similarity Theorem, $\triangle ADE \sim \triangle ABC$. By definition then, $\angle ADE \cong \angle ABC$. Because these 2 angles are congruent corresponding angles of the segments $\overline{DE}$ and $\overline{BC}$, $\overline{DE} \parallel \overline{BC}$.

In an exactly analogous manner, we may prove that $\triangle CFE \sim \triangle CBA$, and $\triangle BDF \sim \triangle BAC$. Hence, $\angle CFE \cong \angle CBA$ and

∢BDF $\overset{\sim}{=}$ ∢BAC. Therefore, $\overline{FE} \parallel \overline{BA}$ and $\overline{DF} \parallel \overline{AC}$.

(b) From part (a), we know that

$$\triangle ADE \sim \triangle ABC$$

$$\triangle CFE \sim \triangle CBA \qquad (1)$$

$$\triangle BDF \sim \triangle BAC.$$

Hence, from equations (1),

$$\frac{DE}{BC} = \frac{AD}{AB} = \frac{1}{2}$$

$$\frac{FE}{BA} = \frac{CF}{CB} = \frac{1}{2} \qquad (2)$$

$$\frac{DF}{AC} = \frac{BD}{BA} = \frac{1}{2}$$

Here, we have used the fact that D, E, and F are midpoints of $\overline{BA}$, $\overline{AC}$, and $\overline{CB}$, respectively. From (2), then,

$$\frac{DE}{BC} = \frac{FE}{BA} = \frac{DF}{AC} = \frac{1}{2}$$

By the S.S.S. (Side Side Side) Similarity Theorem,

$$\triangle DEF \sim \triangle CBA.$$

● **PROBLEM** 6-7

Given: $\overline{AD}$ is an angle bisector of △ABC; point E is on $\overleftrightarrow{AD}$ such that AB · AC = AD · AE. Prove: ∢ B $\overset{\sim}{=}$ ∢ AEC.

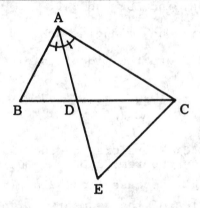

Solution: Whenever there are proportions, the best procedure is to find similar triangles. There are five possible triangles in the figure but only two, △ABD and △AEC, allow us to use the given fact that $\sphericalangle$ BAD $\overset{\sim}{=}$ $\sphericalangle$ EAC. By using this and the information that AB · AC = AD · AE (which show that two pairs of sides are proportional) we can prove $\triangle$ABD $\sim$ $\triangle$AEC by the A.S.A. Similarity Theorem. The congruence of $\sphericalangle$ B and $\sphericalangle$ AEC follows immediately.

| STATEMENT | REASONS |
|---|---|
| 1. $\overline{AD}$ bisects $\sphericalangle$ BAC | 1. Given. |
| 2. $\sphericalangle$ BAD $\overset{\sim}{=}$ $\sphericalangle$ DAC | 2. Definition of an angle bisector. |
| 3. AB · AC = AD · AE | 3. Given. |
| 4. $\dfrac{AB}{AE} = \dfrac{AD}{AC}$ | 4. $\dfrac{a}{b} = \dfrac{c}{d}$ if and only if ad = bc. |
| 5. $\triangle$ABD $\sim$ $\triangle$AEC | 5. S.A.S. Similarity Theorem. |
| 6. $\sphericalangle$ B $\overset{\sim}{=}$ $\sphericalangle$ AEC | 6. Corresponding angles of similar triangles are congruent. |

● **PROBLEM** 6-8

In the accompanying figure, $\triangle$ABC is isosceles with $\overline{AB}$ $\overset{\sim}{=}$ $\overline{AC}$. Segment $\overline{AF}$ is the altitude on $\overline{BC}$. From a point on $\overline{AB}$, call it D, a perpendicular is drawn which is extended to meet $\overleftrightarrow{BC}$. It meets $\overline{BC}$ at point P. Prove that FC : DB = AC : PB.

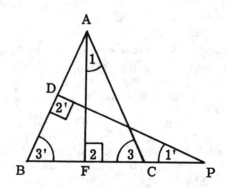

Solution: $\overline{FC}$ and $\overline{AC}$ are sides of $\triangle$FCA and correspond to sides $\overline{DB}$ and $\overline{PB}$ of $\triangle$DBP. By proving $\triangle$FCA $\sim$ $\triangle$DBP, we can conclude that FC : DB = AC : PB is a proportion, because there is a theorem which states that corresponding sides of similar triangles are proportional.

89

The corresponding angles of ΔFCA and ΔDBP have been numbered, in the diagram, by a "prime and no prime" system.

Similarity will be proved by showing two pairs of corresponding angles congruent.

| STATEMENT | REASON |
|---|---|
| 1. $\overline{AB} = \overline{AC}$ | 1. Given. |
| 2. ∢ 3 $\overset{\sim}{=}$ ∢ 3' | 2. If two sides of a trignale are congruent, then the angles opposite these sides are congruent. |
| 3. $\overline{AF} \perp \overline{BC}$ | 3. An altitude drawn to a side is perpendicular to that side. |
| 4. $\overline{PD} \perp \overline{AB}$ | 4. Given. |
| 5. ∢ 2 and ∢ 2' are right angles | 5. Perpendicular lines intersect forming right angles. |
| 6. ∢ 2 $\overset{\sim}{=}$ ∢ 2' | 6. All right angles are congruent. |
| 7. ΔFCA ∿ ΔDBP | 7. A.A. $\overset{\sim}{=}$ A.A. |
| 8. $\dfrac{FC\ (opp.∢ 1)}{DB\ (opp.∢ 1')} = \dfrac{AC\ (opp.\ ∢ 2)}{PB\ (opp.\ ∢ 2')}$ | 8. Corresponding sides of similar triangles are proportional. |

● PROBLEM 6-9

Prove that any two regular polygons with the same number of sides are similar.

Solution: For any two polygons to be similar, their corresponding angles must be congruent and their corresponding sides proportional. It is necessary to show that these conditions always exist between regular polygons with the same number of sides.

Let us examine the corresponding angles first. For a regular polygon with n sides, the measure of each central angle is $\dfrac{360}{n}$ and each vertex angle is $\dfrac{(n - 2)\ 180}{n}$. Therefore, two regular polygons with the same number of sides will have corresponding central angles and vertex

90

angles that are all of the same measure and, hence, are all congruent. This fulfills our first condition for similarity.

We must now determine whether or not the corresponding sides are proportional. It will suffice to show that the ratios of the lengths of every pair of corresponding sides are the same.

Since the polygons are regular, the sides of each one will be equal. Call the length of the sides of one polygon $\ell_1$ and the length of the sides of the other polygon $\ell_2$. Hence, the ratio of the lengths of corresponding sides will be $\ell_1/\ell_2$. This will be a constant for any pair of corresponding sides and, hence, the corresponding sides are proportional.

Thus, any two regular polygons with the same number of sides are similar.

# PROPORTIONS INVOLVING ANGLE BISECTORS

● **PROBLEM** 6-10

The sides of a triangle have lengths 15, 20 and 28. Find the lengths of the segments into which the bisector of the angle with the greatest measure divides the opposite side.

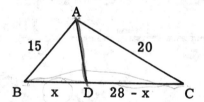

Solution: An angle bisector of any triangle divides the side of the triangle opposite the angle into segments proportional to the sides adjacent to the angle. Therefore,

(i) $$\frac{BD}{DC} = \frac{AB}{AC} .$$

If we let BD = x, then DC = 28 − x. Substituting in equation (i), we have

(ii) $$\frac{x}{28 - x} = \frac{15}{20} .$$

Reducing the fraction on the right to lowest terms,

(iii) $$\frac{x}{28 - x} = \frac{3}{4}$$

For real numbers a, b, c, d, it must be true that if

91

$\frac{a}{b} = \frac{c}{d}$ , then ad = cb. Therefore, from equation (iii), we have

(iv)                    4x = 3(28 - x).

Multiplying out, we have

(v)                    4x = 84 - 3x

Adding 3x to both sides,

(vi)                   4x + 3x = 84 - 3x + 3x

(vii)                  7x = 84

Dividing by 7 leaves

(viii)                 x = 12.

Then,

(ix)                   BD = 12

(x)                    DC = 28 - 12 = 16.


● **PROBLEM 6-11**

A right triangle has legs of length 6 and 8 inches. $\overline{CD}$ bisects the right angle. Find the lengths of $\overline{AD}$ and $\overline{DB}$.

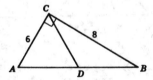

Solution: We must somehow relate the unknown segment lengths to the given data to derive the required results.

Recall that the bisector of one angle of a triangle divides the opposite side so that the lengths of its segments are proportional to the lengths of the adjacent sides. Thus,

$$\frac{6}{8} = \frac{AD}{DB} .$$

We see that $\frac{8}{8} = \frac{DB}{DB}$ is always true. Hence, adding this to the above proportion, we obtain

$$\frac{6 + 8}{8} = \frac{AD + DB}{DB} .$$

92

But, AD + DB = AB, the hypotenuse of a right triangle. Applying the Pythagorean theorem, $a^2 + b^2 = c^2$, where a = 6, b = 8, we obtain

$$6^2 + 8^2 = c^2$$

$$36 + 64 = c^2$$

$$100 = c^2.$$

Thus, c = 10, or hypotenuse AB = 10. Substituting we obtain

$$\frac{6 + 8}{8} = \frac{AD + DB}{DB}$$

$$\frac{14}{8} = \frac{AB}{DB}$$

$$\frac{14}{8} = \frac{10}{DB} .$$

Since, in a proportion, the product of the means is equal to the product of the extremes, we obtain

$$14 \cdot DB = 8 \cdot 10,$$

$$DB = \frac{80}{14} = \frac{40}{7} .$$

To find AD, we notice that

$$AD = AB - DB$$

$$= 10 - \frac{40}{7} = \frac{30}{7} .$$

Therefore, $\qquad AD = \frac{30}{7}$ and $DB = \frac{40}{7} .$

# PROPORTIONS INVOLVING RIGHT TRIANGLES

● PROBLEM 6-12

In the figure below, ∆ABC is a right triangle. $\overline{AD}$ is an altitude on the hypotenuse $\overline{BC}$. $\overline{BD}$ = 2, DC = 8. Find AD, AB, and AC.

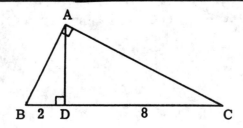

<u>Solution</u>: The geometric mean of two numbers x and z, is
defined as that number, y, such that

$$\frac{x}{y} = \frac{y}{z} .$$

In the right triangle, the altitude to the hypotenuse is
the geometric mean between the segments of the hypotenuse.
Therefore,

(i) $$\frac{BD}{AD} = \frac{AD}{DC}$$

Substituting in the values, BD = 2 and DC = 8, the
equation becomes

(ii) $$\frac{2}{AD} = \frac{AD}{8} .$$

For the proportionality to be true, the product of
the means must equal the product of the extremes.

The equation then becomes

(iii) $$(AD)^2 = 2 \cdot 8 = 16$$

(iv) $$AD = \sqrt{16} = 4.$$

To find AB, we note that AB is the hypotenuse of right
triangle $\triangle ABD$. Since we know the lengths of both legs, we
can use the Pythagorean theorem,

(v) $$c^2 = a^2 + b^2.$$

Substituting, we obtain

(vi) $$(AB)^2 = (BD)^2 + (AD)^2$$

(vii) $$(AB)^2 = 2^2 + 4^2 = 4 + 16 = 20$$

(viii) $$AB = \sqrt{20} = \sqrt{4 \cdot 5} = \sqrt{4} \cdot \sqrt{5} = 2 \cdot \sqrt{5}.$$

Another method of solving for AB is to realize that
there is another geometric mean implicit in the triangle.
The altitude to the leg divides the hypotenuse so that
either leg is the geometric mean between the hypotenuse
and the segment of the hypotenuse adjacent to that leg.
Therefore, it must be that

(ix) $$\frac{BD}{AB} = \frac{AB}{BC}$$

We substitute in the values BD = 2 and BC = 10,

(x) $$\frac{2}{AB} = \frac{AB}{10} ,$$

(xi) $$(AB)^2 = 2 \cdot 10 = 20,$$

(xii) $$AB = \sqrt{20} \quad \text{or} \quad 2\sqrt{5}.$$

We find AC in a similar manner. AC is the geometric mean of DC and BC. Therefore,

(xiii) $$\frac{DC}{AC} = \frac{AC}{BC} ,$$

(xiv) $$\frac{8}{AC} = \frac{AC}{10} .$$

Remember: the product of the means must equal the product of the extremes,

(xv) $$(AC)^2 = 8 \cdot 10 = 80$$

(xvi) $$AC = \sqrt{80} = \sqrt{16 \cdot 5} = \sqrt{16} \cdot \sqrt{5} = 4\sqrt{5}.$$

● **PROBLEM** 6-13

An altitude and an angle bisector are drawn to the hypotenuse of a right triangle whose sides are 8, 15, and 17 inches long. Find the length of the segment joining the points where the altitude and angle bisector intersect the hypotenuse (see figure). Express your answer to the nearest hundredth.

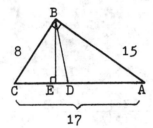

**Solution:** In the accompanying figure, ΔABC is a right triangle with AB = 15, BC = 8, and AC = 17. $\overline{BD}$ is the bisector of the right angle and $\overline{BE}$ is the altitude drawn to the hypotenuse. We wish to find DE. With the given information, we can determine (1) DC and (2) EC. Since DE = DC − EC, we can then solve for DE.

(1) To solve for DC, note that the angle bisector divides the opposite side into segments proportional to the sides.

(i) $$\frac{AD}{DC} = \frac{AB}{BC}$$

Note AB = 15 and BC = 8. Since AD + DC = AC = 17, AD can be expressed as 17 − DC. Substituting these results, we have

(ii) $$\frac{17 - DC}{DC} = \frac{15}{8} .$$

95

We have one equation and one unknown. To solve for DC, multiply both sides by 8 · DC:

(iii)                    8 (17 – DC) = 15 · DC

(iv)                    136 – 8DC = 15 DC

Adding 8DC to both sides and dividing by 23, we obtain

(v)                     $DC = \frac{136}{23}$ .

(2) To solve for EC, note that $\overline{BE}$ is an altitude drawn to the hypotenuse of a right triangle and cuts segments $\overline{AE}$ and $\overline{EC}$ on the hypotenuse. Since the length of each leg of the given triangle is the mean proportional between the hypotenuse length and the adjacent segment, we have

(vi)                    $BC^2 = EC · AC.$

We substitute BC = 8, AC = 17, and solve for EC:

(vii)                   $8^2 = EC · 17$

(viii)                  $EC = \frac{64}{17}$

Having found values for DC and EC, we can now solve for DE:

(ix)                    $DE = DC – EC$

(x)    $DE = \frac{136}{23} - \frac{64}{17} = \frac{17(136) - 64(23)}{23(17)}$

(xi)   $DE = \frac{840}{391} \cong 2.15.$

● **PROBLEM 6-14**

D and E are respective points of side $\overline{AB}$ and $\overline{BC}$ of $\triangle ABC$, so that $\frac{AD}{DB} = \frac{2}{3}$ and $\frac{BE}{EC} = \frac{1}{4}$. If $\overline{AE}$ and $\overline{DC}$ meet at P, find $\frac{PC}{DP}$ .

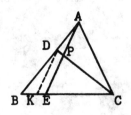

<u>Solution</u>: We are asked to find ratio $\frac{PC}{DP}$. To find the value of a ratio $\frac{a}{b}$, we can either (1) find exact values of a and b; (2) express the values of a and b in terms of a common length; or (3) form a proportion with $\frac{a}{b}$ as one side and a known ratio on the other side. Here, no values are given. Thus, PC and DP cannot be solved exactly. Neither is there a common length in which DP and PC can be expressed. The third method calls for a proportion. Proportions imply (1) similar triangles; (2) a triangle cut by a line parallel to one side; and (3) sets of parallel lines. To create proportional sides, draw segment $\overline{DK}$ parallel to $\overline{AE}$ such that K is between B and C. Note that in $\triangle CDK$, line $\overline{PE}$ is parallel to side DK. Therefore, $\frac{PC}{DP} = \frac{EC}{EK}$. Our proportional is formed. $\frac{PC}{DP}$ is on one side. The term on the other side, $\frac{EC}{EK}$, can be found since both EC and EK can be found in terms of BC.

To find EK in terms of BC, we show, (1) in $\triangle BAE$, $\overset{\leftrightarrow}{DK}$ || side $\overline{AE}$. Therefore, sides $\overline{BA}$ and $\overline{BE}$ are cut proportionally.

$$\frac{KE}{KB} = \frac{AD}{DB} . \text{ Since } \frac{AD}{DB} = \frac{2}{3}, \quad \frac{KE}{KB} = \frac{2}{3} .$$

(2) From $\frac{KE}{KB}$, we can find KE in terms of BE. $\frac{KE}{KB} = \frac{2}{3}$. Then, $KE = \frac{2}{3} KB$, or $KB = \frac{3}{2} KE$. Since $BE = KE + BK$, $BE = KE + \frac{3}{2} KE = \frac{5}{2} KE$. Thus,

$$KE = \frac{2}{5} BE.$$

(3) We can find BE in terms of BC. From the given $\frac{BE}{EC} = \frac{1}{4}$ or $BE = \frac{1}{4} EC$ or $EC = 4BE$. Since $BC = BE + EC = BE + 4BE = 5BE$, then

$$BE = \frac{1}{5} BC.$$

(4) We can combine the results of 2 and 3 to find KE in terms of BC. $KE = \frac{2}{5} BE$ and $BE = \frac{1}{5} BC$. Therefore, $KE = \frac{2}{5} \left[\frac{1}{5} BC\right] = \frac{2}{25} BC$.

To find EC in terms of BC, note that $\frac{BE}{EC} = \frac{1}{4}$ or $BE = \frac{1}{4} EC$. Since $BC = BE + EC = \frac{1}{4} EC + EC = \frac{5}{4} EC$, then $EC = \frac{4}{5} BC$.

Combining these two results, we have

$$\frac{EC}{KE} = \frac{\frac{4}{5} BC}{\frac{2}{25} BC} = 10.$$

Earlier, we found $\frac{PC}{DP} = \frac{EC}{KE}$. Therefore, $\frac{PC}{DP} = 10$.

# PROPORTIONS INVOLVING MEDIANS

● **PROBLEM** 6-15

In triangle ABC, medians $\overline{AD}$, $\overline{BE}$, and $\overline{CF}$ intersect at P, as seen in the figure. If AD = 24 in., find the length of $\overline{AP}$.

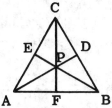

**Solution:** A theorem tells us that the medians of a triangle are concurrent at a point whose distance from any vertex is two-thirds the distance from that vertex to the midpoint of the opposite side. The vertex in question is A, the point of concurrency is P, and the distance to the midpoint of the side opposite A is given by AD. Therefore, the length of $\overline{AP}$ equals $\frac{2}{3}$ the length of $\overline{AD}$. Algebraically, this means

$$AP = \frac{2}{3} AD$$

$$AP = \frac{2}{3}(24") = 16".$$

Therefore, the length of $\overline{AP}$ is 16".

● **PROBLEM** 6-16

Show that the medians of a triangle are concurrent at a point on each median located two-thirds of the way from each vertex to the opposite side.

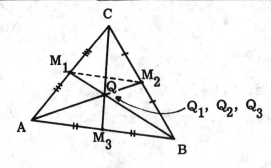

<u>Solution</u>: Referring to the figure above, we must show (1) $Q$ is a point on $\overline{AM_2}$, $\overline{BM_1}$, and $\overline{CM_3}$; and (2) that $AQ = \frac{2}{3} AM_2$, $BQ = \frac{2}{3} BM_1$, and $CQ = \frac{2}{3} CM_3$. Since $AM_2 = AQ + QM_2$, $QM_2 = AM_2 - AQ = AM_2 - \frac{2}{3} AM_2 = \frac{1}{3} AM_2$, or $QM_2 = \frac{1}{3} AM_2$. Thus, to prove the second part, we need to show that the point of concurrency divides the median $AM_2$ into two segments such that the segment near the vertex is twice the length of the segment near the side. In algebraic notation, what we must show for the second part is that $\frac{AQ}{QM_2} = \frac{BQ}{QM_1} = \frac{CQ}{QM_3} = 2$.

Wherever there are proportions, it is wise to look for similar triangles. Suppose we first wish to show that $\frac{AQ}{QM_2} = \frac{2}{1}$. Then we find two triangles such that $\overline{AQ}$ and $\overline{QM_2}$ are corresponding sides. $\triangle AQB$ and $\triangle M_2QM_1$ are such triangles. We show similarity by the A-A Similarity Theorem. Then $\frac{AQ}{QM_2} = \frac{BQ}{QM_1} = \frac{AB}{M_1M_2}$. $\frac{AB}{M_1M_2}$ is known. $\overline{M_1M_2}$ is a midline of $\triangle ABC$. Therefore, $AB = 2 \cdot M_1M_2$, $\frac{AB}{M_1M_2} = 2$, and $\frac{AQ}{QM_2} = 2$, proving the second part. We can repeat the procedure for the two other sides.

NOTE: It may seem that we have proven the second part without actually showing that the lines are indeed concurrent, but we really don't need the concurrency to show the two-thirds division. In fact, the exact reverse is true. We show that the intersection of any two medians is a point two-thirds the length of each median from the respective vertex. Since there is only one point that is two-thirds the median length from the vertex, the points of intersection must be the same. Concurrency (part one) follows from the two-thirds division (part two).

Given: $\overline{AM_2}$, $\overline{BM_1}$, and $\overline{CM_3}$ are medians of $\triangle ABC$.

Prove: (1) $Q$ is a point on $\overline{AM_2}$, $\overline{BM_1}$, and $\overline{CM_3}$.

(2) $AQ = \frac{2}{3} AM_2$, $BQ = \frac{2}{3} BM_1$, $CQ = \frac{2}{3} CM_3$.

| Statements | Reasons |
|---|---|
| 1. $\overline{AM_2}$, $\overline{BM_1}$, and $\overline{CM_3}$ are medians of $\triangle ABC$ | 1. Given. |
| 2. $Q_1$ is the intersection of $\overline{AM_2}$ and $\overline{BM_1}$. | 2. Two non-parallel, non-co-incident, lines intersect in a point. |
| 3. $\sphericalangle AQ_1B \cong \sphericalangle M_2Q_1M_1$ | 3. Opposite angles formed by two intersecting lines are congruent. |
| 4. $\overline{M_1M_2}$ is a midline of $\triangle ABC$ | 4. The segment that connects the midpoints of two sides of a triangle is a midline of the triangle. |
| 5. $\overline{M_1M_2} \parallel \overline{AB}$ | 5. The midline of a triangle is parallel to the third side. |

6. $\angle M_1 M_2 Q \cong \angle QAB$

7. $\triangle M_1 Q M_2 \sim \triangle AQB$

8. $\dfrac{M_2 Q}{AQ} = \dfrac{M_1 Q}{BQ} = \dfrac{M_1 M_2}{AB}$

9. $AB = 2 \cdot M_1 M_2$ or $\dfrac{M_1 M_2}{AB} = \dfrac{1}{2}$

10. $\dfrac{M_2 Q}{AQ} = \dfrac{M_1 Q}{BQ} = \dfrac{1}{2}$

11. $AM_2 = AQ + M_2 Q$

$BM_1 = BQ + M_1 Q$

12. $M_2 Q = \dfrac{1}{2} AQ_1$

$M_1 Q_1 = \dfrac{1}{2} BQ_1$

13. $AM_2 = 1\dfrac{1}{2} AQ_1$

$BM_1 = 1\dfrac{1}{2} BQ_1$

14. $AQ_1 = \dfrac{2}{3} AM_2$

$BQ_1 = \dfrac{2}{3} BM_1$

15. $Q_2$ is the intersection of $\overline{AM_2}$ and $\overline{CM_3}$

16. $AQ_2 = \dfrac{2}{3} AM_2$

$CQ_2 = \dfrac{2}{3} CM_3$

17. $Q_3$ is the intersection of medians $\overline{CM_3}$ and $\overline{BM_1}$

18. $CQ_3 = \dfrac{2}{3} CM_3$

$BQ_3 = \dfrac{2}{3} BM_1$

19. $Q_1$ is a point on segment $\overline{AM_2}$ such that $AQ_1 = \dfrac{2}{3} AM_2$.

$Q_2$ is a point on segment $\overline{AM_2}$ such that $AQ_2 = \dfrac{2}{3} AM_2$.

20. Point $Q_1$ is point $Q_2$

---

6. Alternate interior angles of a transversal are congruent.

7. If two angles of one triangle are congruent with the corresponding two angles of a second triangle, then the two triangles are similar.

8. The corresponding sides of similar triangles are proportional.

9. The midline of a triangle is half the length of the third side.

10. Substitution Postulate.

11. $Q_1$ is the intersection of two segments $AM_2$ and $BM_1$. Therefore $Q_1$ must lie between the endpoints of the segment. The equations at left follow from the definition of betweenness.

12. Multiplication Postulate and Step 10.

13. Substitution of Step 12 into 11.

14. Multiplication Postulate

15. Two non-parallel, non-coincident lines intersect in a unique point.

16. Obtained by repeating procedure used from Steps 3 through 13. The midline is now $M_1 M_3$ not $\overline{M_1 M_2}$.

17. Two non-parallel non-coincident lines intersect in a unique point.

18. Obtained by repeating procedure used from Steps 3 through 13. The midline is now $\overline{M_1 M_3}$.

19. Repetition of results from Steps 14 and 16.

20. On a given segment, there is only one point on the segment that is a given distance from a given endpoint.

21. $Q_2$ is a point on segment $\overline{CM_3}$ such that $CQ_2 = \frac{2}{3} CM_3$. $Q_3$ is a point on segment $\overline{CM_3}$ such that $CQ_3 = \frac{2}{3} CM_3$.

21. Repetition of results from Steps 16 and 18.

22. Point $Q_2$ is point $Q_3$

22. Same reason as Step 20.

23. Let point $Q = Q_1 = Q_2 = Q_3$

23. From Steps 20 and 22, we have shown $Q_1 = Q_2 = Q_3$ and here we give this common point of intersection of the three medians a more general name.

24. $Q$ is a point on $\overline{AM_2}$, $\overline{BM_1}$, and $\overline{CM_3}$

24. Follows from Step 23 and the definitions of $C_1, C_2$, and $C_3$.

25. $AQ = \frac{2}{3} AM_2$
    $BQ = \frac{2}{3} BM_1$
    $CQ = \frac{2}{3} CM_3$

25. Substitution Postulate (Substitute $Q$ for $Q_1$, $Q_2$, and $Q_3$ in Steps 14, 16, and 18.)

# PYTHAGOREAN THEOREM AND APPLICATIONS

● **PROBLEM 6-17**

The legs of a certain right triangle are equal and the hypotenuse is $\sqrt{8}$. What is the length of either leg of the triangle?

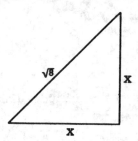

**Solution:** Recall the Pythagorean Theorem, $a^2 + b^2 = c^2$, where a and b are the lengths of the two legs of a right triangle, and c is the length of the hypotenuse. We can use this to solve for the length of the legs. Let x = the length of each of the equal legs. Substituting in the above formula, $x = a = b$ and $\sqrt{8}$ for c,

$$x^2 + x^2 = (\sqrt{8})^2$$

$$2x^2 = 8$$

$$x^2 = 4$$

$$x = 2$$

Therefore, each leg is 2 units in lengths.

• **PROBLEM** 6-18

In an isosceles triangle, the length of each of the congruent sides is 10 and the length of the base is 12. Find
the length of the altitude drawn to the base.

**Solution:** In the figure shown, altitude $\overline{BD}$ has been drawn.
By a theorem, we know that $\overline{BD} \perp \overline{AC}$ and that $\overline{BD}$ bisects
$\overline{AC}$. Therefore, $\overline{AD} \cong \overline{DC}$ and they both measure 6.

Since $\overline{BD} \perp \overline{AC}$, we can conclude that $\triangle BDC$ is a
right triangle and then apply the Pythagorean Theorem.
As applied here, it states that

$$(DC)^2 + (BD)^2 = (BC)^2.$$

We were given that BC = 10, and we have found that
DC = 6. If we let x = BD and substitute into the equation
above, we arrive at

$$6^2 + x^2 = 10^2$$

$$36 + x^2 = 100$$

$$x^2 = 64$$

$$x = 8.$$

Therefore, the length of the altitude drawn to the base is
8.

• **PROBLEM** 6-19

Let $\triangle ABC$ be an equilateral triangle of side length s.
Let D be the midpoint of $\overline{BC}$. Compute AD. (See figure.)

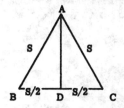

<u>Solution</u>:  We will apply the Pythagorean Theorem to ΔABD to obtain AD.

$$(AB)^2 = (AD)^2 + (BD)^2$$

Hence,  $$(AD)^2 = (AB)^2 - (BD)^2$$

$$AD = \sqrt{(AB)^2 - (BD)^2}$$

Since BD = DC = s/2, and AB = s, therefore,

$$AD = \sqrt{s^2 - s^2/4}$$

$$AD = \sqrt{3s^2/4} = s\,\frac{\sqrt{3}}{2}$$

● **PROBLEM** 6-20

The lengths of the diagonals of the rhombus shown in the figure are 30 and 40. Find the perimeter of the rhombus.

<u>Solution</u>:  Since the diagonals of a rhombus are perpendicular bisectors of each other, ΔAEB is a right triangle in which EB = ½(30), or 15, and AE = ½ (40), or 20. With this in mind, we can calculate the length of the hypotenuse $\overline{AB}$, of ΔAEB by using the Pythagorean Theorem:

$$(AB)^2 = (EB)^2 + (AE)^2.$$

$\overline{AB}$ is one side of a rhombus. All sides of a rhombus are congruent, thus, the perimeter can be calculated by multiplying AB by 4. If we let AB = x, by substitution,

$$x^2 = (15)^2 + (20)^2 = 225 + 400$$

or  $$x^2 = 625; \text{ solving } x = 25.$$

Then, the perimeter = 4x or 4 (25) = 100.

● **PROBLEM** 6-21

Suppose that the area of a rectangle is 300 sq. in., and that the length of its diagonal is 25 in. Find the lengths of the sides of the rectangle.

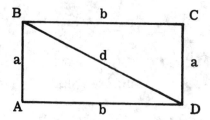

**Solution:** Let the sides of the rectangle be labeled as in the figure. Then the area of the rectangle A(R) is

$$A(R) = ba = 300 \text{ sq. in.} \tag{1}$$

Since $\triangle ABD$ is a right triangle,

$$d^2 = a^2 + b^2 \tag{2}$$

by Pythagoras' Theorem. Noting that d = 25 in., we can write:

$$625 \text{ sq. in.} = a^2 + b^2 \tag{3}$$

We now have 2 equations ((1) and (2)) and 2 unknowns (a and b). We may, therefore, solve explicitly for a and b. First solve (1) for a:

$$a = \frac{300 \text{ sq. in.}}{b} \tag{4}$$

Inserting (4) into (3),

$$625 \text{ sq. in.} = \left(\frac{300 \text{ sq. in.}}{b}\right)^2 + b^2$$

$$625 \text{ sq. in.} = \frac{90000 \text{ in}^4}{b^2} + \frac{b^4}{b^2}$$

$$625 \text{ sq. in.} = \frac{b^4 + 90000 \text{ in}^4}{b^2}$$

$$b^4 - (625 \text{ sq. in.}) \, b^2 + 90000 \text{ in}^4 = 0$$

Let

$$x = b^2 \tag{5}$$

then,

$$x^2 - (625 \text{ sq. in.}) \, x + 90000 \text{ in}^4 = 0 \tag{6}$$

We solve this by means of the quadratic formula. If an equation is of the form

$$ax^2 + bx + c = 0,$$

its roots are

$$x = \frac{-b \pm \sqrt{b^2 - 4ac}}{2a} \tag{7}$$

In equation (6), a = 1, b = - 625 sq. in., and c = 90,000 in⁴. Using these in (7) yields

$$x = \frac{625 \text{ sq. in.} \pm \sqrt{(- 625 \text{ sq. in.})^2 - (4)(1)(90,000 \text{ in}^4)}}{(2)(1)}$$

$$x = \frac{625 \text{ sq. in.} \pm \sqrt{30625 \text{ in}^4}}{2}$$

$$x = \frac{625 \text{ sq. in.} \pm 175 \text{ sq. in.}}{2}$$

x = 400 sq. in.    or 225 sq. in.

But, from (5),    $x = b^2$; hence,

$b^2$ = 400 sq. in.   or 225 sq. in.

Therefore,    b = 20 in. or 15 in.                    (8)

(Negative roots are eliminated because b is a distance and must be positive.)

Using (8) in (4), we find

$a = \frac{300}{20}$ in.,        or    $\frac{300}{15}$ in.

a = 15 in., or 20 in.

Hence, the lengths are

a = 15 in., b = 20 in.

or,        a = 20 in., b = 15 in.

● **PROBLEM** 6-22

A chord, 16 inches long, is 6 inches from the center of a circle. Find the length of the radius of the circle.

Solution: The distance of a chord from the center of a circle is measured on a line perpendicular to the chord from the center of the circle. Therefore, as labeled in the accompanying figure, $\overline{OC} \perp \overline{AB}$ and $\triangle OCB$ is a right triangle.

In addition to being perpendicular to $\overline{AB}$, the segment $\overline{OC}$ also intersects chord $\overline{AB}$ at its midpoint. Hence, $\overline{OC}$ bisects $\overline{AB}$. Therefore, $\overline{AC} \cong \overline{BC}$, and they both measure 8 in. We are given that OC = 6 in.

Since $\triangle OCB$ is a right triangle, we can apply the Pythagorean Theorem to calculate the length of the hypotenuse of the triangle, which is also the radius of the circle.

In this problem,

$$(OB)^2 = (OC)^2 + (CB)^2.$$

If we let r = the length of radius $\overline{OB}$, by substitution

$$r^2 = 6^2 + 8^2$$

$$r^2 = 36 + 64$$

$$r^2 = 100$$

$$r = 10.$$

Therefore, the length of the radius of the circle is 10 inches.

● **PROBLEM** 6-23

In a circle, angle ABC, formed by diamater $\overline{AB}$ end chord $\overline{BC}$, is 30°. If the length of the diameter of the circle is 20, find the length of chord $\overline{AC}$ and, in radical form, the length of chord $\overline{BC}$.

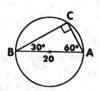

Solution: From the figure shown, we see that ∢ BCA is inscribed in a semi-circle, therefore is 90°. Angle CAB is the third angle of $\triangle ABC$, and it measures 180° − (m ∢ ABC + m ∢ BCA), or 180° − (30° + 90°) = 60°. Therefore, $\triangle ABC$ is a 30-60-90 triangle.

Chord $\overline{AC}$ is opposite the 30° angle, and, accordingly, measures one-half of the length of hypotenuse $\overline{AB}$. Therefore,

$$\overline{AC} = \tfrac{1}{2}\,\overline{AB} = \tfrac{1}{2}(20) = 10.$$

Chord $\overline{BC}$ is opposite the 60° angle, and its length is given by $\tfrac{1}{2}$ the length of the hypotenuse times $\sqrt{3}$. Thus,

$$\overline{BC} = \tfrac{1}{2}\ \overline{AB}\ \sqrt{3} = \tfrac{1}{2}\ (20)\ \sqrt{3} = 10\ \sqrt{3}.$$

Therefore, the length of $\overline{AC}$ is 10 and the length of $\overline{BC}$ is $10\ \sqrt{3}$.

● PROBLEM 6-24

Which of the following are Pythagorean Triples?
(a) 1, 2, 3; (b) 3, 4, 5 ; (c) 5, 6, 7; (d) 5, 12, 13;
(e) 11, 60, 61; (f) 84, 187, 205.

Solution: A set of 3 positive integers, a, b, and c, (where c is the largest of the set) is a Pythagorean Triple if and only if

$$c^2 = a^2 + b^2$$

(i.e. they satisfy Pythagorean Theorem).

(a) For (1, 2, 3) to be a Pythagorean triple, it must be true that

$$3^2 = 2^2 + 1^2 \qquad \text{or} \qquad 9 = 4 + 1 = 5.$$

Since $9 \neq 5$, therefore, (1, 2, 3) is not a Pythagorean Triple.

(b) c = 5, a = 3, b = 4.

$$c^2 \overset{?}{=} a^2 + b^2$$

$$25 \overset{?}{=} 9 + 16$$

Since $\qquad$ 25 = 25,

(3, 4, 5) is a Pythagorean Triple.

(c) c = 7, a = 5, b = 6

$$c^2 \overset{?}{=} a^2 + b^2$$

$$49 \overset{?}{=} 25 + 36$$

$$49 \neq 61$$

Therefore, (5, 6, 7) is not a Pythagorean Triple.

(d) c = 13, a = 5, b = 12.

$$c^2 \overset{?}{=} a^2 + b^2$$

$$169 \overset{?}{=} 25 + 144$$

$$169 = 169$$

Hence, (5, 12, 13) is a Pythagorean Triple.

(e) c = 61, a = 11, b = 60

$$c^2 \overset{?}{=} a^2 + b^2$$

$$3721 \overset{?}{=} 121 + 3600$$

$$3721 = 3721$$

Therefore, (11, 60, 61) is a Pythagorean Triple.

(f) c = 205, a = 84, b = 187

$$c^2 \overset{?}{=} a^2 + b^2$$

$$42025 \overset{?}{=} 7056 + 34969$$

$$42025 = 42025$$

Therefore, (84, 187, 205) is a Pythagorean Triple.

● **PROBLEM 6-25**

A 25-foot ladder leans against the wall such that the base of the ladder is 20 feet from the wall. The ladder slides until the base is 24 feet from the wall. Locate the point X that is common to both ladder positions (see diagram).

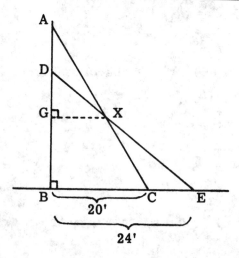

Solution: $\overline{AC}$ is the original position of the ladder; $\overline{DE}$, the final position. The length of the ladder is constant. Hence, AC = DE = 25 ft. The original distance from the base of the ladder to the wall, BC = 20; the final distance BE = 24. To find the height of the ladder top in both cases, by using the Pythagorean Theorem:

108

The original height

$$AB = \sqrt{(AC)^2 - (BC)^2} = \sqrt{25^2 - 20^2} = \sqrt{225} = 15 \text{ ft.}$$

The final height

$$DB = \sqrt{(DE)^2 - (BE)^2} = \sqrt{25^2 - 24^2} = \sqrt{49} = 7 \text{ ft.}$$

We wish to find the point X common to $\overline{DE}$ and $\overline{AC}$.

We draw the line $\overline{GX} \perp \overline{AB}$. Remember that a line drawn through two sides of a triangle and parallel to the third side forms 2 similar triangles. Thus, $\triangle AGX \sim \triangle ABC$ and also $\triangle DGX \sim \triangle DBE$. We can relate these two similarities to find GX and AG. By the Pythagorean Theorem, we can find AX. Thus, we will have the location of X: a distance AX from the top of the ladder in the original position.

$\triangle AGX \sim \triangle ABC$ by the A.A. Similarity Theorem ($\sphericalangle A \overset{\sim}{=} \sphericalangle A$, and $\sphericalangle AGX \overset{\sim}{=} \sphericalangle ABC$ = right angles). Similarly, $\triangle DGX \sim \triangle DBE$, since $\sphericalangle D \overset{\sim}{=} \sphericalangle D$ and $\sphericalangle AGX \overset{\sim}{=} \sphericalangle ABC$. Since corresponding sides of similar triangles are proportional, we have

(i) $\qquad \dfrac{AG}{GX} = \dfrac{AB}{BC} = \dfrac{15}{20} = \dfrac{3}{4}$

(ii) $\qquad \dfrac{DG}{GX} = \dfrac{DB}{BE} = \dfrac{7}{24} \cdot$

We can relate AG and DG by expressing AG in terms of GX and GX in terms of DG. From (i) and (ii), we obtain

(iii) $\qquad AG = \dfrac{3}{4} GX$

(iv) $\qquad DG = \dfrac{7}{24} GX \qquad \text{or} \qquad GX = \dfrac{24}{7} DG.$

By substitution, we have,

(v) $\qquad AG = \dfrac{3}{4} GX = \dfrac{3}{4} \left[ \dfrac{24}{7} DG \right] = \dfrac{18}{7} DG.$

To solve for AG and DG, we need only one more relation. Note that AG = AD + DG. AD is the difference in ladder heights, AB − DB = 15 − 7 = 8. Then, by substitution,

(vi) $\qquad AG = AD + DG = 8 + DG, \quad \text{or} \quad DG = AG - 8.$

Combining (v) and (vi), we obtain:

(vii) $\qquad AG = \dfrac{18}{7} (AG - 8) = \dfrac{18}{7} AG - \dfrac{144}{7}$

(viii) $\qquad \dfrac{18}{7} AG - AG = \dfrac{144}{7}$

109

(ix) $\qquad \frac{11}{7} AG = \frac{144}{7}$ or $AG = \left(\frac{7}{11}\right)\left(\frac{144}{7}\right) = \frac{144}{11}$ .

Thus, $AG = \frac{144}{11}$ . To find GX, remember that by (iii),
$AG = \frac{3}{4} GX$. Then, $GX = \frac{4}{3}\left(\frac{144}{11}\right) = \frac{192}{11}$ .

We could stop here and say that point X, in terms of
the original ladder position, is $\frac{144}{11}$ ft. down from the top
of the wall and $\frac{192}{11}$ ft. from the wall; but it may be easier
to measure distances along the ladder. Therefore, we can
find AX. Note that AX is the hypotenuse of right $\triangle AGX$. By
the Pythagorean Theorem,

$$(AX)^2 = (AG)^2 + (GX)^2 = \left(\frac{144}{11}\right)^2 + \left(\frac{192}{11}\right)^2.$$

---

DIGRESSION: Whenever cumbersome calculations present
themselves, it is best to look for easier methods. We are
asked to square two larger numbers and then to find a
square root. We wonder, therefore, whether or not we are
squaring unnecessary factors. Note that

$$\frac{144}{11} = \frac{48}{11} (3) \quad \text{and} \quad \frac{192}{11} = \frac{48}{11} (4).$$

Then, $(AX)^2 = \left(\frac{48}{11} \times 3\right)^2 + \left(\frac{48}{11} \times 4\right)^2$

$\qquad = \left(\frac{48}{11}\right)^2 \times 3^2 + \left(\frac{48}{11}\right)^2 \times 4^2 = \left(\frac{48}{11}\right)^2 (3^2 + 4^2)$

$\qquad = \left(\frac{48}{11}\right)^2 (9 + 16) = \left(\frac{48}{11}\right)^2 (25).$

Then, $AX = \sqrt{\left(\frac{48}{11}\right)^2 (25)} = \sqrt{\left(\frac{48}{11}\right)^2} \sqrt{25} = \frac{48}{11} (5) = \frac{240}{11}$

Therefore, the point X is $\frac{240}{11}$ feet down from the top
end of the ladder.

Thus, the point in space that is occupied by the ladder
in the original position <u>and</u> the final position is $\frac{240}{11}$ or
21.8 ft. from the top of the ladder along the original line
of the ladder.

# TRIGNOMETRIC RATIOS

A ladder 25 feet long leans against a building and reaches a point 23.5 feet above the ground. Find, to the nearest degree, the angle which the ladder makes with the ground.

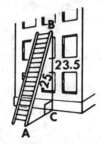

Solution: As seen in the accompanying drawing, the building forms a right triangle with the ground. Angle A is the angle the question asks us to determine. We are given the length of the side opposite ∢ A, 23.5, and the length of the hypotenuse (the ladder) 25. With this information, we can calculate the measure of the angle by using the sine ratio.

$$\text{Sin A} = \frac{\text{length of leg opposite} \angle A}{\text{length of hypotenuse}} = \frac{BC}{AB} \cdot$$

By substitution, Sin A = $\frac{23.5}{25}$ = 0.9400.

Now, we consult a standard sine table to determine which angles have sines near 0.9400.

We find that Sin 70° = 0.9397 and Sin 71° = 0.9455. Since 0.9400 is closer to Sin 70°, we can conclude that m ∢ A is closer to 70°.

Therefore, the ladder makes a 70° angle with the ground.

A guy wire reaches from the top of a pole to a stake in the ground. The stake is 10 feet from the foot of the pole. The wire makes an angle of 65° with the ground. Find, to the nearest foot, the length of the wire.

Solution: A right triangle is formed by the pole, the wire and the ground. The wire acts as the hypotenuse of this triangle, and its length is the unknown to be determined. An acute angle and the length of the side adjacent to it are given and, to find the length of the hypotenuse, the cosine ratio can be applied.

$$\text{Cos } S = \frac{\text{length of leg adjacent to } \sphericalangle S}{\text{length of hypotenuse}} = \frac{SB}{ST} \cdot$$

Let $x = ST$ and, by substitution, $\text{Cos } 65° = \frac{10}{x}$.
In a standard cosine table, we find $\text{Cos } 65° = 0.4226$.

Substitute this value into the equation

$$0.4226 = \frac{10}{x}$$

$$x = \frac{10}{0.4226} = 23.6.$$

Therefore, the guy wire is 24 feet long, correct to the nearest foot.

● **PROBLEM 6-28**

From the top of a lighthouse 160 ft. above sea level, the angle of depression of a boat at sea is 35°. Find, to the nearest foot, the distance from the boat to the foot of the lighthouse.

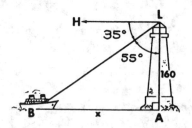

Solution: The distance from the foot of the lighthouse to the boat is represented by BA, (see figure), which is the unknown we wish to find. We will determine BA by an application of the tangent ratio.

The angle of depression, $\sphericalangle$ BLH, is complementary to $\sphericalangle$ BLA. Since m $\sphericalangle$ BLH = 35°, the measure of $\sphericalangle$ BLA is 90° − 35°, or 55°. We cannot use the angle of depression because it is on the exterior of the right triangle.

Given the measure of an acute angle of a right triangle and the length of the side adjacent to it, we can determine the length of the opposite side by a direct application of the tangent ratio.

$$\tan \sphericalangle \text{BLA} = \frac{\text{length of leg opposite } \sphericalangle \text{ BLA}}{\text{length of leg adjacent } \sphericalangle \text{ BLA}} = \frac{\text{BA}}{\text{LA}}$$

Let x = BA, thus $\tan 55° = \frac{x}{160}$ . Consult a standard tangent table to find tan 55° = 1.4281, and substitute this to obtain

$$1.4281 = \frac{x}{160}$$

$$x = (1.4281)\ 160$$

$$x = 228.496$$

Therefore, the boat is 228 ft. away from the foot of the lighthouse (to the nearest foot).

● **PROBLEM** 6-29

In a circle whose radius is 4 in., find, to the nearest inch, the length of the minor arc intercepted by a chord 6 inches in length.

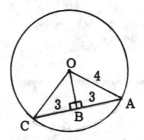

Solution: To find the length of minor arc $\overset{\frown}{\text{AC}}$, we must first find the measure of the arc in degrees. Then we will apply the arc length formula which states that

$$\text{arc length} = \frac{\text{degree measure of arc}}{360} \times \text{Circumference.}$$

Circumference = C = 2πr, where r = radius of circle. By substitution, C = 2π(4) = 8π. ∡AOC is the central angle of the arc in question, AC. m∡AOC is what we wish to determine. Δ AOC is isosceles because, as radii ofcircle O, $\overline{\text{OC}} \cong \overline{\text{OA}}$. Draw the altitude to $\overline{\text{AC}}$. By a theorem, we know that altitude $\overline{\text{OB}}$ bisects vertex angle ∡AOC. Therefore, m∡AOC = m∡AOB + m∡COB and, since $\overline{\text{OB}}$ is the bisector of ∡AOC, m∡AOB = m∡COB = 1/2m∡AOC.

Hence, m∡AOC = 2(m∡AOB). ΔAOB is a right triangle, since OB⊥AC.

Since we know the hypotenuse and the side opposite ∢AOB, we can use the sine ratio to determine the measure of ∢AOB.

$$\text{Sin} (\angle AOB) = \frac{\text{leg opposite} \angle AOB}{\text{hypotenuse}} = \frac{AB}{OA}$$

$\overline{OA}$ is a radius given to be 4 in. Since a line drawn from the center of a circle perpendicular to a chord bisects that chord, AB = 1/2(AC) = 1/2(6) = 3

Therefore, sin (∢AOC) = $\frac{3}{4}$ = 0.75

The measure of the angle whose sine is closest to 0.75 is 49 .

Hence, by substitution

m∢AOC = 2(m∢AOB) = 2(49) = 98°

Then, length of minor arc $\overset{\frown}{AC}$ = $\frac{98}{360}$ x 8π = 2.2π

Using π = 3.14, 2.2π = 6.9

Therefore, to the nearest inch, length of minor arc $\overset{\frown}{AC}$ = 7in.

● **PROBLEM 6-30**

In circle O, $\overline{AB}$ is a diameter. Radius $\overline{OC}$ is extended to meet tangent $\overline{BD}$ at D. The measures of arc $\overset{\frown}{AC}$ and arc $\overset{\frown}{CB}$ are in the ratio 2:1 and $\overline{AB}$ = 32.

(a) Find the number of degrees contained in arc $\overset{\frown}{CB}$.
(b) Find, to the nearest integer, the perimeter of the figure bounded by $\overline{BD}$, $\overline{DC}$ and arc $\overset{\frown}{CB}$. [π = 3.14]
(See figure)

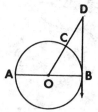

Solution: (a) To find the measure of arc $\overset{\frown}{CB}$, we must make use of two known facts. First, arc $\overset{\frown}{ACB}$ is a semi-circle, and, as such, contains 180°. Second, the composite arcs of $\overset{\frown}{ACB}$; $\overset{\frown}{AC}$ and $\overset{\frown}{CB}$, have measures in a ratio of 2:1. If we let x = the measure of arc $\overset{\frown}{CB}$, then 2x = the measure of arc $\overset{\frown}{AC}$. Since the measure of $\overset{\frown}{ACB}$ = measure of $\overset{\frown}{AC}$ + measure of $\overset{\frown}{CB}$, and $\overset{\frown}{ACB}$ is a semicircle, we may write 180° = 2x + x = 3x or x = 60°. Therefore, the number of degrees contained in arc $\overset{\frown}{CB}$ is 60°.

(b) To find the perimeter of the figure in question, we must determine the lengths of arc $\overset{\frown}{CB}$ and segments

$\overline{DC}$ and $\overline{DB}$, and then sum these quantities. We will first calculate the length of arc $\overset{\frown}{CB}$.

length of arc $\overset{\frown}{CB} = \dfrac{\text{measure of central angle COB}}{360°} \times$ Circumference

of circle O. Arc $\overset{\frown}{CB}$ has a measure of 60°, and its central angle, ∢COB, by theorem, has the same measure. Circumference of circle O = $2\pi r$, where r is the radius of circle O. We are given diameter AB = 32. Therefore, any radius = $\frac{1}{2}$(32) or 16.

Circumference of circle O = $2\pi(16) = 32\pi = 32(3.14) = 100.5$. Therefore, length of arc $\overset{\frown}{CB} = \dfrac{60°}{360°} \times 100.5 = 16.75$.

Next, we need to find BD and DC. ΔODB is a right triangle, since tangent $\overline{BD}$ is perpendicular to radius $\overline{OB}$. (A tangent to a circle is always perpendicular to a radius drawn to the point of tangency.) Hence, the various trigonometric ratios can be employed to find the lengths of the unknown segments. We know m∢DOB = 60°, and the leg adjacent to it, $\overline{OB}$, has a length of 16. We can find the length of the opposite leg, $\overline{DB}$, by using the tangent ratio, and the length of the hypotenuse, $\overline{OD}$, by using the cosine ratio.

$\tan(∢DOB) = \dfrac{\text{length of leg opposite } ∢DOB}{\text{length of leg adjacent } ∢DOB} = \dfrac{DB}{OB}$ .

By substitution, $\tan 60° = \dfrac{DB}{16}$. According to a standard tangent table, $\tan 60° = 1.7321$, hence $1.7321 = \dfrac{DB}{16}$, DB = (16)(1.7321). Therefore, BD = 27.7. The final segment, whose length we need, is DC. $\underline{DC = OD - OC}$. We know OC = 16, because it is a radius of O. $\overline{OD}$ is the hypotenuse of rt. ΔODB. We will use the cosine ratio to find its length.

$\text{cosine}(∢DOB) = \dfrac{\text{length of leg adjacent } ∢COB}{\text{length of hypotenuse}} = \dfrac{OB}{OD}$

OB = 16 and m∢DOB = 60°. By substitution, $\cos 60° = \dfrac{16}{OD}$

$OD = \dfrac{16}{\cos 60°}$. According to a standard cosine table, $\cos 60° = .5$.

$$OD = \dfrac{16}{5} = 32$$

Therefore, length of $\overline{DC}$ = OD - OC = 32 - 16 = 16. Hence, the perimeter of the figure bounded by $\overline{BD}$, $\overline{DC}$, and arc $\overset{\frown}{CB}$ is the sum of the measures of these individual parts, or 27.7 + 16 + 16.75 = 60.45. The perimeter of the required figure is 60, to the nearest integer.

# INTERIOR AND EXTERIOR ANGLES

● PROBLEM 6-31

If an exterior angle of a polygon is obtuse, what can one say about the corresponding interior angle?

Solution: The exterior angle of a polygon and the corresponding interior angle are supplementary. This means that the sum of the measures of these angles is 180°. If one of the 2 angles is obtuse (i.e. has measure greater than 90°), then the other angle must have a measure less than 90° (i.e., it is acute).

● PROBLEM 6-32

Show that the measure of the exterior angle of a regular n-sided polygon is given by the formula $\frac{360}{n}$ .

Solution: An exterior angle of a polygon is defined to be an angle that forms a linear pair (i.e., supplementary) with an interior angle of a polygon. Thus,

(i)    m ⊀ exterior + m ⊀ interior = $180^\circ$ .

To find m ⊀ interior, recall that the sum of the interior angles of an n-sided polygon is $(n-2) \cdot 180^\circ$. Since all interior angles of a regular polygon are congruent, each of the n interior angles has measure $\frac{(n-2) \cdot 180^\circ}{n}$ . Substituting m ⊀ interior = $\frac{(n-2)}{n} \cdot 180^\circ$ in equation (i), we obtain

(ii)    m ⊀ exterior + $\frac{n-2}{n} \cdot 180^\circ = 180^\circ$ .

Solving for m ⊀ exterior, we have:

(iii)    m ⊀ exterior = $180^\circ - \frac{n-2}{n} \cdot 180^\circ$

$$= 180^\circ (1 - \frac{n-2}{n}) = 180^\circ (\frac{2}{n})$$
$$= \frac{360^\circ}{n} .$$

● PROBLEM 6-33

Find the number of degrees contained in each interior angle of a regular hexagon.

Solution: A regular hexagon is a 6 sided polygon in which all sides and all interior angles are of equal measure. A theorem tells us that the measure of each interior angle of a regular polygon of n sides is $\frac{180^\circ (n-2)}{n}$ . In this case, n equals 6.

Therefore, each angle's measure is calculated as follows:

$$\frac{180^\circ (n-2)}{n} = \frac{180^\circ (6-2)}{6} = \frac{180^\circ (4)}{6} = 120^\circ .$$

Therefore, each angle of a regular hexagon measures $120^\circ$ .

116

$\overline{AX}$ and $\overline{BX}$ are two adjacent sides of a regular polygon. If the measure of angle ABX equals $\frac{1}{3}$ the measure of angle AXB, how many sides has the regular polygon?

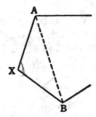

Solution: We first determine the measure of vertex ∡ AXB. Since we are told the polygon is regular, the number of sides will be uniquely determined. The measure of each vertex angle of a regular polygon is given by the expression $\frac{180(n-2)}{n}$ , where n is the number of sides. We will set m ∡ AXB = $\frac{180(n-2)}{n}$ and solve for n.

Draw $\overline{AB}$ to complete △ AXB. Since $\overline{AX}$ and $\overline{BX}$ are sides of a regular polygon, $\overline{AX} \cong \overline{BX}$ . Therefore, △ AXB is isosceles.

The measures of the base angles of an isosceles triangle are equal. As such, m ∡ ABX = m ∡ XAB. We are given that m ∡ AXB = 3 m ∡ ABX. The measure of the angles of a triangle sum to 180. Therefore, m ∡ AXB + m ∡ ABX + m ∡ XAB = 180. By substitution,

$$3m \angle ABX + m \angle ABX + m \angle ABX = 180$$
$$5m \angle ABX = 180$$
$$m \angle ABX = \frac{180}{5} = 36°.$$

Therefore, m ∡ AXB = 3(36) = 108. Set $108 = \frac{180(n-2)}{n}$ and solve for n.

$$108n = 180n - 360$$
$$-72n = -360$$
$$n = \frac{360}{72} = 5.$$

Therefore, the regular polygon has 5 sides, i.e. it is a pentagon.

For a regular polygon of six sides, find the number of degrees contained in (a) each central angle, (b) each interior angle (c) each exterior angle. (See figure.)

Solution: (a) The central angle of a regular polygon is an angle formed by two radii of the polygon drawn to consecutive vertices of the polygon. Its measure is equal to $\frac{360°}{n}$ , where n = the number of sides in the polygon. In the figure shown, ⟩AOB is a central angle. Hence, m⟩AOB = $\frac{360°}{6}$ = 60°.

Therefore, each central angle contains 60°.

(b) An interior angle of a regular polygon is formed by two consecutive sides of the polygon meeting at a vertex. ⟩ABC is such an angle. Its measure is given by $\frac{(n - 2)\ 180°}{n}$ , where n = the number of sides. In this example, n = 6 and, therefore, by substitution, each angle measures $\frac{(6 - 2)\ 180°}{6}$ , or 120°.

Therefore, each interior angle contains 120°.

(c) An exterior angle of a regular polygon is formed outside the regular polygon by one side and the outward extension of an adjacent side. ⟩CBG is an exterior angle. (See figure.) Its measure equals $\frac{360}{n}$ degrees. In this problem $\frac{360°}{n}$ = $\frac{360°}{6}$ = 60°.

Therefore, each exterior angle contains 60°.

# CHAPTER 7

# CIRCLES

## CENTRAL ANGLES AND ARCS

● **PROBLEM** 7-1

In a circle whose radius is 8 inches, find the number of degrees contained in the central angle whose arc length is 2π inches.

_Solution_:  The measure of a central angle is equal to the measure of the arc it intercepts.

The ratio of arc length to circumference, in linear units, will be equal to the ratio of arc length to circumference as measured in degrees.

If n = the number of degrees in the arc 2π inches long,

Then 
$$\frac{\text{length of arc}}{\text{circumference}} = \frac{n}{360°}$$

By substitution, 
$$\frac{2\pi \text{in.}}{2\pi(8 \text{ in.})} = \frac{n}{360°}$$

$$\frac{1}{8} = \frac{n}{360°}$$

$$360° = 8n$$

$$n = 45°$$

Therefore, the central angle contains 45°.

● **PROBLEM** 7-2

Find the number of degrees, to the nearest degree, in an angle subtended at the center of a circle by an arc 5 ft. 10 in. in length.  The radius of the circle is 9 ft. 4 in.

<u>Solution</u>: Let us convert the mixed unit measures into sin-
gle unit measure.

$$(12 \text{ in.} = 1 \text{ ft.})$$

$$5 \text{ ft. } 10 \text{ in.} = 5(12) + 10 = 70 \text{ in.}$$

$$9 \text{ ft. } 4 \text{ in.} = 9(12) + 4 = 112 \text{ in.}$$

We solve this problem by determining what fraction of
the total circumference the arc occupies and then multiplying this by 360° to find the degree measure of the arc.
The angle subtended at the center is a central angle and
contains the same number of degrees as the arc.

Circumference C =π2 r, where r = the radius length.
By substitution, C = 2π(112) = 224π in. The fraction of
the total circumference is given by $\frac{70}{224\pi} = \frac{70}{(224)(3.14)} = \frac{70}{704}$.

Hence, there are $(360)\left(\frac{70}{704}\right)$ or 35° 48' contained in this
arc and in its central angle. To the nearest degree, the
answer is 36°.

● **PROBLEM** 7-3

In circle O, the measure of $\overset{\frown}{AB}$ is 80° Find the measure of ∢A.

80°

<u>Solution</u>: The accompanying figure shows that $\overset{\frown}{AB}$ is inter-
cepted by central angle ∢AOB. By definition, we know that
the measure of the central angle is the measure of its intercepted arc. In this case,

$$m\overset{\frown}{AB} = m∢AOB \text{ or } m∢AOB = 80°$$

Radius $\overline{OA}$ and radius $\overline{OB}$ are congruent and form two
sides of △OAB. By a theorem, the angles opposite these two
congruent sides must, themselves, be congruent. Therefore,
m∢A = m∢B.

The sum of the measures of the angles of a triangle is
180°. Therefore,

$$m∢A + m∢B + m∢AOB = 180°.$$

Since m∢A = m∢B, we can write

$$m\sphericalangle A + m\sphericalangle A + 80° = 180° \text{ or}$$

$$2m\sphericalangle A = 100° \text{ or}$$

$$m\sphericalangle A = 50°.$$

Therefore, the measure of $\sphericalangle A$ is 50°

● **PROBLEM** 7-4

In circle O, in the figure shown, $\overline{OS} \perp \overline{RT}$. Prove $\overarc{RS} \cong \overarc{ST}$.

**Solution:**  We can prove the two arcs congruent by proving that their central angles are congruent.  Congruent central angles intercept congruent arcs.  The central angles of $\overarc{RS}$ and $\overarc{ST}$ are $\sphericalangle ROS$ and $\sphericalangle SOT$, respectively.

These two angles are contained, respectively, in ΔOER and ΔOET.  By proving these two triangles to be congruent to each other, we can conclude that the required central angles are congruent to each other.

| Statement | | Reason |
|---|---|---|
| 1. | $\overline{OS} \perp \overline{RT}$ | 1. | Given. |
| 2. | $\sphericalangle OER$ and $\sphericalangle OET$ are right angles. | 2. | Perpendicular lines intersect in right angles. |
| 3. | $\sphericalangle OER \cong \sphericalangle OET$ | 3. | All right angles are congruent. |
| 4. | $\overline{OR} \cong \overline{OT}$ | 4. | Radii of the same circle are congruent. |
| 5. | $\overline{OE} \cong \overline{OE}$ | 5. | Reflexive property of congruence. |
| 6. | ΔOER $\cong$ ΔOET | 6. | Hypotenuse-Leg Theorem. |
| 7. | $\sphericalangle ROS \cong \sphericalangle SOT$ | 7. | Corresponding angles of congruent triangles are congruent. |
| 8. | $\overarc{RS} \cong \overarc{ST}$ | 8. | Congruent central angles of the same circle intercept congruent arcs. |

$\overline{CE} \cong \overline{DF}$. In the accompanying figure, if $\angle COD \cong \angle FOE$, prove that

**Solution:** In this problem, we will make use of the theorem that congruent chords always intercept congruent arcs in the same circle. The converse of this is also true: congruent arcs have congruent chords.

| Statement | Reason |
|---|---|
| 1- $\angle COD \cong \angle FOE$ | 1- Given. |
| 2- $\overset{\frown}{CD} \cong \overset{\frown}{FE}$ | 2- Congruent central angles intercept congruent arcs. |
| 3- $\overset{\frown}{DE} \cong \overset{\frown}{DE}$ | 3- Reflexive property of congruence. |
| 4- $\overset{\frown}{CD} + \overset{\frown}{DE} \cong \overset{\frown}{FE} + \overset{\frown}{DE}$ or $\overset{\frown}{CE} \cong \overset{\frown}{FD}$ | 4- Congruent quantities added to congruent quantities result in congruent quantities. |
| 5- $\overline{CE} \cong \overline{FD}$ | 5- Congruent arcs have congruent chords. |

# INSCRIBED ANGLES AND ARCS

In the circle shown, if $m\overset{\frown}{PR} = 70$ and $m\overset{\frown}{QR} = 80$, find $m\angle P$, $m\angle Q$, and $m\angle R$.

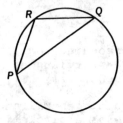

Figure 1

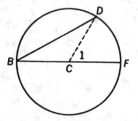

Figure 2

Solution: By definition, the three angles whose measure we are asked to determine are inscribed angles. We will prove the theorem which states that the measure of an inscribed angle is equal to one-half the measure of the intercepted arc. This theorem can be proved in three cases. One where the center of the circle lies on a side of the angle, one where it lies in the interior of the angle, and one where it is assumed to be on the exterior of the angle.

Case 1: We have a circle with C as the center and ∡DBF inscribed so that $\overline{BF}$ is a diameter (figure 2). We draw radius $\overline{CD}$. Since they are radii, $\overline{BC} \cong \overline{CD}$. In $\triangle BCD$, ∡B $\cong$ ∡D because when a triangle has two sides congruent, the angles opposite those sides are congruent. ∡1 and ∡C are, by definition, supplementary. Therefore, m∡1 + m∡C = 180. Since they are the three angles of $\triangle BCD$,

$$m∡D + m∡B + m∡C = 180.$$

Therefore, by transitivity,

$$m∡D + m∡B = m∡1.$$

Since ∡1 is a central angle, $m∡1 = m\overset{\frown}{DF}$ and

$$2(m∡B) = m\overset{\frown}{DF} \text{ and}$$

$$m∡B = \frac{1}{2} m\overset{\frown}{DF}.$$

Case 1 is now established and will be instrumental in proving Cases 2 and 3.

Case 2: Now C is in the interior of ∡DBF (figure 3). If we draw diameter $\overline{AB}$, as shown, then m∡DBF = m∡1 + m∡2. Angles 1 and 2 are both inscribed angles with one side of each containing the center of the circle and, as such, their measures can be found by referring to case 1.

$$m∡1 = \frac{1}{2}m\overset{\frown}{FA} \quad \text{and} \quad m∡2 = \frac{1}{2} m\overset{\frown}{AD}$$

$$m∡1 + m∡2 = \frac{1}{2} m\overset{\frown}{FA} + \frac{1}{2} m\overset{\frown}{AD}$$

$$= \frac{1}{2} (m\overset{\frown}{FA} + m\overset{\frown}{AD}).$$

As the figure shows, $\overset{\frown}{FA}$ and $\overset{\frown}{AD}$ compose $\overset{\frown}{FD}$.

Therefore, $m\overset{\frown}{FA} + m\overset{\frown}{AD} = m\overset{\frown}{FD}$.

$$m∡1 + m∡2 = \frac{1}{2} m\overset{\frown}{FD}.$$

By substitution, then, $m∡DBF = \frac{1}{2} m\overset{\frown}{FD}$.

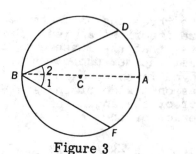

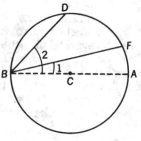

| Figure 3 | Figure 4 |

Case 3: Here, C is in the exterior of the inscribed angle (figure 4), but a technique similar to case 2 is used. Introduce the diameter to from an angle like that covered by case 1.

$$m\angle DBF = m\angle 2 - m\angle 1 .$$

But, by the case 1 result, since $\angle 2$ and $\angle 1$ both have one side that includes the circle's center,

$$m\angle 2 = \tfrac{1}{2}m\overarc{DA} \quad \text{and} \quad m\angle 1 = \tfrac{1}{2}m\overarc{FA}.$$

By substitution, $m\angle DBF = \tfrac{1}{2}m\overarc{DA} - \tfrac{1}{2}m\overarc{FA}$

$$= \tfrac{1}{2}(m\overarc{DA} - m\overarc{FA}).$$

Since $\overarc{DA}$ is composed of $\overarc{DF}$ and $\overarc{FA}$, the $m\overarc{DA} - m\overarc{FA} = m\overarc{DF}$.

By substitution, $m\angle DBF = \tfrac{1}{2}m\overarc{DF}$.

Now we can use the theorem that states if an angle is inscribed, its measure is equal to $\tfrac{1}{2}$ the measure of the intercepted arc, to answer the original question.

We were told that $m\overarc{PR} = 70$ and $m\overarc{QR} = 80$. Therefore, since a circle contains a measure of 360, $m\overarc{PQ} = 360 - (70+80)$ or $m\overarc{PQ} = 210$. $\angle P$, $\angle Q$, and $\angle R$ are all inscribed angles. This allows us to find their measure by using the theorem we have just proved. $\angle P$ intercepts $\overarc{QR}$, $\angle Q$ intercepts $\overarc{PR}$, and $\angle R$ intercepts $\overarc{PQ}$.

Therefore, $m\angle P = \tfrac{1}{2}m\overarc{QR} = \tfrac{1}{2}(80) = 40$

$$m\angle Q = \tfrac{1}{2}m\overarc{PR} = \tfrac{1}{2}(70) = 35$$

$$m\angle R = \tfrac{1}{2}m\overarc{PQ} = \tfrac{1}{2}(210) = 105.$$

● **PROBLEM 7-7**

In a circle, as shown in the accompanying figure, congruent chords $\overline{AB}$ and $\overline{CD}$ are extended through B and D, respectively, until they intersect at P. Prove that triangle APC is an isosceles triangle.

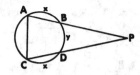

**Solution:** To show that ΔAPC is isosceles, we must show PA ≅ PC. This can be done by showing ⦓A ≅ ⦓C.

The proof of this last point will involve using the theorem which states that congruent chords have arcs of equal measure. This, along with the reflexive property of arc measure, will show that ⦓A and ⦓C are inscribed in arcs of equal measure, which implies the necessary congruence condition.

| Statement | | Reason |
|---|---|---|
| 1. Chord $\overline{AB}$ ≅ Chord $\overline{CD}$. | 1. | Given. |
| 2. m$\overarc{BD}$ = m$\overarc{BD}$ = y | 2. | Reflexive Property of Equality. |
| 3. m$\overarc{AB}$ = m$\overarc{CD}$ = x | 3. | In a circle, congruent chords have equal arcs. |
| 4. m$\overarc{ABD}$ = x + y and m$\overarc{BDC}$ = x + y | 4. | The measure of an arc is equal to the sum of the measures of its parts. |
| 5. m$\overarc{ABD}$ = m$\overarc{BDC}$ | 5. | Transitive Property of Equality |
| 6. ⦓A ≅ ⦓C | 6. | In a circle, if inscribed angles intercept equal arcs, the angles are congruent. |
| 7. $\overline{PA}$ ≅ $\overline{PC}$ | 7. | In a triangle, if two angles are congruent, the sides opposite these angles are congruent. |
| 8. ΔAPC is an isosceles triangle | 8. | An isosceles triangle is a triangle that has two congruent sides. |

● **PROBLEM 7-8**

Let m⦓A = 90° in ΔABC. Let D, E, and F be the midpoints of AB, AC, and BC, respectively. Prove that F is the center of a semicircle which contains B, A, and C.

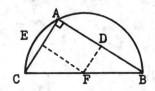

125

__Solution:__ The figure shows △ABC and part of the circle on which A, B, and C lie. To show that F is the center of the circle, we will prove that $\overline{FE}$ and $\overline{FD}$ are perpendicular bisectors of chords $\overline{CA}$ and $\overline{AB}$. Since the perpendicular bisectors of the chords of a circle meet at the center of the circle, we will be able to show that F is the center of the circle passing through A, B, and C. Since an angle inscribed in a semi-circle is a right angle, and ∡A is a right angle inscribed in a circle, we will be able to conclude that $\overset{\frown}{CAB}$ is a semi-circle, and F is its center.

First, note that E and D are the midpoints of $\overline{CA}$ and $\overline{AB}$, as the problem states. Hence, $\overline{EF} \parallel \overline{AB}$ and $\overline{DF} \parallel \overline{AC}$. Since the corresponding angles of 2 parallel lines cut by a transversal are congruent, ∡CEF ≅ ∡CAD and ∡BDF ≅ ∡BAC. Therefore, $\overline{FE} \perp \overline{CA}$ and $\overline{FD} \perp \overline{AB}$. Because E bisects $\overline{CA}$ and D bisects $\overline{AB}$, $\overline{FE}$ and $\overline{FD}$ are the perpendicular bisectors of chords $\overline{CA}$ and $\overline{AB}$. As explained above, the perpendicular bisectors of the chords of a circle intersect at the center of the circle. Hence, F is the center of the circle containing points A, B, and C. (See figure.) Furthermore, ∡A is inscribed in circle F and has measure 90°. Hence, ∡A must intercept a semi-circle i.e. CAB is a semi-circle, with center at F.

• **PROBLEM 7-9**

---

**Given:** Points A, B, C, and D are in ⊙P; $\overset{\frown}{AB} \cong \overset{\frown}{AD}$; $\overset{\frown}{BC} \cong \overset{\frown}{DC}$.
**Prove:** ∡B ≅ ∡D.

---

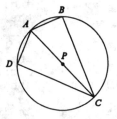

__Solution:__ There are two ways of solving this problem. The first is to prove △ADC ≅ △ABC and then, ∡B ≅ ∡D follows by corresponding parts. The second method is to show ∡B and ∡D both intercept equal arcs.
Method 1: In the same circle, or in congruent circles, if two arcs are congruent, then their chords are congruent. Therefore, $\overset{\frown}{AD} \cong \overset{\frown}{AB}$, which is given, implies $\overline{AD} \cong \overline{AB}$ and $\overset{\frown}{BC} \cong \overset{\frown}{DC}$, which is given, implies $\overline{BC} \cong \overline{DC}$. △ADC ≅ △ABC follows by the SSS Postulate.

| Statements | Reasons |
|---|---|
| 1. Points A, B, C, and D are in ⊙P; $\overset{\frown}{AB} \cong \overset{\frown}{AD}$; $\overset{\frown}{BC} \cong \overset{\frown}{DC}$ | 1. Given. |

| | |
|---|---|
| 2. $\overline{AB} \cong \overline{AD}$; $\overline{BC} \cong \overline{DC}$ | 2. In the same circle, congruent arcs intercept congruent chords. |
| 3. $\overline{AC} \cong \overline{AC}$ | 3. Reflexivity Property. |
| 4. $\triangle ABC \cong \triangle ADC$ | 4. The SSS Postulate. |
| 5. $\angle B \cong \angle D$ | 5. Definition of congruenct triangles. |

Method 2:

| Statements | Reasons |
|---|---|
| 1. Points A, B, C, and D in ⊙P; $\overarc{AB} \cong \overarc{AD}$; $\overarc{BC} \cong \overarc{DC}$ | 1. Given |
| 2. $m\overarc{AB} + m\overarc{BC} = m\overarc{AD} + m\overarc{DC}$ | 2. Addition Postulate. |
| 3. $m\overarc{ABC} = m\overarc{ADC}$ | 3. Substitution. |
| 4. $\overarc{ABC} \cong \overarc{ADC}$ | 4. Definition of Congruent Arcs. |
| 5. $\angle B \cong \angle D$ | 5. Inscribed angles that intercept congruent arcs are congruent. |

● **PROBLEM** 7-10

Given two intersecting chords of a circle, show that the measure of the angle formed by the intersection is one-half the sum of the measures of the arcs intercepted by the angle and its vertical angle.

Solution: We are required to relate $\angle AEM$ to $\overarc{AM}$ and $\overarc{NF}$. Here, by drawing $\overline{MF}$, we can express $\overarc{AM}$ and $\overarc{NF}$ in terms of inscribed angles $\angle NMF$ and $\angle AFM$. $\angle NEF$ can also be expressed in terms of these two angles, since $\angle NEF$ is an exterior angle of $\triangle MEF$. Thus, we solve for $\angle NEF$ in terms of $\angle NMF$ and $\angle AFM$. Then we solve for $\angle NMF$ in terms of $\overarc{NF}$ and for $\angle AFM$ in terms of $\overarc{AM}$. Substituting into the expression for $\angle NEF$, we will then have an equation for $\angle NEF$ in terms of the intercepted arcs.

Given: $\overline{AF}$ and $\overline{MN}$ are chords of ⊙P that intersect at E.

Prove: $m\angle NEF = \frac{1}{2}(m\overarc{AM} + m\overarc{NF})$

127

| Statements | Reasons |
|---|---|
| 1. $\overline{AF}$ and $\overline{MN}$ are chords of ⊙P that intersect at E. | 1. Given. |
| 2. $m\sphericalangle AFM = \frac{1}{2}m\widehat{AM}$<br><br>$m\sphericalangle NMF = \frac{1}{2}m\widehat{NF}$ | 2. The measure of the inscribed angle is equal to one-half the measure of the intercepted arc. |
| 3. $\sphericalangle NEF$ is an exterior angle of $\triangle MEF$ | 3. An exterior angle of a triangle is an angle that forms a linear pair with one of the interior angles of the angle. |
| 4. $m\sphericalangle NEF = m\sphericalangle AFM + m\sphericalangle NMF$ | 4. The measure of the exterior angle of a triangle equals the sum of the measure of the two remote interior angles. |
| 5. $m\sphericalangle NEF = \frac{1}{2}m\widehat{AM} + \frac{1}{2}m\widehat{NF}$<br>or<br>$m\sphericalangle NEF = \frac{1}{2}(m\widehat{AM} + m\widehat{NF})$ | 5. Substitution Postulate (Steps 2 and 4) |

# CHORDS

● **PROBLEM** 7-11

Prove that the line containing the midpoints of the major and minor arcs of a chord of a circle is the perpendicular bisector of the chord.

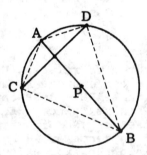

Solution: A perpendicular bisector is a line, all of whose points are equidistant from the endpoints of the given segment. We show that two points, the midpoints of the major and minor arcs, are equidistant from the endpoints of the chord and thus that the line determined by these points must be the perpendicular bisector. To show A and B, the midpoints of the arcs, are equidistant from chord endpoints C and D, we show $\overline{AC} \cong \overline{AD}$ and $\overline{CB} \cong \overline{DB}$. However, from the given $\overset{\frown}{AC} \cong \overset{\frown}{AD}$ and $\overset{\frown}{CB} \cong \overset{\frown}{BD}$, and the congruence of the segments follows.

Given: $\overline{CD}$ is a chord of ⊙P. A is the midpoint of the minor arc $\overset{\frown}{CD}$. B is the midpoint of major arc $\overset{\frown}{CD}$.

Prove: $\overleftrightarrow{AB}$ is the perpendicular bisector of $\overset{\frown}{CD}$.

| Statements | Reasons |
|---|---|
| 1. A is the midpoint of minor arc $\overset{\frown}{CD}$.<br>B is the midpoint of major arc $\overset{\frown}{CD}$. | 1. Given |
| 2. $m\overset{\frown}{AC} = m\overset{\frown}{AD} = 1/2\ m\overset{\frown}{CD}$<br>$m\overset{\frown}{BC} = m\overset{\frown}{BD} = \tfrac{1}{2}m\overset{\frown}{CD}$ | 2. The midpoint of an arc divides the arc into two congruent arcs. |
| 3. $\overline{AC} \cong \overline{AD}$ ; $\overline{CB} \cong \overline{BD}$ | 3. If two arcs are congruent, their chords are also congruent. |
| 4. A is equidistant from C and D.<br>B is equidistant from C and D. | 4. Definition of equidistance. |
| 5. $\overleftrightarrow{AB}$ is the perpendicular bisector of $\overline{BC}$. | 5. If a line contains two points equidistant from the endpoints of the segment, then the line is the perpendicular bisector of the segment. |

● **PROBLEM** 7-12

Two chords intersect in the interior of a circle, thus determining two segments in each chord. Show that the product of the length of the segments of one chord equals the product of the lengths of the segments of the other chord.

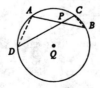

Solution: Restating the above problem, in terms of the figure, we obtain AP · PB = DP · PC. We can rewrite this (divide both sides by PB · DP) as $\frac{AP}{DP} = \frac{PC}{PB}$. To prove the proportionality, we show that two triangles are similar. In this case, $\triangle APD \sim \triangle CPB$ by the A-A Similarity Theorem.

Given: Chords $\overline{AB}$ and $\overline{CD}$ of $\odot Q$ intersect at point P.
Prove: AP · PB = DP · PC.

| Statements | Reasons |
|---|---|
| 1. Chords $\overline{AB}$ and $\overline{CD}$ of $\odot Q$ intersect at point P. | 1. Given. |
| 2. $\angle ADC \cong \angle ABC$. | 2. Inscribed angles that cut the same arc are congruent. |
| 3. $\angle APD \cong \angle CPB$. | 3. Vertical angles are congruent. |
| 4. $\triangle APD \sim \triangle CPB$. | 4. The A-A Similarity Theorem. |
| 5. $\frac{AP}{PD} = \frac{PC}{PB}$ | 5. The sides of similar triangles are proportional. |
| 6. AP · PB = PC · PD. | 6. In a proportion, the product of the means must equal the product of the extremes. |

● **PROBLEM 7-13**

In the figure below, if $m\widehat{BN} = 50$ and $m\angle OFG = 35$, find $m\widehat{OG}$.

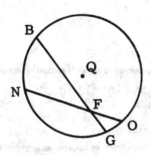

Solution: We know that given two intersecting chords in a circle, the measure of the angle formed by the intersection is equal to one-half the sum of the measures of the arcs intercepted by the angle and its vertical angle. Here, $\widehat{BN}$ and $\widehat{OG}$ are the intercepted arcs of $\angle OFG$ and its vertical angle. Therefore,

(i) $m\angle OFG = \frac{1}{2}(m\widehat{BN} + m\widehat{OG})$.

Substituting in the values m$\overarc{BN}$ = 50 and m∡OFG = 35, we obtain:

(ii)   $35 = \frac{1}{2}(50 + m\overarc{OG})$

(iii)   $(2)35 = 50 + m\overarc{OG}$

(iv)   $m\overarc{OG} = (2)35 - 50 = 70 - 50 = 20$

● **PROBLEM** 7-14

...neter $\overline{BC}$ is drawn in circle ...to chord $\overline{CD}$. Prove that ...to the measure of arc ED,

Checkout Receipt

NEWARK LIBRARY
Phone: 740-349-5555
10/11/11  03:05PM
************************************

ID: 1636891

The high school geometry tutor /
ITEM: 32487008091341
# DUE DATE: 11/08/11
************************************
Cracking the ACT /
ITEM: 32487010641125
# DUE DATE: 11/08/11
************************************

TOTAL: 2


************************************
Get your geek on at the Library!
www.geekthelibrary.org
************************************


www.lickingcountylibrary.info

...given circle, arcs of equal
...equal measure.  Radius $\overline{OD}$,
...rsal of parallel segments
...a transversal of these lines.
...we have shown that the arcs
...intercept are also equal.

**Reason**

One and only one straight
line may be drawn through
two points.

Given.

If two parallel lines are
cut by a transversal, the
alternate interior angles
are congruent and of equal
measure.

Radii of a circle are congruent.

5.   m∡DOE = m∡OCD.

5.   If two parallel lines are
cut by a transversal, the
corresponding angles are
congruent and of equal
measure.

6.   m∡OCD = m∡CDO.

6.   If two sides of a triangle
are congruent, the angles

opposite these sides are
congruent and of equal
measure.

7. m∡BOE = m∡CDO.

7. Transitive property of
equality.

8. m∡BOE ≅ m∡EOD.

8. Same as reason 7.

9. $\overarc{BE}$ ≅ $\overarc{ED}$.

9. In a circle, central angles
whose measures are equal
intercept congruent arcs.

● **PROBLEM** 7-15

In the circle shown, $\overline{BE} \perp \overline{AC}$ and B is the midpoint of arc
$\overarc{AC}$. Prove $\overline{AE} \cong \overline{CE}$.

<u>Solution:</u> In this proof, we must use the theorem that con-
gruent arcs have congruent chords. To show $\overline{AE} \cong \overline{CE}$, we
first prove ΔABE ≅ ΔCBE. To show ΔABE ≅ ΔCBE, we use the
Hypotenuse Leg Theorem. Right angles BEA and BEC are con-
gruent. $\overline{BE} \cong \overline{BE}$. For the third congruence, we note that
$\overline{AB}$ and $\overline{BC}$ are chords that intersect congruent arcs. From
the above theorem, it follows that $\overline{AB} \cong \overline{BC}$.

| Statement | Reason |
|---|---|
| 1. $\overline{BE} \perp \overline{AC}$ | 1. Given. |
| 2. ∡BEA and ∡BEC are right angles. | 2. Perpendicular lines inter-sect to form right angles. |
| 3. ΔABE and ΔBCE are right triangles. | 3. A triangle containing a right angle is a right triangle. |
| 4. B is the midpoint of $\overarc{AC}$. | 4. Given. |
| 5. $\overarc{AB} \cong \overarc{BC}$. | 5. A midpoint of an arc divides the arc into two congruent sections. |
| 6. $\overline{AB} \cong \overline{BC}$ | 6. Congruent arcs have con-gruent chords. |
| 7. $\overline{BE} \cong \overline{BE}$ | 7. Reflexive property of con-gruence. |

8.  ΔABE ≅ ΔCBE.

9.  $\overline{AE}$ ≅ $\overline{CE}$.

8.  hy. leg ≅ hy. leg.

9.  Corresponding sides of con-
    gruent triangles are con-
    gruent.

● **PROBLEM 7-16**

Given:  Point  Q  is in the interior of  ⊙P;  $\overrightarrow{QP}$  intersects  ⊙P  in  R;
S  is any point on  ⊙P.

Prove:  RQ > SQ  (Hint:  Use  $\overline{SP}$).

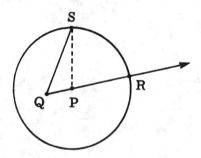

Solution:  We must show  RQ > SQ.  Since  RQ = RP + PQ, this is the
same as proving  RP + PQ > SQ.

To relate  SQ  and  PQ, we use the Triangle Inequality Theorem –
that is, in  Δ SPQ, SQ < QP + SP.  Since  $\overline{SP}$  and  $\overline{PR}$  are radii,
$\overline{SP}$ ≅ $\overline{PR}$  and  QP + SP = QP + PR.  The inequality then becomes   SQ < QP +
PR  or  SQ < RQ.

| Statements | Reasons |
|---|---|
| 1. (see problem statement) | 1. Given |
| 2. QR = QP + PR | 2. Definition of betweenness. |
| 3. SQ < QP + PS | 3. Triangle Inequality Theorem. |
| 4. SP = PR | 4. All radii of a circle are congruent. |
| 5. SQ < QP + PR | 5. Substitution Postulate (Step 3,4) |
| 6. SQ < QR | 6. Substitution Postulate (Step 5,2) |

● **PROBLEM 7-17**

Given:  $\overline{AB}$ and $\overline{CD}$ are chords of circle P;
$\overline{PM} \perp \overline{AB}$ at M; $\overline{PN} \perp \overline{CD}$ at N; $\overline{PM}$ ≅ $\overline{PN}$.  Prove:  $\overline{AB}$ ≅ $\overline{CD}$.

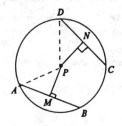

133

**Solution:** To prove congruence of lines, we must look for congruent triangles. Here, in drawing the radii $\overline{AP}$ and $\overline{DP}$, we make use of the fact that all radii of a given circle are congruent. After proving $\triangle AMP \cong \triangle DNP$, we have $\overline{AM} \cong \overline{DN}$. We could then repeat the procedure, drawing radii $\overline{PC}$ and $\overline{PB}$, and prove $\overline{NC} \cong \overline{MB}$, but that is unnecessary. The line containing the center of the circle and perpendicular to any chord bisects that chord. Therefore, if $\overline{AM} \cong \overline{DN}$; $\overline{AB}$ (which equals $2 \cdot AM$) must be congruent to $\overline{CD}$ (which equals $2 \cdot DN$).

| | Statements | | Reason |
|---|---|---|---|
| 1. | $\overline{AB}$ and $\overline{CD}$ are chords of circle P; $\overline{PM} \perp \overline{AB}$ at M; $\overline{PN} \perp \overline{CD}$ at N; $\overline{PM} \cong \overline{PN}$. | 1. | Given |
| 2. | $AP = DP$. | 2. | All radii of a circle are equal in measure. |
| 3. | $\triangle AMP \cong \triangle DNP$. | 3. | If the hypotenuse and a leg of a right triangle are congruent to the hypotenuse and leg of another right triangle, then the two triangles are congruent. |
| 4. | $AM = DN$. | 4. | Corresponding parts of congruent triangles are congruent. |
| 5. | M is the midpoint of $\overline{AB}$; N is the midpoint of $\overline{CD}$. | 5. | The line containing the center of the circle and perpendicular to the chord intersects the chord at its midpoint. |
| 6. | $AB = 2AM$ $CD = 2DN$ | 6. | Property of the midpoint. |
| 7. | $AB = CD$. | 7. | Multiplication Postulate and Substitution Postulate. |
| 8. | $\overline{AB} \cong \overline{CD}$ | 8. | Two line segments are congruent if they are of the same length. |

● **PROBLEM** 7-18

Show that in the same circle (or in congruent circles) if two chords are not congruent, then the longer chord is nearer the center of the circle than the shorter chord.

**Solution:** Consider chords $\overline{AB}$ and $\overline{CD}$ in the accompanying figure. $AB < CD$. We want to show $PM > PN$.

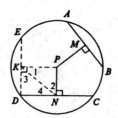

The inequality AB < CD could lead us to an inequality of angles, if $\overline{AB}$ and $\overline{CD}$ were sides of a triangle. Similarly, if $\overline{PM}$ and $\overline{PN}$ were sides of a triangle, then by showing the angle opposite $\overline{PM}$ is greater than the angle opposite $\overline{PN}$, we could reach the desired conclusion.

We can create the necessary triangles by constructing chord $\overline{ED} \cong \overline{AB}$. Consider point K, the midpoint of $\overline{ED}$. Then, KD = ½ED. Also, DN = ½DC.

Since DC > ED, then DN > KD. In triangle Δ DKN, m ⊀ 3 > m ⊀ 4. Because ⊀ DKP and ⊀ DNP are right angles, m ⊀ 3 + m ⊀ 1 = m ⊀ 4 + m ⊀ 2 = 90°. Since m ⊀ 3 > m ⊀ 4, m ⊀ 1 < m ⊀ 2. PK > PN and the distance of chord $\overline{AB}$ from the center, PM = PK, is greater than the distance of the longer chord $\overline{DC}$ from the center, $\overline{PN}$.

Given: $\overline{AB}$ and $\overline{CD}$ are chords of ⊙ P; $\overline{PM} \perp \overline{AB}$ at M;
$\overline{PN} \perp \overline{CD}$ at N; CD > AB.
Prove: PN < PM.

| Statements | Reasons |
|---|---|
| 1. $\overline{AB}$ and $\overline{CD}$ are chords of ⊙ P; $\overline{PM} \perp \overline{AB}$ at M; $\overline{PN} \perp \overline{CD}$ at N; CD > AB | 1. Given. |
| 2. Construct chord $\overline{ED}$ such that ED = AB and E and P are on the same side of DC. | 2. From any point on the circle, a chord can be constructed of a given length, provided the length is less than the diameter. |
| 3. K is the midpoint of $\overline{ED}$ | 3. Every line segment $\overline{AB}$ has one and only one point C such that AC = CB. |
| 4. KD = ½ED | 4. Definition of the midpoint of a segment. |
| 5. $\overline{PK} \perp \overline{ED}$ | 5. The line joining the center of the circle and the midpoint of a chord is the perpendicular bisector of the chord. |
| 6. PK = PM | 6. In the same circle (or congruent circles), chords are congruent if and only if they are equidistant from the center of the circle. |
| 7. DN = ½DC | 7. The perpendicular from the center of the circle to a chord bisects the chord. |
| 8. DC > ED | 8. Substitution Postulate |
| 9. DN > KD | 9. Halves of unequal quantities are unequal in the same sense. |
| 10. m ⊀ 3 > m ⊀ 4 | 10. In a triangle, if the length of the side opposite the first angle is greater than the length of the side opposite the second angle, the first |

11. m ∢ 3 + m ∢ 1 = 90°
    m ∢ 4 + m ∢ 2 = 90°

11. If two angles form a right angle, their measures sum to 90°.

12. m ∢ 1 = 90° - m ∢ 3
    m ∢ 2 = 90° - m ∢ 4

12. Equals subtracted from equals leave equals.

13. 90° - m ∢ 4 > 90° - m ∢ 3

13. If a = b and c < d, then a - c > b - d. (The equality is 90° = 90°; the inequality comes from Step 10.)

14. m ∢ 2 > m ∢ 3

14. Substitution Postulate.

15. PK > PN

15. In a triangle, if the measure of the angle opposite the first side is greater than the measure of the angle opposite the second side, then the length of the first side is greater than the length of the second.

16. PM > PN

16. Substitution Postulate (Steps 15 and 6)

# TANGENTS, LINES AND CIRCLES

● PROBLEM 7-19

Prove that if two circles are tangent externally, tangents drawn to the circles from any point on their common internal tangent are equal in length. (See figure)

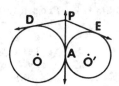

Solution: A common internal tangent is a line which is tangent to both circles and intersects their line of center. The line of center has endpoints O and O'. $\overleftrightarrow{PA}$ is the common internal tangent of circles O and O', and $\overleftrightarrow{PD}$ and $\overleftrightarrow{PE}$ are external tangents drawn from a point P on the common internal tangent. If both $\overleftrightarrow{PE}$ and $\overleftrightarrow{PD}$ can be shown to be equal in length to the same line segment, then we can conclude that they are equal to each other.

| Statement | Reason |
|---|---|
| 1. $\overleftrightarrow{PD}$ and $\overleftrightarrow{PA}$ are tangents to circle O. | 1. Given |
| 2. PD = PA. | 2. The lengths of tangents drawn to a circle from an external point are equal. |
| 3. $\overleftrightarrow{PE}$ and $\overleftrightarrow{PA}$ are tangents to circle O'. | 3. Given. |

4.  PA = PE.

4.  Same as Reason 2.

5.  If PD = PA and PE =
    PA, then PD = PE.

5.  Transitive Property of
    Equality.

● **PROBLEM** 7-20

A belt moves over two wheels which are the same size and crosses itself at right angles as shown in the figure. A,B,C, and D are points of tangency; E is the intersection of the tangents; and O is the center of one of the circles. The radius of each wheel is 7 inches.

(a)  Show that m⧸AOE = 45°.

(b)  Find

   (1)  the length of $\overline{AE}$

   (2)  the length of major arc $\overset{\frown}{AC}$.  $\left[\text{Use } \pi = \dfrac{22}{7}\right]$

   (3)  the length of the entire belt.

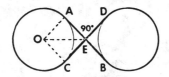

Solution:  (a)  We will first show that AOCE is a square in order to prove that ⧸AOC is a right angle. Then we will show that diagonal $\overline{OE}$ bisects ⧸AOC. If m⧸AOC = 90°, then ⧸AOE must equal 1/2 of 90° or 45°.

| Statement | Reason |
|---|---|
| 1.  $\overline{OA} \cong \overline{OC}$ | 1.  Radii of a circle are congruent. |
| 2.  $\overline{AE}$ and $\overline{CE}$ are tangents at points A and C respectively. | 2.  Given. |
| 3.  $\overline{OA} \perp \overline{AE}$ and $\overline{OC} \perp \overline{CE}$ | 3.  If a line is tangent to a circle, the line is perpendicular to the radius drawn to the point of contact. |
| 4.  ⧸OAE and ⧸OCE are right angles. | 4.  Perpendicular lines intersect to form right angles. |
| 5.  ⧸AEC is a right angle. | 5.  Given. |
| 6.  ⧸OAE is supplementary to ⧸AEC. | 6.  Any two right angles are supplementary. |

137

| | |
|---|---|
| 7. $\overline{OA} \parallel \overline{EC}$ | 7. If interior angles on the same side of a transversal are supplementary, then the lines are parallel. |
| 8. ∡OCE is supplementary to ∡AEC. | 8. Any two right angles are supplementary. |
| 9. $\overline{OC} \parallel \overline{AE}$ | 9. Same as reason 7. |
| 10. AOCE is a square. | 10. A quadrilateral in which (1) all opposite sides are parallel; (2) there exists two adjacent sides which are congruent; and (3) at least one vertex angle is a right angle is a square. |
| 11. ∡AOC is a right angle. | 11. All vertex angles of a square are right angles. |
| 12. m∡AOC = 90° | 12. Right angles measure 90°. |
| 13. $\overline{OE}$ bisects ∡AOC | 13. The diagonal of a square bisects the vertex angles through which it is drawn. |
| 14. m∡AOC = 2m∡AOE | 14. An angle bisector divides the angle into two angles of equal measure. |

| Statement | Reason |
|---|---|
| 15. 2(m∡AOE) = 90°. | 15. Substitution Postulate. |
| 16. m∡AOE = 45°. | 16. Division Property of Equality. |

(b) 1. Since all four sides of a square are of equal measure, AE = OC. $\overline{OC}$ is a radius (r) given to be 7 in. in length.

Therefore, AE = 7 in.

2. Since central angle AOC measures 90°, minor arc $\overset{\frown}{AC}$ = 90°. Therefore, major arc $\overset{\frown}{AC}$ = 360 - 90 or 270.

arc length = $\dfrac{\text{degree measure of the arc}}{360}$ x Circumference.

Circumference = C = 2πr, where r is the radius. By substitution, C = 2π(7) = 14π. Using π = $\dfrac{22}{7}$, we obtain C = $\dfrac{14 \times 22}{7}$ = 44 in. Therefore, length of major arc $\overset{\frown}{AC}$ = $\dfrac{270}{360}$(44) = $\dfrac{3}{4}$(44) = 33. Therefore, length of major arc $\overset{\frown}{AC}$ = 33 in.

3. From the diagram, we find that length of entire belt = length of major arc $\overset{\frown}{AC}$ + $\overline{AE}$ + $\overline{EC}$ + $\overline{ED}$ + $\overline{EB}$ + length of major arc $\overset{\frown}{BD}$. We know that $\overline{AE}$ = $\overline{EC}$ = 7 inches, and that the length of major arc $\overset{\frown}{AC}$ = 33 inches.
Using the same manner we employed to find the above measurements, we can derive $\overline{ED}$, $\overline{EB}$ and length of major arc $\overset{\frown}{DB}$.

138

If we drew the radii from D and B to the center of the circle on the right, they would form a square symmetric to AOCE and, as such, $\overline{ED} = \overline{EB}$ = radius of that circle. We are given the radius = 7 in. for both circles. Therefore, $\overline{ED} = \overline{EB}$ = 7 in.

By a similar symmetry argument, we prove major arc $\overset{\frown}{BD}$ has the same length of major arc $\overset{\frown}{AC}$. Therefore, major arc $\overset{\frown}{BD}$ = 33 in.

By substitution, length of entire belt = 33 + 7 + 7 + 7 + 7 + 33 = 94

Therefore, the length of the entire belt = 94 in.

● **PROBLEM** 7-21

Given:   Circles E and F; $\overleftrightarrow{AB}$ and $\overleftrightarrow{CD}$ tangent to both circles at A, B, C, and D.   Prove: $\overline{AB} \cong \overline{CD}$.

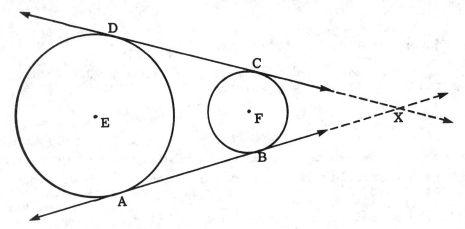

Solution:   Extend $\overleftrightarrow{CD}$ and $\overleftrightarrow{AB}$ to the right until they intersect at a point X.

Since A, B, C, and D are points of tangency, $\overleftrightarrow{AX}$ and $\overleftrightarrow{DX}$ will be tangent to ⊙E and $\overleftrightarrow{BX}$ and $\overleftrightarrow{CX}$ will be tangents to ⊙F. Two tangents drawn to a circle from an external point are of equal length. Therefore, $\overline{AX} \cong \overline{DX}$ and $\overline{BX} \cong \overline{CX}$.

We know that the length of the whole segment is equal to the sum of the lengths of its parts. Hence, $\overline{AX} = \overline{AB} + \overline{BX}$ and $\overline{DX} = \overline{DC} + \overline{CX}$. Accordingly, $\overline{AB} = \overline{AX} - \overline{BX}$ and $\overline{DC} = \overline{DX} - \overline{CX}$. Since $\overline{AX} \cong \overline{DX}$ and $\overline{BX} \cong \overline{CX}$, we can conclude that $\overline{AB} \cong \overline{DC}$.

● **PROBLEM** 7-22

Circles A and B are externally tangent at C.   Prove that A, C, and B are collinear.

139

Solution: If two adjacent angles are right angles, then their non-common sides form a straight angle. Since the rays of a straight angle form a straight line, any points on these rays are collinear.

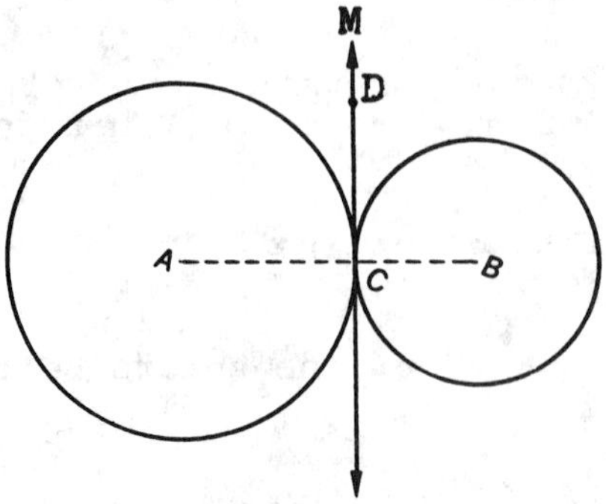


C is the point of tangency of line m and circle B. Since radii of a circle are perpendicular to tangent lines at the points of tangency, therefore, radius $\overline{CB}$ is perpendicular to line m. Accordingly, radius $\overline{AC}$ is also perpendicular to line m.

Since perpendicular lines intersect to form right angles, adjacent angles DCB and DCA are right angles.

Hence, the non-common sides of ∢DCB and ∢DCA form a straight angle, and the points A, C, and B are collinear.

**• PROBLEM 7-23**

Given two circles with a common tangent at a point A such that the second circle passes through the center of the first. Show that every chord of the first circle that passes through A is bisected by the second circle. (See figure.)

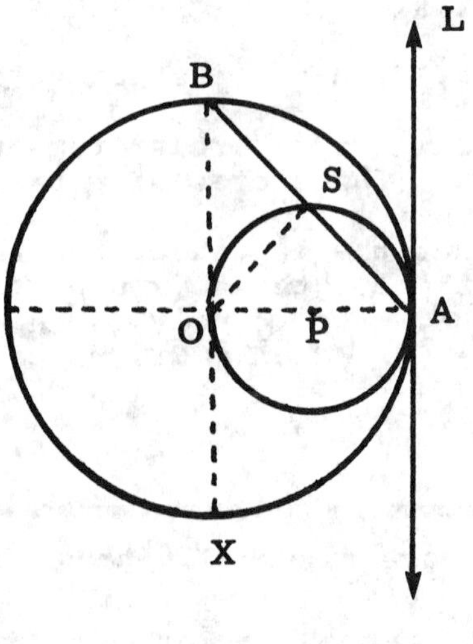

Solution: We are asked to show that if circles P and O are tangent at A, and O lies on circle P, then $\overline{AB}$ is bisected by circle P at point S. We will do this by showing that $\overline{OS}$ is the perpendicular bisector of $\overline{BA}$.

First, note that $\overline{OPA}$ connects the centers of 2 circles tangent at the same point (See figure.) Hence, $\overline{OPA}$ is a straight line passing through the center of circle P. $\overline{OPA}$ is, therefore, a diameter of P, which implies that $\angle OSA$ is inscribed in a semicircle ($\overparen{OSA}$). This means that $\angle OSA$ is a right angle, and that $\overline{OS} \perp \overline{BA}$. However, any line segment drawn from the center of a circle perpendicular to a chord of the same circle bisects the chord. Since $\overline{OS} \perp \overline{BA}$ at S, $\overline{BS} \cong \overline{SA}$.

● **PROBLEM 7-24**

Circles A, B, and C are tangent to one another. Find the radii of the three circles if AB = 7, AC = 5, and BC = 9.

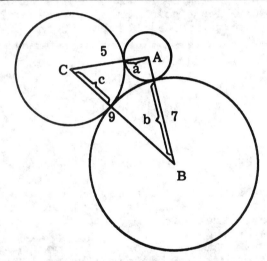

Solution: The segment connecting the centers of tangent circles passes through the point of tangency on the circumference of the circles. Thus, the distance to the point of tangency from the center of ⊙C is the radius, c, from the center of ⊙A is the radius, a, and from the center of ⊙B is the radius, b. Therefore, the length of the segments between the centers is the sum of the radii. Hence,

$$AC = c + a$$
$$AB = a + b$$
$$BC = b + c$$

Since AC = 5, AB = 7, and BC = 9, we have

(i)  $5 = c + a$
(ii)  $7 = a + b$
(iii)  $9 = b + c$

141

Solving for a in terms of c 5= c + a, a = 5 - c.  Substituting this result in the other equations, we obtain:

(ii)   7 = (5-c) + b = 5 + b - c or 2 = b - c
(iii)  9 = b + c

Adding both equations, we eliminate c.

$$11 = 2b \quad or \quad b = 5.5$$

Since 9 = b + c, c = 9 - 5.5 = 3.5  Hence a = 5 - c = 5 - 3.5 = 1.5.  Thus, a = 1.5, b = 5.5, and c = 3.5.

## INTERSECTING CIRCLES

Given:  Circles P and Q intersect at points A and C; chord $\overline{AB}$ of ⊙P is tangent to ⊙Q; chord $\overline{AD}$ of ⊙Q is tangent to ⊙P; E is a point on ⊙Q; F is a point on ⊙P.  Prove: ΔABC ∿ ΔDAC and AC is the mean proportional between BC and DC.

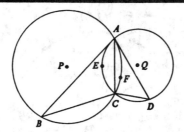

Solution:  To show similar triangles, we use either (1) A-A Similarity Theorem, (2) SAS Similarity Theorem, or  (3) SSS Similarity Theorem.  There are no obvious proportions between the sides.  Therefore, we try to find an A-A Similarity.  We are to prove ΔABC ∿ ΔDAC, therefore, ⦨ABC corresponds to ⦨CAD. ⦨B is an inscribed angle that intercepts arc AFC and, thus, m⦨B = $\frac{1}{2}$mAFC.  ⦨CAD is an angle formed by a chord and a tangent of ⊙P and has a measure equal to $\frac{1}{2}$ the intercepted arc or $\frac{1}{2}$mÂFC.  Therefore, both m⦨B and m⦨CAD equal $\frac{1}{2}$mÂFC and ⦨B ≅ ⦨CAD.

        In a similar manner, we show ⦨BAC ∿ ⦨CDA.  Thus, ΔABC ∿ ΔDAC.  By definition of similar triangles, we show AC is the mean proportional between BC and DC.

| Statements | Reasons |
| --- | --- |
| 1.  (See problem statement) | 1.  Given. |

2. $m\sphericalangle B = \frac{1}{2}m\overset{\frown}{AFC}$ in $\odot$P.

   $m\sphericalangle D = \frac{1}{2}m\overset{\frown}{AEC}$ in $\odot$Q.

2. The measure of the inscribed angle equals one-half the measure of the intercepted arc.

3. $m\sphericalangle CAD = \frac{1}{2}m\overset{\frown}{AFC}$ in $\odot$P.

   $m\sphericalangle BAC = \frac{1}{2}m\overset{\frown}{AEC}$ in $\odot$Q.

3. The measure of an angle formed by a chord and a tangent of a circle equals one-half the intercepted arc.

4. $m\sphericalangle B = m\sphericalangle CAD$, or,
   $\sphericalangle B \cong \sphericalangle CAD$
   $m\sphericalangle D = m\sphericalangle BAC$, or,
   $\sphericalangle D \cong \sphericalangle BAC$.

4. Transitivity Postulate and Definition of Congruence of Angles.

5. $\triangle ABC \sim \triangle DAC$.

5. The A-A Similarity Theorem.

6. $\dfrac{BC}{AC} = \dfrac{AC}{DC}$

6. The sides of similar triangles are proportional.

7. $AC^2 = BC \cdot DC$.

7. For a proportion to hold, the product of the means equal the product of the extremes.

8. AC is the mean proportional between BC and DC.

8. Defintion of the mean proportional.

● **PROBLEM 7-26**

Given: Circles P and Q intersect at points A and C; $\overline{PQ}$ meets $\overrightarrow{BA}$ and $\overrightarrow{DC}$ at T, a point of circle P. Prove that $\overline{AB} \cong \overline{CD}$.

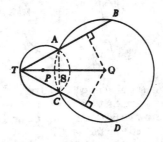

Solution: Construct segment $\overline{AC}$ so that it intersects $\overline{PQ}$ at point S. Draw perpendicular line segments from Q to $\overline{AB}$ and $\overline{CD}$. The perpendicular to $\overline{AB}$ intersects $\overline{AB}$ at E, and the perependicular to $\overline{CD}$ intersects $\overline{CD}$ at F. (See figure.)

We first prove that $\overline{TPSQ}$ is the perpendicular bisector of $\overline{AC}$. This will enable us to show that $\triangle ATS \cong \triangle CTS$, which implies that $\sphericalangle ATS \cong \sphericalangle CTS$. We will then have enough data to prove that $\triangle QET \cong \triangle QFT$ or that $\overline{QE} \cong \overline{QF}$. Since chords which are equidistant from the center of a circle are congruent, we will have shown that $\overline{AB} \cong \overline{CD}$.

Circles P and Q intersect at points A and C. Hence, $\overline{QA}$ and $\overline{QC}$ are radii of circle Q, and points A and C are equidistant from point Q. Similarly, A and C are equidistant from point P. Since the locus of points equidistant from two points is the perpendicular bisector of the line segment joining the two points, P and Q must lie on the perpendicular bisector of $\overline{AC}$. Furthermore, since two points determine a line, $\overline{PQ}$ is the perpendicular bisector of $\overline{AC}$. By construction, S and T lie on $\overline{PQ}$. $\overline{TPSQ}$ is the perpendicular bisector of $\overline{AC}$. We use this fact to show that $\triangle ATS \cong \triangle CTS$.

$\overline{AS} \cong \overline{CS}$ and $\angle AST \cong \angle CST$ because $\overline{TPSQ}$ is the perpendicular bisector of $\overline{AC}$. $\overline{TS} \cong \overline{TS}$. By the S.A.S. Postulate, $\triangle ATS \cong \triangle CTS$, and $\angle ATS \cong \angle CTS$. A lies on $\overline{TE}$, C lies on TF, and $\overline{TPSQ}$ is a straight line. Hence, the last statement can be rewritten as $\angle ETQ \cong \angle FTQ$. By construction, $\angle TEQ \cong \angle TFQ$. $\overline{TQ} \cong \overline{TQ}$ and, by the A.A.S. Postulate, $\triangle QET \cong \triangle QFT$. Hence, $\overline{QE} \cong \overline{QF}$ or QE = QF. This means that $\overline{AB}$ and $\overline{CD}$ are equally distant from Q (because $\overline{QE} \perp \overline{AB}$ and $\overline{QF} \perp \overline{CD}$). Therefore, since chords drawn equidistantly from the center of a circle are congruent, $\overline{AB} \cong \overline{CD}$.

● **PROBLEM 7-27**

Two equal circles are drawn so that the center of each is on the circumference of the other. Their intersection points are A and B. Prove that if, from A, any line is drawn cutting the circles at D and C, then ∆BCD is equilateral.

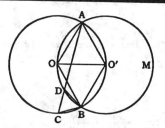

Solution: In the accompanying figure, ⊙O and ⊙O' intersect at A and B. $\overline{AD}$ is an arbitrary line that intersects ⊙O' at D and ⊙O at C. To show ∆BCD is an equilateral triangle, we must either show (1) sides DC = CB = BD or (2) ∠DCB ≅ ∠CBD ≅ ∠BDC. We will show that m∠DCB = 60° and m∠ BDC = 60°. Therefore, m∠CBD = 180 - m∠DCB - m∠BDC = 60 . Thus, we will be able to conclude that ∆BCD is an equilateral triangle.

To show m∠DCB = 60°, note that ∠DCB is the same angle as ∠ACB which is an inscribed angle of ⊙O. Thus, m∠ACB = m∠DCB = $\frac{1}{2}$m $\overset{\frown}{AO'B}$.

To find m $\overset{\frown}{AO'B}$, we consider ∆OAO' and ∆OBO'. Because equal circles have equal radii, OA = OO' = O'A and OO' = OB = BO'. Thus ∆OAO' and ∆OBO' are equilateral triangles

144

and m∡AOO' = m∡BOO' = 60°. m∡AOB = m∡AOO' + m∡BOO' =
60 + 60 = 120°. Thus, m $\overarc{AO'B}$ = m∡AOB = 120°. Since
m∡DCB = $\frac{1}{2}$m $\overarc{AO'B}$, m∡DCB = $\frac{1}{2}$(120°) = 60°.

To show m∡CDB = 60°, we show that its supplement, exterior angle ∡ADB, has a measure of 120°. Note that ∡ADB
is an inscribed angle of ⊙O'. Thus, m∡ADB = $\frac{1}{2}$ $\overarc{AMB}$. Since

m$\overarc{AMB}$ + m$\overarc{AOB}$ = 360, then m$\overarc{AMB}$ = 360 - m$\overarc{AOB}$ = 360 - 120 = 240.
Substituting, we have m∡ADB = $\frac{1}{2}$(240) = 120.

Because exterior angle ∡ADB forms a linear pair with
∡CDB, m∡ADB + m∡CDB = 180. Thus, m∡CDB = 180 - m∡ADB = 180
- 120 = 60.

Finally, in ΔBCD, if m∡DCB = 60° and m∡CDB = 60°, then
m∡DBC = 180 - m∡DCB - m∡CDB = 180 - 60 - 60 = 60°.

Thus, all angles of ΔBCD are equal and ΔBCD is an equilateral triangle.


# TANGENTS, SECANTS AND CHORDS

● **PROBLEM** 7-28

> Prove that the measure of the angle formed by a tangent and
> a chord of a circle is one-half the measure of its intercepted arc.

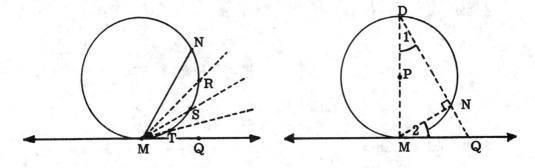

Figure 1                         Figure 2

<u>Solution:</u> To see why the statement must be true, consider
the inscribed angle ∡NMR. We know that m∡NMR = $\frac{1}{2}$$\overarc{NR}$. Similarly, for the larger angle ∡NMS, it is true that m∡NMS =
$\frac{1}{2}$m$\overarc{NRS}$. Even as we pick points on the circle closer to M,
the statement continues to be true. At the limit, the series
of lines $\overleftrightarrow{MR}$, $\overleftrightarrow{MS}$, $\overleftrightarrow{MT}$ ... approach the tangent $\overline{MQ}$, and what
we shall prove here is that the relationship still holds:

$m \sphericalangle NMQ = \frac{1}{2} m \overgroup{NSM}.$

There are two methods for proving the relation and both involve relating the angle $\sphericalangle NMQ$ with some inscribed angle of the circle that intercepts the same arc.

Method 1: Let D be the point on the circle such that $\overline{DM}$ is a diameter. Define Q such that Q is the intersection of $\overleftrightarrow{DN}$ and the tangent. Inscribed angle $\sphericalangle 1 = \frac{1}{2} m \overgroup{MN}$. If we prove $\sphericalangle 2 \cong \sphericalangle 1$, then $\sphericalangle 2 = \frac{1}{2} m \overgroup{MN}$ and the proof is complete. We prove $\sphericalangle 2 \cong \sphericalangle 1$ by showing $\triangle NMQ \sim \triangle MDQ$ by the A-A Similarity Theorem.

Given: $\overleftrightarrow{MQ}$ is tangent to $\odot P$;
$\overline{DM}$ is a diameter of $\odot P$;
$\overline{MN}$ is a chord of $\odot P$.

Prove: $m \sphericalangle NMQ = \frac{1}{2} m \overgroup{MN}$

| Statement | Reason |
|---|---|
| 1. $\overleftrightarrow{MQ}$ is tangent to $\odot P$; $\overline{DM}$ is a diameter of $\odot P$; $\overline{MN}$ is a chord of $\odot P$. | 1. Given. |
| 2. $\overline{PM} \perp \overline{MQ}.$ | 2. The tangent to a circle is perpendicular to the radius of the circle drawn to the point of intersection. |
| 3. $\sphericalangle DMQ$ is a right angle. | 3. Definition of perpendicularity. |
| 4. $\triangle DMN$ is a right triangle. | 4. If one side of a triangle inscribed in circle is a diameter, then the triangle is a right triangle with the hypotenuse being the diameter. |
| 5. $\sphericalangle DNM$ is a right angle. | 5. Definition of a right triangle. |
| 6. $\sphericalangle MNQ$ is a right angle | 6. If one angle of a linear pair is a right angle, then the other angle is also a right angle. |
| 7. $\sphericalangle MNQ \cong \sphericalangle DMQ$ | 7. All right angles are congruent. |
| 8. $\sphericalangle NQM \cong \sphericalangle NQM$ | 8. A-A Similarity Theorem. |
| 9. $\sphericalangle 1 \cong \sphericalangle 2$ | 9. Corresponding angles of similar triangles are congruent. |

| 10. $m\angle 1 = \frac{1}{2}m\overset{\frown}{MN}$ | 10. The measure of an inscribed angle equals one-half the measure of the intercepted arc. |
|---|---|
| 11. $m\angle 2 = \frac{1}{2}m\overset{\frown}{MN}$ | 11. Substitution Postulate |

Method 2: Here, again, we show $\angle 1 \cong \angle 2$. By showing $\angle 1$ and $\angle DMN$ are complementary, and $\angle 2$ and $\angle DMN$ are complementary, we can equate $\angle 1$ and $\angle 2$ and, therefore, $m\angle 1 = m\angle 2 = \frac{1}{2}m\overset{\frown}{MN}$.

| <u>Statement</u> | <u>Reason</u> |
|---|---|

The first 5 steps are the same as the last proof.

| 6. $\angle 1$ and $\angle DMN$ are complementary. | 6. The acute angles of a right triangle are complementary. |
|---|---|
| 7. $\angle 2$ and $\angle DMN$ are complementary | 7. If the sum of two angles is 90°, then they are complementary. |
| 8. $\angle 1 \cong \angle 2$ | 8. Two angles that are complementary to the same angle are congruent. |
| 9. $m\angle 1 \cong \frac{1}{2}m\overset{\frown}{MN}$ | 9. The measure of an inscribed angle equals one-half the measure of the intercepted arc. |
| 10. $m\angle 2 = \frac{1}{2}m\overset{\frown}{MN}$ | 10. Substitution Postulate. |

● **PROBLEM** 7-29

The angle formed by two tangents drawn to a circle from the same external point measures 80°. Find the measure of the minor intercepted arc.

<u>Solution:</u> The measure of an angle formed by two tangents drawn to a circle from an outside point is equal to one-half the difference of the measures of the intercepted arcs.

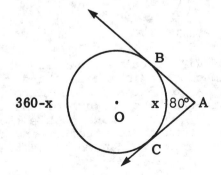

147

If we let x = the measure of minor arc $\overarc{BC}$, then 360°-x = the measure of the major arc $\overarc{BC}$.  Applying the above rule,

$$m\sphericalangle BAC = \frac{1}{2}(m(major\ \overarc{BC}) - m(minor\ \overarc{BC})).$$

By substitution,

$$80° = \frac{1}{2}(360° - 2x).$$

80° = 180° - x, which implies x = 100°.  Therefore, the measure of the minor intercepted arc is 100°.

An alternative solution for this problem is as follows. Draw $\overline{BC}$.  Since tangents to a circle from the same external point are congruent, triangle ABC is an isosceles triangle. Hence, m$\sphericalangle$ABC = m$\sphericalangle$ACB.  But the sum of the measures of the angles of any triangle is 180°.  Therefore,

$$m\sphericalangle BAC + m\sphericalangle ABC + m\sphericalangle ACB = 180°.$$

Since m$\sphericalangle$ABC = m$\sphericalangle$ACB and m$\sphericalangle$BAC =  80°, we obtain

$$m\sphericalangle ABC = m\sphericalangle ACB = 50°.$$

Angle ABC is formed by a tangent and a chord.  There-fore, its measure equals $\underset{2}{1}$ the measure of the intercepted

arc; i.e., m$\sphericalangle$ABC = $\frac{1}{2}$m$\overarc{BC}$.  By substituting 50° for the m$\sphericalangle$ABC, we can calculate the m$\overarc{BC}$ to be 100°.  This method is less direct than the first, but is a valid option.

● PROBLEM 7-30

As shown in the diagram, $\overline{BD}$ bisects $\sphericalangle$ABC, which is inscribed in circle O.  $\overarc{EC}$ is tangent to circle O at point C.  Prove that $\sphericalangle$ABD ≅ $\sphericalangle$DCE.

Solution:  This proof will involve recalling that both the measure of an inscribed angle in a circle and the measure of an angle formed by a tangent and a chord to that tangency point are equal to one-half the measure of the intercepted arc.  With this in mind, we can prove $\sphericalangle$DCE ≅ $\sphericalangle$DBC.  By ap-plying the definition of an angle bisector and the transi-tive property of congruence, we can conclude that $\sphericalangle$ABD = $\sphericalangle$DCE.

| Statement | Reason |
|---|---|
| 1. $\overline{BD}$ bisects ⦨ABC | 1. Given. |
| 2. ⦨ABD ≅ ⦨DBC | 2. A bisector divides an angle into two congruent angles. |
| 3. $\overleftrightarrow{EC}$ is tangent to the circle. | 3. Given. |
| 4. m⦨DCE = $\frac{1}{2}$m$\overarc{DC}$ | 4. The measure of an angle formed by a tangent and a chord at the point of tangency is equal to one-half the measure of the intercepted arc. |
| 5. m⦨DBC = $\frac{1}{2}$m$\overarc{DC}$ | 5. The measure of an inscribed angle is equal to one-half the measure of the intercepted arc. |
| 6. m⦨DBC = m⦨DCE | 6. Transitive property of equality. |
| 7. ⦨DBC ≅ ⦨DCE | 7. Two angles are congruent if their measures are equal. |
| 8. ⦨ABD ≅ ⦨DCE | 8. Transitive property of congruence. |

● **PROBLEM** 7-31

Two secant lines of the same circle share an endpoint in the exterior of the circle. Show that the product of the lengths of one secant segment and its external segment equal the product of the lengths of the other secant segment and its external segment.

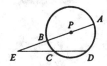 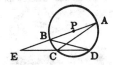

Solution: The secant segment is the portion of the secant line bounded by the common endpoint and the point of intersection with the circle farthest from this point.

Restating the problem in terms of the above figure, we must show that EB · EA = EC · ED. We can rewrite this as the proportion $\frac{EB}{ED} = \frac{EC}{EA}$. To prove the proportion, we show ΔEBD ∿ ΔECA by the A-A Similarity Theorem.

Given: $\overline{ABE}$ and $\overline{DCE}$ are secant segments of ⊙P. Point E is

exterior to OP.
Prove: EB · EA = EC · ED.

| Statements | Reasons |
|---|---|
| 1. $\overline{ABE}$ and $\overline{DCE}$ are secant segments of OP. Point E is exterior to OP. | 1. Given. |
| 2. $m\sphericalangle BAC = \frac{1}{2}m\overset{\frown}{BC}$  $m\sphericalangle BDC = \frac{1}{2}m\overset{\frown}{BC}$ | 2. The measure of an inscribed angle equals one-half the measure of the subtended arc. |
| 3. $m\sphericalangle BAC = m\sphericalangle BDC$ | 3. Transitivity Postulate. |
| 4. $\sphericalangle BAC \cong \sphericalangle BDC$ | 4. Definition of congruence of angles. |
| 5. $\sphericalangle E \cong \sphericalangle E$ | 5. An angle is congruent to itself. |
| 6. $\triangle EBD \sim \triangle ECA$ | 6. The A-A Similarity Theorem. |
| 7. $\frac{EB}{ED} = \frac{EC}{EA}$ | 7. The sides of similar triangles are proportional. |
| 8. $EB \cdot EA = EC \cdot ED$. | 8. In a proportion, product of the means must equal the product of the extremes. |

● **PROBLEM 7-32**

In the accompanying figure, the length of a radius of circle O is 4. From a point P outside circle O, tangent $\overline{PA}$ is drawn. If the length of $\overline{PA}$ is 3, find the distance from P to the circle.

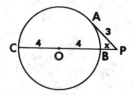

Solution: Let B be the point of intersection of the circle with the segment connecting point P to the center of OO. $\overline{PB}$ is the shortest segment that can be drawn from P to any point on the circle. Therefore, PB is the distance from P to the circle.

Now locate point C such that $\overline{PC}$ intersects the circle at B and C and passes through both O and P.

150

From this, we can determine that $\overline{PC}$ is a secant to circle O and, as such, the tangent $\overline{PA}$ will be, by theorem, the mean proportional between the length of the secant, $\overline{PC}$, and the length of its external segment, $\overline{PB}$. Thus, PC:PA = PA:PB is the proportion.

Diameter CB = 8, since we are given the radius of the circle as 4.

If we let x = the length of $\overline{PB}$, then x + 8 = the length of $\overline{PC}$. By substitution, (x+8):3 = 3:x. As stated in prior examples, the product of the means equals the product of the extremes. Therefore, x(x+8) = 9. By the distributive property, this becomes $x^2$ + 8x = 9 or $x^2$ + 8x - 9 = 0. To solve for x, factor the left side of the equation and set each factor equal to zero. (x-1) and (x+9) are the factors. x-1 = 0 implies x = 1 and x+9 = 0 implies x = -9. The negative value has no geometric significance and is rejected. Therefore, the distance from P to the circle, PB, equals 1.

● **PROBLEM 7-33**

In the accompanying figure, we are given that m$\widehat{AE}$ = 80° and m∡C = 20°. Find the measures of ∡1, ∡2 and $\widehat{BD}$.

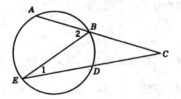

Solution: ∡2 is an inscribed angle which intercepts an arc, $\widehat{AE}$, of 80°. Recall that the measure of an inscribed angle is equal to one-half the measure of its intercepted arc. Hence, ∡2 = 40.

We can derive m$\widehat{BD}$ by noticing that it is intercepted by ∡C. ∡C is formed by the intersection of two secants outside the circle. Recall that an angle formed in this way is equal to one-half the difference of its intercepted arcs. The intercepted arcs of ∡C are $\widehat{AE}$ and $\widehat{BD}$. Therefore, ∡C = $\frac{1}{2}$($\widehat{AE}$ - $\widehat{BD}$). By substituting the given values for ∡C and $\widehat{AE}$, we can solve for m$\widehat{BD}$.

$$20° = \frac{1}{2}(80° - \widehat{BD})$$

$$40° = 80° - \widehat{BD}$$

$$\widehat{BD} = 40°.$$

Since ∡1 is an inscribed angle which intercepts this 40° arc, ∡1 must measure one-half of 40°, or 20°.

Therefore, m∡1 = 20°, m∡2 = 40°, and m$\widehat{BD}$ = 40°.

Line segment $\overline{CD}$ is the diameter of circle O, as seen in the diagram, and $\overline{AD}$ is tangent to the same circle. Given that $\overline{ABC}$ is a straight line, prove that $\triangle ABD$ and $\triangle DBC$ are mutually equiangular.

Solution: To show that two triangles are mutually equiangular, we must prove that all three angles in one triangle are congruent to the corresponding angles of the other triangle. In familiar notation, this states that A.A.A. $\cong$ A.A.A. for mutually equiangular triangles to exist.

The proof will proceed in three stages, each one dealing with a different angle.

| Statement | Reason |
|---|---|
| 1. $\overline{CD}$ is a diameter in circle O. | 1. Given. |
| 2. ∢CBD is a right angle | 2. An angle inscribed in a semi-circle is a right angle. |
| 3. $\overline{ABC}$ is a straight line. | 3. Given. |
| 4. ∢ABD is supplementary to ∢CBD. | 4. If two adjacent angles have their non-common sides lying on a straight line, the angles are supplementary. |
| 5. ∢ABD is a right angle. | 5. The supplement of a right angle is a right angle. |
| 6. ∢CBD ≅ ∢ABD | 6. All right angles are congruent. |
| 7. $\overline{AD}$ is tangent to circle O. | 7. Given. |
| 8. ∢CDA is a right angle. | 8. A tangent to a circle is perpendicular to a radius at the point of contact. |
| 9. ∢ADB is complementary to ∢BDC. | 9. Two angles are complementary if the sum of their measures is 90°. |
| 10. $\triangle BCD$ is a right triangle. | 10. Any triangle that contains a right angle is a right triangle. |

152

| | |
|---|---|
| 11. ∢BCD is complementary to ∢BDC. | 11. The acute angles of a right triangle are complementary. |
| 12. ∢BCD ≅ ∢ADB | 12. If two angles are complements of the same angle, they are congruent. |
| 13. ∢BDC ≅ ∢BAD | 13. If two angles in one triangle are congruent to two angles in another triangle, the third angle in these triangles are congruent. |
| 14. △ABD and △DBC are mutually equiangular. | 14. If three angles in one triangle are congruent to three angles in another triangle, the triangles are mutually equiangular. |

● **PROBLEM** 7-35

In the accompanying figure, △MBC is formed by the intersection of three tangents, two of which, $\overline{MN}$ and $\overline{MP}$, are fixed lines. The third tangent, $\overline{BC}$, is a variable tangent. Prove that no matter where point A lies, the angle, BOC, is constant in measure.

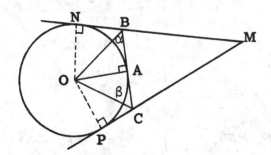

Solution: We wish to show m∢BOC does not change as the tangency point, A, changes. We do this by expressing m∢BOC in terms of m∢M. Since m∢M does not change as point A changes, m<BOC is constant.

Given: ⊙O with fixed tangents $\overline{MN}$ and $\overline{MP}$. The tangent at point A intersects $\overline{MN}$ at B and $\overline{MP}$ at C. Prove: m∢BOC is constant regardless of the position of A.

| Statements | Reasons |
|---|---|
| 1. (See given) | 1. Given. |
| 2. m∢M is constant. | 2. If the sides of an angle are fixed, the angle does not change. |

| | |
|---|---|
| 3. $m\angle M + m\angle MBC + m\angle MCB$ $= 180°$. | 3. The angle sum of a triangle equals 180°. |
| 4. $m\angle MBC + m\angle MCB = 180 - m\angle M$. | 4. Subtraction Property of Equality. |
| 5. $m\angle NBC + m\angle MBC = 180$ $m\angle BCP + m\angle MCB = 180$ | 5. Pairs of angles that form a linear pair sum to 180°. |
| 6. $m\angle NBC + m\angle BCP +$ $m\angle MBC + m\angle MCB = 360$ | 6. Addition Property of Equality. |
| 7. $m\angle NBC + m\angle BCP = 360 -$ $(m\angle MBC + m\angle MCB) = 360$ $- (180 - m\angle M) = 180 +$ $m\angle M$. | 7. The Subtraction Property of Equality. The property that the sum of the interior angles of a triangle equals 180, together with the substitution postulate. |
| 8. $\angle ONB$ is a right angle $\angle OPC$ is a right angle | 8. The intersection of a tangent with a radius at point of tangency forms a right angle. |
| 9. $\overline{OB} \cong \overline{OB}$ | 9. Reflexive property. |
| 10. $\overline{OB}$ is a hypotenuse | 10. A sides of a triangle opposite a right angle is the hypotenuse. |
| 11. $\overline{ON} \cong \overline{OP} \cong \overline{OA}$ | 11. All radii of a circle are equal. |
| 12. $\triangle ONB \cong \triangle OAB$ | 12. The Hypotenuse-Leg Theorem. |
| 13. $\triangle OAC \cong \triangle OPC$ | 13. The Hypotenuse-Leg Theorem. |
| 14. $\angle NBO \cong \angle ABO$ ($\overline{OB}$ bisects $\angle AON$ $\angle NBA$) $\angle OCA \cong \angle OCP$ ($\overline{OC}$ bisects $\angle AOP$ $\angle ACP$) | 14. Corresponding parts of congruent triangles are congruent, and definition of angle bisector. |
| 15. $m\angle NBO = m\angle ABO =$ $\frac{1}{2}m\angle NBC$. $m\angle OCA = m\angle OCP =$ $\frac{1}{2}m\angle BCP$. | 15. The Angle Addition Postulate, |
| 16. $m\angle ABO + m\angle OCA =$ $\frac{1}{2}(m\angle NBC + m\angle BCP) =$ $\frac{1}{2}(180 + m\angle M)$. | 16. Angle Addition Postulate, and Substitution Postulate from step 7. |
| 17. $m\angle BOC + m\angle ABO +$ $m\angle OCA = 180$. | 17. The angle sum of a triangle is 180°. |

| 18. | m⊀BOC + $\frac{1}{2}$(180 + m⊀M) = 180°. | 18. | Substitution Postulate. |
|---|---|---|---|
| 19. | m⊀BOC = 180 - $\frac{1}{2}$(180 + m⊀M) = 90 - $\frac{1}{2}$m⊀M. | 19. | Subtraction Property of Equality. |
| 20. | 90 - $\frac{1}{2}$m⊀M is a constant. | 20. | The subtraction of a constant from a constant is a constant. |
| 21. | m⊀BOC is a constant. | 21. | If a quantity equals a constant, then the quantity is a constant. |

# CYCLIC QUADRILATERALS

● **PROBLEM** 7-36

In the figure below, the measures of angles are as indicated. Are the points B, C, D, and E concyclic? What is m⊀DEB?

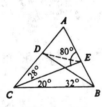

Figure 1

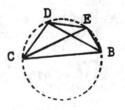

Figure 2

**Solution:** Inscribed angles of the same circle must be congruent if they intercept the same arc. Therefore, if points B, C, D, and E lie on the same circle, the inscribed angles ⊀CDB and ⊀CEB must be congruent. In fact, the reverse is true. If we show that inscribed angles ⊀CDB and ⊀CEB are congruent, B, C, D, and E must be concyclic. (The theorem we use here is usually stated in terms of the quadrilateral determined by the four points. If one side of a quadrilateral subtends congruent angles at the two nonadjacent vertices, then the quadrilateral is cyclic.)

Proof: ⊀CEB is supplementary to ⊀CEA. Therefore

m⊀CEB = 180 - m⊀CEA = 180 - 80 = 100.

In triangle △CDB, m⊀CDB + m⊀DCB = m⊀DBC = 180. Since the measure of the whole is equal to the sum of its parts, m⊀DCB = m⊀DCE + m⊀ECB. Therefore by substitution, m⊀CDB =

155

180 - 28 - 20 - 32 = 100.

m∢CEB = m∢CDB. Therefore, inscribed angles ∢CEB and ∢CDB are congruent, and points B, C, D, and E are concyclic.

To find m∢DEB, we use two facts: (1) B, C, D, and E are concyclic, which means ∢DEB is an inscribed angle. (2) DCB, DE, and EB comprise the entire circle and therefore

(i)   m⌢DCB + m⌢DE + m⌢EB = 360.

Because D̂E is the intercepted arc of inscribed ∢DBE and ∢DCE, it must be true that m⌢DE = 2 · m∢DCE. Since m∢DCE = 28, m⌢DE = 2 · 28 = 56.

Similarly, ÊB is the intercepted arc of inscribed angle ∢ECB and thus m⌢EB = 2 · m∢ECB = 2·20 = 40.

Substituting these results in equation (i), we obtain:

(ii)   m⌢DCB + 56 + 40 = 360

(iii)   m⌢DCB + 360 - 56 - 40 = 264.

Since the unknown, ∢DEB, is the inscribed angle that intercepts D̂CB, then

(iv)   m∢DEB = $\frac{1}{2}$m⌢DCB = $\frac{1}{2}$ · 264 = 132.

A shorter method would have been to note that the opposite angles in an inscribed quadrilateral are supplementary. Therefore,

m∢DEB = 180 - m∢DCB = 180 - (m∢DCE + m∢ECB) = 180 - (20 + 28) = 180 - 48 = 132.

● **PROBLEM** 7-37

Given: Isosceles △DEC with $\overline{DE} \cong \overline{DC}$; $\overline{ADC}$; $\overline{AB}$ intersects $\overline{DE}$ in F; m∢A = 1/2 m∢ABE. Prove: Points A, B, D, and E are concyclic.

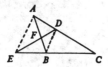

Solution: We show points A, B, D, and E are concyclic by showing quadrilateral ABDE cyclic. Since the vertices of a cyclic quadrilateral lie on a common circle, we will have shown that A, B, D, and E are concyclic.

To show a quadrilateral cyclic, we show that one side of a quadrilateral subtends congruent angles at the two non-

156

adjacent vertices. The side we choose is $\overline{BD}$. The angles we must show congruent are ⦟A (⦟BAD) and ⦟E (⦟BED).

To show ⦟A ≅ ⦟E, we relate the triangles △AFD and △EFB. Note: Since the angle sum of a triangle is 180°, m⦟A + m⦟AFD + m⦟FDA = 180° and m⦟E + m⦟EBF + m⦟EFB = 180°. Thus,

(1)  m⦟A + m⦟AFD + m⦟FDA = m⦟E + m⦟EBF + m⦟EFB. But ⦟AFD and ⦟EFB are opposite angles. Thus, m⦟AFD = m⦟EFB, and we delete them from the equation.

(2)  m⦟A + m⦟FDA = m⦟E + m⦟EBF. We are given that m⦟A = $\frac{1}{2}$m⦟ABE = $\frac{1}{2}$m⦟FBE or m⦟FBE = 2 · m⦟A

(3)  m⦟A + m⦟FDA = m⦟E + 2m⦟A.

We have an equation relating ⦟A, ⦟E, and the unwanted ⦟FDA. We rid ourselves of ⦟FDA by showing m⦟FDA = 2 · m⦟E. Note that ⦟FDA is an exterior angle of △EDC. Its measure equals the sum of remote interior angles ⦟E and ⦟C. But △EDC is isosceles. Thus, ⦟E ≅ ⦟C. Since m⦟FDA = m⦟E + m⦟C, m⦟FDA = 2 · m⦟E. Using this result in (3), we have:

(4)  m⦟A + 2 · m⦟E = m⦟E + 2 · m⦟A

(5)  m⦟A = m⦟E or ⦟A = ⦟E.

Since side $\overline{DB}$ intercepts congruent angles from the non-adjacent vertices, quadrilateral ABDE is cyclic.

| Statements | Reasons |
|---|---|
| 1. (See the problem statement.) | 1. Given. |
| 2. ⦟E ≅ ⦟BCD | 2. The base angles of an isoceles triangle are congruent. |
| 3. m⦟ADE = m⦟E + m⦟DCE = 2 · m⦟E. | 3. The measure of an exterior angle of the triangle equals the sum of the measures of the remote interior angles. |
| 4. m⦟AFD ≅ m⦟EFB. | 4. Opposite angles formed by intersecting lines are congruent. |
| 5. m⦟AFD + m⦟A + m⦟ADF = 180  m⦟E + m⦟EFB + m⦟FBE = 180 | 5. The sum of the angles of a triangle equals 180°. |
| 6. m⦟AFD + m⦟A + 2 · m⦟E = 180  m⦟AFD + m⦟E + 2 · m⦟A = 180. | 6. Substitution Postulate, (Steps 5, 4, 3, and 1). |
| 7. m⦟E - m⦟A = 0. | 7. Subtraction Postulate. |

| 8. | $m\sphericalangle E = m\sphericalangle A$. | 8. | Addition Postulate. |
|---|---|---|---|
| 9. | Quadrilateral ABDE is concyclic. | 9. | If a side of a quadrilateral subtends congruent angles with non-adjacent vertices, then the quadrilateral is cyclic. |
| 10. | A, B, D, and E are concyclic. | 10. | The vertices of cyclic polygons are cyclic (Definition of concyclic polygon.) |

● **PROBLEM** 7-38

Given: $\overline{AB}$ is a diameter of ⊙Q; $\overline{CQ} \perp \overline{AB}$ at Q; $\overline{AC}$ intersects ⊙Q at D; $\overline{BC}$ intersects ⊙Q at F. Prove: Quadrilateral CDQB is cyclic; $\sphericalangle QDB \cong \sphericalangle QCA$.

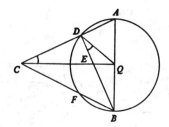

Solution: To show that a quadrilateral is cyclic, we show a side of the quadrilateral subtends congruent angles with the nonadjacent vertices of the quadrilateral.

To prove CDQB cyclic, we must show side QB subtends $\sphericalangle BDQ$ and $\sphericalangle BCQ$ such that $\sphericalangle BDQ \cong \sphericalangle BCQ$. Also, we will have to show $\sphericalangle QDB \cong \sphericalangle QCA$.

| Statements | Reasons |
|---|---|
| 1. AB is a diameter of ⊙Q; $\overline{CQ} \perp \overline{AB}$ at Q; $\overline{AC}$ intersects ⊙Q at D; $\overline{BC}$ intersects ⊙Q at F. | 1. Given. |
| 2. $\overline{DQ} = \overline{QB}$. | 2. All radii of a circle are congruent. |
| 3. $\sphericalangle QDB \cong \sphericalangle QBD$. | 3. If two sides of a triangle are congruent, the angles opposite them are congruent. |
| 4. $\sphericalangle ADB$ is a right angle. | 4. Any angle inscribed in a semicircle is a right angle. |

158

| | |
|---|---|
| 5. ∢DAB and ∢QBD are complementary. | 5. The acute angles of right triangle ADB are complementary. |
| 6. ∢AQC and ∢BQC are right angles. | 6. Perpendicular lines intersect at right angles. |
| 7. ∢ACQ and ∢DAB are complementary. | 7. The acute angles of right triangles △CAQ are complementary. |
| 8. ∢ACQ ≅ ∢QBD. | 8. Angles complementary to congruent angles are congruent. |
| 9. $\overline{CQ} \cong \overline{CQ}$. | 9. A segment is congruent to itself. |
| 10. $\overline{AQ} \cong \overline{QB}$. | 10. The radii of a circle are congruent. |
| 11. ∢AQC ≅ ∢BQC. | 11. All right angles are congruent. |
| 12. △AQC ≅ △BQC. | 12. The SAS Postulate. |
| 13. ∢ACQ ≅ ∢BCQ. | 13. Corresponding parts of congruent triangles are congruent. |
| 14. ∢BCQ ≅ ∢QBD. | 14. Substitution Postulate. (Steps 13, 8). |
| 15. ∢BCQ ≅ ∢QDB. | 15. Substitution Postulate. (Steps 14, 3) |
| 16. Quadrilateral CDQB is cyclic. | 16. If a side of a quadrilateral subtends equal angles with the two nonadjacent vertices, then the quadrilateral is cyclic. |

# CIRCLES INSCRIBED IN POLYGONS

● PROBLEM 7-39

Show that in a quadrilateral circumscribed about a circle, the sum of the lengths of a pair of opposite sides equals the sum of the lengths of the remaining pair of opposite sides.

Solution: In the accompanying figure, quadrilateral AGEC is circumscribed about ⊙O and is tangent to ⊙O at points H, F, D, and B. We are asked to show

159

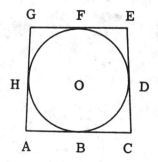

(i)   GE + AC = AG + CE.

We can accomplish this by rewriting each side of the equation in terms of segments such that each segment length on the left side of the equation has a segment equal in length to it on the opposite side.

To find these congruent segments, we use the result that the two tangent segments to a circle from an external point are congruent.  Consider a vertex G and the two segments drawn to the circle, $\overline{GF}$ and $\overline{GH}$.  Since $\overline{GH}$ is tangent to $\odot O$ at H and $\overline{GF}$ is tangent to $\odot O$ at F, $\overline{GF}$ and $\overline{GH}$ are tangent segments drawn from external point G and, thus, $\overline{GF} = \overline{GH}$. If we consider E, C, and A as external points, then we relate the tangent segments by the congruencies $\overline{EF} \cong \overline{ED}$, $\overline{CD} \cong \overline{CB}$, and $\overline{AB} \cong \overline{AH}$.

We can rewrite the equation to be proved in terms of the tangent segments.  Note that GE = GF + FE, AC = AB + BC, GA = GH + HA, and EC = ED + DC.  Substituting these results in (i), we obtain:

(ii)   GF + FE + AB + BC = GH + HA + ED + DC.

Since GF = GH, FE = ED, AH = AB, and CB = CD, the equation holds and, thus, GE + AC = AG + CE.

● **PROBLEM 7-40**

Find the radius of a circle inscribed in a triangle whose sides have lengths 3, 4 and 5.

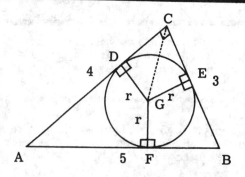

**Solution:** In the accompanying figure, ΔABC circumscribes circle G. AC = 4, BC = 3, and AB = 5. Points D, E, and F are the points of tangency of ⊙G with the sides of ΔABC. We are asked to find GE - the length of the radius of the inscribed circle. We will do this by (1) finding the length of tangent segment, CE, and (2) showing ΔCEG is isosceles with $\overline{GE} \cong$ tangent segment $\overline{CE}$. Thus, the radius, r, will equal CE.

(1) To find the lengths of the tangent segments, we use the theorem which states that, from an external point (such as C), the tangent segments (DC and CE) drawn to the circle (G) are congruent ($\overline{DC} \cong \overline{CE}$). Thus, if we consider C, A, and B respectively as the external point, we obtain:

(i) DC = CE (C is the external point)
(ii) AD = AF (A is the external point)
(iii) BF = BE (B is the external point)

But from the figure, we know that

(iv) AD + DC = AC = 4
(v) CE + EB = CB = 3
(iv) AF + FB = AB = 5.

We have 6 equations with 6 variables. To solve for tangent segment CE, we first eliminate AD, BE, and DC by substituting in equations (iv), (v), and (vi) the values AD = AF, BE = BF, and DC = CE.

(vii) AF + CE = 4
(viii) CE + BF = 3
(ix) AF + FB = 5.

We now have 3 equations in 3 unknowns. Eliminate AF by substituting (ix) in (vii).

(x) CE - FB = 4 - 5 = -1
(xi) CE + FB = 3

We eliminate FB by adding (x) and (xi).

(xii) 2 · CE = 2 or CE = 1.

(2) Thus, we have a value for CE.

To show ΔCEG is isosceles, we will show m∡ECG = m∡EGC = 45°. In order to show m∡ECG = 45°, we prove ∡DCG ≅ ∡ECG. By the Hypotenuse Leg Theorem, ΔDCG ≅ ΔECG, since points D and E are points of tangency, radii $\overline{DG} \perp \overline{DC}$ and $\overline{GE} \perp \overline{CE}$ and, thus, m∡CDG = m∡CEG = 90°. Since $\overline{DG}$ and $\overline{GE}$ are radii, $\overline{DG} \cong \overline{GE}$ and $\overline{CG} \cong \overline{CG}$. Thus, ∡DCG ≅ ∡ECG because they are corresponding angles of congruent triangles. Because a 3-4-5 triangle is a right triangle, ∡ACB is a right angle. Thus, we have

m∡DCG + m∡ECG = m∡ACB.

By substitution, 2·m∡ECG = 90°
m∡ECG = 45°.

161

We will now show m∢CGE also equals 45°. Since m∢ECG = 45° and m∢GEC = 90°, then to find m∢CGE, we have the following:

$$m\angle GCE + m\angle GEC + m\angle CGE = 180°$$
$$45° + 90° + m\angle CGE = 180°$$
$$m\angle CGE = 45°.$$

Since m∢CGE ≅ m∢GCE, ΔCGE is isosceles. Therefore, GE ≅ CE, and r = GE = CE = 1. The radius of the inscribed circle equals 1.

● **PROBLEM** 7-41

Given: ΔABC with sides of length a, b, and c. The inscribed circle, Q, intersects $\overline{AB}$ at D, $\overline{BC}$ at E, and $\overline{CA}$ at F. Find the lengths AD and DB in terms of a, b, and c.

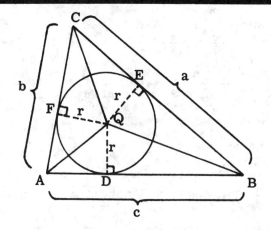

<u>Solution</u>: We are asked to find AD and DB, the lengths of the segments into which the tangency point, D, divides side AB of ΔABC, in terms of the sides of the triangle. We know therefore, that we must (1) use the properties of the inscribed circle Q; and (2) relate segments $\overline{AD}$ and $\overline{DB}$ to the other sides of ΔABC.

Because D, E, and F are the points of tangency, the radii $\overline{QD}$, $\overline{QE}$, and $\overline{QF}$ are all radii to the points of tangency and, therefore, perpendicular to the sides.

Thus, from the fact that ⊙Q is the inscribed circle, we know that (1) QD = QE = QF (because all radii are congruent); and (2) $\overline{QD} \perp \overline{AB}$, $\overline{QE} \perp \overline{CB}$, and $\overline{QF} \perp \overline{AC}$.

We now relate segments $\overline{AD}$ and $\overline{DB}$ to the corresponding sides. Note, from the problem statement, that $\overline{AD}$ and $\overline{DB}$ are segments divided by the point of tangency. We can use the same procedure as we are using now to find AF and FC, or CE and EB. Therefore, it should not be surprising that the expressions for these segments be, in some way, similar to the expressions for AD and DB. Nor should it be unexpected that,

162

when we relate segments AD and DB to side AC, those segments
correspond to segments AF and FC.  In fact, we can relate
segment $\overline{AD}$ to $\overline{AF}$, they are congruent.  Consider $\triangle AQD$ and $\triangle AQF$.
$\overline{QF} = \overline{QD}$ because they are radii of $\odot Q$.  $\measuredangle QFA$ and $\measuredangle QDA$ are
both right angles and therefore congruent.  $\overline{AQ} \cong \overline{AQ}$ is true
by the reflexive property.  Since the hypotenuse and the leg
of right triangle $\triangle AQD$ are congruent to the hypotenuse and
the leg of right triangle $\triangle AQF$, $\triangle AQD \cong \triangle AQF$.  By corresponding parts, $\overline{AD} \cong \overline{AF}$.

In relating segments $\overline{AD}$ and $\overline{DB}$ to side $\overline{CB}$, we note that
$\triangle QDB \cong \triangle QEB$ and, therefore, $\overline{DB} \cong \overline{EB}$.  Segments CF and CE
cannot be related to $\overline{AD}$ and $\overline{DB}$, but they can be related to
each other.  By showing $\triangle QFC \cong \triangle QEC$, we know by corresponding parts that $\overline{CF} \cong \overline{CE}$.

We have (1) used the properties of inscribed circle Q
and (2) related $\overline{AD}$ and $\overline{DB}$ to the sides of $\triangle ABC$.  We collect
our data, and solve for AD and DB.

Because F, E, and D are points on $\overline{AC}$, $\overline{BC}$, and $\overline{AB}$, respectively, we have from the definition of "betweenness"
that:

$$AB = AD + DB$$
$$AC = AF + FC$$
$$BC = BE + EC.$$

From the properties of the inscribed circles we have
shown that

$$\overline{AD} \cong \overline{AF}$$
$$\overline{DB} \cong \overline{EB}$$
$$\overline{FC} \cong \overline{EC}$$

From the given, we know that $BC = a$
$$AC = b$$
$$AB = c.$$

We substitute a, b, c for BC, AC, and AB and substitute
AD, DB, and FC for AF, EB, and EC in the above "betweenness"
equations to obtain the following:

$$c = AD + DB$$
$$b = AD + FC$$
$$a = DB + FC$$

Here, we have three equations in three unknowns.  FC is
a variable for which we do not wish to solve.  Therefore, we
eliminate that variable first.  Since b = AD + FC, FC = b -
AD.  Substituting this result in the equation, we obtain the
following:

$$c = AD + DB$$
$$a = DB + (b-AD) = -AD + DB + b$$

Adding the equations, we eliminate AD.

$$c + a = (AD-AD) + DB + DB + b = 2DB + b$$

163

$$DB = \frac{c + a - b}{2}$$

To solve for AD, remember that c = AD + DB and, therefore, AD = c - DB.

$$AD = c - \frac{c + a - b}{2} = \frac{2c - (c+a-b)}{2} = \frac{c + b - a}{2}$$

Remember the earlier supposition that the expressions would probably be similar? Segment $\overline{DB}$ touches vertex B, and its formula can be written as

$$\frac{\left(\begin{array}{l}\text{sum of the length of the}\\ \text{sides of } \triangle ABC \text{ that touch B}\end{array}\right) - \left(\begin{array}{l}\text{length of the}\\ \text{third side}\end{array}\right)}{2}.$$

The same formula can be written for AD. For any segment that touches an arbitrary vertex X, the formula for the length is

$$\frac{\left(\begin{array}{l}\text{sum of the lengths of}\\ \text{sides that touch x}\end{array}\right) - \left(\begin{array}{l}\text{length of the}\\ \text{third side}\end{array}\right)}{2}$$

● **PROBLEM 7-42**

Find the radius, r, of the inscribed circle of right triangle ABC in terms of leg lengths a and b and hypotenuse length c.

<u>Solution</u>: In the accompanying figure, circle O of radius r is inscribed in right $\triangle ABC$ with AB = c, BC = a, and AC = b. Points P, Q, and S are points of tangency of the circle with the triangle. Point R is the intersection of $\overline{AB}$ and the extension of $\overline{OP}$. g is the length $\overline{OR}$. We must find r in terms of a, b, and c.

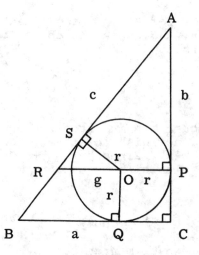

First, we will show $\triangle ARP \sim \triangle ABC$, which will give a relationship involving (known) a, b, and c and (unknown) g and

164

r.   Second, we will show $\triangle$ORS $\sim$ $\triangle$ABC, which will give us a second relationship involving unknown g and r.  With two equations in two unknowns, we can then solve for r in terms of a, b, and c.

To show $\triangle$ARP $\sim$ $\triangle$ABC, we use the A-A Similarity Theorem. Because P is a point of tangency, $\overline{OP} \perp \overline{AC}$ and $\angle$OPA is a right angle.  $\angle$BCA is given to be a right angle.  Thus $\angle$OPA = $\angle$BCA.  $\angle$RAP $\cong$ $\angle$BAC by the reflexive property.  Thus, $\triangle$ARP $\sim$ $\triangle$ABC.  Because corresponding sides of similar triangles are proportional, $\frac{RP}{BC} = \frac{AP}{AC}$.  Note: RP = RO + OP = g + r, BC = a and AC = b.  Furthermore, quadrilateral OPCQ is a parallelogram.  (Since corresponding angles $\angle$BQO and $\angle$BCP are congruent, $\overline{QO} \parallel \overline{PC}$.  Similarly, $\overline{OP} \parallel \overline{QC}$.  Since both pairs of opposite sides are parallel, OPCQ is a parallelogram.)  Opposite sides of a parallelogram are congruent. Thus, QC = OP = r, and PC = OQ = r.  Thus, AP = AC - PC = b - r.  Substituting these values, we obtain the following:

(i)   $\dfrac{g+r}{a} = \dfrac{b-r}{b}$

Crossmultiplying, we obtain

(ii)   gb + rb = ab - ar.

Solving for g, we obtain

(iii)   g = (ab - ar - rb)/b.

Now we find a second relationship by showing $\triangle$ORS $\sim$ $\triangle$ABC.  Note:  S is the point of tangency.  Therefore, the radius $\overline{OS} \perp \overline{AB}$ and $\angle$OSR is a right angle.  Since $\angle$ACB is a right angle, $\angle$OSR $\cong$ $\angle$ACB.  Furthermore, note that OPCQ is a parallelogram and therefore $\overline{OP} \parallel \overline{QC}$.  Since $\overline{RO}$ is an extension of $\overline{OP}$ and $\overline{BC}$ an extension of $\overline{QC}$, $\overline{RO} \parallel \overline{BC}$.  Since corresponding angles of parallel lines are congruent, $\angle$SRO $\cong$ $\angle$CBA.  By the A-A Similarity Theorem, we have $\triangle$ORS $\sim$ $\triangle$ABC. Because corresponding sides of similar triangles are proportional, $\frac{OR}{SO} = \frac{AB}{AC}$.  Note:  OR = g, OS = r, AB = c, and AC = b. Substituting these values in the proportion, we obtain

(iv)   $\dfrac{g}{r} = \dfrac{c}{b}$.

Solving for g, we obtain

(v)   g = $\dfrac{rc}{b}$ .

Now we have two relations involving g and r.  From (iii), we know that g = (ab - ar - rb)/b.  From (v), we know that g also equals $\frac{rc}{b}$.  By equating the two expressions for g, we obtain an expression involving only the unknown, r, and the known, a, b, and c.

(vi)   $\dfrac{rc}{b} = \dfrac{(ab-ar-rb)}{b}$

Solving for r, we obtain

(vii)   rc = ab−ar−rb
(viii)  ra+rb+rc = ab
(ix)    r(a+b+c) = ab
(x)     $r = \dfrac{ab}{a+b+c}$

# CIRCLES CIRCUMSCRIBING POLYGONS

● PROBLEM 7-43

Prove that the sum of the alternate angles of any hexagon in-scribed in a circle is equal to four right angles.

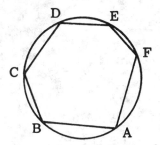

Solution: We see from the figure that each angle is an in-scribed angle of the circle. As such, each angle has a mea-sure equal to $\frac{1}{2}$ the measure of its intercepted arc. If the alternate angles of the hexagon sum to 360°, the measure of four right angles, then we have proved the desired results.

We choose ∢A, ∢E, and ∢C as the alternate angles.

$$m\angle A = \tfrac{1}{2}m\overparen{BCDEF}$$

$$m\angle E = \tfrac{1}{2}m\overparen{FABCD}$$

$$m\angle C = \tfrac{1}{2}m\overparen{DEFAB}$$

Hence, $m\angle A + m\angle E + m\angle C = \tfrac{1}{2}(m\overparen{BCDEF} + m\overparen{FABCD} + m\overparen{DEFAB})$

We now show that these three arcs form two entire cir-cular angles. Note:

$$m\overparen{BCDEF} = m\overparen{BC} + m\overparen{CD} + m\overparen{DE} + m\overparen{EF}$$
$$m\overparen{FABCD} = m\overparen{FA} + m\overparen{AB} + m\overparen{BC} + m\overparen{CD}$$
$$m\overparen{DEFAB} = m\overparen{DE} + m\overparen{EF} + m\overparen{FA} + m\overparen{AB}$$

Adding these three equations, we obtain

166

$$m\overset{\frown}{BCDEF} + m\overset{\frown}{FABCD} + m\overset{\frown}{DEFAB} = (m\overset{\frown}{BC} + m\overset{\frown}{CD} + m\overset{\frown}{DE} + m\overset{\frown}{EF} + m\overset{\frown}{FA} + m\overset{\frown}{AB}) + (m\overset{\frown}{BC} + m\overset{\frown}{CD} + m\overset{\frown}{DE} + m\overset{\frown}{EF} + m\overset{\frown}{FA} + m\overset{\frown}{AB})$$

Note, though, that $m\overset{\frown}{BC} + m\overset{\frown}{CD} + m\overset{\frown}{DE} + m\overset{\frown}{EF} + m\overset{\frown}{FA} + m\overset{\frown}{AB}$ contains the whole circle or 360°. Thus, $m\overset{\frown}{BCDEF} + m\overset{\frown}{FABCD} + m\overset{\frown}{DEFAB} = 2 \cdot 360 = 720$.

In other words, if we start at point B and trace the three arcs in the sum, then we will find that we have made two entire trips around the circle. Therefore, the sum of the arcs is 2(360°) or 720°. By substitution

$$m\angle A + m\angle E + m\angle C = \frac{1}{2}(720) = 360 .$$

With similar reasoning, it can be shown $m\angle B + m\angle F + m\angle D = 360°$. Hence, we conclude that the sum of the alternate angles of a hexagon will always sum to the measure of four right angles.

● **PROBLEM 7-44**

Given: Regular hexagon ABCDEF. Prove: Quadrilateral ABDE is a rectangle.

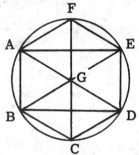

Solution: To show quadrilateral ABDE is a rectangle, we can either show (1) it has four right angles, (2) it is a parallelogram with one right angle, or (3) it is a parallelogram with congruent diagonals. Since there is not any given data concerning right angles, the third method is suggested.

We show ABDE is a parallelogram by showing both pairs of opposite sides are congruent. Then, we show that, since the diagonals of the parallelogram pass through the center of the hexagon, their lengths are both equal to twice the length of the radii of the hexagon and, as such, the diagonals are congruent.

| STATEMENTS | REASONS |
|---|---|
| 1. Regular hexagon ABCDEF | 1. Given. |
| 2. $\overline{AB} \cong \overline{DE} \cong \overline{AF} \cong \overline{FE} \cong \overline{BC} \cong \overline{CD}$ | 2. The sides of a regular polygon are congruent. |

167

| Statements | Reasons |
|---|---|
| 3. $\angle F \cong \angle C$ | 3. The interior angles of a regular polygon are congruent. |
| 4. $\triangle AFE \cong \triangle BCD$ | 4. The SAS Postulate. |
| 5. $\overline{AE} \cong \overline{BD}$ | 5. Corresponding parts of congruent triangles are congruent. |
| 6. Quadrilateral ABDE is a parallelogram | 6. If both pairs of opposite sides of a quadrilateral are congruent, then the quadrilateral is a parallogram. |
| 7. G is the center of ABCDEF | 7. Every regular polygon has a center that is concurrent with the centers of the inscribed and circumscribed circles. |
| 8. $\overline{AG} \cong \overline{BG} \cong \overline{CG} \cong \overline{DG} \cong \overline{EG} \cong \overline{FG}$ | 8. The radii of a regular polygon are congruent. |
| 9. $\triangle AGB \cong \triangle AGF \cong \triangle FGE \cong \triangle EGD \cong \triangle DGC \cong \triangle CGB$ | 9. The SSS Postulate. |
| 10. $\angle AGF \cong \angle FGE \cong \angle EGD \cong \angle DGC \cong \angle CGB \cong \angle BGA$ | 10. Corresponding parts of congruent triangles are congruent. |
| 11. $m\angle AGF + m\angle FGE + m\angle EGD + m\angle DGC + m\angle CGB + m\angle BGA = 360°$ | 11. Angles that form a complete circle sum to 360°. |
| 12. $6 \cdot m\angle AGF = 360°$ | 12. Substitution Postulate. |
| 13. $m\angle AGF = 60°$ | 13. Division Property of Equality. |
| 14. $m\angle AGD = m\angle AGF + m\angle FGE + m\angle EGD$ <br> $m\angle BGE = m\angle BGA + m\angle AGF + m\angle FGE$ | 14. Angle Addition Postulate. |
| 15. $m\angle AGD = 60° + 60° + 60° = 180°$ <br><br> $m\angle BGE = 60° + 60° + 60° = 180°$ | 15. Substitution Postulate. |
| 16. $\angle AGD$ and $\angle BGE$ are straight angles and $\overline{AGD}$ and $\overline{BGE}$ | 16. A straight angle has measure 180°. |
| 17. $AD = AG + DG = 2 \cdot AG$ <br> $BE = BG + EG = 2 \cdot AG$ | 17. Definition of "Betweenness" and Substitution |

| 18. AD = BE | 18. Transitivity Postulate. |
| 19. $\overline{AD} \cong \overline{BE}$ | 19. Definition of congruence of segments. |
| 20. Quadrilateral ABDE is a rectangle | 20. A parallelogram whose diagonals are congruent is a rectangle. |

● **PROBLEM 7-45**

Find the length of an arc intercepted by a side of a regular hexagon inscribed in a circle whose radius is 18 in.

6 sides

Solution:  Since a regular hexagon consists of 6 sides of equal measure, the degree measure of each arc intercepted by a side must equal $\frac{1}{6}$ the total degree measure of the circle, or $\frac{1}{6}(360°) = 60°$.

$$\text{arc length} = \frac{\text{degree measure of arc}}{360°} \times \text{Circumference}$$

The circumference (C) of the circle of radius r is C = 2πr. By substitution, C = 2π(18 in.) = 36π in.  Therefore,

$$\text{arc length} = \frac{60°}{360°}(36\pi)\,\text{in.} = \frac{60}{10}\pi \text{ in} = 6\pi \text{ in.}$$

Using π = 3.14, arc length = 6(3.14 in.) = 18.84 in.  Therefore, the length of the arc intercepted by a side of a regular hexagon in the circle of radius 18 in. is 18.84 in.

● **PROBLEM 7-46**

The product of two sides of a triangle is equal to the product of the altitude to the third side and the diameter of the circumscribed circle. Prove this. (Hint: consider the diameter that passes through the included vertex of the first two sides.)

Solution: In the folowing figure, ⊙ O is circumscribed about ΔABC. $\overline{BD}$ is an altitude. We are asked to show that AB · BC = BE · BD.

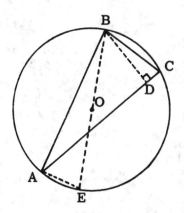

Whenever there are products, proportions are also present; and whenever proportions are present, we are well advised to search for similar triangles. If AB · BC = BE · BD, then, dividing both sides by BE · BC, we obtain, $\frac{AB}{BE} = \frac{BD}{BC}$ . It is sufficient for this proof to prove this proportion.

These are proportions that correspond to ΔABE and ΔDBC. Thus, if we prove that ΔABE ∿ ΔDBC, then the proof is almost complete.
Note that ΔABE is a triangle inscribed in a semicircle (since $\overline{BE}$ is a diameter). Therefore, ΔABE is a right triangle and ∢BAE is a right angle. Since $\overline{BD}$ is an altitude, ∢ BDC is also a right angle and ∢ BAE $\overset{\sim}{=}$ ∢ BDC. Thus, one pair of corresponding angles are congruent. Note also that ∢ AEB and ∢ DCB are inscribed angles that intercept the same arc, $\overset{\frown}{AB}$. Therefore, ∢ AEB $\overset{\sim}{=}$ ∢ DCB. By the A.A. Similarity Theorem, ΔABE ∿ ΔDBC. Since corresponding sides of similar triangles are proportional,

$$\frac{AB}{BE} = \frac{BD}{BC} \quad \text{or AB · BC = BE · BD.}$$

Thus, the product of two sides of a triangle is equal to the product of the altitude on the third side and the diameter of the circumscribed circle.

● **PROBLEM 7-47**

Given: ΔABC is inscribed in ⊙P; $\overline{AD}$ is an altitude of ΔABC; $\overline{APE}$ is a diameter of ⊙P.  Prove:  AB · AC = AD · AE.

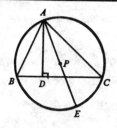

**Solution:**  $AB \cdot AC = AD \cdot AE$ can be rewritten as $\frac{AB}{AD} = \frac{AE}{AC}$. This is a proportion between similar triangles $\triangle ABD$ and $\triangle AEC$. We can show $\triangle ABD \sim \triangle AEC$ by the A-A Similarity Theorem, and thus the proportion holds.

| Statements | Reasons |
|---|---|
| 1. $\triangle ABC$ is inscribed in $\overline{OP}$; $\overline{AD}$ is an altitude of $\triangle ABC$; $\overline{APE}$ is a diameter of $OP$. | 1. Given |
| 2. $m \angle ABC \cong \frac{1}{2}m\widehat{AC}$ <br> $m \angle AEC \cong \frac{1}{2}m\widehat{AC}$ | 2. The measure of an inscribed angle equals one-half the intercepted arc. |
| 3. $m \angle ABC \cong m \angle AEC$ <br> or $\angle ABC \cong \angle AEC$ | 3. Transitivity and Definition of Congruent Angles. |
| 4. $\angle ADB$ is a right angle. | 4. The altitude to a given side is perpendicular to the side |
| 5. $\angle ACE$ is a right angle. | 5. An angle inscribed in a semicircle is a right angle. |
| 6. $\angle ADB \cong \angle ACE$ | 6. All right angles are congruent. |
| 7. $\triangle ABD \sim \triangle AEC$ | 7. The A.A. Similarity Theorem |
| 8. $\frac{AB}{AD} = \frac{AE}{AC}$ | 8. The sides of similar triangles are proportional. |
| 9. $AB \cdot AC = AE \cdot AD$ | 9. The product of the means equals the product of the extremes. |

● **PROBLEM** 7-48

Using Ptolemy's Theorem show that if a and b, with $a \geq b$, are chords of two arcs of a circle of unit radius, then
$d = (a/2)(4-b^2)^{\frac{1}{2}} - (b/2)(4-a^2)^{\frac{1}{2}}$ is the chord of the difference of the two arcs.

**Solution:**  In circle $O$, chord $AC = a$, $AB = b$. DC is a diameter. The difference $\widehat{AC} - \widehat{AB} = \widehat{BC}$. We must find the length of chord $\overline{BC}$. The hint in this problem is to use Ptolemy's Theorem which reads: The product of the diagonals of a cyclic quadrilateral equals the sum of the products of the opposite sides. Thus, we search for some convenient cyclic quadrilateral, each of whose diagonals and sides are known except for $\overline{BC}$. Using Ptolemy's Theorem, BC can then be solved.

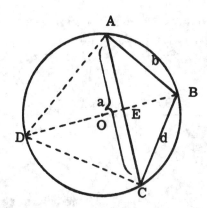

Consider the quadrilateral determined by diameter $\overline{DC}$, cyclic quadrilateral ABCD. Side $\overline{AB}$ has known length b. Diagonal $\overline{AC}$ has known length a. Diagonal $\overline{DB}$ is a diameter and has known length 2 · radius or 2. Furthermore, because DB is a diameter, $\triangle DAB$ and $\triangle DCB$ are triangles inscribed in a semicircle and therefore are right triangles. Side $\overline{DA}$ is thus a leg of right $\triangle DAB$ and can be expressed in terms of known quantities using the Pythagorean Theorem. $DA^2 = DB^2 - AB^2$ or, substituting the given, $DA^2 = 2^2 - b^2$ or $DA = \sqrt{4-b^2}$.

Of the six elements (4 sides, 2 diagonals) used in Ptolemy's Theorem, we have solved for 4, one element is the unknown, and DC is an element that is also unknown but for which we are not solving. We recap our information up to this point:

$$AB = b, \quad AC = a, \quad DB = 2, \quad AD = \sqrt{4-b^2}.$$

(i)  By Ptolemy's Theorem, $DB \times AC = AD \times BC + AB \times DC$.

(ii)  Because of rt. $\triangle DCB$, $DC^2 + BC^2 = DB^2$.

Substituting our known values in (i) and (ii), we obtain:

(iii)  $2 \cdot a = \sqrt{4-b^2} \cdot BC + b \cdot DC$

(iv)  $DC^2 + BC^2 = 4$.

We then solve (iv) for DC in terms of BC. Then we substitute for DC in (iii) to obtain an expression totally in BC: From (iv), we have $DC = \sqrt{4-BC^2}$ .

(v)  $2 \cdot a = \sqrt{4-b^2} \cdot BC + b\sqrt{4-BC^2}$.

We now have an expression for BC, but we have a long algebraic road between (v) and a solution for BC. First, we eliminate all BC's in radicals by subtracting $\sqrt{4-b^2} \cdot BC$ from both sides and squaring.

(vi)  $(2a - \sqrt{4-b^2}BC)^2 = (\sqrt{4-b^2}BC + b\sqrt{4-BC^2} - \sqrt{4-b^2}BC)^2$

(vii)  $(2a - \sqrt{4-b^2} \cdot BC)^2 = (b\sqrt{4-BC^2})^2$

(viii)   $4a^2 - 4a \cdot BC \cdot \sqrt{4-b^2} + 4BC^2 - BC^2 \cdot b^2 = 4b^2 - b^2 BC^2$

Gathering terms on the left side, we have:

(ix)   $4BC^2 - (4a\sqrt{4-b^2})BC + (4a^2 - 4b^2) = 0$

We now divide each side by 4 and use the quadratic formula.

(x)   $BC^2 + (-a\sqrt{4-b^2})BC + (a^2-b^2) = 0.$

$qx^2 + px + r = 0$, $x = \dfrac{-p \pm \sqrt{p^2-4qr}}{2q}$ . In this equation (ix),

$q = 1$; $p = -a\sqrt{4-b^2}$; $r = (a^2-b^2)$.

(xi)   $BC = \dfrac{+a\sqrt{4-b^2} \pm \sqrt{(4a^2-a^2 b^2) - 4(a^2-b^2)}}{2}$

(xii)   $BC = \dfrac{a\sqrt{4-b^2} \pm \sqrt{4b^2 - a^2 b^2}}{2}$

(xiii)   $BC = \dfrac{a}{2}\sqrt{4-b^2} \pm \dfrac{b}{2}\sqrt{4-a^2}$ .

There would seem to be two answers, $BC = \dfrac{a}{2}\sqrt{4-b^2} + \dfrac{b}{2}\sqrt{4-a^2}$ and $BC = \dfrac{a}{2}\sqrt{4-b^2} - \dfrac{b}{2}\sqrt{4-a^2}$. But $\dfrac{a}{2}\sqrt{4-b^2} + \dfrac{b}{2}\sqrt{4-a^2}$ equals the sum of arcs a and b and therefore cannot be their difference. (Consult the previous problem.)  Therefore the difference

$$d = \dfrac{a}{2}\sqrt{4-b^2} - \dfrac{b}{2}\sqrt{4-a^2}.$$

Note:  To see where the extra answer crept in, remember that in step (vi), we squared each side, a procedure that sometimes leads to an extra root in the equation.

# CHAPTER 8

# AREAS OF PLANE REGIONS

## SQUARES AND RECTANGLES

● **PROBLEM 8-1**

Find the area of a square whose perimeter is 20 ft.

**Solution:** The perimeter, p, of a square is given by 4 times the length of one side, s; that is, p = 4s.
But, by substitution,
$$p = 20 \text{ ft.}$$
$$20 \text{ ft.} = 4s$$
$$5 \text{ ft.} = s \quad .$$
The area of a square is given by $s^2$ . Hence, $A = s^2$ and, by substitution,
$$A = (5 \text{ ft.})^2 = 25 \text{ ft.}^2$$
Therefore, the area of the square is 25 sq. ft.

● **PROBLEM 8-2**

A man has a rectangular piece of property measuring 200 x 300 ft. He plans to put a concrete sidewalk 3 ft. wide around the edge. What will the area of the sidewalk be?

**Solution:** We assume that the man puts the sidewalk down as shown in the figure. We must find the area of the shaded region. First, find the area of the figure bounded by the outer border (the large rectangle). Next, find the area of the small rectangle and subtract this from the area of the large rectangle. We will then have the area of the sidewalk.

Area of large rectangle = (206 ft.)(306 ft.)
= 63036 sq. ft.

Area of small rectangle = (300 ft.)(200 ft.)
= 60000 sq. ft.

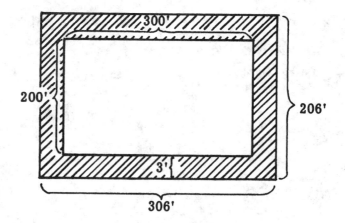

Area of sidewalk     = (63036 - 60000) sq. ft.
                     = 3036 sq. ft.

This is much more efficient than breaking up the sidewalk region into
rectangles, calculating their areas, and summing them up.

● PROBLEM 8-3

A man wishes to put linoleum tile on a rectangular floor which
measures 5 x 7 yd.  If each piece of linoleum tile is a 9 in. square,
how many pieces of tile will be needed?  If a quart of tile adhesive
covers 10 sq. ft., how many quarts will he need?

Solution:     The actual problem is to find out how many tiles (9" per
side) are needed to cover the surface of a rectangle 5 x 7 yd.
     The area of the rectangle (the floor) is made up of the sum of
the areas of the square tiles.  Let us represent the number of tiles
needed by  x.  Then the previous statement may be written, mathematic-
ally, as

$$x(\text{Area of 1 tile}) = \text{Area of floor}. \tag{1}$$

The area of 1 tile is $(9 \text{ in.})^2$ = 81 sq. in., since each tile is a
square.  The area of the floor is (5 yd.)(7 yd.) = 35 sq. yd., since
the floor is rectangular.  Using these results in (1), we obtain

$$x(81 \text{ sq. in.}) = 35 \text{ sq. yd.}$$

Dividing both sides by 81 sq. in.,

$$x = \frac{35 \text{ sq. yd.}}{81 \text{ sq. in.}} \tag{2}$$

Now, we have mixed units in (2),  In order to get a pure number in
(2) (which we must, since the number of tiles (x) is dimensionless)
we must change either sq. yds. to sq. ins., or vice versa.  We take
the former course.

$$1 \text{ sq. yd. } (1 \text{ yd.})^2 = (36 \text{ in.})^2 = 1296 \text{ sq. in.}$$

Using this in (2),

$$x = \frac{(35 \text{ sq. yd.})(1296 \text{ sq. in./sq. yd.})}{(81 \text{ sq. in.})} = 560 \quad.$$

The man will need 560 tiles to cover his floor.
     As for the adhesive, we know that each quart of adhesive covers

10 sq. ft. We must cover the area of the floor, which is, from the above calculations, 35 sq. yd. Since

$$1 \text{ sq. yd.} = (1 \text{ yd.})^2 = (3 \text{ ft.})^2 = 9 \text{ sq. ft.}$$

the floor area is (35)(9) sq. ft. = 315 sq. ft.
The man will therefore need

$$\frac{315}{10} = 31.5 \quad \text{quarts of adhesive.}$$

# TRIANGLES

In right triangle ABC, ∢ C measures 90°, $\overline{AB}$ is of length 20 in., and the length of $\overline{AC}$ is 16 in. Find the area of triangle ABC.

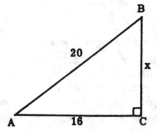

**Solution**: Assume, as in the accompanying figure, that $\overline{AC}$ is the base of triangle ABC. Since ∢ C is a right angle, $\overline{BC}$ is the altitude to the base of the triangle.

The area (A) of a right triangle is given by one-half the product of the length of the base (b) times the length of the corresponding altitude (h). A = ½bh .

We are not given the length of the altitude, but can calculate it by applying the Pythagorean Theorem to ΔABC. If we let x = the length of the altitude, then,

$$x^2 + (16 \text{ in.})^2 = (20 \text{ in.})^2$$
$$x^2 + 256 \text{ in.}^2 = 400 \text{ in.}^2$$
$$x^2 = 144 \text{ in.}^2$$

which implies $\qquad$ x = 12 in.

The area of ΔABC = ½bh. By substitution,

$$\text{area of } \Delta ABC = \tfrac{1}{2}(16 \text{ in.})(12 \text{ in.}) = 96 \text{ in.}^2$$

Therefore, the area of ΔABC is 96 sq. in.

The area of a certain triangle is 52 square feet and the height is 13 feet. What is the measure of the base of the triangle?

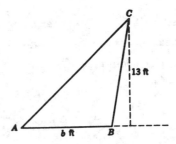

Solution: Recall the formula for the area of a triangle, $A = \frac{1}{2}bh$, where $b$ = length of a base and $h$ = corresponding height of the triangle. Since we wish to find the length of the base, $b$, let us solve the equation for $b$:

$$A = \frac{1}{2}bh$$

$$\frac{2A}{h} = b .$$

We are given that $A$ = 52 sq. ft. and $h$ = 13 ft. Substituting into the above equation we have:

$$\frac{2(52 \text{ ft.}^2)}{13 \text{ ft.}} = b$$

$$8 \text{ ft.} = b .$$

Therefore, the measure of the base of the triangle is 8 feet.

● **PROBLEM 8-6**

Find the length of a side of an equilateral triangle whose area is $4\sqrt{3}$ .

Solution: The area of an equilateral triangle, of side length $s$, is given by the formula

$$\text{Area} = \frac{s^2 \sqrt{3}}{4} .$$

Substituting the given area into this formula, we obtain,

$$4\sqrt{3} = \frac{s^2 \sqrt{3}}{4}$$

$$4 = \frac{s^2}{4}$$

$$16 = s^2$$

$$4 = s .$$

Therefore, the length of the side is 4.

● **PROBLEM 8-7**

Show that the median of any triangle separates the triangle into two regions of equal area.

Solution: The area of a triangle with base length $b_1$ and corresponding height $h_1$ is $\frac{1}{2}b_1 h_1$ . For any triangles with the same base

177

length, $b_1$, and measured height, $h_1$, the expressions for their areas are the same, hence, their areas must be equal. Therefore, to show that two triangles have the same area, it is sufficient to show that their base lengths and their heights are equal.

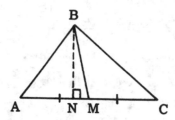

Consider as the base the side of the triangle to which the median is drawn. Then, the base of the triangle is divided into two equal segments by the median. The bases of the two triangular regions created by the median are equal; i.e., $\overline{AM} = \overline{MC}$. The median does not affect the height $\overline{BN}$; both regions have the same height to the bases $\overline{AM}$ and $\overline{MC}$, respectively. Since the two triangular regions have the same height and base length, they have the same area.

Given:    $\overline{BM}$ is a median of $\triangle ABC$.

Prove:    Area of $\triangle ABM$ = Area of $\triangle CBM$.

| Statements | Reasons |
|---|---|
| 1. $\overline{BM}$ is the median of $\triangle ABC$. | 1. Given. |
| 2. M is the midpoint of $\overline{AC}$. | 2. Definition of the median of a triangle. |
| 3. AM = MC. | 3. Definition of the midpoint of a line segment. |
| 4. Locate N in $\overleftrightarrow{AC}$ so that $\overline{BN} \perp \overleftrightarrow{AC}$. | 4. Through a point external to a line, there is one and only one line perpendicular to the given line. |
| 5. $\overline{BN}$ is an altitude of both $\triangle ABM$ and $\triangle CBM$. | 5. Definition of an altitude of a triangle. |
| 6. Area of $\triangle ABM$ = Area of $\triangle CBM$. | 6. Two triangles have equal areas if their bases have the same length and the altitudes to their bases have the same length. |

● **PROBLEM 8-8**

The semiperimeter  s  of a triangle of sides  a, b, and  c  is defined as half the perimeter, or,
$$\frac{a+b+c}{2}.$$
Find an expression for the area of $\triangle ABC$ and show that it is equivalent to  $\sqrt{s(s-a)(s-b)(s-c)}$ .

Solution: The area of a triangle equals $\frac{1}{2}Q \cdot H$ where  Q  is the length of the base and  H  is the altitude. If, in $\triangle ABC$, we choose $\overline{AB}$ as

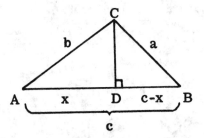

the base, then $Q = AB = c$. Then the altitude $H$ must be $\overline{CD}$, or

$$H = \overline{CD} = \frac{1}{2c} \sqrt{(b+a+c)(b+c-a)(a+c-b)(a+b-c)} \quad.$$

The area, therefore, equals $\frac{1}{2}Q \cdot H$ or

$$\frac{1}{2}(c)\left[\frac{1}{2c} \sqrt{(a+b+c)(b+c-a)(a+c-b)(a+b-c)}\right]$$

or

$$\frac{1}{4} \sqrt{(a+b+c)(b+c-a)(a+c-b)(a+b-c)} \quad.$$

Consider the expression $\sqrt{s(s-a)(s-b)(s-c)}$ :

if $\quad s = \frac{a+b+c}{2}; \; s-a = \frac{a+b+c}{2} - a = \frac{b+c-a}{2} \;$ ;

$s-b = \frac{a+b+c}{2} - b = \frac{a+c-b}{2} \;$ ; and $\quad s-c = \frac{a+b+c}{2} - c = \frac{a+b-c}{2}$ .

Then, $\quad \sqrt{s(s-a)(s-b)(s-c)} = \sqrt{\left(\frac{a+b+c}{2}\right)\left(\frac{b+c-a}{2}\right)\left(\frac{a+c-b}{2}\right)\left(\frac{a+b-c}{2}\right)}$

Factoring out the $\frac{1}{2}$'s, we have

$$\sqrt{\frac{1}{16}(a+b+c)(a+b-c)(a+c-b)(b+c-a)}$$

or

$$\frac{1}{4} \sqrt{(a+b+c)(b+c-a)(a+c-b)(a+b-c)} \quad.$$

Thus, the two expressions we have found are equivalent. Therefore, Heron's Formula, $\sqrt{s(s-a)(s-b)(s-c)}$ is a valid formula for the area of a triangle, if

$$s = \frac{a+b+c}{2}$$

where $a,b,$ and $c$ are the lengths of the sides of the triangle.

● **PROBLEM** 8-9

Show that the ratio of the areas of two similar triangles equals the square of their ratio of similitude.

Solution: Suppose each side of $\Delta 1$ is $a$ times larger than the corresponding sides of $\Delta 2$. Then, Area of $\Delta 2 = \frac{1}{2}b_2 h_2$ and the

area of $\Delta 1 = \frac{1}{2}b_1 h_1$ . Since $b_1 = ab_2$ and $h_1 = ah_2$ ,
area of $\Delta 1 = \frac{1}{2}(ab_2)(ah_2) = a^2(\frac{1}{2}b_2 h_2)$ or $a^2$ times larger
than the area of $\Delta 2$ .

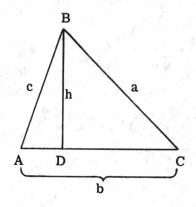
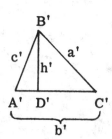

Given: $\Delta ABC \sim \Delta A'B'C'$ ; $\overline{BD}$ and $\overline{B'D'}$ are the altitudes of their respective triangles. The lengths are indicated in the figure.

Prove: $\dfrac{\text{Area of } \Delta ABC}{\text{Area of } \Delta A'B'C'} = \left(\dfrac{b}{b'}\right)^2$ where $\dfrac{b}{b'}$ is the ratio of similitude.

| Statements | Reasons |
|---|---|
| 1. $\Delta ABC \sim \Delta A'B'C'$; $\overline{BD}$ and $\overline{B'D'}$ are the altitudes of their respective triangles. $\angle BDC$ and $\angle B'D'C'$ are right angles. | 1. Given. |
| 2. $\dfrac{a}{a'} = \dfrac{b}{b'}$ | 2. The sides of similar triangles are proportional. |
| 3. Area of $\Delta ABC = \frac{1}{2}bh$ <br> Area of $\Delta A'B'C' = \frac{1}{2}b'h'$ | 3. The area of a triangle of base length b and altitude h equals $\frac{1}{2}bh$. |
| 4. $\dfrac{\text{Area of } \Delta ABC}{\text{Area of } \Delta A'B'C'} = \dfrac{\frac{1}{2}bh}{\frac{1}{2}b'h'} = \dfrac{bh}{b'h'}$ | 4. Multiplicative Property. |
| 5. $\angle BDC \cong \angle B'D'C'$ . | 5. All right angles are congruent. |
| 6. $\angle C \cong \angle C'$ . | 6. Corresponding angles of similar triangles are congruent. |
| 7. $\Delta BDC \sim \Delta B'D'C'$ . | 7. If two pairs of corresponding angles of two triangles are congruent, then the triangles are similar. |
| 8. $\dfrac{a}{a'} = \dfrac{h}{h'}$ . | 8. The sides of similar triangles are proportional. |
| 9. $\dfrac{h}{h'} = \dfrac{b}{b'}$ . | 9. Transitive Property (Step 2). |
| 10. $\dfrac{\text{Area of } \Delta ABC}{\text{Area of } \Delta A'B'C'} = \dfrac{b^2}{(b')^2} = \left(\dfrac{b}{b'}\right)^2$ | 10. Substitution Postulate. |

180

In trapezoid ABCD , as in the accompanying diagram, the larger base, $\overline{AB}$, measures 24 in., the smaller base, $\overline{DC}$, measures 8 in., and the altitude, $\overline{FG}$, measures 6 in.. The nonparallel sides $\overline{AD}$ and $\overline{BC}$ are extended to meet at E.
a)  In triangle DEC: (a) Find EF, the measure of the altitude from E to $\overline{DC}$;
b)  Find the area of  △DEC.

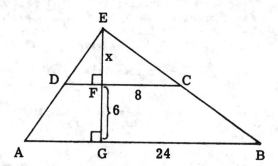

**Solution**:  In the trapezoid ABCD, $\overline{DC} \parallel \overline{AB}$ .  Then, △DEC ∼ △AEB, because a line parallel to one side of a triangle, which intersects the other two sides at different points, creates a triangle similar to the given triangle.  Therefore, by corresponding parts, the proportion

$$\frac{\text{length of altitude } \overline{EF}}{\text{length of altitude } \overline{EG}} = \frac{\text{length of base } \overline{DC}}{\text{length of base } \overline{AB}}$$

is valid.  Let  x = EF, then  x + 6" = EG.  By substitution,

$$\frac{x}{x+6"} = \frac{8"}{24"} = \frac{8}{24} .$$

Since, in a proportion, the product of the means equals the product of the extremes,

$$24x = 8x + 48"$$
$$16x = 48"$$
$$x = 3" .$$

Therefore, the altitude of  △DEC  to  $\overline{DC}, \overline{EF}$, measures 3 in.

b)  The area, A, of  △DEC = ½bh = ½DC × EF .  By substitution,

$$A = \tfrac{1}{2}(8 \text{ in.} \times 3 \text{ in.})^2 = 12 \text{ in.}^2 .$$

Therefore, the area of  △DEC = 12 sq. in.

Let the two congruent sides of an isosceles triangle have lengths a, and let the included angle have measure  θ.  Choosing the third side as a base, let the corresponding altitude be of length  r.  Prove that the area enclosed by the triangle is given by the formula

$$A = r^2 \tan \theta/2 .$$

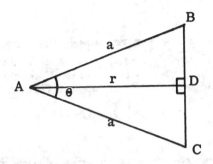

Solution: The figure shows isosceles $\triangle ABC$, with altitude $\overline{AD}$ of length r. By definition of an altitude, $\overline{AD} \perp \overline{BC}$, as indicated. We will use the general formula for the area of a triangle, and "tailor" it to the special properties of an isosceles triangle to prove that $A = r^2 \tan \theta/2$.

The area, A, of any triangle with base length b and corresponding altitude length h is

$$A = \tfrac{1}{2}bh.$$

In the $\triangle ABC$, the length of the base is BC, and the length of the altitude $\overline{AD}$ is r. Hence,

$$A = \tfrac{1}{2}(BC)r .$$

It is now necessary to find BC in terms of the known quantities r and $\theta$. In order to do this, we must digress for a moment.

We note that

$$BC = BD + DC \tag{1}$$

Therefore, if we can find BD and DC, in terms of r and $\theta$, our problem will be solved. We will do this by proving $\triangle ADB \cong \triangle ADC$, and concluding that BD = DC. Finding either BD or DC in terms of r and $\theta$, and using (1), we will have finished the problem.

First, note that $\triangle ABC$ is an isosceles triangle. By definition, this means that AB = AC. Furthermore, AD = AD. Now, the sum of the measures of the angles of any triangle is $180°$. Applying this fact to $\triangle ABD$ and $\triangle ACD$,

$$m \angle BAD + m \angle ADB + m \angle DBA = 180° \tag{2}$$

$$m \angle CAD + m \angle ADC + m \angle DCA = 180° .$$

But $m \angle ADB = m \angle ADC = 90°$, and $m \angle DBA = m \angle DCA$. (The last equality follows from the fact that $\triangle ABC$ is an isosceles triangle.) Using these facts, (2) may be written

$$m \angle BAD + 90° + m \angle DBA = 180° \tag{3}$$

$$m \angle CAD + 90° + m \angle DBA = 180° .$$

Comparing the 2 equations in (3), we conclude that $m \angle BAD = m \angle CAD$, or $\angle BAD \cong \angle CAD$. By the S.A.S. (side-angle-side) Postulate, $\triangle ADB \cong \triangle ADC$. Hence, $\overline{BD} \cong \overline{DC}$ and BD = DC, upon which (1) becomes

$$BC = 2BD . \tag{4}$$

Using (4) in the formula $A = \tfrac{1}{2}(BC)r$ yields

$$A = (BD)r. \tag{5}$$

We may write BD in terms of $\theta$ and r by introducing the concept of the tangent of an angle (abbreviated tan). The tangent of an angle of a right triangle is defined as the ratio of the length of the side of the triangle opposite the angle and the length of the side of the triangle adjacent to the angle, so long as neither of the sides are the hypotenuse. For instance, in the figure,

$$\tan(m \not\angle BAD) = \frac{BD}{DA} = \frac{BD}{r}$$

or

$$BD = r \tan(m \not\angle BAD) \ . \tag{6}$$

Since $m \not\angle BAC = m \not\angle BAD + m \not\angle DAC$, and $\triangle ADB \cong \triangle ADC$, (which means that $m \not\angle BAD = m \not\angle DAC$), we have

$$m \not\angle BAC = 2m \not\angle BAD.$$

But, $m \not\angle BAC = \theta$,

$$\theta = 2m \not\angle BAD$$

or

$$m \not\angle BAD = \theta/2 \ . \tag{7}$$

Using (7) in (6),

$$BD = r \tan \theta/2 \ .$$

Inserting this in (5) yields

$$A = r^2 \tan \theta/2 \ .$$

This is a formula for the area of $\triangle ABC$ in terms of $r$ and $\theta$, as defined by the figure.

# PARALLELOGRAMS

● **PROBLEM 8-12**

The lengths of two consecutive sides of a parallelogram are 10 inches and 15 inches, and these sides include an angle of $63°$. (As shown in the figure). a) Find, to the nearest tenth of an inch, the length of the altitude drawn to the longer side of the parallelogram. b) Find, to the nearest square inch, the area of the parallelogram.

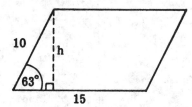

**Solution:** Let $h$ = the length of the altitude.

a) When the altitude is drawn, a right triangle is formed (see figure). We know an acute angle, the length of the hypotenuse, and we wish to determine the length of the leg opposite the given angle. Therefore, we can apply the sine ratio:

$$\sin 63° = \frac{h}{10}$$

and, according to a standard sine table, $\sin 63° = 0.8910$. By substitution, $0.8910 = \frac{h}{10}$ in.

$$h = 8.910 \text{ in.}$$

Therefore, the altitude is 8.9 in., to the nearest tenth of an inch.

b) The area of a parallelogram, A, equals the product of the lengths of the base (b) and altitude (h). A = bh. By substituting,

$$b = 15 \text{ in. and } h = 8.9 \text{ in.}$$

$$A = (15)(8.9) \text{ in.}^2 = 133.5 \text{ in.}^2$$

Therefore, the area equals 134 sq. in., to the nearest square inch.

In parallelogram ABCD, M is the midpoint of side $\overline{DC}$, as shown in the figure. Line segment $\overline{AM}$, when extended, intersects $\overleftrightarrow{BC}$ at K.

a)  Prove that triangle ADM is congruent to triangle KCM.
b)  Prove that triangle AKB is equal in area to parallelogram ABCD.

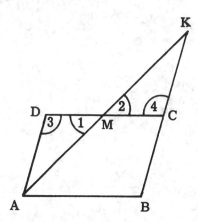

Solution:  a)  In this proof, we will prove congruence of the two triangles by the A.S.A. ≅ A.S.A. method.

| Statements | Reasons |
|---|---|
| 1. ABCD is a ▱ | 1. Given. |
| 2. $\overleftrightarrow{KA}$ and $\overleftrightarrow{KB}$ are straight lines | 2. Given. |
| 3. ∡ 1 ≅ ∡ 2 | 3. If two angles are vertical angles then they are congruent. |
| 4. $\overline{AD} \parallel \overline{BC}$. | 4. The opposite sides of a parallelogram are parallel. |
| 5. ∡ 3 ≅ ∡ 4 | 5. If two parallel lines are cut by a transversal, then the alternate interior angles are congruent. |
| 6. $\overline{DM} \cong \overline{CM}$ | 6. A midpoint divides a line into two congruent segments. |
| 7. △ADM ≅ △KCM. | 7. A.S.A. ≅ A.S.A. |

b)  To prove that the area of △AKB is equal to the area of ▱ABCD, we must show that the sum of the areas of quadrilateral ABCM and △KCM is equal to the sum of the areas of quadrilateral ABCM and △ADM. The first sum is precisely the area of △AKB; the second sum is the area of ▱ABCD.

| Statements | Reasons |
|---|---|
| 1. △KCM ≅ △ADM. | 1. Proved in part (a). |
| 2. Area of △KCM = Area of △ADM. | 2. If two triangles are congruent, then they are equal in area. |
| 3. Area of ABCM = Area of ABCM. | 3. Reflexive Property of Equality. |
| 4. Area of △KCM + Area of ABCM = Area of △ADM + Area of ABCM. | 4. Equal quantities added to equal quantities sum to equal quantities (see step (2)). |
| 5. Area of △KCM + Area of ABCM = Area of △AKB and Area of △ADM + Area of ABCM = Area of ▱ABCD. | 5. If a polygon which encloses a region is separated into several polygons which do not overlap, |

then its area is the sum of the
areas of these several polygons.
(Area-Addition Postulate).

6. Area of $\triangle$AKB = Area of $\square$ABCD.   6. Substitution Postulate.

● **PROBLEM 8-14**

Find the area of a rhombus, each of whose sides is 10 in., and one of whose diagonals is 16 in.

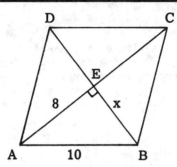

**Solution:** Since the area of a rhombus is equal to one-half the product of the lengths of the diagonals, we must determine the length of the second diagonal before the area can be calculated. (It has been represented in the accompanying figure).

Since the diagonals of a rhombus bisect each other at right angles, we can conclude that $\overline{AE} \perp \overline{BD}$, and that AE = EC = ½AC. $\overline{AC}$ is assumed to be the given 16 in. diagonal. Therefore,

$$AE = \tfrac{1}{2}(16 \text{ in.}) = 8 \text{ in.}$$

Because $\triangle$AEB is a right triangle we can apply the Pythagorean Theorem to determine the length of half-diagonal $\overline{EB}$. Let x = EB. Then,

$$x^2 + (8 \text{ in.})^2 = (10 \text{ in.})^2$$
$$x^2 + 64 \text{ in.}^2 = 100 \text{ in.}^2$$
$$x^2 = 36 \text{ in.}^2$$
$$x = 6 \text{ in.}$$

Therefore, the whole diagonal $\overline{BD}$ measures twice EB or BD = 2EB = 2(6 in.) = 12 in.

Area of a rhombus = ½$d_1 d_2$, where $d_1$ and $d_2$ are the lengths of the rhombus diagonals. By substitution,

$$\text{Area} = \tfrac{1}{2}(12)(16)\text{in.}^2$$
$$= 6(16)\text{in.}^2 = 96 \text{ in.}^2$$

Therefore, the area of rhombus ABCD = 96 sq. in.

● **PROBLEM 8-15**

In the accompanying figure, $\overline{AB}$ and $\overline{DC}$ are the bases of trapezoid ABCD. Diagonals $\overline{AC}$ and $\overline{BD}$ intersect in E. Prove that triangle ADE is equal in area to triangle BCE.

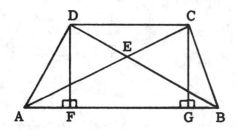

**Solution**: The purpose of this proof is to show that the area of △ADB is equal to the area of △ACB. We will then prove that the difference between the areas of △ADB and △AEB (which is the area of △ADE), is equal to the difference between the areas of △BCA and △AEB (which is the area of △BCE.)

We will construct the altitudes of △ADB and △BCA and prove equality of the two areas by showing that two triangles having congruent bases and altitudes are equivalent.

This is derived from the formula for the area of a triangle, A = ½bh, where b and h are the base length and height, respectively.

| Statements | Reasons |
|---|---|
| 1. Draw $\overline{DF} \perp \overline{AB}$ and $\overline{CG} \perp \overline{AB}$. | 1. An altitude may be drawn to a side of a triangle. |
| 2. $\overline{AB}$ and $\overline{DC}$ are bases of trapezoid ABCD. | 2. Given. |
| 3. $\overline{DC} \parallel \overline{AB}$ . | 3. The bases of a trapezoid are parallel. |
| 4. DF = CG or $\overline{DF} \cong \overline{CG}$ . | 4. Parallel lines are everywhere equidistant. |
| 5. $\overline{AB} \cong \overline{AB}$ . | 5. Reflexive Property of Congruence. |
| 6. Area of △ADB = area of △BCA . | 6. Two triangles which have congruent bases and congruent altitudes are equal in area. |
| 7. Area of △AEB = area of △AEB. | 7. Reflexive Property of Equality. |
| 8. Area of △ADB - area of △AEB = area of △BCA - area of △AEB | 8. Equal quantities subtracted from equal quantities yield equal differences. |
| 9. Area of △ADB - area of △AEB = area of △ADE and, Area of △BCA - area of △AEB = area of △BCE. | 9. Area-addition postulate: If a polygon is made up of several non-overlapping polygons, then the area of any one of the composite polygons is equal to the area of the larger polygon minus the sum of the areas of the remaining composite polygons. (See figure.) |
| 10. Area of △ADE = area of △CEB. | 10. Substitution Postulate. |

● **PROBLEM 8-16**

In isosceles trapezoid ABCD , $\overline{CF}$ and $\overline{DE}$ are altitudes drawn to base $\overline{AB}$, and the measure of ∢ B is 60° (as shown in the figure). If CD exceeds AD by 5 and the perimeter of ABCD is 110, find, in radical form, the area of the trapezoid.

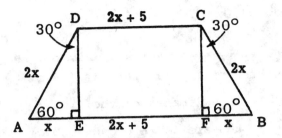

<u>Solution</u>: To find the area, we must first determine the length of both bases and the length of the altitude of trapezoid ABCD.

Triangle AED is a right triangle; and since m $\not\angle$ DAE = $60^\circ$, then the m $\not\angle$ ADE = $30^\circ$.

In a 30-60-90 triangle, the length of the side opposite the $30^\circ$ angle equals ½ the length of the hypotenuse.

Therefore, AD = 2AE . Let AE = x. Then, AD = 2x. We are told that $\overline{CD}$ exceeds $\overline{AD}$ by 5. Therefore, CD = 2x + 5.

Since DCFE is a rectangle, EF = CD = 2x + 5.

Because ABCD is isosceles, $\triangle DAE \cong \triangle CBF$, by A.S.A. $\cong$ A.S.A.

(AD = BC = 2x; m $\not\angle$ ADE = m $\not\angle$ BCF = $30^\circ$; and m $\not\angle$ DAE = m $\not\angle$ CBF = $60^\circ$.)

By corresponding parts, AE = FB = x.

Referring to the diagram, we see that $\overline{AE} + \overline{EF} + \overline{FB} + \overline{BC} + \overline{CD} + \overline{DA}$ = perimeter of ABCD. By substitution,

$$x + (2x+5) + x + 2x + (2x+5) + 2x = 110$$
$$10x + 10 = 110$$
$$10x = 100$$
$$x = 10 .$$

Therefore, the length of base $\overline{CD}$ = 2(10) + 5, or 25. The length of base $\overline{AB}$ = 10 + (2(10) + 5) + 10 = 45.

To calculate the altitude DE of trapezoid ABCD we apply the Pythagorean Theorem to right triangle AED. Let h = length of altitude $\overline{DE}$ .

We have found that AD = 20 and AE = 10. By substitution,

$$(20)^2 = h^2 + (10)^2$$
$$400 = h^2 + 100$$
$$h^2 = 300$$
$$h = \sqrt{300} = \sqrt{100}\sqrt{3} = 10\sqrt{3} .$$

Therefore, since the area of a trapezoid = ½h(b+b'), by plugging in the values we have determined, we obtain

$$A = \tfrac{1}{2}(10\sqrt{3})(25+45)$$
$$= \tfrac{1}{2}(10\sqrt{3})(70)$$
$$= 35(10\sqrt{3})$$
$$= 350\sqrt{3} .$$

Therefore, the area of the trapezoid is $350\sqrt{3}$ .

# AREA OF A CIRCLE

The circumference of a tree trunk is 6.6 ft.

    a) What is the diameter of the trunk?

    b) What is the area of a cross-section of the tree trunk?

Solution: To a first approximation, we may assume that the tree trunk is cylindrical, and that its cross-section is circular.

    a) The circumference, C, of a circle of diameter, d, is

$$C = \pi d.$$

In our case, we want d and we know C. Hence,

$$d = \frac{C}{\pi} = \frac{6.6}{3.14} \text{ ft.} = 2.10 \text{ ft.}$$

    b) The area, A, of a circle of radius, r, is

$$A = \pi r^2 \tag{1}$$

Since 2r = d, where d is the circle's diameter, we may rewrite (1) as

$$A = \pi (d/2)^2 = \frac{\pi d^2}{4}$$

Using the value of d found in part (a), we have

$$A = \frac{(3.14)}{(4)} (2.10 \text{ ft})^2$$

$$A = 3.46 \text{ ft.}^2$$

Find the area of a circle of radius 4. What is the area of the sector subtended by a central angle of $45°$ .

Solution: The area of the circle is $\pi r^2$ . Therefore, for a circle of radius 4, the area is $\pi(4)^2 = 16\pi$ .

The area of a sector with radius r and a central angle of measure n equals

$$\frac{n}{360} \cdot \pi r^2 .$$

In this case, n = $45°$ and area equals $\frac{45}{360} \cdot \pi(4)^2 = \frac{1}{8} \cdot \pi 16 = 2\pi$ .

In a circle whose radius is 12, find the area of a minor segment whose arc has a central angle of 60°. [Leave the answer in terms of π, and in radical form.]

**Solution**: A segment of a circle is the union of an arc of the circle, its chord and the region bounded by the arc and the chord. While there is no formula for the area of a segment, a general rule that can be applied is to subtract the area of the triangle formed by the rays of the central angle and chord of the arc from the area of the sector bounded by the rays of the central angle and the arc. In the accompanying figure, Area of segment ASB = Area of sector OASB
- area of triangle AOB.

$$\text{Area of sector } OASB = \frac{\text{measure of central angle}}{360°} \times \pi r^2 ,$$

where r is the radius of the circle O. By substitution,

$$\text{Area of sector } OASB = \frac{60°}{360°} \times \pi(12)^2 = \frac{1}{6}(144)\pi = 24\pi .$$

Since $\overline{OA}$ and $\overline{OB}$ are radii of a circle, $\overline{OA} \cong \overline{OB}$, and, since the angle included between them is given to be 60°, △AOB is equilateral. As such, its area equals $\frac{s^2}{4}\sqrt{3}$, where s is the length of 1 side of the △. We are told s = 12 and, by substitution,

$$\text{Area of } \triangle AOB = \frac{(12)^2}{4}\sqrt{3} = \frac{144}{4}\sqrt{3} = 36\sqrt{3} .$$

Therefore,

Area of segment ASB = Area of sector OASB - Area of triangle AOB

$$= 24\pi - 36\sqrt{3} .$$

Therefore, Area of segment ASB = $24\pi - 36\sqrt{3}$ .

The ratio of the area of two circles is 16:1. If the diameter of the smaller circle is 3, find the diameter of the larger circle.

**Solution**: The area of a circle equals $\pi r^2$ and, from this, we can conclude the ratio of areas is equal to the square of the ratio of radii length. However, we know that r = ½d, where d = diameter, therefore, by substitution,

$$A = \pi(\tfrac{1}{2}d)^2 = \tfrac{1}{4}\pi d^2 .$$

This shows the ratio of any two areas will be equal to the square of the ratio of the diameters. Let A/A' = the ratio of areas. Also, d' = the smaller diameter, and d = the larger diameter. Then,

$$\frac{A}{A'} = \left(\frac{d}{d'}\right)^2 .$$

By substitution,

$$\frac{16}{1} = \left(\frac{d}{3}\right)^2$$

$$\frac{16}{1} = \frac{d^2}{9}$$

$$144 = d^2 \implies d = 12 .$$

Therefore, the diameter of the larger circle is 12.

● **PROBLEM 8-21**

Given:   P is a point on $\overarc{AB}$ of circle Q, so that $\overarc{AP} \cong \overarc{BP}$; $\overarc{ANB}$ is an arc of circle P; $\overline{AQB}$ .

Prove:   The area of the shaded region = $(PQ)^2$ .

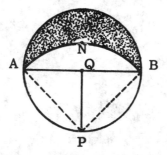

Solution: To find the area of any irregular region, look for areas that can be calculated and that either sum or form, by their difference, the desired region. Here, the shaded region is the difference of semi-circle Q minus the region ANBQ. The area of semicircle Q can be found with the formula $\frac{1}{2}\pi r^2$ . The region ANBQ is the difference of sector PANB and △APB. Therefore, the area of region ANBQ equals the area of the sector PANB minus the area of △APB.

| Statements | Reasons |
|---|---|
| 1. P is a point on $\overarc{AB}$ of circle Q, so that $\overarc{AP} \cong \overarc{BP}$; $\overarc{ANB}$ is an arc of circle P; $\overline{AQB}$ . | 1. Given. |
| 2. AB is a diameter. | 2. Any chord that passes through the center of the circle is a diameter. |
| 3. m $\angle$ AQB = 180° . | 3. The measure of a straight angle is 180° . |
| 4. $\angle$ AQP $\cong$ $\angle$ PQB . | 4. Central angles that intercept congruent arcs are congruent. |
| 5. m $\angle$ AQP + m $\angle$ PQB = m $\angle$ AQB. | 5. Angle Addition Postulate. |
| 6. 2m $\angle$ AQP = 180 or m $\angle$ AQP = m $\angle$ PQB = 90° . | 6. Substitution Postulate. |
| 7. AQ = QB = PQ . | 7. All radii are congruent. |

190

8. $PB^2 = BQ^2 + PQ^2 = 2 \cdot PQ^2$ .

8. Pythagorean Theorem and Substitution Postulate.

9. $\triangle APB$ is a right triangle.

9. Any triangle inscribed in a semi-circle with the diameter as a side is a right triangle, with the hypotenuse being the diameter.

10. $\angle APB$ is a right angle.

10. Definition of right triangle.

11. Area of sector PANB = $\dfrac{90}{360} \cdot \pi \cdot PB^2$ .

11. The area of a sector with radius r and central angle n is $\dfrac{n}{360} \cdot \pi r^2$ .

12. Area of sector PANB = $\frac{1}{4} \pi (2PQ^2) = \frac{1}{2} \pi\, PQ^2$ .

12. Substitution Postulate and Step 8.

13. Area of $\triangle APB = \frac{1}{2} AB \cdot QP$ .

13. The area of a triangle with base b and altitude h is $\frac{1}{2}bh$ .

14. Area of $\triangle APB = \frac{1}{2} PQ \cdot (2PQ)$
    $= (PQ)^2$ .

14. Substitution Postulate.

15. Area of region ANBQ = (Area of sector PANB) - (Area of $\triangle APB$) = $\frac{1}{2}\pi PQ^2 - PQ^2$ .

15. The area of non-overlapping regions is the sum of the areas of each region. Also, Substitution Postulate.

16. Area of semicircle with diameter $\overline{AQB} = \frac{1}{2}\pi (AQ)^2$ .

16. Area of a semicircle of radius r equals $\frac{1}{2}\pi r^2$ .

17. Area of shaded area = (Area of semicircle $\overline{AQB}$) - (Area of region ANBQ).

17. The area of non-overlapping regions is the sum of the areas of each region.

18. Area of shaded region = $\frac{1}{2}\pi(AQ)^2 - (\frac{1}{2}\pi PQ^2 - PQ^2)$ .

18. Substitution Postulate.

19. $(\frac{1}{2}\pi - \frac{1}{2}\pi + 1)PQ^2 = PQ^2$ .

19. Substitution Postulate and Factoring.

● **PROBLEM** 8-22

A farmer is cutting a field of oats with a machine which takes a 5 ft. cut. The field he is cutting is circular and when he has been round it 11½ times (starting from the perimeter) he calculates that he has cut half the area of the field. How large is the field? (Answer to the nearest 100 sq. yds.)

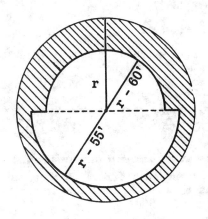

191

<u>Solution</u>: In the accompanying figure, the shaded area is the area already cut; r is the radius of the field. Originally the entire field was uncut and the uncut area was a circle of radius r. The first trip around, he reduces the uncut area from a circle of radius r to a circle of radius r - 5. On the nth trip, he reduces the uncut area from a circle of radius r - 5(n-1) to a circle of radius r - 5n. Thus, on the 11th trip, the uncut area is a circle of radius r - 55. Because the farmer made 11 and ½ trips, the uncut area consists of a semicircle of radius r - 55 and a semicircle of radius r - 60.

We are given that the area of the uncut portion equals the area of the cut portion. Thus, the area of the unplowed area is one-half the area of the field. The area of the uncut portion is the sum of the areas of the semicircle of radius r - 55 and the area of semicircle of radius r - 60. Given that the formula of the semicircle of radius x is $\frac{1}{2}\pi x^2$ , we have

(i) area of semicircle of r - 55 = $\frac{1}{2}\pi(r-55)^2$

(ii) area of semicircle of r - 60 = $\frac{1}{2}\pi(r-60)^2$

(iii) area of unplowed area = $\frac{1}{2}\pi(r-55)^2 + \frac{1}{2}\pi(r-60)^2$

$$= \tfrac{1}{2}\pi((r-55)^2 + (r-60)^2)$$

(vi) area of field = 2 · area of unplowed area.

(v) $\pi r^2 = 2 \cdot \frac{1}{2}\pi((r-55)^2 + (r-60)^2)$

(vi) $r^2 = r^2 - 110r + 3025 + r^2 - 120r + 3600$

(vii) $r^2 - 230r + 6625 = 0$

Using the quadratic formula,

$$ax^2 + bx + c = 0, \quad x = \frac{-b \pm \sqrt{b^2 - 4ac}}{2a} \quad ,$$

we obtain for the radius of the field,

(viii) $r = \dfrac{230 \pm \sqrt{230^2 - 4(6625)}}{2} = \dfrac{230 \pm \sqrt{26400}}{2}$

(ix) $r = \dfrac{230 \pm 162.48}{2}$ = 196.24 or 33.76.

Note that the answer r = 33.76 makes no sense since this would imply that the radius of the unplowed portion would be r = 33.76 - 55 = -21.24. Thus, r = 196.24 ≈ 196 ft. is the only solution.

To find the area of the circular field, remember that the area of the circle is $\pi r^2$ .

(x) Area of field = $\pi(196)^2 = 38416\pi$

$38416\,\pi \approx 120687$ sq. ft.

Since 1 sq. ft. = $\frac{1}{9}$ sq. yd.,

(xi) Area of field = $120687(\frac{1}{9}$ sq. yd.) = 13,400 sq. yd.

# AREA BY THE PYTHAGOREAN THEOREM

• **PROBLEM** 8-23

A rectangle is inscribed in a circle whose radius is 5 inches. The base of the rectangle is 8 inches. Find the area of the rectangle. (See figure.)

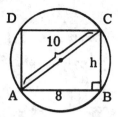

**Solution:** The diagonal of the rectangle is a diameter of the circle and as such, each of the two triangles shown in the figure is inscribed in a semi-circle. Therefore, they are right triangles.

Since $\triangle BAC$ is a right triangle, we can use the Pythagorean Theorem to determine the altitude, h, of ABCD, as indicated in the figure. We will need this to calculate the area of the rectangle. Therefore,

$$h^2 + (8 \text{ in.})^2 = (10 \text{ in.})^2$$
$$h^2 + 64 \text{ in.}^2 = 100 \text{ in.}^2$$
$$h^2 = 36 \text{ in.}^2 \quad \text{and}$$
$$h = 6 \text{ in.}$$

Now, Area = bh. Let b = 8 in., h = 6 in. By substitution,

$$A = (8 \times 6) \text{ in.}^2 = 48 \text{ in.}^2$$

Therefore, the area of the inscribed rectangle is 48 sq. in.

● **PROBLEM 8-24**

Find, in terms of $\pi$, the area of the shaded region in the diagram.

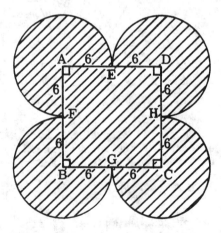

**Solution:** The shaded region consists of square ABCD, whose side is 12, and four major sectors whose areas are equal because their radii and central angles are equal. We will calculate the area of the square and the major sectors, and then sum them, to determine the area of the shaded region.

$$\text{Area of the square} = (AB)^2 = (12)^2 = 144.$$

Each sector spans $270°$, since the corners of the square cut off arc lengths that measure $90°$ from each circle. Since the area of a sector is proportional to the central angle, the area of each sector is

$$\frac{270°}{360°} ,$$

or  3/4 of the area of each entire circle.

$$\text{Area of each sector} = \frac{3}{4} \pi r^2$$

$$= \frac{3}{4} \pi (6)^2$$

$$= \frac{3}{4} (36\pi)$$

$$= 27\pi.$$

Area of shaded region = area of square + area of 4 sectors

$$= 144 + 4 (27\pi)$$

$$= 144 + 108 \pi$$

Therefore, area of shaded region = 144 + 108π.

Find the area of a circle inscribed in a rhombus whose perimeter is 100 in. and whose longer diagonal is 40 in.

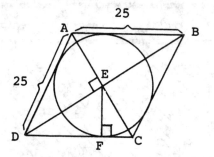

25

25

**Solution**:  In the accompanying figure, rhombus ABCD circumscribes circle E.  DB, the length of the longer diagonal, equals 40.  Since all four sides of a rhombus are congruent and the perimeter equals 100, then

$$AD = DC = CB = AB = \frac{100}{4} = 25.$$

To find the area of  ⊙E, we must first find the radius.  To find the radius, we (1) show point  E, the center of the circle is the intersection of the diagonals and thus  $\overline{EF}$  is a radius of  ⊙E;

(2) Show  ΔDEC  is a right triangle;
(3) We take advantage of the proportions involving the altitude of a right triangle to find  EF, since  $\overline{EF}$  is the altitude drawn to the hypotenuse.

To show point  E  is the intersection of the diagonals, we recall that  E, the center of the circle, is equidistant from all four sides. Consider the intersection of the diagonals  E .  In a rhombus, the diagonals bisect the angles of the rhombus.  Therefore,  E   is on the

angle bisector of each vertex angle. Because E is on the bisector
of ∢ DAB, E is equidistant from sides $\overline{AD}$ and $\overline{AB}$. Because E
is on the bisector of ∢ ABC, E is equidistant from sides $\overline{AB}$ and
$\overline{BC}$. Because E is on the bisector of ∢ BCD, E is equidistant
from sides $\overline{BC}$ and $\overline{DC}$. Combining these three facts and using the
transitive property, we have that E is equidistant from all four
sides. Therefore, E, the center of the inscribed circle, is the same
point as E , the intersection of the diagonals.

To show the second step, that △DEC is a right triangle, we
remember that the diagonals of a rhombus are perpendicular to each
other. Therefore, ∢ DEC is a right angle and △DEC is a right triangle.

In right △DEC, we have the length of the hypotenuse, DC = 25.
Because the diagonals of a parallelogram bisect each other, we have
that the measure of the leg DE = ½DB = ½(40) = 20. By the Pythagorean Theorem,
$$EC^2 = DC^2 - DE^2 = 25^2 - 20^2 = 225;$$
or
$$EC = 15.$$

We wish to find the radius EF. EF, as the altitude to the hypotenuse, is the mean proportional of the hypotenuse segments, DF
and FC. To find DF and FC, remember that the adjacent leg is the
mean proportional of the segment and the hypotenuse. Thus,
$$\frac{DF}{DE} = \frac{DE}{DC} \quad \text{or} \quad DF = \frac{DE^2}{DC} = \frac{20^2}{25} = 16.$$

Then, DF = 16 and FC = DC - DF = 25 - 16 = 9.

Since altitude $\overline{EF}$ is the mean proportional of the base segments,
we obtain
$$\frac{DF}{EF} = \frac{EF}{FC} \quad \text{or} \quad EF^2 = DF \cdot FC = 16 \cdot 9 = 144.$$

Then EF = $\sqrt{144}$ = 12.

Since the radius of the inscribed circle, EF, equals 12, the area
of the circle = $\pi r^2 = \pi(12)^2 = 144\pi$ .

● **PROBLEM 8-26**

A circle is inscribed in an equilateral triangle, whose side is
12. Find, to the nearest integer, the difference between the area of
the triangle and the area of the circle. (Use π = 3.14 and $\sqrt{3}$ =
1.73.)

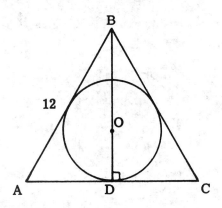

Solution:   By determining the area of the triangle, and then subtracting the area of the inner circle, the required area can be found.

$\triangle ABC$   is an equilateral triangle and its area is equal to

$$\frac{s^2}{4}\sqrt{3}\ ,$$

where   s   is the length of a side of the triangle.   Therefore, the area of

$$\triangle ABC = \frac{s^2}{4}\sqrt{3} = \frac{(12)^2}{4}\sqrt{3} = 36\sqrt{3}\ .$$

Using   $\sqrt{3} = 1.73$, area of

$$\triangle ABC = 36(1.73) = 62.28$$

In order to calculate the area of the circle, remember that its radius equals $\frac{1}{3}$ the altitude of the circumscribing equilateral triangle. We must first determine the length of the altitude $\overline{BD}$. Let the length of $\overline{BD}$ be h. Since altitude $\overline{BD} \perp \overline{AC}$ and bisects it, $\triangle ABD$ is a right triangle and h can be found by applying the Pythagorean Theorem.

$$(AB)^2 = (AD)^2 + h^2\ .$$

But   AB = 12, and   $AD = \frac{1}{2}AC = \frac{1}{2}(12) = 6$.   By substitution,

$$(12)^2 = (6)^2 + h^2$$
$$144 = 36 + h^2$$
$$108 = h^2$$
$$h = \sqrt{108} = \sqrt{36}\sqrt{3} = 6\sqrt{3}\ .$$

In an equilateral triangle, the radius of the inscribed circle equals one third the altitude. Therefore, the length of radius $\overline{OD} = r = \frac{1}{3}(h)$. By substitution, $r = \frac{1}{3}(6\sqrt{3}) = 2\sqrt{3}$ .

$$\text{Area of circle}\ \ 0 = \pi r^2 = \pi(2\sqrt{3})^2 = 12\pi\ .$$

Using   $\pi = 3.14$,
Area of circle   $0 = 12(3.14) = 37.68$.
Difference in area = area of triangle   ABC - area of circle   0

$$= 62.28 - 37.68 = 24.6.$$

Therefore, the difference in area, to the nearest integer, is   25.

● **PROBLEM 8-27**

By how much does the area of the circumscribed circle exceed the area of the inscribed circle of a square of side 8.

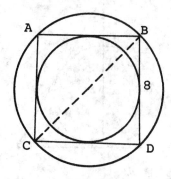

196

<u>Solution</u>:    The diameter of the inscribed circle equals the side of
the square.  Therefore, the area equals  $\pi r^2 = \pi(4)^2 = 16\pi$ .

The diameter of the circumscribed circle is the diagonal of the
square.  The diagonal of a square is the hypotenuse of the right triangle  formed by any two sides of the square adjacent at a vertex
not intersected by the diagonal.  Its length can be found by applying
the Pythagorean Theorem, since we know the length of two sides of
right  $\triangle ABC$.

$$(AC)^2 + (AB)^2 = (BC)^2$$

AC = AB = 8 and accordingly, by substitution,

$$(8)^2 + (8)^2 = (BC)^2$$
$$2(64) = (BC)^2$$
$$BC = \sqrt{128} = \sqrt{64}\,\sqrt{2} = 8\sqrt{2}$$

The diagonal equals  $8\sqrt{2}$,  therefore,  r = $4\sqrt{2}$.  The area of the circle
equals  $\pi(4\sqrt{2})^2 = 32\pi$ .  The area of the circumscribed circle exceeds
the area of the inscribed circle by  $32\pi - 16\pi = 16\pi$ .  In general, for
a given square, the area of the circumscribing circle is twice the area
of the inscribed circle.

● **PROBLEM** 8-28

The side of a regular pentagon is 20 inches in length.  (a) Find,
to the nearest tenth of an inch, the length of the apothem of the pentagon.  (b) Using the result obtained in part (a), find, to the nearest ten square inches, the area of the pentagon.

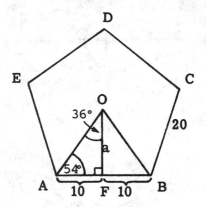

<u>Solution</u>:  (a) When the central angle  AOB  is drawn, as shown in the
figure, its rays, along with side  $\overline{AB}$  of pentagon ABCDE  form a
triangle.  The central-angle theorem states that the measure of a
central angle of a regular polygon equals  $360°$  divided by the number
of sides of the polygon.  Therefore, the measure of  ∡ AOB  is  $360°/5$,
or  $72°$,  where  5  is the number of sides in the pentagon.

By theorem, apothem  $\overline{OF}$  bisects central angle  AOF  and pentagon
side  $\overline{AB}$.  Since  $\overline{OF} \perp \overline{AB}$,  therefore, $\triangle OFA$  is a right triangle.

$$m \angle AOF = \tfrac{1}{2}(m \angle AOB) = \tfrac{1}{2}(72°) = 36° \ .$$

Therefore, m ∡ FAO = $180°$ - (m ∡ AOF + m ∡ OFA).

By substitution, m ∡ FAO = $180°$ - ($36° + 90°$) = $54°$ .  We also know,

197

$\overline{AF} = \frac{1}{2}\overline{AB} = \frac{1}{2}(20 \text{ in.}) = 10 \text{ in.}$

Since $\triangle OAF$ is a right triangle, knowing an angle measure and the length of its adjacent side, we can calculate the length of $\overline{OF}$ by using the tangent ratio.

$$\tan \not{\prec} OAF = \frac{\text{length of leg opposite } \not{\prec} OAF}{\text{length of leg adjacent } \not{\prec} OAF} .$$

Let $a$ = length of leg opposite $\not{\prec}$ OAF (see figure.) Then, by substitution,

$$\tan 54° = \frac{a}{10 \text{ in.}} .$$

From a standard tangent table, we find $\tan 54° = 1.3764$. Therefore,

$$1.3764 = \frac{a}{10 \text{ in.}}$$

$$a = (10 \text{ in.})(1.3764) = 13.764 \text{ in.}$$

The length of apothem $\overline{OF}$ is 13.8 in.

(b) The area of a regular polygon is given by $A = \frac{1}{2}$(apothem length) (perimeter) = $\frac{1}{2}ap$. The perimeter, $P$, of pentagon ABCDE = 5(20) in. = 100 in. Therefore, by substitution,

$$A = \frac{1}{2}(13.8)(100) \text{ in.}^2 = (50)(13.8) \text{ in.}^2 = 690 \text{ in.}^2 .$$

Therefore, the area of pentagon ABCDE is 690 sq. in.

● **PROBLEM 8-29**

Draw a circle circumscribed about a square of edge length s. What is the area of the region outside the square but inside the circle?

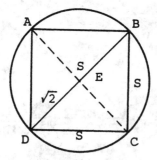

**Solution:** Let the area of the region inside the circle but outside the square be A(R). Furthermore, let the area of the circle be A(C) and the area of the square A(s). From the figure, we have

(1)     $A(R) = A(C) - A(s) .$

Since the square is of edge length s, $A(s) = s^2$. To find $A(C) = \pi r^2$, we must first find the radius r.

We first show that the diameter of the circle equals the diagonal of the square. Let E be the center of the

198

circumscribing circle. To show $\overline{DB}$ is a diameter, we must show $\overline{DEB}$ is a straight line. We will show this by showing that ⧸DEA and ⧸BEA form a straight angle. From an earlier theorem, we know that the central angles of a regular polygon are congruent. Therefore, m⧸DEA = m⧸AEB = m⧸BEC = m⧸CED = $\dfrac{360^{\circ}}{4}$ = 90°. m⧸DEA + m⧸BEA = 90° + 90° = 180°.

Since m⧸DEA + m⧸BEA = m⧸DEB, m⧸DEB = 180°, then ⧸DEB is a straight angle and D, E, and B are collinear. Thus $\overline{DB}$, the diagonal, is also a diameter.

To find DB, note that △DBC is a right triangle.

Using the Pythagorean Theorem, we have $DB^2 = DC^2 + CB^2 = s^2 + s^2 = 2s^2$. Thus, $DB = \sqrt{2s^2} = \sqrt{2}s$.

The radius of the circle equals ½ the diameter DB or $\frac{1}{2}(\sqrt{2}s)$. The area of the circle equals

$$\pi r^2 = \pi \left[\frac{\sqrt{2}}{2} s\right]^2 = \frac{\pi s^2}{2} .$$

Returning to equation (1), we obtain

$$A(R) = \frac{\pi s^2}{2} - s^2 = s^2 \left[\frac{\pi}{2} - 1\right]$$

● **PROBLEM** 8-30

The area of pentagon ABCDE is 18 sq. in.; the area of a similar pentagon A'B'C'D'E' is 32 sq. in. The diagonal AC is 6 in.; find the length of A'C' .

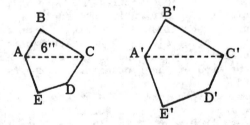

Solution: For two polygons to be similar, all corresponding angles are congruent, and all corresponding sides must be proportional. We will first show that the ratio of similitude of the diagonals, A'C'/AC, is the same as the ratio of similitude of the sides, A'B'/AB. Then, we find this ratio of similitude of the two polygons using the fact that the ratio of the area of similar polygons equals the square of the ratio of similitude.

To show that A'C'/AC = ratio of similitude, we show

$$\triangle ABC \sim \triangle A'B'C' .$$

Note ⧸ B ≅ ⧸ B' and $\dfrac{A'B'}{AB} = \dfrac{B'C'}{BC}$ because ABCDE and A'B'C'D'E' are similar polygons, By the S.A.S. Similarity Theorem, △ABC ~△A'B'C', and thus $\dfrac{A'C'}{AC} = \dfrac{A'B'}{AB}$ .

Since $\dfrac{A'B'}{AB}$ is the ratio of similitude, $\dfrac{A'C'}{AC}$ = ratio of similitude. To find the ratio of similitude, remember that

$$(\text{ratio of similitude})^2 = \frac{\text{area of A'B'C'D'E'}}{\text{area of ABCDE}} = \frac{32}{18} = \frac{16}{9}$$

$$\text{ratio of similitude} = \sqrt{\frac{16}{9}} = \frac{4}{3} .$$

Thus, $\dfrac{A'C'}{AC} = \dfrac{4}{3}$ . Since AC = 6, then $\dfrac{A'C'}{6} = \dfrac{4}{3}$ or A'C' = $\dfrac{4}{3}$(6) = 8 in.

● **PROBLEM 8-31**

Prove that the area of an inscribed regular octagon is equivalent to that of a rectangle whose dimensions are the sides of the inscribed and circumscribed squares.

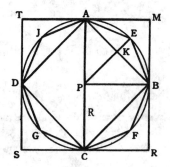

<u>Solution</u>: In the accompanying figure, AEBFCGDJ is the inscribed octagon; ABCD, the inscribed square; MRST, the circumscribed square. We are given circle P with radius of length r.

We will proceed by first determining the area of the octagon. Second, we determine the sides of the inscribed and circumscribed squares, which are the width and length of the rectangle. From this, we calculate the area of the rectangle. If the two areas are equal our work is done.

The area of octagon AEBFCGDJ = area of ABCD + area of $\triangle$AEB + area of $\triangle$BFC + area of $\triangle$DGC + area of $\triangle$AJD.

The area of ABCD = $AB^2$. To find AB, note that it is the hypotenuse of isosceles right triangle APB. The legs are formed by radii of $\odot$P. Hence, by the Pythagorean Theorem,

$$AB^2 = r^2 + r^2 = 2r^2 \quad \text{and} \quad AB = r\sqrt{2} .$$

The area of ABCD = $(r\sqrt{2})^2 = 2r^2$ . By the S.S.S. Postulate, all the triangles are congruent and the expression reduces to area of ABCD + 4(area of $\triangle$AEB), area of $\triangle$AEB = ½(base)(altitude) = ½(AB)(EK). We know AB = $r\sqrt{2}$ .

EK = r - KP . KP can be found and, hence, EK will be known (in terms of r).

Since the octagon is regular, AE = EB. In the same circle congruent chords intercept congruent arcs which have congruent central angles. Hence, $\angle$ APK $\cong$ $\angle$ BPK or $\overline{PK}$ is the angle bisector of the vertex angle of isosceles triangle APB. As such, $\overline{PK}$ is the perpendicular bisector of $\overline{AB}$. Therefore, $AK = KB = \frac{1}{2}(AB) = \frac{1}{2}r\sqrt{2}$. $\triangle AKP$ is a right triangle. Hence, we can apply the Pythagorean Theorem to find KP, given that we know $AP = r$ and $AK = \frac{1}{2}r\sqrt{2}$,

$$(AP)^2 = (AK)^2 + (KP)^2$$
$$r^2 = (\tfrac{1}{2}r\sqrt{2})^2 + (KP)^2$$
$$r^2 - \tfrac{1}{2}2r^2 = (KP)^2$$
$$\tfrac{1}{2}r^2 = (KP)^2$$
$$\frac{\sqrt{2}}{\sqrt{2}} \cdot \frac{1}{\sqrt{2}}r = KP$$

$$\tfrac{1}{2}r\sqrt{2} = KP$$

As such, $EK = r - \frac{1}{2}r\sqrt{2}$.

Area of $\triangle AEB = \frac{1}{2}(r\sqrt{2})(r - \frac{1}{2}r\sqrt{2})$
$$= \tfrac{1}{2}(r^2\sqrt{2} - \tfrac{1}{2}2r^2) = \tfrac{1}{2}r^2(\sqrt{2} - 1).$$

Recall, area of AEBFCGDJ = area of ABCD + 4(area of $\triangle AEB$).
By substitution,
$$= 2r^2 + 4(\tfrac{1}{2}r^2(\sqrt{2} - 1))$$
$$= 2r^2 + 2r^2(\sqrt{2} - 1)$$

Therefore, Area of octagon = $2r^2\sqrt{2}$. We have one side of the required rectangle, $AB = r\sqrt{2}$. We will now find MR, the other side.

Since MRST is a square, $\overline{MT} \parallel \overline{SR}$ and MR is the perpendicular distance between $\overline{MT}$ and $\overline{SR}$. A and C are points of tangency. As such, $\overline{CA} \perp \overline{MT}$ and $\overline{CA} \perp \overline{SR}$ and CA is also a $\perp$ distance between $\overline{MT}$ and $\overline{SR}$. Since parallel lines are everywhere equidistant, MR = CA. CA is a diameter of OP. Hence, CA = 2r and MR = 2r.

The proposed rectangle has sides 2r and $r\sqrt{2}$. Its area then equals $2r^2\sqrt{2}$. Since this is the area of the octagon, we have shown the desired results.


# AREA BY THE TRIGONOMETRIC FUNCTIONS

● **PROBLEM** 8-32

> Using the fact that the area of an n sided regular polygon is $nr^2 \tan \pi/n$, find the area of a circle. (Here, the polygon is composed of n isosceles triangles, with height r. See figure.)

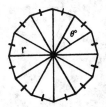

Solution: The figure shows the situation for n = 12. The idea here is that a circle is the limit of a regular polygon as the number of its sides increases without limit. We obtain the desired result by letting n get very large in the formula for the area of an n-sided regular polygon.

First, note that as n gets larger, tangent of $\pi/n$ gets very small. Now, the tangent of any small angle is approximately equal to the angle itself. Hence,

$$\text{as } n \to \infty, \tan \pi/n \to \pi/n.$$

Then, using this in the formula given in the problem

$$\text{as } n \to \infty, nr^2 \tan \pi/n \to nr^2 \ \pi/n = \pi r^2.$$

Hence, the area of a circle of radius r is $\pi r^2$.

● PROBLEM 8-33

> Prove that the area bounded by a regular polygon of n sides circumscribed about a circle with a radius of length r is given by the formula $A = nr^2 \tan \pi/n$.

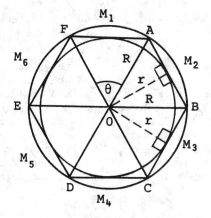

Solution: The figure shows the situation for the case where n = 6. In general, we see that we may consider the polygon of n sides to be composed of n triangles (for example, $\triangle AOB$, $\triangle BOC$, etc.). Since the polygon is circumscribed about circle O, $\overline{OM_2} \perp \overline{AB}$. This makes $\overline{OM_2}$, of length r, an altitude of $\triangle AOB$. If $\triangle AOB$ were isosceles, we could find its area by using the formula $A = r^2 \tan \theta/2$. We now prove that $\triangle AOB$ is, indeed, isosceles.

In the figure, we have circumscribed a circle about the polygon, By definition, the center of a regular polygon is also the center of the inscribed and circumscribed circles. Now, look at $\triangle AOB$. $\overline{AO} \cong \overline{BO}$, since both are radii of the larger circle. Hence, $\triangle AOB$ is isosceles. Its area is, then,

$$A = r^2 \tan \theta/2$$

where r and $\theta$ are as shown.

Now we prove that each triangle (of which there are n) is congruent to every other triangle of the polygon. Consider $\triangle AOB$ and $\triangle BOC$, $\overline{AO} \cong \overline{CO}$, since both are radii of the large circle. $\overline{OB} \cong \overline{OB}$. $\overline{AB} \cong \overline{CB}$, because the sides of a regular polygon are all congruent. Therefore, by the S.S.S. (side-side-side) Postulate, $\triangle AOB \cong \triangle BOC$. This may be done n times to prove that all the triangles comprising the polygon are congruent. Hence, they all have the same area. Since the n-sided polygon is composed of the n adjacent triangles (see figure), the area of the polygon is the sum of the areas of each of the n triangles. Hence,

$$A_p = nr^2 \tan \theta/2 .$$

But

$$n\theta = 2\pi$$

or

$$\theta/2 = \pi/n .$$

Hence,

$$A_p = nr^2 \tan \pi/n .$$

● PROBLEM 8-34

Find the area of a regular hexagon circumscribed about a circle of radius r. Calculate the area explicitly if
a) r = 4; b) r = 9; c) r = 16; d) r = 25.

Solution: The area of a regular n-sided polygon circumscribed about a circle of radius r is given by

$$A = nr^2 \tan \pi/n .$$

In a hexagon, n = 6. $\tan \pi/6 = \sqrt{3}/3$

Thus

$$A = 6r^2 \tan \pi/6 = 2r^2 \sqrt{3}$$

a) For  r = 4,      $A = 2(16)\sqrt{3} = 32\sqrt{3}$

b) For  r = 9,      $A = 2(81)\sqrt{3} = 162\sqrt{3}$

c) For  r = 16,     $A = 2(256)\sqrt{3} = 512\sqrt{3}$

d) For  r = 25,     $A = 2(625)\sqrt{3} = 1250\sqrt{3} .$

# CHAPTER 9

# CONSTRUCTIONS

## LINES AND ANGLES

> Construct a line perpendicular to a given line through a given point outside the line.

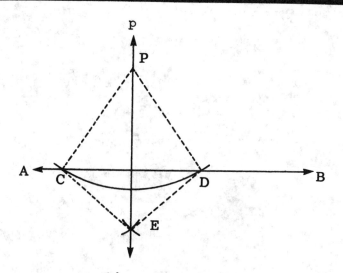

Solution: We are given line $\overleftrightarrow{AB}$ and point P, not on $\overleftrightarrow{AB}$, as in the figure shown. We wish to construct a line through P, perpendicular to $\overleftrightarrow{AB}$. Call this line p.

There is a segment $\overline{CD}$ on $\overleftrightarrow{AB}$ such that line p is the perpendicular bisector of $\overline{CD}$. To perform the construction we will (1) locate $\overline{CD}$ ; (2) construct the perpendicular bisector of $\overline{CD}$.

(1) Using P as a center, and any convenient radius, construct

an arc which intersects $\overleftrightarrow{AB}$ at C and D . Since $\overline{PC}$ and $\overline{PD}$ are radii of the same arc, we have PC = PD . Since point P is equidistant from points C and D, point P must be on the perpendicular bisector of $\overline{CD}$ .

(2) Construct the perpendicular bisector of $\overline{CD}$ .

The perpendicular bisector contains point P and is perpendicular to given line $\overleftrightarrow{AB}$. Thus, the perpendicular bisector is the required line p.

● PROBLEM 9-2

Bisect a given angle.

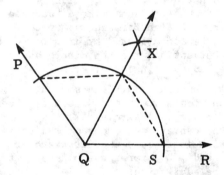

Solution: $\overrightarrow{QX}$ bisects ∢PQR if and only if ∢PQX ≅ ∢XQR . Let T be a point on QP and S be a point on QR such that ΔQTX ≅ ΔQSX . Then ∢PQX and ∢XQR are corresponding parts of congruent triangles and ∢PQX ≅ ∢XQR . Therefore, if we construct ΔQTX and ΔQSX such that ΔQTX ≅ ΔQSX , then $\overrightarrow{QX}$ bisects ∢PQR. We construct the triangles by the SSS Postulate.

Construction:
1. Using Q as the center and any radius, construct an arc of a circle that intersects $\overline{QP}$ at T and $\overline{QR}$ at S. Since radii of a circle are equal, QS = QT . By reflexivity, QX = QX .

2. Since SX must equal TX for ΔQTX ≅ ΔQSX , as required by the earlier reasoning, we make certain of this by construction.
Using S as a center and a radius of more than half ST, make an arc in the interior of ∢PQR.
Using T as a center and the same radius, make an arc in the interior of ∢PQR.
Since the radii are the same, SX = TX.

3. Draw $\overrightarrow{QX}$ . Since $\overline{QX} \cong \overline{QX}, \overline{TX} \cong \overline{SX}, \overline{QS} \cong \overline{QT}$ , then ΔQTX ≅ ΔQSX by the SSS Postulate. Therefore, ∢TQX ≅ ∢XQS, and $\overrightarrow{QX}$ bisects ∢PQR .

Construct an angle containing 60°, whose vertex is a given point. (See figure).

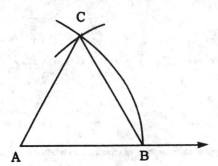

**Solution**: Since all angles in an equilateral triangle measure 60° (or $\frac{1}{3}(180)°$), by constructing such a triangle a 60° angle can be readily determined. This may seem like a "back door" method; however, there exists a fairly straightforward way to construct an equilateral triangle. This can be accomplished by drawing two radii of a circle whose points of intersection with the circle are a linear distance apart equal to the length of the radius.

1. Given point A, construct any line segment $\overline{AB}$.
2. Using A as the center, and a radius whose length is equal to AB, construct an arc of a circle.
3. Using B as the center, and the same radius as before, mark off another arc which intersects the first arc at C.
4. Construct $\overline{CA}$ and $\overline{CB}$, forming equilateral triangle ABC. The triangle will be equilateral because all three sides are radii of arcs which have been constructed with radii of the same length.

Since ΔABC is equilateral, and, as such, equiangular, m ⊰ CAB = $\frac{1}{3}$ of 180°, the total of the measures of the angles of a triangle. Hence, m ⊰ CAB = 60°, the required angle to be constructed.

Divide a given line segment into parts proportional to given line segments.

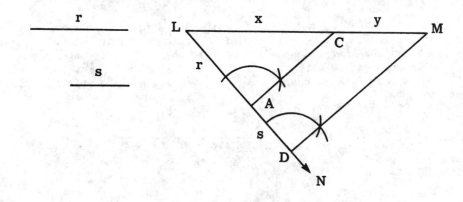

<u>Solution</u>: We know that a line intersecting two sides of a triangle, and parallel to the third side, will divide the two sides proportionally. First, we construct a triangle with (1) the first side equal in length to the given segment; and (2) a second side that can be easily divided into segments proportional to the given segments. Then we construct a line parallel to the third side that divides the second side into parts proportional to the given segment. By the above, we know that this line must also cut the first side, the given length, proportionally.

To find the second side that can be easily divided, note that there is no restriction on the length on the second side. Therefore, we construct the second side to be the length of the given segments combined.

1. Given segment $\overline{LM}$ and line segments of lengths r and s, draw $\overleftrightarrow{LN}$ making any convenient angle MLN.

2. On $\overleftrightarrow{LN}$, construct $\overline{LA}$ so that LA = r and construct $\overline{AD}$ so that AD = s.

3. Construct $\overleftrightarrow{DM}$ to complete the triangle, △DML.

4. Through A, construct $\overleftrightarrow{AC}$ parallel to $\overleftrightarrow{DM}$. C is the intersection of $\overleftrightarrow{AC}$ and $\overleftrightarrow{LM}$.

5. $\overline{LC}$ and $\overline{CM}$ are the required segments of length x and y.

The construction makes $\overleftrightarrow{AC} \parallel \overleftrightarrow{DM}$. Therefore, x:y = r:s because a line parallel to one side of a triangle and intersecting the other two sides divides the other two sides proportionally.

● **PROBLEM** 9-5

Construct the mean proportional between two given segments.

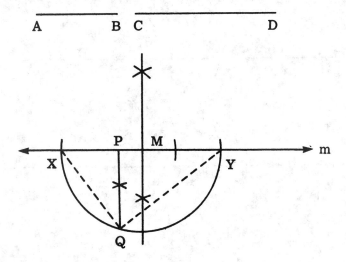

<u>Solution</u>: The mean proportional of two numbers a and b is defined as that number c such that a/c = c/b . The key here is "mean proportional". What geometric figures have properties involving the mean proportional?

207

In the right triangle, the altitude to the hypotenuse is the mean proportional of the segments of the hypotenuse.

Therefore, we construct a right triangle whose altitude divides the hypotenuse into segments of length AB and CD. The altitude will then be the mean proportional.

Given: $\overline{AB}$ and $\overline{CD}$ .

Wanted: $\overline{PQ}$ such that $\dfrac{AB}{PQ} = \dfrac{PQ}{CD}$ .

Construction:

(1) Construction of the hypotenuse: Choose a point P on any line. (P will be the intersection of the altitude and hypotenuse).

(2) On each side of P, construct segments $\overline{PX}$ and $\overline{PY}$ such that PX = AB and PY = CD. ($\overline{XY}$ is the hypotenuse.)

(3) Construction of the right triangle: (Any triangle inscribed in a semicircle is a right triangle and its hypotenuse is the diameter. We now construct the semicircle.) Bisect $\overline{XY}$ in order to find the mid-point M.

(4) Construct a semicircle above m using M as center and MX as radius.

(5) At P, construct a line perpendicular to m, intersecting the semi-circle at Q.

PQ is the mean proportional between AB and CD since $\overline{PQ}$ is the altitude to hypotenuse $\overline{XY}$ of right $\triangle XQY$ .

● **PROBLEM 9-6**

Given a line and a point not on the line, construct the line through the point that is parallel to the given line.

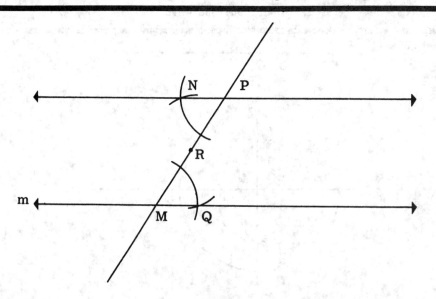

Solution: Two lines are parallel if their alternate interior angles are equal. Therefore, by constructing a transversal to m through point P, and constructing an interior angle on the "left" side congruent to the interior angle on the "right" side, the lines must be parallel.

Given: line  m  and point  P .

Wanted: line  $\overleftrightarrow{NP}$ ‖ m .

Construction:

(1) Let  M  and  Q  be points on  m, with  Q  on the right of  M.
Draw  $\overleftrightarrow{MP}$ .

(2) Let  R  be any point of  $\overleftrightarrow{MRP}$  on the same side of  P  from  M.
On  $\overleftrightarrow{PR}$  construct  ∡ RPN  with  N  to the left of  $\overleftrightarrow{MPR}$  such that
∡ RPN ≅ PMQ .

(3) Draw  $\overleftrightarrow{NP}$ .  ∡ NPR ≅ ∡ RMQ  by construction.  By congruence of
alternate interior angles,  $\overleftrightarrow{NP}$‖ m .

# TRIANGLES

Construct a triangle when two sides and the included angle are
given.  (See figure).

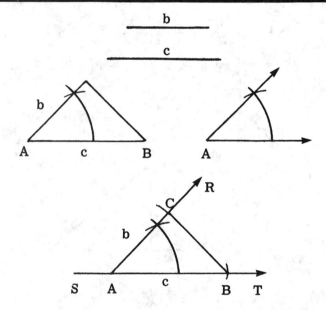

Solution: We are given two sides of lengths  b  and  c, as shown in
the figure, and one angle,  ∡ A.  We will duplicate  ∡ A,  and then
construct segments congruent to  b  and  c  along the sides of  ∡ A.
Then, by connecting the endpoints of the segments farthest away from
the vertex of  ∡ A, a unique triangle can be drawn.

Follow the construction shown in the sketch.

1. On any line  $\overleftrightarrow{ST}$ , use point  A  as the vertex to construct
∡ RAT ≅ ∡ A, the given angle.  (The construction of an angle
congruent to another angle was done previously.)

2. Using point A as a center, and c as the radius length construct $\overline{AB}$, along side $\overrightarrow{AT}$ of ∢ A, congruent to segment c.

3. Using A as the center again, and b as the radius length, construct $\overline{AC}$, along side $\overrightarrow{AR}$ of ∢ A, congruent to segment b.

4. Construct $\overline{BC}$. The required triangle is △ABC.

△ABC is unique because, given any other triangle with side 1 ≅ b, side 2 ≅ c, and the included angle ≅ ∢ A, the two triangles would be congruent by S.A.S. ≅ S.A.S. By corresponding parts, side 3 = $\overline{BC}$. Therefore, all parts of the alternative triangle would be congruent to the corresponding parts of △ABC and the alternative triangle would be indistinguishable from △ABC. This shows that, given two sides and the included angle, a unique triangle can be constructed.

● **PROBLEM 9-8**

Construct an altitude of a given triangle.

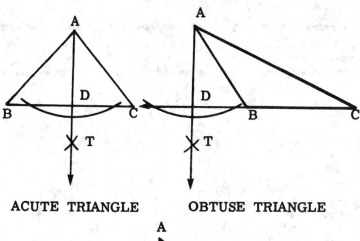

ACUTE TRIANGLE        OBTUSE TRIANGLE

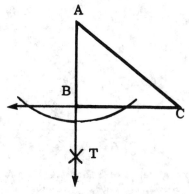

RIGHT TRIANGLE

<u>Solution</u>: This construction will vary slightly, depending upon whether the triangle is obtuse, acute, or right.

The basic idea when constructing an altitude of any triangle is to select a vertex, and draw a line through that vertex perpendicular to the opposite side. In the case of an obtuse triangle, the opposite side will have to be extended, and the point of intersection between the side and the perpendicular will be outside the triangle.

The construction can be followed in the accompanying sketch:

1. Through point A, construct $\overleftrightarrow{AT}$, a line perpendicular to $\overline{CB}$. Extend $\overline{CB}$ if necessary. (The construction of a perpendicular to a line through a given point outside the line has been described previously.)

2. In acute triangle ABC , $\overleftrightarrow{AT}$ intersects $\overline{CB}$ at point D. $\overline{AD}$ is the altitude from vertex A to side $\overline{CB}$.

3. In obtuse triangle ABC, $\overleftrightarrow{AT}$ intersects $\overline{CB}$ extended at point D. Line segment $\overline{AD}$ is the altitude from vertex A to side $\overline{CB}$.

4. In right triangle ABC, the point of intersection of $\overleftrightarrow{AT}$ and side $\overline{BC}$ is a vertex of the triangle, namely vertex B. Therefore, in addition to being one side of the triangle, $\overline{BC}$ is the altitude of right triangle ABC. This is so because ∡ B is a right angle.

● **PROBLEM 9-9**

Construct an isosceles triangle which has the same base as a given scalene triangle, and which is equal in area to it. (See figure).

<u>Solution</u>: The key to this construction lies in the fact that the area of a triangle is equal to ½ × base × height. The isosceles triangle to be constructed is to have the same base as the given scalene triangle. To insure that the isosceles triangle has the same area as the scalene triangle, we must construct it in such a way that both triangles have the same altitude.

If we draw line $\overleftrightarrow{RS}$ parallel to base $\overline{AB}$ , the distance between the two lines will be the altitude of the scalene triangle (△ABC).

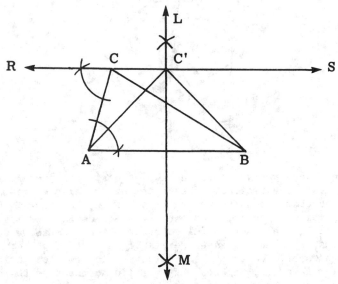

Any other perpendicular distance between $\overleftrightarrow{RS}$ and $\overline{AB}$ will be equal to the altitude of the scalene triangle. The altitude of the isosceles

211

triangle will be one such perpendicular distance.

The construction follows:

1. Through vertex C, construct $\overset{\leftrightarrow}{RS}$ parallel to $\overline{AB}$ . (This parallel line construction was done previously.)

2. Construct $\overset{\leftrightarrow}{LM}$, the perpendicular bisector of base $\overline{AB}$ . (This was also shown earlier).

3. $\overset{\leftrightarrow}{RS}$ and $\overset{\leftrightarrow}{LM}$ intersect at the point C' .

4. Construct $\overline{AC'}$ and $\overline{BC'}$ to form isosceles triangle ABC' .

Because $\overline{AC'}$ and $\overline{BC'}$ are drawn to the same point on perpendicular bisector $\overset{\leftrightarrow}{LM}$, $\overline{AC'} \cong \overline{BC'}$ . It therefore follows that $\triangle ABC'$ must be isosceles.

We have constructed $\overset{\leftrightarrow}{RS} \parallel \overset{\leftrightarrow}{AB}$ . Since parallel lines are everywhere equidistant, the heights of the triangles, which equal the distance between the parallel lines , must be equal. With common bases and equal heights, the area of the isosceles triangle must be the same as the area of the given scalene triangle.


# CIRCLES

● **PROBLEM 9-10**

Locate the center of a given circle.

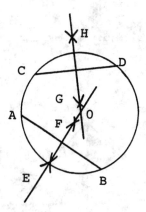

**Solution:** In any given construction, the special properties of the figure must be exploited. The center of the circle has many special properties that belong to no other points in the circle. Several of the properties, such as, "the center is equidistant from every point on the circle," are not useful to our problem because we do not know the radius, nor can we measure distances except in the crudest manner. We can, however, construct perpendicular bisectors of various chords. By earlier theorems, we know that the line connecting the center of the circle and the midpoint of a chord is the perpendicular bisector of the chord. This holds for every chord in the circle. Therefore, the center of the circle is on the perpendicular bisector of every chord in the circle. By choosing two non-parallel chords (so that their perpendicular bisectors do not coincide) and constructing their perpendicular bisectors, we know that only the point that lies on both bisectors can be the center.

Given:   Any circle.

Wanted:  The center, O, of the circle.

Construction:

(1) Draw any two nonparallel chords and label them $\overline{AB}$ and $\overline{CD}$ .

(2) Construct the perpendicular bisector of each chord. Name them $\overleftrightarrow{EF}$ and $\overleftrightarrow{GH}$, respectively.

(3) The intersection of $\overleftrightarrow{EF}$ and $\overleftrightarrow{GH}$ is O, the center of the circle.

● **PROBLEM 9-11**

Construct the lines tangent to a circle through a point external to the circle.

<u>Solution</u>: Let  P  be the point of tangency. A line is tangent to a circle at point  X, if the line is perpendicular to the radius drawn to point  X. Therefore, in the figure shown, $\overline{BP} \perp \overline{PA}$ or ∡ BPA  is a right angle and △BPA  is a right triangle. Thus, there are two requirements for point  P: (i) P, the point of tangency, must be on circle  A ; and (ii) △BPA  must be a right triangle. The locus of

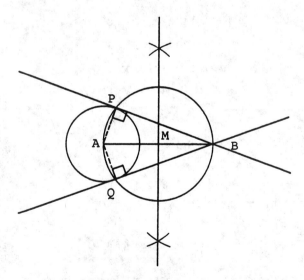

points satisfying condition (i) is the circle  A. The locus of points satisfying condition (ii) is the circle (not the semicircle) with  $\overline{BA}$ as the diameter. (To see this, remember that any triangle inscribed in a semicircle is a right triangle with the hypotenuse as the diameter. The converse is also true. All right triangles with given hypotenuse length can be inscribed in a semicircle with diameter equal to the hypotenuse.)

The intersection of the loci are thus the possible points of tangency, point P and Q .

Given:   Point B in the exterior of ⊙A .

Wanted: The lines through B tangent to ⊙A .

Construction:

(1)  Draw and bisect $\overline{AB}$ . Label the midpoint M .

(2)  With M as center and MB as the radius construct the circle through A and B. Circle M, with diameter $\overline{AB}$ , intersects ⊙A at P and Q .

(3)  Draw $\overrightarrow{BP}$ and $\overrightarrow{BQ}$ , the required tangents.

# POLYGONS

● **PROBLEM 9-12**

Construct a rectangle that has a given base length and is equal in area to the area of a given parallelogram.  (See figure).

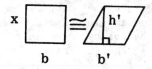

**Area of Rectangle = Area of Parallogram**

$$b\,x = b'h'$$

$$b : b' = h': x$$

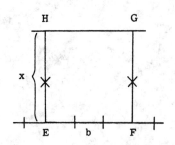 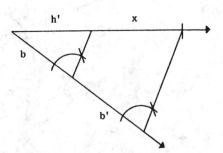

<u>Solution</u>: We are given parallelogram ABCD, with base of length b' and altitude of length h' . Accordingly, area of ▱ ABCD = b'h' .

The rectangle we want to construct has a known base length of b, and an unknown altitude, say x. Then, area of rectangle to be constructed = bx .

Since we want the area of the rectangle to equal the area of the parallelogram, it must be that bx = b'h' . Therefore,

$$\frac{b}{b'} = \frac{h'}{x}$$

214

or  b: b' = h':x  is a proportion. We must find the fourth proportional of  b,b'  and  h, (i.e., x), and then construct the rectangle with base  b  and altitude  x.

Follow the construction in the accompanying sketch:

(1)  Construct  $\overline{DR}$, the altitude of  $\square$ ABCD, whose length has been represented by  h' .

(2)  Construct the fourth proportional to  b,b', and  h' , (i.e., x). (This construction is vitally important to the problem.  It was done previously.)

(3)  The segment we have just determined, whose length is  x, is congruent to the altitude of the required rectangle.

(4)  Let  $\overline{EF}$  represent the base of the rectangle of length  b.  At points  E  and  F, construct perpendiculars to  $\overline{EF}$  of length  x; these are the altitudes of the rectangle.  (This construction has also appeared previously.)

(5)  Through points  H  and  G, construct  $\overline{HG}$ .  Since  $\overline{HE} \cong \overline{FG}$ , $\overline{HE} \parallel \overline{FG}$  and  $\angle$ HEF  is a right angle. EFGH  is the required rectangle, whose base is a segment of length  b, and whose area is equal to the area of  $\square$ ABCD .

Since the construction makes  x  the fourth proportional of b,b'  and  h' , then  b:b' = h': x  or  bx = b'h' .  Since the area of  $\square$ABCD = b'h' , and the area of rectangle  EFHG = bx , the area of rectangle  EFGH = area of  $\square$ABCD.  Therefore, EFGH is the rectangle we set out to construct.

● **PROBLEM 9-13**

Inscribe a regular hexagon in a circle.

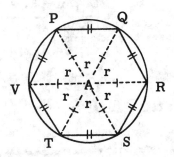

Solution:  Consider the n-sided regular polygon in the figure above (n, in this case, equals  6).  From the center of the circumscribed circle, draw the radii to the vertices.  Because all radii are congruent, two sides of every triangle must be congruent to two sides of every other triangle.  Because this is a regular polygon, all the sides, $\overline{VT}$, $\overline{VP}$, $\overline{PQ}$, etc., must be congruent.  By the SSS Postulate, all the triangles must be congruent, and, by corresponding parts, all the central angles must be congruent.  Since the central angles must sum to 360 , the measure of the central angle of each side of an n-sided regular polygon must be  360/n .

This is the crux of every problem that involves inscribing a regular polygon in a circle. If we are able to construct an angle of measure 360/n , then the polygon can be constructed by constructing n isosceles triangles (each with two sides of length r and vertex angle of measure 360/n ) side by side. In the case of the square, this critical angle is 360/4 or 90°— a right angle. Therefore, the inscription of a square in a circle is possible. (Note that the inscribed square is usually constructed by constructing two perpendicular diameters - or four right angles.) In the case of a heptagon, the critical angle is 360/7 or $51\frac{3}{7}$. We cannot construct this angle. Therefore this construction is impossible by our method.

In this problem, we are asked to inscribe a hexagon. The central angle is 360/6 = 60. We can construct an angle of 60° , and a hexagon can be inscribed in a circle by constructing 6 isosceles triangles with vertex angle = 60° and the vertex at the center of the circle.

However, much of the work can be omitted. In this case, the triangle to be constructed is an isosceles triangle with vertex angle = 60° . This is an equilateral triangle. Therefore, the side of the triangle that also forms a chord with the circle, must be equal to the radius. Consequently, for a hexagon inscribed in a circle, the measure of a side of the hexagon equals the measure of the radius.

This is extremely useful. We know the vertices are points on the circle and that they are spaced a distance r apart. There is no need for central triangles at all.

Given:   Circle A.

Wanted:   A regular hexagon inscribed in ⊙A .

Construction:
(1)   Find the center of ⊙A .

(2)   Choose any point P on the circle to be the first vertex. Using P as the center, and the radius of ⊙A as the radius, construct an arc intersecting the circle at Q. Since Q is on the circle and also a distance r from vertex P, Q is also a vertex.

(3)   Repeat this process to locate points R, S, T, and V .

(4)   Join these points to form $\overline{PQ}$, $\overline{QR}$, $\overline{RS}$, $\overline{ST}$, $\overline{TV}$, and $\overline{VP}$ . PQRSTV is the inscribed hexagon.

# COMPLEX CONSTRUCTIONS

● **PROBLEM 9-14**

Construct a triangle equal in area to a given pentagon. (See figure).

Solution: We have already shown that two triangles with a common base which both have a vertex on a line parallel to that base will be of equal area. This fact will guide our construction.

We can divide the pentagon ABCDE into three triangles by drawing diagonals $\overline{DB}$ and $\overline{DA}$ . If we can find 2 triangles equal in area to $\triangle AED$ and $\triangle BCD$ which, when placed adjacent to $\triangle ABD$ form a triangle, our task if complete.

216

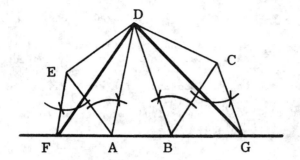

1. Given pentagon ABCDE, extend $\overline{AB}$ both to the left and to the right.

2. Construct diagonal $\overline{DB}$.

3. Through vertex C, construct $\overleftrightarrow{CG}$ parallel to $\overline{DB}$. [The construction of a line parallel to a fixed line through a given point was done previously.]

   $\overleftrightarrow{CG}$ intersects $\overleftrightarrow{AB}$ at G.

4. Construct $\overline{DG}$. At this point, $\triangle BCD$ and $\triangle BGD$ have been constructed.

5. Construct diagonal $\overline{DA}$.

6. Through vertex E, construct $\overleftrightarrow{EF}$ parallel to $\overline{DA}$. $\overleftrightarrow{EF}$ intersects $\overleftrightarrow{BA}$ at F.

7. Construct $\overline{DF}$. Now, $\triangle$'s AED and AFD have been completed.

8. $\triangle FDG$ is the required triangle, which is equal in area to pentagon ABCDE.

   The construction makes $\overline{EF} \parallel \overline{DA}$. Therefore, the area of $\triangle AFD$ = the area of $\triangle AED$ because the two triangles have a common base, $\overline{DA}$, and vertices F and E lie on a line parallel to the base. A previously solved problem gives proof of this.

   Similarly, since $\overline{CG} \parallel \overline{DB}$, the area of $\triangle BGD$ = the area of $\triangle BCD$.

   The area of $\triangle ABD$ = the area of $\triangle ABD$, by reflexivity.

   Pentagon ABCDE is composed of $\triangle$'s AED, BCD and ABD. Triangle FDG is composed of $\triangle$'s AFD, BGD and ABD.

   Therefore, area of triangle DFG = area of pentagon ABCDE since the sums of equal quantities will be equal quantities. The area of $\triangle AFD$ + the area of $\triangle ABD$ + the area of $\triangle BGD$ = the area of $\triangle AED$ + the area of $\triangle ABD$ + the area of $\triangle BCD$, and the sums of the areas of the respective components of triangle DFG and pentagon ABCDE are equal.

● **PROBLEM 9-15**

Using a straight edge only, construct the perpendicular to a given diameter of a circle from any point off the diameter.

Solution: This construction is quite different from most others in this section in that it restricts you to only using a straight edge without a compass. Hence, the usual ways of dropping a perpendicular from a point to a line cannot be used here. We are given point P

217

and circle O with diameter AB and asked to drop the perpendicular from P to $\overline{AB}$ .

Complete triangle PAB and note the points of intersection of PA and PB with the circle, points C and D, respectively.

Join point C to vertex B and point D to vertex B. Angles ACB and BDA are angles inscribed in a semi-circle and, as such, are right angles. Therefore, $\overline{BC} \perp \overline{AP}$ and $\overline{AD} \perp \overline{PB}$ .

By the definition of an altitude of a triangle, $\overline{BC}$ is the altitude to $\overline{AP}$ and $\overline{AD}$ is altitude $\overline{PB}$ .

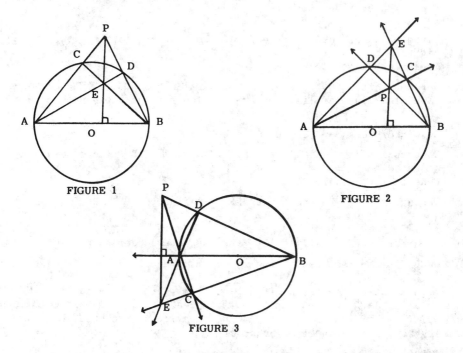

FIGURE 1

FIGURE 2

FIGURE 3

We have a theorem that tells us the three altitudes of a triangle are always concurrent at a point. Since $\overline{AD}$ and $\overline{BC}$ intersect at E, the altitude from P to $\overline{AB}$ must also pass through E. Two points determine a line. Therefore, by extending $\overline{PE}$ to intersect $\overline{AB}$ we will have drawn the third altitude and, hence, the perpendicular to $\overline{AB}$ from P.

The drawing in figure 1 has two restrictions. The first is that P is outside the circle and the second is that $\triangle PAE$ is acute. Either of these restrictions can be lifted and the construction will still work.

In figure 2, P is located in the interior of the circle. Draw $\overline{AP}$ and $\overline{BP}$ extended to C and D, respectively. By extending $\overline{AD}$ and $\overline{BC}$ complete triangle EAB. $\overline{AC}$ and $\overline{BD}$ are the respective altitudes to $\overline{BE}$ and $\overline{EA}$ . Again $\overline{PE}$ extended to $\overline{AB}$ is the required perpendicular.

The altitude in figure 3 from P to $\overline{AB}$ will lie outside $\triangle PAB$ and this will show that our construction works when $\triangle PAB$ is obtuse.

Draw $\overline{PA}$ and $\overline{PB}$ and extend $\overline{PA}$ so that it intersects the circle at C. Draw $\overline{BC}$ and $\overline{AD}$ and continue them until they intersect at point E. Once again the line from E to P will be perpendicular to diameter $\overline{AB}$ .

218

Given two parallel lines and a transversal $\overleftrightarrow{FG}$ , construct the
circle tangent to both the parallel lines and the transversal.

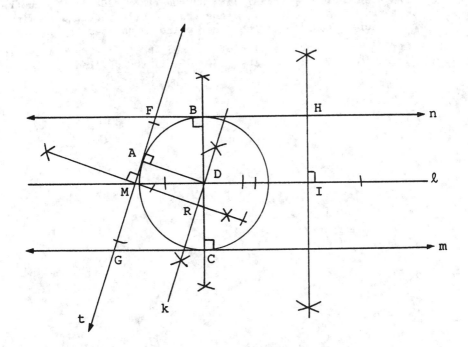

**Solution**: To construct a circle, we must find (a) the center; and
(b) the radius.

(a) The center: Consider the radii drawn to the tangent points,
$\overline{AD}$, $\overline{BD}$, and $\overline{CD}$. Because these are radii drawn to tangent points,
$\overline{AD} \perp$ line t, $\overline{BD} \perp$ line n, and $\overline{CD} \perp$ line m. Then, by definition,
AD, BD, and CD are the distances from lines t, n, and m to point
D. Therefore, D, the center of the circle, which must be equidistant
from t, m, and n.

The locus of points that are equidistant from n and m is the
line parallel to n and m and equidistant from both. Find the midpoint of the transversal segment cut by n and m and construct
line $\ell$ parallel to n. The distance BD between n and $\ell$ must
be the radius of the circle. The center must also be a distance HI
from t. The locus of points a distance HI from t is two parallel
lines a distance HI from t. The center of the circle is the intersection of $\ell$ and the lines parallel to t.

(b) The radius is the length of $\overline{HI}$ where $\overleftrightarrow{BD}$ is a line perpendicular to n, m, and $\ell$ .

Given: Two parallel lines n and m, and a transversal t. Let F
and G be the points of intersection of the transversal
with n and m.

Wanted: Construct the circle tangent to both the parallel lines and
the transversal.

Construction:
(1) Locate the midpoint of $\overline{FG}$, label it M.

(2) Construct line $\ell$ through M parallel to n.

(3)  Construct line $\overset{\leftrightarrow}{HI}$ perpendicular to  n  such that point  H  is on line  n  and point  I  is on line  $\ell$ .

(4)  Construct $\overset{\leftrightarrow}{MR}$ perpendicular to  t, such that  $\overline{MR} \cong \overline{HI}$ .

(5)  Construct line  k  through point  R  such that  k $\parallel$ t. (By constructing another parallel line on the other side of  t, another centerpoint may be found.  Since you are only required to find one circle, location of the other point is unnecessary.)

(6)  Let  D  be the intersection of  k  and  $\ell$ .  Construct a circle centered at  D  with radius  $\overline{HI}$.  OO  is the desired circle.

# CHAPTER 10

# COORDINATE GEOMETRY

## PLOTTING POINTS

● **PROBLEM 10-1**

Describe the location of the point (-1,-2) and then plot it
on coordinate graph paper.

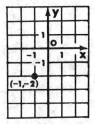

**Solution:**  The first number in the point, the abscissa, is -1
and represents the number of horizontal units along the x-axis
that will be moved left of the origin of the Cartesian plane
when plotting this point.  The second number, the ordinate, is
-2 which represents the vertical distance to be moved downward
from the origin.

With this in mind, we can plot the required point on the
graph.  We find that (-1,-2) will lie in the lower left region of the graph, Quadrant III, 2 units below the x-axis and
1 unit to the left of the y-axis.

● **PROBLEM 10-2**

Give the coordinates of points A,B,C,D,E,and F in the figure
below and determine the quadrants in which they lie.

**Solution:**  To find the coordinates of a point, z for example,
imagine a line parallel to the y axis passing through z.

Where that line intersects the x-axis, gives the x-coordinate. Similarly, the imaginary line parallel to the x-axis passing through z, gives the y coordinate. For example, the y-coordinate of A is 2. Similarly, the x-coordinate of A is 2.

Repeating the procedure for points B,C,D,E, and F, we obtain the table below.

| Point | Coordinate | Quadrant |
|-------|------------|----------|
| A | (2, 2) | I |
| B | (-3, -3) | III |
| C | (-2, 0) | on the x-axis |
| D | (-4, 3) | II |
| E | (0, -2) | on the y-axis |
| F | (4, -3) | IV |

In determining the quadrant of a point, note that any point above the x-axis and to the right of the y-axis is in the first quadrant. A more common way of expressing first quadrant is to use the Roman numeral notation. Thus the first quadrant becomes Quadrant I. Similarly, if the point is above the x-axis but to the left of the y-axis, it is said to be in the second quadrant, or Quadrant II. Points below the x-axis and to the left of the y-axis are in Quadrant III; and points below the x-axis but to the right of the y-axis are in Quadrant IV. Points that lie on the x or y axis are said to lie on the x or y axis and are not in any quadrant.

There is a second method of determining the quadrant of the point. Note that all points above the x-axis have positive y-coordinates. Similarly, all points below the x-axis have negative y-coordinates. Points to the right of the y-axis have positive x-coordinates. Points to the left of the y-axis have negative x-coordinates. Since all points in Quadrant I are above the x-axis and to the right of the y-axis, all points in Quadrant I have the form (positive, positive). Repeating the procedure for the other five cases, we obtain:

> Quadrant II: (Negative, positive)
> Quadrant III: (negative, negative)
> Quadrant IV: (positive, negative)
> On the x-axis: (positive or negative, 0)
> On the y-axis: (0, positive or negative).

Given the graph and asked to find the quadrant of the point, method 1 is easier. If we are given the coordinates, method 2 is better.

## DETERMINING DISTANCE

● **PROBLEM** 10-3

**Problem:** Show that the triangle with vertices A(6,7), B(-11,0), and C(1,-5) is isosceles.

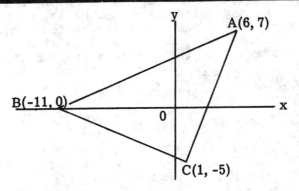

**Solution:** To prove that triangle ABC is isosceles, we must find two equal sides. Calculate the length of the sides using

223

the formula for distance in the plane: The length of the line segment determined by the two points $P_1(x_1, y_1)$, $P_2(x_2, y_2)$ is given by

$$P_1P_2 = \sqrt{(x_1-x_2)^2 + (y_1-y_2)^2}$$

Plugging in the values for A, B, C, we have

$$AB = \sqrt{(6-(-11))^2 + (7-0)^2}$$

$$= \sqrt{17^2 + 7^2} = \sqrt{338}$$

$$AC = \sqrt{(6-1)^2 + (7-(-5))^2} = \sqrt{5^2 + 12^2}$$

$$= \sqrt{25 + 144} = \sqrt{169} = 13.$$

$$BC = \sqrt{((-11)-1)^2 + (0-(-5))^2} = \sqrt{(-12)^2 + (+5)^2}$$

$$= 13.$$

Since  AC =  BC , triangle ABC is isosceles.

● PROBLEM 10-4

A circle whose center is at C(-4,2) passes through the point D(-3,5). Find R, the length of the radius, in radical form.

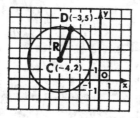

Solution: Since the length of the radius is, by definition, the length of a line segment drawn from the center of the circle to any point on the circle, R can be found by determining the length of $\overline{CD}$. On the Cartesian plane the length of a line segment is governed by the distance between its endpoints. The general formula for the distance between two points is $d = \sqrt{(x_1-x_2)^2 + (y_1-y_2)^2}$. Let

$$C = (x_1, y_1), \quad \text{then} \quad x_1 = -4 \quad y_1 = 2$$

$$D = (x_2, y_2), \quad \text{then} \quad x_2 = -3 \quad y_2 = 5$$

and  R = distance (length of the radius).

By substitution, $R = \sqrt{(-4-(-3))^2 + (2-5)^2} = \sqrt{(-1)^2 + (-3)^2}$

$$= \sqrt{1 + 9} = \sqrt{10}$$

The length of the radius is $\sqrt{10}$.

Prove, using coordinate geometry, that the diagonals of a rectangle are congruent.

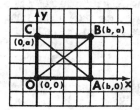

Solution: Prior to getting into the proof, let us draw a rectangle on the Cartesian plane. (See figure). Place one vertex at the origin and side $\overline{OA}$ along the x-axis, as shown. Extend side $\overline{AB}$ into quadrant I, so that vertex B is the point (b,a). The coordinates of the vertices of the rectangle are O(0,0), A(b,0), B(b,a), and C(0,a).

Since ABCO is given to be a rectangle, with $\overline{OB}$ and $\overline{CA}$ as the diagonals, proving OB = CA will be sufficient to prove that the diagonals of a rectangle are congruent.

We can use the general formula for the distance between two points, $d = \sqrt{(x_1-x_2)^2 + (y_1-y_2)^2}$, to obtain the desired results. Here, $(x_1,y_1)$ and $(x_2,y_2)$ are the coordinates of the 2 points. Distance OB is given by

$$OB = \sqrt{(0-b)^2 + (0-a)^2} = \sqrt{b^2 + a^2}.$$

Distance AC is given by

$$AC = \sqrt{(b-0)^2 + (0-a)^2} = \sqrt{b^2 + a^2}.$$

Therefore, since OB = AC we can conclude that $\overline{OB} \cong \overline{AC}$.

# MIDPOINTS

Find the coordinates of the midpoint of the line segment which joins the point R(4,6) and the point S(8,-2). (See figure)

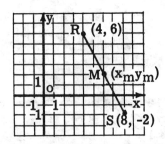

Solution: By a theorem, we know that the coordinates of the midpoint of a line segment are equal to one-half the sum of the corresponding x and y coordinates of the endpoints of the line segment. (These results can be checked by applying the general formula for the distance between two points). Let $M = (x_m, y_m)$, the midpoint of segment $\overline{RS}$.

Also let $R = (x_1, y_1)$ where $x_1 = 4$, $y_1 = 6$

and $S = (x_2, y_2)$ where $x_2 = 8$, $y_2 = -2$.

Then, $x_m = \frac{1}{2}(x_1 + x_2) = \frac{1}{2}(4+8) = \frac{1}{2}(12) = 6$

and $y_m = \frac{1}{2}(y_1 + y_2) = \frac{1}{2}(6-2) = \frac{1}{2}(4) = 2$.

To check that $M = (6,2)$ is the midpoint of $\overline{RS}$, calculate RM and MS by using the general distance formula to verify that they are equal.

$$RM = \sqrt{(x_1 - x_m)^2 + (y_1 - y_m)^2}$$

By substitution, $RM = \sqrt{(4-6)^2(6-2)^2} = \sqrt{(-2)^2 + (4)^2} = \sqrt{4+16}$

$$RM = \sqrt{20}$$

$$MS = \sqrt{(x_m - x_2)^2 + (y_m - y_2)^2}$$

By substitution, $MS = \sqrt{(6-8)^2 + (2-(-2)^2} = \sqrt{(-2)^2 + (4)^2} = \sqrt{4+16}$

$$MS = \sqrt{20}$$

Therefore, $RM = MS$

Therefore, the coordinates of the midpoint of line segment $\overline{RS}$ are $x = 6$, $y = 2$ or $(6,2)$.

● PROBLEM 10-7

The midpoints of the sides of a triangle are (2,5), (4,2), (1,1). Find the coordinates of its three vertices.

226

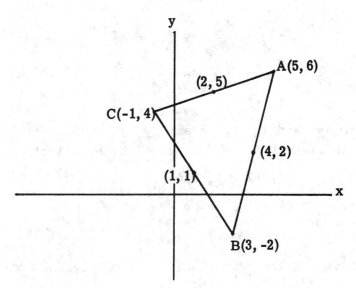

**Solution:** This problem will involve applying the midpoint formula and then solving a system of simultaneous equations.

For any segment, with endpoints (a,b) and (c,d), the midpoint is given by $(\frac{a+c}{2}, \frac{b+d}{2})$.

Let the triangle have vertices A,B, and C with coordinates $(x_1,y_1)$, $(x_2,y_2)$ and $(x_3,y_3)$, respectively. (2,5) is the midpoint of $\overline{AC}$. (4,2) is the midpoint of $\overline{AB}$. (1,1) is the midpoint of $\overline{CB}$. Hence, by applying the midpoint formula,

$$(2,5) = \left(\frac{x_1+x_3}{2}, \frac{y_1+y_3}{2}\right) \quad (4,2) = \left(\frac{x_1+x_2}{2}, \frac{y_1+y_2}{2}\right)$$

$$(1,1) = \left(\frac{x_2+x_3}{2}, \frac{y_2+y_3}{2}\right)$$

Now, we can write

$$\frac{x_1+x_3}{2} = 2 \; , \qquad x_1+x_3 = 4 \qquad (1)$$

$$\frac{x_1+x_2}{2} = 4 \; , \qquad x_1+x_2 = 8 \qquad (2)$$

$$\frac{x_2+x_3}{2} = 1 \; , \qquad x_2+x_3 + 2 \qquad (3)$$

Sum (1) and (2) to obtain $2x_1+x_3+x_2 = 12$.

But (3) tells us $x_3+x_2 = 2$. Hence, by substitution, we have

$$2x_1+2 = 12 \text{ and } x_1 = 5.$$

From (1), $x_3 = 4-x_1 = 4-5 = -1 = x_3$

From (2), $x_2 = 8-x_1 = 8-5 = 3 = x_2$

Also,

$$\frac{y_1 + y_3}{2} = 5, \quad y_1 + y_3 = 10 \qquad (4)$$

$$\frac{y_1 + y_2}{2} = 2, \quad y_1 + y_2 = 4 \qquad (5)$$

$$\frac{y_2 + y_3}{2} = 1, \quad y_2 + y_3 = 2 \qquad (6)$$

Again sum (4) and (5) to obtain $2y_1 + y_2 + y_3 = 14$

But (6) tells us $y_3 + y_2 = 2$. Hence, by substitution,
we have
$$2y_1 + 2 = 14 \text{ and } y_1 = 6.$$

From (4), $y_3 = 10 - y_1 = 10 - 6 = 4 = y_3$

From (5), $y_2 = 4 - y_1 = 4 - 6 = -2 = y_2$

The vertices of the triangle in this problem are A = (5,6),
B = (3,-2), and C = (-1,4).

# SLOPES

● **PROBLEM** 10-8

What is the slope of the line that passes through the origin
and point (1,2)? the slope of a horizontal line? a vertical
line?

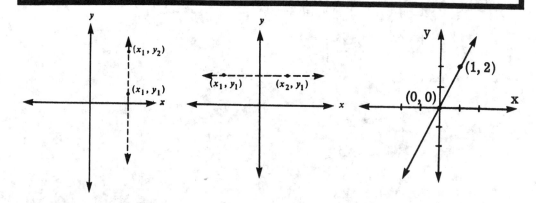

<u>Solution</u>: The slope of the line determined by two points,
$(x_1, y_1)$ and $(x_2, y_2)$ such that $x_1 \neq x_2$ and is the same as m,
the slope of any segment of the line. The line that passes
through the origin and point (1,2) is determined by the
points (0,0) and (1,2), Therefore, the slope of the line is
the same as m, the slope of the line segment between (0,0)
and (1,2).

$$\text{(i)} \quad m = \frac{\Delta y}{\Delta x} = \frac{y_2 - y_1}{x_2 - x_1} = \frac{2 - 0}{1 - 0} = 2 .$$

228

A horizontal line is, by definition, parallel to the
x-axis. Therefore all the ordinates must be equal. Let
$(x_1,y_1)$ and $(x_2,y_2)$ be two distinct points on the horizontal
line. Then the slope of the line equals

$$\text{(ii)} \quad m = \frac{\Delta y}{\Delta x} = \frac{y_2 - y_1}{x_2 - x_1} \ .$$

Since $(x_1,y_1)$ and $(x_2,y_2)$ lie on the horizontal line,
$y_2 = y_1$. Therefore, the numerator $y_2 - y_1 = 0$, and $m = 0$.
The slope of a horizontal line equals zero.

A vertical line is, by definition, parallel to the
y-axis, and, consequently, all abscissas are equal: For
all points $(x_1,y_1)$ and $(x_2,y_2)$ on the line, $\underline{x_1 = x_2}.$

Therefore, we cannot apply the above theorem since the theorem requires that the line be determined by two points
$(_1,y_1)$ and $(x_2,y_2)$ such that $x_1 \neq x_2$. No two such points
exist on the vertical line and we are left to conclude that
a vertical line has no slope.

If we did try to find the slope using the formula, then
we would obtain $m = \frac{\Delta y}{\Delta x} = \frac{y_2 - y_1}{x_2 - x_1}$ . For a vertical line,
$x_2 = x_1$; thus $x_2 - x_1 = 0$ and $m = \frac{y_2 - y_1}{0}$ . Because the denominator is zero, the value of $m$ is not defined.

● **PROBLEM 10-9**

---

Prove that points A(2,3), B(4,4), and C(8,6) are collinear.

---

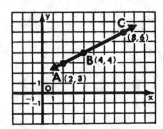

**Solution:** Three points are collinear if the slope of the
line segment between the first and second point is equal to
the slope of the line segment between the second and third
points.

Let   A = $(x_1,y_1)$ = (2,3)

      B = $(x_2,y_2)$ = (4,4)

      C = $(x_3,y_3)$ = (8,6)

These three points have been plotted on the accompanying graph. If the slope of $\overline{AB}$ equals the slope of $\overline{BC}$, the points are collinear.

Slope of $\overline{AB} = \dfrac{y_2 - y_1}{x_2 - x_1} = \dfrac{4 - 3}{4 - 2} = \dfrac{1}{2}$

Slope of $\overline{BC} = \dfrac{y_3 - y_2}{x_3 - x_2} = \dfrac{6 - 4}{8 - 4} = \dfrac{2}{4} = \dfrac{1}{2}$

Since the slope of $\overline{AB}$ = slope of $\overline{BC}$, the points A, B, and C all lie on the same straight line, $\overleftrightarrow{AC}$, and are, therefore, collinear.

● **PROBLEM 10-10**

Prove, by means of slope, that the triangle plotted in the accompanying graph, whose vertices are A(0,2), B(2,3), and C(1,5), is a right triangle.

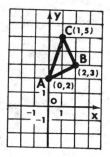

**Solution:** We can prove that lines $\overline{CB} \perp \overline{AB}$, making $\triangle ABC$ a right triangle, by demonstrating that the slope of $\overline{CB}$ is the reciprocal of the slope of $\overline{AB}$.

Let $\quad A = (x_1, y_1) = (0, 2)$

$\quad\quad B = (x_2, y_2) = (2, 3)$

$\quad\quad C = (x_3, y_3) = (1, 5)$,

then,

$$\text{Slope of } \overline{AB} = \frac{y_2 - y_1}{x_2 - x_1} = \frac{3 - 2}{2 - 0} = \frac{1}{2}$$

$$\text{Slope of } \overline{CB} = \frac{y_3 - y_2}{x_3 - x_2} = \frac{5 - 3}{1 - 2} = -\frac{2}{1}$$

The slope of $\overline{AB}$ is the negative reciprocal of the slope of $\overline{CB}$ because $(\frac{1}{2})(-2) = 1$. Therefore, $\overline{AB} \perp \overline{BC}$. Hence, $\triangle ABC$ is a right triangle because it contains a right angle.

230

Given A(-4,-2), B(1,-3), and C(3,1) find the coordinates of D, in the 2nd quadrant such that quadrilateral ABCD is a parallelogram.

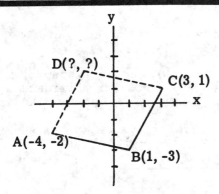

Solution: The many properties of a parallelogram allow us several methods of proceeding; however, not all of them are equally straightforward. We know, for example, that opposite sides of a parallelogram are congruent and, therefore, AD = CB and DC = AB. However, to use the distance formula

$$d = \sqrt{(x_1 - x_2)^2 + (y_2 - y_1)^2}$$

would yield two equations with square roots of unknowns. Similarly, any attempt to show congruence of angle would bring more complications than it would solve. The best method is to use the property which states that opposite sides of a parallelogram are parallel. In coordinate geometry, this reduces down to the problem of showing that the slopes of the opposite sides are equal. Let the coordinates of D be (x,y)

Slope of $\overline{AB} = \frac{-2 - (-3)}{-4 - 1} = -\frac{1}{5}$

Slope of $\overline{DC} = \frac{y - 1}{x - 3}$

Slope of $\overline{CB} = \frac{1 - (-3)}{3 - 1} = \frac{4}{2} = 2$

Slope of $\overline{DA} = \frac{y - (-2)}{x - (-4)} = \frac{y + 2}{x + 4}$

By the properties of the parallelogram, $\overline{AB} \parallel \overline{DC}$

       (i) slope of $\overline{AB}$ = slope of $\overline{DC}$

       (ii)       $-\frac{1}{5} = \frac{y - 1}{x - 3}$

By crossmultiplication,

       (iii) x - 3 = -5(y-1) = -5y + 5

       (iv) x + 5y - 3 = 5

       (v)   x + 5y = 8

Since $\overline{DA}$ and $\overline{CB}$ are also opposite sides,

(vi) slope of $\overline{DA}$ = slope of $\overline{BC}$

(vii) $\quad 2 = \dfrac{y + 2}{x + 4}$

(viii) $y + 2 = 2(x+4) = 2x + 8$

(ix) $-2x + y + 2 = 8$

(x) $-2x + y = 6$

Equations (v) and (x) form a system of two simultaneous equations in two unknowns. We can eliminate x from the equation by multiplying equation (v) by 2 and adding the result to equation (x):

(xi) $\qquad 2x + 10y = 16$

(x) $\underline{+ \ -2x + \quad y = \quad 6}$

(xii) $\qquad\qquad\quad 11y = 22$

(xiii) $\qquad\qquad\quad\quad y = \dfrac{1}{11} \cdot 22 = 2$

Substitution y = 2 into equation (v), we obtain:

(xiv) $x + 5(2) = 8$

(xv) $x = 8 - 5(2) = 8 - 10 = -2$.

Therefore, D = (-2,2) for ABCD to be a parallelogram.

● **PROBLEM 10-12**

Given: A(0,0), B(6,0), and C(3,3), find the equation for the median to side $\overline{AB}$.

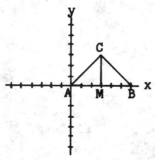

Solution: To find the equation of a line, we need two points on the line. Let $\overline{CM}$ be the median to $\overline{AB}$. Then vertex C is one point on the median. Similarly M, the midpoint of $\overline{AB}$, is also on the median. Using the Midpoint Formula,

$$M = \left(\frac{x_1+x_2}{2}, \frac{y_1+y_2}{2}\right) = \left(\frac{0+6}{2}, \frac{0+0}{2}\right) = (3,0).$$

Thus, with M(3,0), C(3,3), the equation of the median is

given by the Point-slope form.

Form: $y-y_1 = m(x-x_1)$, where $(x_1,y_1)$ is point M(3,0) and

the slope m = $\frac{\Delta y}{\Delta x} = \frac{3-0}{3-3} = \frac{3}{0}$ or undefined.

The only straight lines whose slopes are undefined are vertical lines. The equation of a vertical line is x=c, where c is the abscissa of any point on the line. Since the slope of $\overleftrightarrow{CM}$ is undefined, $\overleftrightarrow{CM}$ is a vertical line containing points (3,3) and (3,0). 3 is the common abscissa. Therefore, the equation of $\overleftrightarrow{CM}$ is x=3.

There is one last step. x=3 is an equation of a line. A median is a line segment. Therefore, we must make it clear that the endpoints are (3,3) and (3,0) – that the ordinates must be between 3 and 0. Equation of the median:

x=3 where $0 \le y \le 3$.

## LINEAR EQUATIONS

● PROBLEM 10-13

a) Draw a line with slope 3 through the origin. b) Write the coordinates of the points whose x coordinates are -2, -1, 0, 1, 2, 3. c) Write the equation of the line. d) Describe the set of coordinates of the line two ways using set builder notation. e) Verify that the coordinates of part (b) satisfy the equation of part (c).

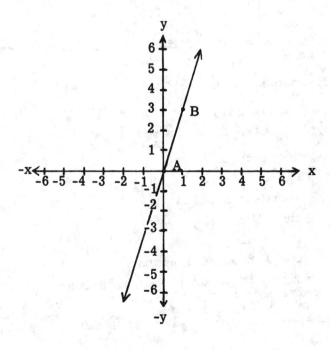

**Solution:** a) The fact that the line passes through the origin indicates that the point (0,0) lies on the line. This is
indicated by point A in the figure. Since the slope of the
line is 3, all points whose y and x distances from (0,0) are
in the ratio of 3 to 1 also lie on the line. One such point
is (1,3), indicated in the figure as point B. Since two points
determine a line, $\overline{AB}$ is the line which satisfies the given c
conditions, as shown in the figure.

b) Let the coordinates of a point be (x,y). Then
the y distance of (x,y) from (0,0) is y - o = y. The x distance of (x,y) from (0,0) is x - 0 = x. From part (a), we
realize that all points which lie on $\overline{AB}$ satisfy the relationship $\frac{y}{x} = \frac{3}{1}$

Multiplying both sides by x,
$$y = 3x \qquad\qquad (1)$$

We may therefore set up the following table:
The entries in the last column are the coordinates of the
points with the absissas given in the first column.

| x | y = 3x | (x, y) |
|---|--------|--------|
| -2 | -6 | (-2, -6) |
| -1 | -3 | (-1, -3) |
| 0 | 0 | (0, 0) |
| 1 | 3 | (1, 3) |
| 2 | 6 | (2, 6) |
| 3 | 9 | (3, 9) |

c) The equation of the line is given, from part
(c), in equation (1).

d) An example of set builder notation is

$$S = \{(x,y) \mid x \in R \text{ and } y \in R\}.$$

The various symbols used have the meanings given below:

" = "      consists of

"{ }"      the set of

"(x,y)"      coordinate pairs, x,y

" | "      such that

" e"      is an element of

" R"      the set of real numbers

The above expression, therefore; reads, "S consists of the set
of coordinate pairs x,y such that x is an element of the set
of real numbers and y is an element of the set of real numbers." Now, the points (x,y) lying on $\overline{AB}$ may be described in

234

two alternative ways. First, the line AB consists of all co-ordinate pairs (x,y) such that x is an element of the set of real numbers, and y is 3x. That is,

$$S = \{(x,y) \mid x \in R, y = 3x\} ,$$

where we have labelled the set of points lying on $\overleftrightarrow{AB}$ as S. Alternatively, the line $\overleftrightarrow{AB}$ consists of all coordinate pairs (x,3x) such that x is an element of the set of real numbers (Here we have used the fact that y = 3x). In set builder notation,

$$S = \{(x,3x) \mid x \in R\}.$$

e) By the table of part (b) and equation (1), all the coordinates of part (b) satisfy the equation of part (c).

● **PROBLEM** 10-14

Write an equation of the line which is parallel to 6x + 3y = 4, and whose y-intercept is -6.

**Solution:** We employ the slope intercept form for the equation to be written, since we are given the y-intercept. Our task is then to determine the slope.

We are given the equation of a line parallel to the line whose equation we wish to find. We also know that the slopes of two parallel lines are equal. Hence, by finding the slope of the given line, we will also be finding the unknown slope. To find the slope of the given equation 6x + 3y = 4, we transform the equation 6x + 3y = 4 into slope intercept form.

$$6x + 3y = 4$$

$$3y = -6x + 4$$

$$y = -\frac{6}{3}x + \frac{4}{3}$$

$$y = -2x + \frac{4}{3}.$$

Therefore, the slope of the line we are looking for is -2. The y-intercept is -6. Applying the slope intercept form, y = mx + b, to the unknown line, we obtain,

$$y = -2x - 6$$

as the equation of the line.

● **PROBLEM** 10-15

Find the equation of the straight line passing through the point (4,-1) and having an angle of inclination of 135°.

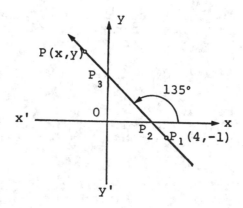

Solution: We are given one point on the line. If we had the slope of the line, we could apply the point slope theorem to determine the equation.

To determine the slope we will make use of the fact that the angle of inclination is 135°. The angle of inclination is the angle between the positive x-axis and the part of the line above the x-axis with the interior of the angle lying to the right of the line.

We shall show that the slope of the line = $-\tan \angle P_3P_2O$ = tan (angle of inclination).

Given points $P_2(x',0)$ and $P_3(0,y')$ on the line we can represent the slope m as

$$m = \frac{y' - 0}{0 - x'} = -\frac{y'}{x'}$$

In right triangle $P_3OP_2$, $y'$ and $x'$ are the respective lengths of sides $\overline{OP_3}$ and $\overline{OP_2}$. Hence, the tangent of $\angle P_3P_2O$ is the

$$\frac{\text{length of leg opposite } \angle P_3P_2O}{\text{length of leg adjacent } \angle P_3P_2O} \quad \text{or}$$

$$\tan \angle P_3P_2O = \frac{y'}{x'} \qquad \text{Since } m = -\frac{y'}{x'} \text{ and}$$

$$\tan \angle P_3P_2O = \frac{y'}{x'},$$

by substitution,

$$m = -\tan \angle P_3P_2O$$

Exterior angle $\angle P_3P_2X$ is given as 135° and can be observed to be the supplement of $\angle P_3P_2O$. Accordingly, $m\angle P_3P_2O = 180° - 135° = 45°$. Hence, by substitution, $m = -\tan 45° = 1$. Now we know a point on the line, $(4,-1)$ and the slope $m = -1$. The point - slope theorem is $(y-y_1) = m(x-x_1)$. Making one final substitution, we obtain

$$(y+1) = -1(x-4)$$

$$y+1 = -x + 4$$

$$y = -x + 3$$

Therefore, the equation of the line is given by $y = -x + 3$ or $y + x = 3$.

● **PROBLEM** 10-16

Find the equation of the perpendicular bisector of that portion of the straight line $5x + 3y - 15 = 0$ which is intercepted by the coordinate axes.

Solution: Prior to finding the midpoint of the segment and the negative reciprocal of its slope, which are essential to determining the equation of the perpendicular bisector, we must more clearly describe the segment.

To determine the slope of the segment, let us rearrange

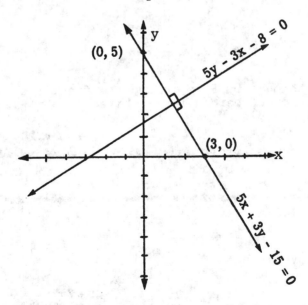

the equation into the form $y = mx + b$, where m is the slope and b is the y-intercept.

$$5x + 3y - 15 = 0$$
$$3y = -5x + 15$$
$$y = -\frac{5}{3}x + 5.$$

Hence, the slope, m, is $-\frac{5}{3}$. The coordinate axes provide the

237

boundary of the segment in question. Since the y-intercept is 5, one endpoint is (0,5).

The other endpoint can be found by setting y = 0 and solving for x.

$$0 = -\frac{5}{3}x + 5$$

$$-5 = -\frac{5}{3}x$$

$$5\left(\frac{3}{5}\right) = x$$

$$3 = x.$$

Hence, the other endpoint is (3,0).

The perpendicular bisector of the segment will have slope $-\frac{1}{m}$, or $\frac{3}{5}$. Also, it will pass through the midpoint of the given segment, $(\frac{0+3}{2}, \frac{5+0}{2})$ or $(\frac{3}{2}, \frac{5}{2})$.

We apply the point-slope form, $(y-y_1) = m(x-x_1)$, to obtain the equation of the perpendicular bisector. Hence,

$$(y - \frac{5}{2}) = \frac{3}{5}(x - \frac{3}{2})$$

$$y - \frac{5}{2} = \frac{3}{5}x - \frac{9}{10}$$

$$y = \frac{3}{5}x + \frac{16}{10}.$$

Multiplying through by 5 to remove the fractions, we obtain, for the equation of perpendicular bisector, 5y - 3x - 8 = 0.

● PROBLEM 10-17

Problem: Find the point of intersection of the two lines, 4x + 2y - 1 = 0, x - 2y - 7 = 0.

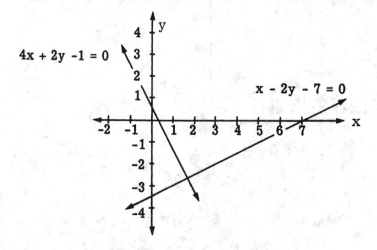

**Solution:** If $P_0(x_0, y_0)$ is the required point, and if we use the two slope intercept forms of these equations, we see that $x_0$ and $y_0$ must satisfy them both. The slope intercept form of $4x + 2y - 1 = 0$ is $y = -2x + \frac{1}{2}$ (just solve for y). Similarly, the slope intercept form of $x - 2y - 7 = 0$ is $y = \frac{1}{2}x - \frac{7}{2}$. Plugging in $(x_0, y_0)$, the points to be determined, yields two expressions for $y_0$,

$$y_0 = -2x_0 + \frac{1}{2} \quad \text{and} \quad y_0 = \frac{1}{2}x_0 - \frac{7}{2}.$$

Substituting the second value for $y_0$ back into the first equation gives us an expression in $x_0$ alone:

$$\frac{1}{2}x_0 - \frac{7}{2} = -2x_0 + \frac{1}{2}.$$

Collecting like terms yields $\frac{5}{2}x_0 = \frac{8}{2}$, or $x_0 = \frac{8}{5}$. Substituting this value into either of the slope-intercept forms gives $y_0 = -\frac{27}{10}$. Thus, the point of intersection is $(\frac{8}{5}, -\frac{27}{10})$.

● **PROBLEM** 10-18

---

a) Draw the graphs of $S = \{(x,y) \mid y = x\}$ and $T = \{(x,y) \mid y = -x\}$.

b) Draw the graph of $U = \{(x,y) \mid y = |x|\}$.

---

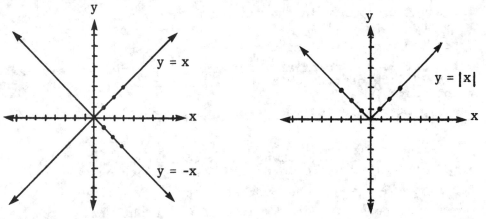

**Solution:** a) The graph of the set S consists of all points $(x,y)$ such that $y = x$. The points $(0,0)$, $(1,1)$, $(2,2)$ and $(3,3)$ all satisfy this requirement. The graph, a straight line, is shown in figure (a).

The graph of the set T consists of all points $(x,y)$ such that $y = -x$. The point $(0,0)$, $(1,-1)$, $(2,-2)$ and $(3,-3)$ satisfy this requirement. The graph, a straight line, is shown in figure (a).

b) The set U consists of all points (x,y) such that y = |x|
The points (0,0), (1,1) (-1,1), (2,2) (-2,2), (3,3) and (-3,3)
all satisfy this requirement. The graph of U is shown in figure (b).

● PROBLEM 10-19

Draw the graph of 3y - 2x = -6, using its slope and y-
intercept.

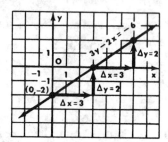

Solution: Prior to discussing the actual graphing, let us
transform the equation into slope intercept form and read off
the necessary information.

$$3y - 2x = -6$$

$$3y = 2x - 6$$

$$y = \frac{2}{3}x - 2$$

The equation is now in the standard form y = mx + b, where
m is the slope of the line, and b is its y-intercept. Therefore, the slope is $\frac{2}{3}$ and the y-intercept is -2. (The y-
intercept is the point at which the graph crosses the y axis.
At the y-intercept, x = 0. Hence, in our case, (0,-2) is the
y-intercept.)

To start drawing the graph, plot the point (0,-2).
(See figure).

Since the slope = $\frac{\text{change in y-coordinate}}{\text{change in x-coordinate}}$, knowing the
slope will allow us to determine other points on the graph.
If slope = $\frac{\Delta y}{\Delta x}$ = $\frac{2}{3}$, then another point on the line will lie
two units above, $\Delta y$, and 3 units to the right, $\Delta x$, of the y-
intercept. This point will be (0 + 3, -2 + 2), or (3,0).
This point is plotted in the accompanying graph.

Similarly, a third point would be 2 units above, and 3
units to the right, of (3,0). Hence, (3 + 3, 0 + 2), or
(6,2) is another point on the graph. This has been plotted.

To conclude the graph, draw a straight line which passes
through the three points plotted.

Note that three points were used but two were sufficient to determine the line.

# AREAS

Plot the points A (- 2, 3), B (1, 5) and C (4, 2) and find the area of △ABC.

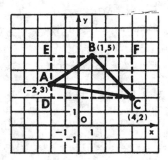

Solution: After plotting the points, as the graph shows, we find that no side is parallel to either of the axes. Therefore, when the altitude is drawn, its length is not easily determined. This makes the standard area formula for a triangle inapplicable.

To overcome this problem, we can inscribe the triangle in a figure whose sides are parallel to the axis, the lengths easier to calculate, and whose area formula can be applied. Any area within this figure but outside of the figure of main concern must be subtracted from the larger area in order to obtain the desired results.

In this problem, construct rectangle EFCD by drawing lines parallel to the x-axis through B and C and lines parallel to the y-axis through A and C.

The area of △ABC = area of rectangle EFCD - sum of the areas of right triangles, CDA, BEA and BFC.

Now, the endpoints of all line segments, whose lengths are needed for the calculation, will match in either the x or y coordinates. The length will be equal to the absolute value of the difference of the non-matching coordinates of the two endpoints for each segment. We will calculate the relevant lengths and then the area.

Since, A = (- 2, 3), B = (1, 5), C = (4, 2)

D = (- 2, 2), E = (- 2, 5), F = (4, 5)

Therefore,

$$ED = |5 - 2| = 3$$

$$EF = |4 - (-2)| = 6$$

$$EA = |5 - 3| = 2$$

$$EB = |1 - (-2)| = 3$$

$$BF = |4 - 1| = 3$$

$$FC = |5 - 2| = 3$$

$$DC = |4 - (-2)| = 6$$

Recall,

$$AD = |3 - 2| = 1$$

Area of ΔABC = area of rectangle EFCD - (area of rt. ΔCDA + area of rt. ΔBEA + area of rt. ΔBFC).

We must now determine the areas on the right side then substitute for the desired results.

Area of rectangle EFCD = bh = DC × ED = 6 × 3 = 18

Area of rt. ΔCDA = ½ leg × leg = ½(AD×DC)= ½(1×6) = 3

Area of rt. ΔBEA = ½ leg × leg = ½(EB×EA)= ½(2×3) = 3

Area of rt. ΔBFC = ½ leg × leg = ½(BF×FC)=½(3×3) = 4.5

Therefore, by substitution,

Area of ΔABC = 18 - (3 + 3 + 4.5) = 18 - 10.5

Therefore, Area of ΔABC = 7.5 sq. units.

● **PROBLEM 10-21**

Find the area of the polygon whose vertices are A (2, 2), B (9, 3), C (7, 6), and D (4, 5).

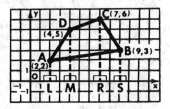

<u>Solution</u>: The polygon described in this question, and drawn on the accompanying graph, does not have any opposite sides parallel to each other, in which case it cannot be a type of parallelogram or trapezoid. Additionally, it is not regular, since no two sides are congruent. Therefore, no standard area formula for quadrilaterals can be applied.

We must therefore use a method for solution in which figures are constructed which have straightforward formulas for area and the length of whose sides and altitudes are known. This will enable us to indirectly determine the area of the given figure.

The usual approach is to extend lines from the vertices, perpendicular to one of the axis and calculate the area of the largest figure bounded by these lines and the sides of the polygon. We then subtract any area lying in this region not in the polygon, whose area we desire to find.

In this problem we draw line $\overrightarrow{AL}$, $\overrightarrow{DM}$, $\overrightarrow{CR}$ and $\overrightarrow{BS}$ all perpendicular to the x-axis. Since they are all perpendicular to the same line, they are all parallel to each other and, as such, will provide the bases of several trapezoids that will be used in this calculation. The trapezoids are LMDA, MRCD, RSBC and LSBA.

The area of polygon ABCD can be found by adding the areas of trapezoids LMDA, MRCD, RSBC and subtracting the area of trapezoid LSBA from the sum.

The formula for the area of a trapezoid with altitude h and bases $b_1$ and $b_2$ is

$$A = \tfrac{1}{2} h (b_1 + b_2).$$

Area of ABCD = (area of trapezoid LMDA + area of trapezoid MRCD + area of trapezoid RSBC) - area of trapezoid LSBA.

We will calculate the area of each trapezoid and substitute it into the above to find the area of ABCD.

The lengths of the bases of the trapezoids will be given as the distance from each vertex to the x-axis; and the altitudes as the horizontal distance between the bases along the x-axis.

Let us determine all necessary base and altitude lengths. The base lengths will equal the y-component of the vertex from which it is drawn, since that represents the vertical distance the vertex is above the x-axis.

Therefore, AL = 2, DM = 5, CR = 6, and BS = 3.

The altitude lengths will be given by the absolute value of the difference between the x-components of the two "vertex points" in each trapezoid.

Therefore,    LM = $|4 - 2|$ = 2

MR = $|4 - 7|$ = 3

RS = $|9 - 7|$ = 2

LS = $|2 - 9|$ = 7

Accordingly,

Area of trapezoid LMDA = $\tfrac{1}{2}$(LM)(AL + DM) = $\tfrac{1}{2}$ (2)(2 + 5)

243

$$= \tfrac{1}{2} \ (2)(7) = 7.$$

Area of trapezoid MRCD $= \tfrac{1}{2}(MR)(DM + CR) = \tfrac{1}{2}(3)(5 + 6)$

$$= \tfrac{1}{2} \ (3)(11) = 16.5$$

Area of trapezoid RSBC $= \tfrac{1}{2}(RS)(CR + BS) = \tfrac{1}{2}(2)(6 + 3)$

$$= \tfrac{1}{2}(2)(9) = 9$$

Area of trapezoid LSBA $= \tfrac{1}{2}(LS)(AL + BS) = \tfrac{1}{2}(7)(2 + 3)$

$$= \tfrac{1}{2} \ (7)(5) = 17.5$$

By substitution,

Area of ABCD $= (7 + 16.5 + 9) - 17. \ 5 = 32.5 - 17.5$

Therefore, the area of ABCD = 15.

## LOCUS

● **PROBLEM** 10-22

Write an equation for the locus of points equidistant from (3, 3) and (4, 4).

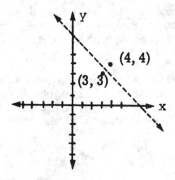

Solution: A perpendicular bisector is defined as the locus of points that are equidistant from the endpoints of a given segment. Therefore, the perpendicular bisector of the segment with endpoints (3, 3) and (4, 4) is the locus that is required.

FINDING THE EQUATION: A perpendicular bisector is a line. To find the equation of a line, we require a point on the line and the slope of the line. Because the perpendicular bisector includes the midpoint of the segment, we know that the midpoint between (3, 3) and (4, 4) is a point on the line. By the Midpoint Formula, we obtain

$$\left( \frac{3 + 4}{2} \ , \ \frac{3 + 4}{2} \right) = \left( \frac{7}{2} \ , \ \frac{7}{2} \right)$$

Because the perpendicular bisector is perpendicular
to the segment, we know m, the slope of the bisector, is the
negative reciprocal of the slope of the segment.
Slope of segment = $\frac{\Delta y}{\Delta x} = \frac{3-4}{3-4} = \frac{-1}{-1} = +1$. Therefore, the

slope of the line must be $-\left(\frac{1}{+1}\right) = -1$.

Because we have the slope, $-1$, and a point, $\left(\frac{7}{2}, \frac{7}{2}\right)$,

of the line, we can find the equation of the line using the
Point-Slope Form. An equation of the line that contains
point $(x_1, y_1)$ and has a slope m is $y - y_1 = m(x - x_1)$.
Thus, by substitution, the equation for the locus is

$$y - \frac{7}{2} = -1 \cdot \left(x - \frac{7}{2}\right).$$

Simplifying, this becomes $x + y = 7$.

● **PROBLEM 10-23**

Prove that the locus of points equidistant from the ends
of a given line segment is the perpendicular bisector of
the line segment. Prove the converse of this statement.

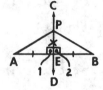     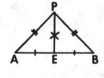

Figure (a)                    Figure (b)

Solution: To prove that a given locus takes on the
characteristics of a geometric figure, we must prove two
statements. First, prove that if a point is on the locus,
it satisfies the given condition. Then, prove either the
converse or inverse of the given statement. The converse
states that if the given conditions are satisfied, the
point is on the locus. The inverse states that if the point
is not on the locus then it does not satisfy the conditions.
In this problem, we will prove the initial statement and
its converse.

In order to prove that the locus is the correct one,
we will (a) prove the statement "If a point is on the
perpendicular bisector of a line segment, it is equidistant
from the ends of the line segment," and, (b) the converse
of this statement, namely, "If a point is equidistant from
the ends of a line segment, it is on the perpendicular bisector of the line segment."

(a) Proof of statement, "If a point is on the
perpendicular bisector of a line segment, it is equidistant

245

from the ends of the line segment ":

Draw the perpendicular bisector $\overleftrightarrow{CD}$ of $\overline{AB}$. Select a point P on $\overleftrightarrow{CD}$ and prove PA = PB.

This can be done by showing $\overline{PA}$ and $\overline{PB}$ are corresponding parts of $\triangle APE$ and $\triangle BPE$, proved congruent by the S.A.S. Postulate.

| STATEMENT | REASON |
|---|---|
| 1. $\overleftrightarrow{CD}$ is the $\perp$ bisector of $\overline{AB}$ and P is a point on $\overleftrightarrow{CD}$. | 1. Given. |
| 2. $\overline{AE} \cong \overline{EB}$ | 2. A bisector divides a line segment into two congruent parts. |
| 3. $\angle 1$ and $\angle 2$ are right angles | 3. Perpendicular lines intersect and form right angles. |
| 4. $\angle 1 \cong \angle 2$ | 4. All right angles are congruent. |
| 5. $\overline{PE} \cong \overline{PE}$ | 5. Reflexive property of congruence. |
| 6. $\triangle APE \cong \triangle BPE$ | 6. S.A.S. $\cong$ S.A.S. |
| 7. $\overline{PA} \cong \overline{PB}$ | 7. Corresponding sides of congruent triangles are congruent. |
| 8. PA = PB | 8. Congruent segments are equal in length. |

(b) Proof of the converse "If a point is equidistant from the ends of a line segment, it is on the perpendicular bisector of the line segment."

Draw a point O, off $\overline{AB}$, such that PA = PB. If we let E be the midpoint of AB and can then show $\overleftrightarrow{PE}$, the bisector of $\overline{AB}$, is perpendicular to $\overline{AB}$, then the proof is done. We will show $\overleftrightarrow{PE} \perp \overline{AB}$ by proving congruence between adjacent angles $\angle PEA$ and $\angle PEB$. $\angle PEA$ and $\angle PEB$ will be shown to be corresponding angles of $\triangle APE$ and $\triangle BPE$, these proved congruent by the S.S.S. $\cong$ S.S.S. Postulate.

| STATEMENT | REASON |
|---|---|
| 1. Let E be the midpoint of $\overline{AB}$. | 1. Every line segment has one and only one midpoint. |

| | |
|---|---|
| 2. Draw $\overleftrightarrow{PE}$. | 2. One and only one straight line can be drawn between two points. |
| 3. $\overline{AE} \cong \overline{EB}$. | 3. A midpoint divides a line segment into two congruent parts. |
| 4. $\overline{PA} \cong \overline{PB}$. | 4. Given. |
| 5. $\overline{PE} \cong \overline{PE}$ | 5. Reflexive property of congruence. |
| 6.  $\triangle APE \cong \triangle BPE$. | 6. S.S.S. $\cong$ S.S.S. |
| 7.  $\sphericalangle PEA \cong \sphericalangle PEB$. | 7. Corresponding angles of congruent triangles are congruent. |
| 8. $\overleftrightarrow{PE} \perp \overline{AB}$. | 8. If two lines intersect forming congruent adjacent angles, the lines are perpendicular (theorem). |
| 9. $\overleftrightarrow{PE}$ is the $\perp$ bisector of $\overline{AB}$. | 9. If a line is perpendicular to a line segment and bisects the line segment, then the line is the perpendicular bisector of the line segment. |

● **PROBLEM 10-24**

Describe the locus of points determined by the equation

$$x^2 + y^2 + z^2 = 2x.$$

(Hint: Complete the square in x.)

Solution: Let us apply the hint first and then see what help this gives us in answering the question.

$$x^2 - 2x + y^2 + z^2 = 0.$$

Completing the square we obtain: $(x - 1)^2 + y^2 + z^2 - 1 = 0$, or:

(1) $\qquad (x - 1)^2 + y^2 + z^2 = 1.$

The square of the distance, d, between any two points $A(x_1, y_1, z_1)$ and $B(x_2, y_2, z_2)$ in 3-space is given by

$$d^2 = (x_1 - x_2)^2 + (y_1 - y_2)^2 + (z_1 - z_2)^2.$$

If A is allowed to be any arbitrary point (x, y, z)

then we have

(2)  $(x - x_2)^2 + (y - y_2)^2 + (z - z_2)^2 = d^2.$

Assuming $(x_2, y_2, z_2)$ and d are given, this is an equation for all points a distance d from $(x_2, y_2, z_2)$. In other words, a sphere of radius d centered at $(x_2, y_2, z_2)$.

By inspection we see that equation (2) is similar to equation (1). In fact, if we take $(x_2, y_2, z_2) = (1, 0, 0)$, and d = 1, the equations are identical. Hence, the locus described by equation (1) and the original equation is a sphere centered at (1, 0, 0) with radius d.

● **PROBLEM** 10-25

Locate the points that are a given distance, d, from a given point S, and are also equidistant from the ends of line segment $\overline{AB}$.

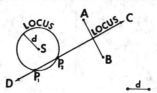

Solution: Conditions for two loci are given in this problem. The problem can be interpreted as one of locating the intersection points of these two loci.

The first condition, that the points of the locus be a given distance d from point S, describes a circle, the length of whose radius is d. This locus is the circle shown in the figure, with center at S.

The locus of points equidistant from the end of the line segment $\overline{AB}$ is the perpendicular bisector of $\overline{AB}$. In the figure, this is line $\overleftrightarrow{CD}$.

If d is less than the distance from S to $\overleftrightarrow{CD}$, then the circle locus and the locus given by $\overleftrightarrow{CD}$ do not intersect at any points and no points satisfy the two conditions.

If d is equal to the distance from S to $\overleftrightarrow{CD}$, then there is one point where both loci will intersect since $\overleftrightarrow{CD}$ will be the tangent of the circle centered at S with radius d. One point will satisfy both conditions.

If d is greater than the distance from S to $\overleftrightarrow{CD}$, then the locus $\overleftrightarrow{CD}$ is a secant to the circular locus and, accordingly, the two loci intersect at two points and these two points, $P_1$ and $P_2$, satisfy both conditions. This final case is exhibited in the figure.

Two concentric circles have radii whose lengths are 2 in. and 6 in. Line m is drawn, in the accompanying figure, tangent to the smaller circle. (a) Describe fully the locus of points equidistant from the two circles. (b) Describe fully the locus of points at a given distance d from line m. (c) How many points are there which satisfy the conditions given in both parts (a) and (b) if: (1) d < 2 in.? (2) d = 2 in.? (3) d = 6 in.? (4) d > 6 in.?

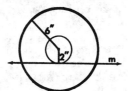

Solution:   (a) The locus of points equidistant from the two concentric circles is a third concentric circle, the length of whose radius is 4 in.

The middle circle represents this locus.

(b) The locus of points at a given distance d from the given line m is a pair of lines, parallel to m, at the distance d from m. The 2 outer parallel lines shown comprise this locus.

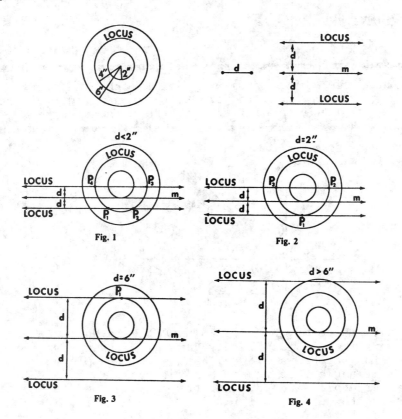

Fig. 1

Fig. 2

Fig. 3

Fig. 4

(c) The accompanying figures, numbered 1 - 4, will be helpful in solving this problem.

(1) d < 2 in.: In this case, there are 4 points of intersection of the loci. In figure 1, they are $P_1$, $P_2$, $P_3$, $P_4$.

(2) d = 2 in.: As the distance between the parallel lines widens, the points of intersection approach each other. In case (1), both parallel lines were secants of the circular locus. However, when d = 2 in., one line becomes a tangent. Therefore, as fig. (2) shows, there are 3 points that satisfy both conditions: $P_1$, $P_2$ and $P_3$.

(3) d = 6 in.: The lowest of the lines in the parallel line locus, as shown in fig. (3), now lies completely outside of the circular locus and has no points of intersection with the latter. The upper line is tangent to the circle and provides the only point of intersection, $P_1$, that satisfies both conditions.

(d) d > 6 in.: The distance from line m to the outermost edge of the circular locus is 6 in. Therefore, when the parallel lines are over 6 in. away from line m, there will be no point which satisfies both conditions.

## COORDINATE PROOFS

● PROBLEM 10-27

Prove that the segment formed by joining the midpoints of two sides of a triangle is parallel to the third side and has a length equal to half that of the third side.

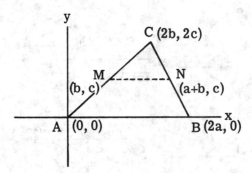

Solution: There may be a certain amount of doubt that the figure above is completely general. If we prove the theorem for the above figure, have we really proven it for all triangles? It would seem that this is a very special triangle, indeed, that has one side on the X-axis and one vertex at the origin.

We could prove the theorem for a triangle anywhere in the X-Y plane, but the notation is less complicated here. Draw a triangle anywhere in the plane and we can translate it and rotate it so that one side of it is on the X-axis and one vertex is at the origin. True we will have changed its position and direction, but the shape of the triangle will remain the same, its sides will have the same length; its angles will have the same measure. If the line between the midpoints of two sides is parallel to the third side, that too is unchanged. In short, ABC can be any triangle, and this proof is just as general as the geometric proof of the midline of a triangle.

GIVEN: $\triangle ABC$: A( 0, 0); B (2a, 0); C (2b, 2c);
M and N are the midpoints of $\overline{AC}$ and $\overline{CB}$ respectively.

PROVE: $\overline{MN} \parallel \overline{AB}$; and MN = ½ AB.

PROOF: If M is the midpoint of $\overline{AC}$, then by the midpoint formula, $M = \left( \dfrac{2b + 0}{2}, \dfrac{2c + 0}{2} \right)$ or M =(b, c).

Similarly, N is the midpoint of $\overline{BC}$. Therefore, $N = \left( \dfrac{2b + 2a}{2}, \dfrac{2c + 0}{2} \right)$ or N=(b + a, c).

To show $\overline{MN} \parallel \overline{AB}$, we find the slopes $\overline{MN}$ and $\overline{AB}$. Slope of $\overline{MN} = \dfrac{\Delta y}{\Delta x} = \dfrac{c - c}{(b + a) - b} = 0$. Because $\overline{AB}$ lies on the X-axis, slope of $\overline{AB} = 0$. Since the two slopes are equal $\overline{AB} \parallel \overline{MN}$.

To show MN = ½ AB, we find the lengths of each using the distance formula.

$AB = \sqrt{ (2a - 0)^2 + (0 - 0)^2 } = 2a.$

$MN = \sqrt{ (b - (a + b))^2 + (c - c)^2 } = \sqrt{ (- a)^2 + 0^2 }$

$= \sqrt{ a^2 } = a$

Therefore, AB = 2 · MN or MN = ½ AB, and the proof is complete.

● **PROBLEM 10-28**

Show that the points A (2, -2), B (- 8, 4), and C (5, 3) are the vertices of a right triangle and find its area.

Solution: We can prove that a triangle is a right triangle by showing that the square of the length of the hypotenuse is equal to the sum of the squares of the lengths of both

251

legs, i.e. showing that the Pythagorean Theorem holds.

The general formula for distance between two points will allow us to determine the required length. The formula tells us that for any two points $(x_1, y_1)$ and $(x_2, y_2)$ the length of the segment between them, $d$, is given by

$$d = \sqrt{(x_2 - x_1)^2 + (y_2 - y_1)^2}.$$

Hence, since $A = (2, -2)$, $B = (-8, 4)$, and $C = (5, 3)$, we can apply the formula to find:

$$AB = \sqrt{(-8 -2)^2 + (4 - (-2))^2} = \sqrt{(-10)^2 + (6)^2} = \sqrt{136}$$

$$BC = \sqrt{(5 - (-8))^2 + (3 - 4)^2} = \sqrt{(13)^2 + (-1)^2} = \sqrt{170}$$

$$CA = \sqrt{(5 - 2)^2 + (3 - (-2))^2} = \sqrt{(3)^2 + (5)^2} = \sqrt{34}$$

$\overline{BC}$ is the longest side of $\triangle ABC$ and, if $\triangle ABC$ is a right triangle, $\overline{BC}$ is the hypotenuse. Therefore, if $(BC)^2 = (AB)^2 + (CA)^2$, then $\triangle ABC$ is a right triangle.

By substitution, we obtain

$$(\sqrt{170})^2 = (\sqrt{136})^2 + (\sqrt{34})^2$$

$$170 = 136 + 34 = 170.$$

Hence, $\triangle ABC$ is a right triangle.

The area of a right triangle is equal to the one-half the product of the lengths of its legs.

Ergo, area of $\triangle ABC = \frac{1}{2} (\sqrt{136})(\sqrt{34}) = \frac{1}{2} \sqrt{4624}$

$$= \frac{1}{2} \sqrt{16} \sqrt{289} = \frac{1}{2} (4)(17) = \frac{1}{2}(68).$$

Therefore, area of $\triangle ABC$ is 34 sq. units.

**● PROBLEM 10-29**

Prove analytically that if the diagonals of a parallelogram are equal, the figure is a rectangle.

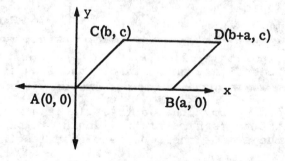

Solution: In the figure shown, ABDC is a general parallelogram positioned on the Cartesian plane in such a way that one side corresponds to the x-axis and one vertex to the origin. Here we are given AD = BC and asked to prove ABCD is a rectangle. To complete the proof, we will employ the fact that a rectangle is a parallelogram with one right angle.

The length of the two diagonals can be represented by using the distance formula.

$$AD = \sqrt{(b + a - 0)^2 + (c - 0)^2} = \sqrt{b^2 + 2ab + a^2 + c^2} \quad \text{and}$$

$$BC = \sqrt{(b - a)^2 + (c - 0)^2} = \sqrt{b^2 - 2ab + a^2 + c^2}$$

We are given AD = BC. Hence,

$$\sqrt{b^2 + 2ab + a^2 + c^2} = \sqrt{b^2 - 2ab + a^2 \cdot c^2}$$

$$b^2 + 2ab + a^2 + c^2 = b^2 - 2ab + a^2 + c^2$$

$$2ab = - 2ab$$

This can only happen if a = 0 or if b = 0. a cannot equal zero or points A and B would coincide and ABDC would not exist as a quadrilateral. Hence, b = 0 is the only possible conclusion in this problem.

We know, then, that the coordinates of ABDC take the form A $(0, 0)$, B $(a, 0)$, C $(0, c)$, and D $(a, c)$. This tells us that $\overline{AC}$ is a segment of the y-axis and $\overline{AB}$ is a segment of the x-axis. Since the two axes are perpendicular, $\overline{AC} \perp \overline{AB}$. Hence ∢ CAB is a right angle and ABCD is a rectangle.

● **PROBLEM** 10-30

Prove analytically that any angle inscribed in a semi-circle is a right angle.

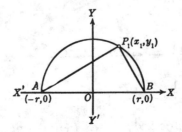

Solution: We will prove that the inscribed angle is a right angle by showing that it is formed by the inter-section of two perpendicular line segments.

We draw a semicircle of radius r centered at the origin, as shown in the figure, the equation of the semi-circle is $x^2 + y^2 = r^2$.

Let $P_1$ have the coordinates $(x_1, y_1)$ and lie anywhere on the semicircle. Since r is the radius of the semicircle, the coordinates of A and B are $(-r, 0)$ and $(r, 0)$.

To prove that $\overline{P_1A} \perp \overline{P_1B}$ by analytical methods, we can show that the slopes of $\overline{P_1A}$ and $\overline{P_1B}$, $m_1$ and $m_2$ respectively, are in the relation $m_1 m_2 = -1$.

By the definition of slope,

Slope of $\overline{P_1A} = m_1 = \dfrac{y_1 - 0}{x_1 - (-r)} = \dfrac{y_1}{x_1 + r}$

Slope of $\overline{P_1B} = m_2 = \dfrac{y_1 - 0}{x_1 - r} = \dfrac{y_1}{x_1 - r}$

Hence, $m_1 m_2 = \left(\dfrac{y_1}{x_1 - r}\right)\left(\dfrac{y_1}{x_1 + r}\right) = \dfrac{y_1{}^2}{x_1{}^2 - r^2}$

Since $P_1$ lies on a circle, the coordinates $(x_1, y_1)$ satisfy the equation of the semicircle. Hence, $x_1{}^2 + y_1{}^2 = r^2$. It follows then that $y_1{}^2 = r^2 - x_1{}^2$, and $-y_1{}^2 = x_1{}^2 - r^2$.

Therefore, by substitution, $m_1 m_2 = \dfrac{y_1{}^2}{-y_1{}^2} = -1$.

Hence, $\overline{P_1A} \perp \overline{P_1B}$ and $\sphericalangle AP_1B$ is a right angle.

● **PROBLEM** 10-31

Prove analytically that the lines joining the midpoints of the adjacent sides of any quadrilateral form a parallelogram.

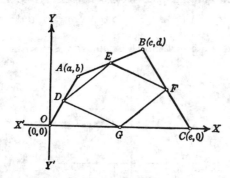

Solution: In plane geometry we can prove a quadrilateral is a parallelogram by proving both pairs of opposite sides are parallel. This condition, in analytic geometry, amounts to proving that opposite sides have the same slope, since line segments with the same slope will always be parallel.

On the accompanying graph, an arbitrary quadrilateral has been positioned with one side on the x-axis and vertices A (a, b), B (c, d), C (e, 0), and O (0, 0) as shown. The midpoints of the sides are E, F, G, and D.

We want to prove that quadrilateral DEFG is a parallelogram. The slopes of the sides of this figure can readily be determined once we know the coordinates of D, E, F, and G.

Since these points are the midpoints of segments whose endpoints are known, by the midpoint formula, their coordinates can be determined.

D is the midpoint of $\overline{AO}$. Hence, D $= \left(\dfrac{a}{2}, \dfrac{b}{2}\right)$.

E is the midpoint of $\overline{AB}$. Hence E $= \left(\dfrac{a + c}{2}, \dfrac{b + d}{2}\right)$.

F is the midpoint of $\overline{BC}$. Hence, F $= \left(\dfrac{c + e}{2}, \dfrac{d}{2}\right)$.

G is the midpoint of $\overline{CO}$. Hence, G $= \left(\dfrac{e}{2}, 0\right)$.

Now we can proceed to calculate the slopes of the sides of DEFG. Recall, for any segment with endpoints $(x_1, y_1)$ and $(x_2, y_2)$ the slope equals $\dfrac{y_2 - y_1}{x_2 - x_1}$.

Slope of $\overline{DE}$ = $\dfrac{\dfrac{b}{2} - \dfrac{b + d}{2}}{\dfrac{a}{2} - \dfrac{a + c}{2}}$ = $\dfrac{\dfrac{b - b - d}{2}}{\dfrac{a - a - c}{2}}$ = $\dfrac{-d}{-c}$ = $\dfrac{d}{c}$

Slope of $\overline{FG}$ = $\dfrac{0 - \dfrac{d}{2}}{\dfrac{e}{2} - \dfrac{c + e}{2}}$ = $\dfrac{-\dfrac{d}{2}}{\dfrac{e - c - e}{2}}$ = $\dfrac{-d}{-c}$ = $\dfrac{d}{c}$

Hence, $\overline{DE} \parallel \overline{FG}$ since their slopes are equal.

Slope of $\overline{EF}$ = $\dfrac{\dfrac{b + d}{2} - \dfrac{d}{2}}{\dfrac{a + c}{2} - \dfrac{c + e}{2}}$ = $\dfrac{\dfrac{b + d - d}{2}}{\dfrac{a + c - c - e}{2}}$ = $\dfrac{b}{a - e}$

Slope of $\overline{DG}$ = $\dfrac{\dfrac{b}{2} - 0}{\dfrac{a}{2} - \dfrac{e}{2}}$ = $\dfrac{b}{a - e}$

By similar reasoning, $\overline{EF} \parallel \overline{DG}$.

Therefore, DEFG is a parallelogram since all of its opposite sides are parallel.

# CHAPTER 11

# SOLID GEOMETRY

## LOCUS

Graph $\{(x, y) : y \geq |x|\}$ where x and y are members of the set $\{-3, -2, -1, 0, 1, 2, 3\}$ .

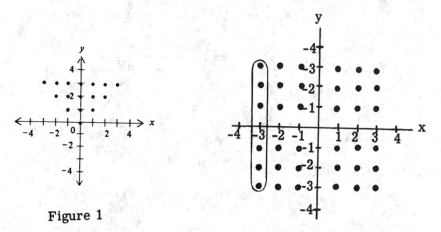

Figure 1

Figure 2

Solution:   In this example, x and y are limited to a finite set of values. Therefore, there are a finite number of points. Thus for this graph, we need only to list all ordered pairs in the set, and plot each point, to complete the graph.

Each point on the graph must satisfy the equation

$$y \geq |x|.$$

To list all the points, we first choose a possible value of x, - 3  for example, and find all the possible values

of y such that y ≥ ]- 3|, or y ≥ 3. y is limited to the
set {- 3, - 2, - 1, 0, 1, 2, 3}. Therefore, the only
possible value of y is 3. Point (- 3, 3) is, consequently,
a point on the graph. Next, choose another value of x,
- 2. for example. For y = 3, it is true that y > |- 2|.
Also for y = 2, it is true that y > |- 2|. Therefore,
points (- 2, 2) and (- 2, 3) are on the graph. We continue
choosing possible values of x and finding the corresponding
y's such that y > |x|, until all x's have been chosen. When
all x's have been tested, then our list of points is complete. The final list of points is (- 3, 3), (- 2, 3),
(- 2, 2), (- 1, 3), (- 1, 2), (- 1, 1), (0, 3), (0, 2),
(0, 1), (0, 0), (1, 3), (1, 2), (1, 1), (2, 3), (2, 2),
(3, 3). The graph is shown in Fig. 1.

WHY THIS METHOD WORKS: If x and y must be members of
the set {- 3, - 2, - 1, 0, 1, 2, 3}, then the graph of all
possible points in the set would be as in Fig. 2. By
selecting x = - 3, we were actually testing all the
circled points in Fig. 2, and listing only those that
satisfy the relation y > |x|. By repeating the procedure
for every possible x, we see that all possible points are
tested.

● **PROBLEM 11-2**

Describe the locus of points equidistant from two concentric
spheres, the length of whose radii are 2 and 6.

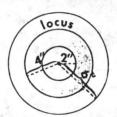

Solution: The locus of points that satisfy the given conditions must lie between the surfaces of the two spheres.

Since the original two spheres are concentric, a radius
of the larger sphere will be concurrent with a radius of the
smaller sphere. The distance between the two surfaces is the
length of the larger radius minus the length of the smaller
radius, i.e. 6 - 2 = 4. One point in the locus must be at
the midpoint of this distance, or 2 units from the inner
spherical surface (or 4 units from the center). Repeating
this process for every radius will result in our plotting a
sphere of radius 4. Therefore, the locus described is a
sphere of radius 4, with the same center as the given spheres.

● **PROBLEM 11-3**

In the figure, if plane M passes through the center, P, of the
sphere S, prove that the intersection set of S and M is a
great circle of S.

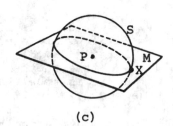

(c)

<u>Solution</u>: If S is a sphere of radius r, then any circle lying on S, with radius r, is a great circle of S. We will first show that the intersection set of S and M lies on sphere S. Then we show that the intersection set is a circle of radius r, and therefore is a great circle see figure.)

Since all the points of S lie on the sphere of radius r, the intersection set of S and M lies on the sphere. Hence, these points must also be members of S.

To show that the set of points is a great circle of P, note that (1) because the set of points are members of M, the set is collinear; (2) because the set of points are members of S, for every point X of the set of points, XP = radius of sphere; (3) P is on plane M.

For a set of coplanar points, if there exists a point P coplanar with the set, such that the point is equidistant from every point of the set, then the set is a circle of center P and radius equal to the distance between each point and P. Therefore, the intersection set is a circle of radius XP = radius of sphere.

The intersection set is thus a circle on sphere S with radius equal to the radius of the sphere - in short, a great circle of S.

● **PROBLEM 11-4**

**Given:** Planes P and Q intersect sphere S in ⊙A and ⊙B, respectively; M is a point of ⊙A; N is a point of ⊙B: $\overline{AS} \cong \overline{BS}$.

**Prove:** ⊙A ≅ ⊙B.

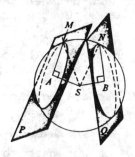

<u>Solution</u>: To prove two circles congruent, we must prove that their radii are congruent, in this case, $\overline{AM}$ and $\overline{BN}$. Whenever two line segments are to be equated, it is wise to look for

congruent triangles. The congruent triangles for which we search must contain $\overline{AM}$ and $\overline{BN}$. In addition, since we are given that $\overline{AS} \cong \overline{BS}$, the triangles should also contain these segments. $\triangle AMS$ and $\triangle BNS$ satisfy these requirements. In proving $\triangle AMS \cong \triangle BNS$, we shall make use of three facts: (1) $\overline{AS} \cong \overline{BS}$ (given); (2) $\angle$ MAS and $\angle$ NBS are right angles (the line connecting the center of the sphere and the center of the intercepted circle is perpendicular to the intercepting plane); and (3) $\overline{MS} = \overline{NS}$ (all radii are equal).

| Statements | Reasons |
|---|---|
| 1. Planes P and Q intersect sphere S in ⊙A and ⊙B, respectively; M is a point of ⊙A; N is a point of ⊙B; $\overline{AS} \cong \overline{BS}$. | 1. Given. |
| 2. $\overline{MS} \cong \overline{NS}$. | 2. All radii of a sphere are congruent. (Definition of a sphere.) |
| 3. $\overline{AS} \perp$ plane P. $\overline{BS} \perp$ plane Q. | 3. If a line contains the center of a sphere, and the center of a circle of intersection of the sphere with a plane not through the center of the sphere, then the line is perpendicular to the intersecting plane. |
| 4. $\overline{AS} \perp \overline{AM}$. $\overline{BS} \perp \overline{BN}$. | 4. A line perpendicular to a plane is perpendicular to every line in the plane that intersects the line. |
| 5. $\angle$A and $\angle$B are right angles. | 5. Definition of perpendicular lines. |
| 6. $\triangle MAS$ and $\triangle NBS$ are right triangles. | 6. Definition of right triangle. |
| 7. $\triangle MAS \cong \triangle NBS$. | 7. If the hypotenuse and a leg of one right triangle are congruent to the hypotenuse and a leg of another right triangle, then the two triangles are congruent. |
| 8. $\overline{MA} \cong \overline{NB}$. | 8. Correspoinding sides of congruent triangles are congruent. |
| 9. ⊙A $\cong$ ⊙B. | 9. Circles are congruent if and only if their radii are congruent. |

259

Show that the locus of points equidistant from two given points is the plane perpendicular to the line segment joining them at their midpoint.

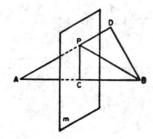

**Solution**:  To prove that a certain set of points is a locus, we must show (1) all points in the set satisfy the conditions, and (2) all points that satisfy the conditions are contained in the set.

We satisfy the first condition by showing that any point P on m is equidistant from A and B (by showing ΔAPC ≅ ΔBPC). We satisfy the second condition by selecting a point outside the plane D on the B-side of the half-space and showing that AD > DB.  Thus, any point not on the plane cannot be equidistant from both points.

> **Given**:  Points A and B, with plane m perpendicular to $\overline{AB}$ and bisecting $\overline{AB}$ at C.
> **To Prove**:  The locus of points equidistant from A and B is plane m ⊥ $\overline{AB}$ at its midpoint C.

| Statements | Reasons |
|---|---|
| 1. From P, any point in plane m, draw $\overline{PA}$, $\overline{PB}$ and $\overline{PC}$. | 1. Two points determine a line. |
| 2. $\overline{AB} \perp \overline{PC}$. | 2. If a line is ⊥ to a plane, then it is ⊥ to any line in the plane passing through the point of intersection. |
| 3. $\overline{PC} \cong \overline{PC}$. | 3. Reflexive Property. |
| 4. $\overline{AC} \cong \overline{BC}$. | 4. Definition of a midpoint. |
| 5. ⦟PCA ≅ ⦟PCB. | 5. All right angles are congruent. |
| 6. ΔPAC ≅ ΔPBC. | 6. The SAS Postulate. |
| 7. PA = PB. | 7. Corresponding parts of congruent triangles are equal in length. |

Thus, every point on plane m is equidistant from A and B.

| | | | |
|---|---|---|---|
| 8. | From D, any point outside m in the B-halfspace, draw $\overline{DA}$ and $\overline{DB}$. | 8. | Two points determine a line. |
| 9. | DP + PB > DB. | 9. | The sum of two sides of a triangle ($\triangle$PDB) exceeds the third. |
| 10. | DP + PA > DB or DA > DB. | 10. | Substitution Postulate. |
| 11. | Only points on m will be in the locus. | 11. | Postulate of Elimination. |

Any point outside plane m is not equidistant from A and B.

● **PROBLEM** 11-6

Show that if a plane intersects two parallel planes, then it intersects them in two parallel lines.

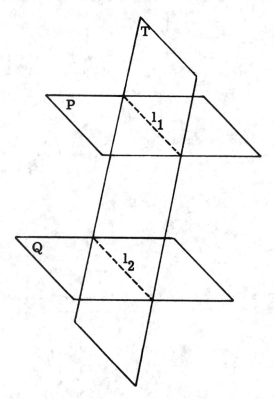

<u>Solution</u>: Two lines are parallel if they are (1) coplanar and (2) they never intersect. Two noncoincident nonparallel planes intersect in a line. Therefore, the intersection of a plane T with two parallel planes are two lines that (1) are both on plane T and (2) never intersect because the planes in

which the lines lie are parallel. As such, the two lines of intersection will be parallel.

Given: Plane T intersects parallel planes P and Q.

Prove: The intersection consists of two parallel lines.

| Statements | Reasons |
|---|---|
| 1. Plane T intersects parallel planes P and Q. | 1. Given. |
| 2. The intersection of T and P is line $\ell_1$. The intersection of T and Q is line $\ell_2$. | 2. The intersection of two non-parallel, noncoincident planes is a line coplanar to both planes. (Plane T cannot be parallel or coincident to P or Q because it would contradict our assumption that T intersects P and Q). |
| 3. $\ell_1$ and $\ell_2$ are coplanar. | 3. From 2, we know that both $\ell_1$ and $\ell_2$ lie on plane T. |
| 4. Either (1) $\ell_1$ intersects $\ell_2$ (2), or $\ell_1$ does not intersect $\ell_2$. | 4. Either a statement or its negation is true. |
| 5. Case (1) $\ell_1$ intersects $\ell_2$. Let r be a point on $\ell_1$ and $\ell_2$. | 5. Definition of intersection of two lines. |
| 6. r lies on P. r lies on Q. | 6. If a line lies on a plane, then all points of the line are common to the plane. |
| 7. There is no point r such that r lies on P and r lies on Q. | 7. Parallel planes have no point in common. |
| 8. $\ell_1$ does not intersect $\ell_2$. | 8. Since statement (1) leads to a contradiction, the negation must be true. |
| 9. $\ell_1 \parallel \ell_2$ or the intersection consists of two parallel lines. | 9. Two coplanar lines that do not intersect are parallel. |

# LINES AND PLANES

Show that if a line is perpendicular to one of two parallel
planes, then it is perpendicular to the other.

<u>Solution</u>: For a line to be perpendicular to a plane, we show
that the line is perpendicular to every line in the plane that
passes through the point of intersection. Suppose $\overleftrightarrow{AB} \perp$ plane
P at point A, plane P ∥ plane Q, and $\ell_1$ intersects plane Q

at point B. Then for every line $\overleftrightarrow{BD}$ in plane Q, there is a
line $\overleftrightarrow{AC}$ in plane P such that $\overleftrightarrow{AC}$ ∥ $\overleftrightarrow{BD}$. Then, interior angles
on the same side of the transversal must be supplementary.
Since for every $\overleftrightarrow{AC}$, $\overleftrightarrow{AC} \perp \overleftrightarrow{AB}$, then $\overleftrightarrow{AB} \perp \overleftrightarrow{BD}$ for every $\overleftrightarrow{BD}$, and
$\overleftrightarrow{AB}$ must be perpendicular to plane Q.

Given: Plane P ∥ plane Q; $\overleftrightarrow{AB} \perp$ P at A. $\overleftrightarrow{AB}$ intersects Q
at point B.

Prove: $\overleftrightarrow{AB} \perp$ Q.

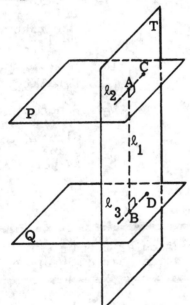

| Statements | Reasons |
|---|---|
| 1. Plane P ∥ plane Q; $\overleftrightarrow{AB} \perp$ P at A, $\overleftrightarrow{AB}$ intersects Q at point B. | 1. Given. |
| 2. Point D is any point in plane Q. | 2. A plane contains an infinite number of points. |
| 3. Plane T is the plane determined by $\overleftrightarrow{AB}$ and $\overleftrightarrow{BD}$. | 3. Two intersecting lines determine a plane. |

4. Plane T intersects P at line $\overleftrightarrow{AC}$.

4. The intersection of two nonparallel, noncoincident planes is a line common to both planes.

5. $\overleftrightarrow{AC} \parallel \overleftrightarrow{BD}$.

5. If a plane intersects two parallel planes, then it intersects them in two parallel lines.

6. $\overline{BA} \perp \overline{AC}$.

6. A line is perpendicular to a plane if, and only if, it is perpendicular to every line in the plane that passes through the point of intersection.

7. ∢BAC is a right angle.

7. Perpendicular lines intersect to form right angles.

8. m∢BAC = 90°.

8. All right angles measure 90°.

9. m∢BAC + m∢ABD = 180 .

9. Interior angles of parallel lines on the same side of the transversal are supplementary.

10. m∢ABD = 90°.

10. Subtraction Property of Equality.

11. $\overleftrightarrow{AB} \perp$ plane Q.

11. Since D could be any point in the plane, $\overleftrightarrow{AB}$ is perpendicular to every line $\overleftrightarrow{BD}$ in plane Q. By definition, $\overleftrightarrow{AB}$ is perpendicular to Q.

● **PROBLEM 11-8**

Given that $\overleftrightarrow{AB}$ is perpendicular to plane P, $\overleftrightarrow{BC}$ and $\overleftrightarrow{BD}$ lie in plane P, and $\overline{BC} \cong \overline{BD}$, prove that $\overline{AC} \cong \overline{AD}$.

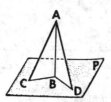

**Solution:** To prove that $\overline{AC} \cong \overline{AD}$, we must prove that the triangles in which these lines are corresponding sides, ΔABC and ΔABD, are congruent. This will be done using the S.A.S. Postulate.

In order to prove that the included angles are congruent,

264

(i.e. $\angle ABC \cong \angle ABD$), we will have to apply the definition of a line perpendicular to a plane. This definition tells us that a line perpendicular to a plane at a point is perpendicular to every line, in the plane, which passes through that point.

| Statement | Reason |
|---|---|
| 1. $\overleftrightarrow{AB} \perp$ plane P. | 1. Given. |
| 2. $\overleftrightarrow{BC}$, $\overleftrightarrow{BD}$ lie in plane P. | 2. Given. |
| 3. $\overleftrightarrow{AB} \perp \overleftrightarrow{BC}$, $\overleftrightarrow{AB} \perp \overleftrightarrow{BD}$. | 3. Definition of a line perpendicular to a plane. |
| 4. $\angle ABD$ and $\angle ABC$ are right angles. | 4. Perpendicular lines intersect forming right angles. |
| 5. $\angle ABC \cong \angle ABD$. | 5. All right angles are congruent. |
| 6. $\overline{BC} \cong \overline{BD}$. | 6. Given. |
| 7. $\overline{AB} \cong \overline{AB}$. | 7. Reflexive Property of Congruence. |
| 8. $\triangle ABC \cong \triangle ABD$. | 8. S.A.S. Postulate. |
| 9. $\overline{AC} \cong \overline{AD}$. | 9. Corresponding sides of congruent triangles are congruent. |

● **PROBLEM 11-9**

Line k is parallel to plane P. Prove that a plane perpendicular to line k is also perpendicular to P.

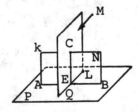

Solution: The best way to present this proof will be in two column format. We will show that the plane perpendicular to line k contains a line perpendicular to two intersecting lines in the parallel plane and is, therefore, perpendicular to that plane.

| Statement | Reason |
|---|---|
| 1. Line k ∥ plane P<br>plane M ⊥ line k. | 1. Given |

| | |
|---|---|
| 2. C is the intersection of line k with plane M. | 2. The intersection of a line and a plane is a point. |
| 3. $\overline{QL}$ is the intersection of planes M and P. | 3. The intersection of two planes is a straight line. |
| 4. Drop $\overline{CE} \perp \overline{QL}$ from point C. | 4. A perpendicular may be drawn in a plane, from a point to a line. |
| 5. Pass a plane through lines k and $\overline{CE}$ intersecting plane P in line $\overleftrightarrow{AB}$. | 5. Two intersecting lines determine a plane. |
| 6. Line k ∥ $\overleftrightarrow{AB}$. | 6. If a line is parallel to a plane, then it is parallel to the intersection of that plane with any plane containing the line. |
| 7. Line k $\perp$ $\overline{CE}$. | 7. A line perpendicular to a plane is perpendicular to every line in the plane passing through its foot. |
| 8. $\overline{AB} \perp \overline{CE}$. | 8. In a plane, if a line is perpendicular to one of two parallel lines, then it is perpendicular to the other. |
| 9. $\overline{CE} \perp \overline{QL}$. | 9. Construction. |
| 10. $\overline{CE} \perp$ plane P. | 10. If a line is perpendicular to two intersecting lines at their point of intersection, then it is perpendicular to the plane determined by the lines. |
| 11. Plane M $\perp$ plane P. | 11. If a line is perpendicular to a given plane, then every plane which contains this line is perependicular to the given plane. |

● **PROBLEM 11-10**

Show that two lines perpendicular to the same plane are parallel.

**Solution:** In the accompanying figure, $\overleftrightarrow{AB}$ and $\overleftrightarrow{CD}$ are perpendicular to plane m. We must prove $\overleftrightarrow{AB} \parallel \overleftrightarrow{CD}$. This can be done in two steps: first prove $\overleftrightarrow{AB}$ and $\overleftrightarrow{CD}$ are coplanar and then show $\overleftrightarrow{AB} \parallel \overleftrightarrow{CD}$. To show $\overleftrightarrow{AB}$ and $\overleftrightarrow{CD}$ are coplanar, we relate $\overleftrightarrow{AB}$ and $\overleftrightarrow{CD}$ to two other lines, $\overline{AD}$ and $\overline{BD}$.

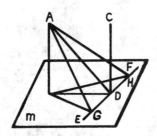

We use the theorem stating that all lines perpendicular
to a line at a point are coplanar. We find a line such that
$\overleftrightarrow{BD}$, $\overleftrightarrow{AD}$, and $\overleftrightarrow{CD}$ are all perpendicular to it at point D. Then
$\overleftrightarrow{CD}$ is coplanar to the plane of $\overleftrightarrow{BD}$ and $\overleftrightarrow{AD}$. Since points A and
B must lie in the plane of $\overleftrightarrow{BD}$ and $\overleftrightarrow{AD}$, so must the line $\overleftrightarrow{AB}$.
Since $\overleftrightarrow{AB}$ and $\overleftrightarrow{CD}$ both lie in the plane determined by $\overleftrightarrow{BD}$ and
$\overleftrightarrow{AD}$, $\overleftrightarrow{AB}$, and $\overleftrightarrow{CD}$ are coplanar. To show that $\overleftrightarrow{AB}$ and $\overleftrightarrow{CD}$ are parallel, we show $\overleftrightarrow{AB} \perp \overleftrightarrow{BD}$ and $\overleftrightarrow{CD} \perp \overleftrightarrow{BD}$. Therefore, $\overleftrightarrow{AB} \parallel \overleftrightarrow{CD}$.

| Statements | Reasons |
|---|---|
| 1. Draw $\overline{BD}$ and $\overline{AD}$. | 1. Two points determine a line. |
| 2. In plane m, construct $\overleftrightarrow{EF} \perp \overleftrightarrow{BD}$. | 2. At any point on a line, a $\perp$ may be drawn. |
| 3. On $\overleftrightarrow{EF}$, construct $\overline{HD} \cong \overline{DG}$ so that $\overleftrightarrow{BD}$ is $\perp$ bisector of $\overline{HG}$. | 3. Congruent line segments may be constructed on a line. |
| 4. Draw $\overline{AH}$, $\overline{GA}$, $\overline{BH}$, and $\overline{BG}$. | 4. Two points determine a line. |
| 5. $\overline{BH} \cong \overline{BG}$. | 5. A point on the $\perp$ bisector of a line segment is equidistant from the ends of the line segment. |
| 6. $\overline{AH} \cong \overline{AG}$. | 6. If line segments drawn from a point in the $\perp$ to a plane meet the plane at equal distances from the foot of the $\perp$, then the line segments are equal. (This can be shown by proving $\triangle ABG \cong \triangle ABH$ by SAS.) |
| 7. $\overline{AD} \perp \overline{HG}$. | 7. The line determined by two points equidistant from the endpoints of the segments is the perpendicular bisector of the segment. |
| 8. $\overleftrightarrow{CD} \perp \overleftrightarrow{EF}$. | 8. If a line is $\perp$ to a plane then it is $\perp$ to any line in the plane passing through its foot. |

| | |
|---|---|
| 9. $\overline{BD}$, $\overline{AD}$ and $\overline{CD}$ lie in the same plane, plane CDB. | 9. All the ⊥'s to a line at a point in the line lie in a plane which is ⊥ to the line at the given point. |
| 10. $\overline{AB}$ lies in the plane of $\overline{BD}$ and $\overline{AD}$. | 10. A line which joins two points in a plane lies wholly within the plane. |
| 11. $\overline{AB} \perp \overline{BD}$ and $\overline{CD} \perp \overline{BD}$. | 11. If a line is ⊥ to a plane, then it is ⊥ to every line in the plane passing through its foot. |
| 12. $\overline{AB} \parallel \overline{CD}$. | 12. Two coplanar lines perpendicular to a third line are parallel to each other. |

● **PROBLEM 11-11**

Show that if each of two intersecting planes is perpendicular to a third plane, then their intersection is perpendicular to the plane.

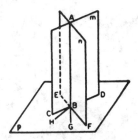

Solution: In the accompanying figure, planes n and m ⊥ p. n and m intersect at $\overleftrightarrow{AB}$; n and p intersect at $\overleftrightarrow{EF}$; and m and p intersect at $\overleftrightarrow{CD}$. We must show $\overleftrightarrow{AB} \perp$ p, and we prove this by finding two lines in p that are perpendicular to $\overleftrightarrow{AB}$.

From an earlier theorem, we know that if two planes are perpendicular to each other, a line drawn in one plane perpendicular to their intersection is perpendicular to the other plane. Consider line $\overleftrightarrow{BH}$ in p such that $\overleftrightarrow{BH} \perp \overleftrightarrow{EF}$. Since $\overleftrightarrow{EF}$ is the intersection of planes n and p, $\overleftrightarrow{BH} \perp$ n. A line perpendicular to a plane is perpendicular to every line in the plane that intersects the perpendicular. Therefore, $\overleftrightarrow{BH} \perp \overleftrightarrow{AB}$. Similarly, a line in p perpendicular to $\overleftrightarrow{CD}$, $\overleftrightarrow{BG}$, is perpendicular to m and thus, $\overleftrightarrow{BG} \perp \overleftrightarrow{AB}$. Remember that a line perpendicular to two lines in a plane is perpendicular to the plane. Since $\overleftrightarrow{AB} \perp \overleftrightarrow{BH}$ and $\overleftrightarrow{AB} \perp \overleftrightarrow{BG}$, and $\overleftrightarrow{BH}$ and $\overleftrightarrow{BG}$ are lines of plane p, $\overleftrightarrow{AB} \perp$ p.

# POLYHEDRAL ANGLES

Prove that the sum of the measures of any two faces of a
trihedral angle is greater than the measure of the third angle
face.

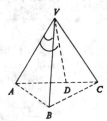

<u>Solution</u>:  A polyhedral angle is the figure formed by three or
more planes that intersect in one point.  The point of intersection of all the planes is called the vertex of the polyhedral angle.  The planes themselves are called the faces; the
lines that form the intersection of the faces are called edges;
and the plane angles formed by the intersection of the two
edges of a face are face angles.  The trihedral angle has three
face angles.  The three face angles are related somewhat like
the sides of a triangle.  To see this, have a plane that is not
a face intersect the tetrahedral angle.  The intersection is a
triangle, the sides of which are partially determined by the
size of the face angles that subtend them.  Therefore, the restrictions upon the sides of a triangle should have some anal-
ogy to the restrictions upon the face angles.

The triangle inequality for plane triangles requires that
the sum of the measures of any two sides of a triangle be
greater than the measure of the third side.  Here, we are asked
to prove the comparable theorem for trihedral angles.  It is
not surprising that we use the Triangle Inequality Theorem.

Given:  Trihedral ⧨V-ABC; ⧨AVC is the face angle of greatest measure.

Prove:  m⧨AVB + m⧨BVC > m⧨AVC.

Proof Outline:  We find point D on the plane VAC such
that ⧨AVC = ⧨AVD + ⧨DVC and ⧨AVD ≅ ⧨AVB.  Then,
to show m⧨AVB + m⧨BVC > m⧨AVC, we need only show
m⧨BVC > m⧨DVC.  By Triangle Inequality Theorem,
we show BC > DC and that ⧨BVC of ΔBVC > ⧨DVC of
ΔDVC.

| Statements | Reasons |
| --- | --- |
| 1.  Trihedral ⧨V-ABC; ⧨AVC is the face angle of greater measure. | 1.  Given. |
| 2.  Draw $\overline{AC}$. | 2.  Two distinct points deter- |

3. Construct, in face VAC, ∢AVD ≅ ∢AVB, such that ADC.

3. If an angle A is larger than a given angle, then a ray can be constructed such that it forms, with one side of ∢A, an angle congruent to the given angle and such that every point of the ray is in the interior of ∢A.

4. $\overline{VD} \cong \overline{VB}$.

4. On a given line, a segment can be determined such that it is congruent to a given segment. (There is no restriction on point B, other than it is on edge $\overleftrightarrow{VB}$ of the trihedral angle. Therefore, we arbitrarily choose point B such that VD = VB.)

5. $\overline{VA} \cong \overline{VA}$.

5. Every segment is congruent to itself.

6. ∆VAB ≅ ∆VAD.

6. SAS Postulate.

7. $\overline{AB} \cong \overline{AD}$

7. Corresponding sides of congruent triangles are congruent.

8. AB + BC > AC.

8. Triangle Inequality Theorem.

9. AC = AD + DC.

9. Definition of Betweenness.

10. AB + BC > AD + DC or BC > DC.

10. Substitution Postulate and Subtraction Postulate.

11. $\overline{VC} \cong \overline{VC}$.

11. Every segment is congruent to itself.

12. m∢BVC > m∢DVC.

12. If two sides of a triangle (∆VDC) are congruent to two sides of a second triangle (∆BVC), then the included angle of the first triangle is greater than the included angle of the second triangle if the third side of the first triangle is greater than the third side of the second.

13. m∢AVC = m∢AVD + m∢DVC.

13. If D is a point on the interior of ∢ABC, then m∢ABC = m∢ABD + m∢DBC (Angle Sum Postulate.)

| 14. m∢BVC + m∢AVB > m∢AVD <br> + m∢DVC. | 14. Substitution from Steps 12 and 3. Also, equals added to both sides of an inequality does not change the inequality. |
| 15. m∢BVC + m∢AVB > m∢AVC. | 15. Substitution Postulate. |

● **PROBLEM** 11-13

From a point within the dihedral angle formed by the intersection of two planes, perpendicular lines are drawn to each plane. (a) Prove that the plane determined by these perpendiculars is perpendicular to the edge of the dihedral angle. (b) If the number of degrees in the dihedral angle is represented by n, express in terms of n the number of degrees in the angle formed by the two perpendicular lines.

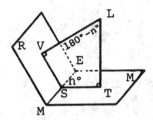

Solution: In the accompanying figure, point L is in the interior of dihedral angle R-ME-N. LT ⊥ plane N and LV ⊥ plane R have been drawn.

We wish to prove plane LVT is ⊥ ME, the edge of the dihedral angle. To do this remember that if a plane is perpendicular to two planes, then it is also perpendicular to their line of intersection. We will show that the plane LTV is perpendicular to planes N and R and thus is perpendicular to ME.

| Statement | Reason |
|---|---|
| 1. LT ⊥ plane N. LV ⊥ plane R. | 1. Given. |
| 2. LV and LT determine plane LVT. | 2. Two intersecting lines determine a line. |
| 3. Plane LTV ⊥ plane N. <br> Plane LTV ⊥ plane R. | 3. A plane containing a line perpendicular to a given plane is perpendicular to the given plane. |
| 4. Plane LTV ⊥ ME. | 4. If a plane is ⊥ to two planes, then it is ⊥ to their line of intersection. |

(b) We wish to find the measure of ∢VLT. This angle is part

271

of a quadrilateral LVTS. The sum of the measures of the angles
of a quadrilateral is 360°.

Since angles V and T each measure 90°, they sum to 180°
and the remaining angles of LVTS, ⊄VST and ⊄VLT, sum to 360° −
180° = 180°. We are given m⊄VST = n, therefore, we can conclude
m⊄VLT = 180° − n.

● **PROBLEM** 11-14

Show that the sum of the measures of the face angles of any
convex polyhedral angle is less than 360°. An informal argument will suffice.

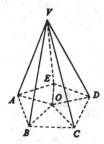

Solution: The only theorem about face angles we have learned
thus far is that, for trihedral angles, the sum of any two
face angles must be greater than the measure of the third.
Here, we use the theorem to relate the supplements of the face
angles to the interior angles of a convex polygon. Let a
plane cut the edges of the polyhedral angle at points A, B, C,
D, E. Let O be any point in the polygon ABCDE. Draw the segments OA, OB, OC, OD, and OE.

Call the n triangles with common vertex O the O-triangles.
Call the n triangles with common vertex V (the triangles formed
by the faces of the polyhedral angle) the V-triangles. Consider the base angles of the V triangles, ⊄ABV, ⊄BAV, ⊄VBC,
⊄VCB, etc., and the base angles of the O-triangles, ⊄OAB, ⊄OBA,
⊄OBC, ⊄OCB, etc. We show that (1) the sum of the base angles
of the V triangles > the sum of the base angles of the O triangles; and, therefore, (2) the sum of the vertex angles (face
angles) of V-triangles is less than the sum of the vertex
angles (⊄AOB, ⊄BOC, ⊄COD, etc.) of O-triangles. Since the vertex angles of O triangles sum to 360°, because a circle centered
at O can be drawn, the sum of face angles must be less than 360°.

Given: Polyhedral angle ⊄V-ABCDE...with n faces; the sum
of the measures of the face angles equals S.
Plane P intersects ⊄V-ABCDE...at points A, B, C,
D, E... .

Prove: S < 360.

| Statements | Reasons |
|---|---|
| 1. Polyhedral angle ⊄V-ABCDE...with n faces; | 1. Given. |

272

the sum of the measures
of the face angles
equals S. Plane P in-
tersects ⁋V-ABCDE...at
point A, B, C, D, E...

2. Select any point O in
the interior of convex
polygon ABCDE...

2. In the interior of the polygon, there are an infinite
number of points.

3. Draw segments from O
to each vertex of
polygon.

3. Two points determine a line
segment. (From this point
on, the triangles formed by
the faces of the polyhedral
angle will be referred to as
V-triangles. Those formed
by the n triangles in polygon ABCDE, will be called
...the O-triangles. The
vertex angles of the V triangles are the face angles.
The vertex of the O-tri-
angles have point O as the
vertex.)

4. In trihedral ⁋B - AVC,
m⁋ABV + m⊄VBC > m⊄ABC.

4. The sum of the measures of
any two face angles of a
trihedral angle is greater
than the measure of the
third.

5. m⁋ABC = m⁋ABO + m⁋OBC.

5. Angle Sum Postulate.

6. m⁋ABV + m⊄VBC > m⊄ABO
+ m⁋OBC.

6. Substitution Postulate.
(Result: Two V-triangle
base angles > two O-tri-
angle base angles.)

7. m⊄BCV + m⊄DCV > m⊄BCO
+ m⁋OCD and m⁋CDV +
m⊄EDV > m⊄ODC + m⊄EDO,
etc.

7. Repeat steps 4-6 for trihedral angles ⊄C-BVD,
⊄D-CVE, etc.

8. m⊄BAV + m⊄ABV + m⊄CBV
+ m⊄BCV... > m⊄ABO +
m⁋OBC + m⊄OCB + m⊄OCD...

8. If a > b and c > d, then
a + c > b + d. [Result:
from Steps 6 and 7, we have
that (sum of all V-triangle
base angles) > (sum of all
O-triangle base angles).]

9. m⊄AOB + m⊄OAB + m⊄OBA =
= 180. m⊄BOC + m⁋OBC
+ m⊄OCB = 180. m⁋COD
+ m⁋OCD + m⊄ODC = 180.
.
.
.
(rest of the O-tri-
angles)

9. The sum of the measures of
the angles of a triangle
is 180°. (Note, the equa-
tions are in the form of
(vertex angle) + (base
angles) = 180°.)

10. (m∡AOB + m∡BOC + m∡COD+..)  10. Addition Property of Equal-
    + (m∡OAB + m∡OBC +               ity. (Note there were n
    m∡OCD + m∡OBA + m∡OCB+...)       triangles, and thus the total
    = 180 · n.                       number of degrees is 180 · n.
                                     Note the expression in the
                                     first parenthesis consists of
                                     all O-triangle vertex angles.
                                     The second expression con-
                                     sists of all O-triangle base
                                     angles.)

11. m∡AVB + m∡VAB + m∡VBA       11. The measures of the angles
    = 180. m∡BVC + m∡VBC            of a triangle sum to 180°.
    + m∡VCB = 180.
                   .
                   .
                   .
    (rest of V-triangles)

12. (m∡AVB+m∡BVC+m∡CVD+...)+    12. Addition Property of Equal-
    (m∡VAB+m∡VBC+∡VCD+m∡VBA+m       ity. (Note the vertex
    VCB+...)=180·n.                 angles are in the first
                                    parenthesis.)

13. (m∡AVB + m∡BVC +           13. Transitivity Property.
    m∡CVD...) + (m∡VAB +           Both expressions in Step
    m∡VBC + ...) = (m∡AOB          10 and 12 equal 180 · n.
    + m∡BOC + m∡COD...) +
    (m∡OAB + m∡OBC...).

14. m∡AVB + m∡BVC +            14. If a > b and c = d, then
    m∡CVD... > m∡AOB +             c − a < d − b. In this
    m∡BOC + m∡COD... .             case a and b correspond to
                                   Step 8.

15. m∡AOB + m∡BOC... =         15. The measure of the sum of
    360°.                          angles that form a circle
                                   is 360°.

16. m∡AVB + m∡BVC +            16. Given.
    m∡CVD = S.

17. S < 360°.                 17. Substitution of Steps 15
                                  and 16 in 14.

## RECTANGULAR SOLIDS AND CUBES

● **PROBLEM** 11-15

A spider on the ceiling in one corner of a 18' × 15' × 8' room
sees a fly on the floor at the opposite corner (See Figure 1.).
Find the shortest path that the spider can take.

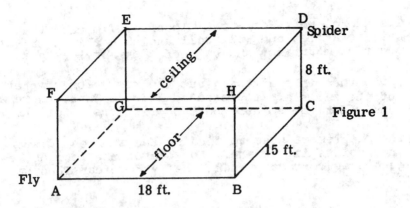

Figure 1

**Solution:** The elimination of confusing and irrelevant factors is the main difficulty in distance problems. For example, a person may drive in as straight a line as possible from New York to California, but because of mountains, valleys, and potholes in the road, the distance travelled will be greater than the straight line distance between New York and California. To determine the straight line distance, one must be able to eliminate the mountains and valleys.

In this problem, we are not concerned with the number of direction changes or transitions from wall to ceiling.

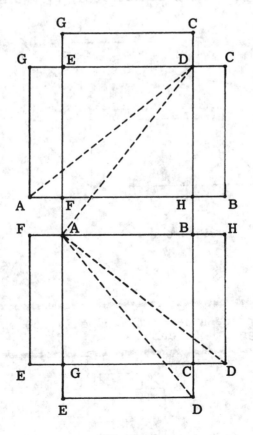

Figure 2

275

Therefore, we re-draw the picture, eliminate the wall-ceiling angles and wall-wall angles - this problem's equivalent of mountains and valleys. (See Figure 2.)

[Note that in flattening out the room, for completeness, three of the walls are represented twice. Thus, there are two locations D for the spider and two positions A for the fly.]

The problem reduces to finding the shortest distance between two points in a plane. Any one of the four dotted lines in Figure 2 is correct. Using the Pythagorean Theorem, we obtain:

(i)   $AD^2 = AH^2 + DH^2$

(ii)  $AD^2 = (AF + FH)^2 + (15 \text{ ft.})^2$

(iii) $AD^2 = (8 \text{ ft.} + 18 \text{ ft.})^2 + (15 \text{ ft.})^2$

(iv)  $AD^2 = 676 \text{ ft.}^2 + 225 \text{ ft.}^2$

(v)   $AD = \sqrt{901 \text{ ft.}^2} \cong 30 \text{ ft.}$

The shortest path is illustrated in Figure 3.

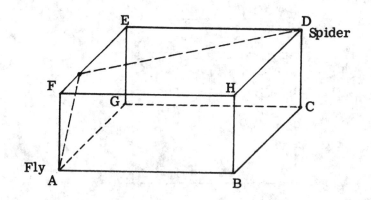

Figure 3

● PROBLEM 11-16

If the total surface area of the cube is 150 sq. in., find the length of an edge of the cube.

276

Solution:  We have previously established that for a rectangular solid the total area, or T, is given by T = S + 2B, where S is the lateral area, and B is the base area.  A cube is a specific case of a rectangular solid.  Let e = the length of an edge.  e is the same for all edges of a cube.  If h is the cube's altitude, and p is the perimeter of the base, S = hp, For a cube, h = e and p = 4e.  Therefore,

$$S = e(4e) = 4e^2 \qquad B = e^2.$$

As such, $T = 4e^2 + 2(e^2) = 6e^2$.

In this case, $T = 150$ in.$^2$.  By substitution,

$$T = 150 \text{ in.}^2 = 6e^2$$
$$25 \text{ in.}^2 = e^2$$
$$5 \text{ in.} = e.$$

Therefore: the length of an edge at the cube is 5 in.

● **PROBLEM** 11-17

Find the lateral area and the total surface area of a rectangular solid in which the dimensions of the base are 5 in. and 4 in. and the length of the altitude is 3 in.

Solution:  The lateral area of a rectangular solid is the sum of the areas of its lateral faces, i.e. those perpendicular to the base.  The total surface area is the lateral area plus the sum of the areas of the two bases.

Let the dimensions of the base be, in general, $\ell$ and w, and let the length of the altitude be h.  Since opposite faces of a rectangular solid are of equal area, and all lateral faces have a height h, two opposing faces will have dimensions $\ell$ by h while two other opposing faces will have dimensions w by h.  Based on the concept that the area of a rectangle is equal to the product of the lengths of its sides, it is correct to determine the lateral surface area by the equation

$\ell h + wh + \ell h + wh = $ Lateral Area.

Factoring, we obtain lateral area = $h(\ell + w + \ell + w)$.  Since $\ell + w + \ell + w = p$ (the perimeter of the base), then S (the lateral area of a rectangular solid) = hp.  The total surface area in-

277

cludes the sum of the areas of the two bases plus the lateral area.

Total area = hp + 2(ℓw) or S + 2B, where B = ℓw.

In this problem, the perimeter of the base = (5+4+5+4) in. = 18 in. The altitude of the solid is h = 3 in. Lateral area of the solid = S = hp = (3×18) in.$^2$ = 54 in.$^2$. Area of the base = (5×4) in.$^2$ = (20) in.$^2$ = B. Total surface area = S + 2(B) = $\left(54+2(20)\right)$ in.$^2$ = 94 in.$^2$. Therefore, Lateral area = 54 sq. in.; Total area = 94 sq. in.

● PROBLEM 11-18

In the rectangular solid shown, $\overline{DA}$ = 4 in., $\overline{DC}$= 3, and $\overline{GC}$ = 12.

(a) Find the length of $\overline{CA}$, a diagonal of the base ABCD.

(b) Using the result found in part (a), find the length of $\overline{GA}$, a diagonal of the solid.

(c) If $\overline{DA}$ = ℓ, $\overline{DC}$ = w, and $\overline{GC}$ = h, represent the length of $\overline{GA}$ in terms of ℓ, w, and h.

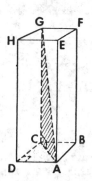

Solution: All three parts of this problem will involve applying the Pythagorean Theorem in a solid geometry setting. Recall that the Pythagorean Theorem tells us that in a right triangle, the square of the length of the longest side, the hypotenuse, is equal to the sum of the squares of the lengths of the legs.

ABCD is a rectangle because the base of a rectangular solid is a rectangle. The diagonal of a rectangle partitions it into two right triangles. Knowing the length of two adjacent sides, $\overline{DC}$ and $\overline{DA}$, the length of the diagonal can be determined, as mentioned, by the Pythagorean Theorem.

In right ΔCDA, $(CA)^2 = (DA)^2 + (DC)^2$. By substitution, $(CA)^2 = (4)^2 + (3)^2 = 16 + 9 = 25$

278

CA $= \sqrt{25} = 5$. Therefore, CA = 5.

(b) Since the edge of a rectangular solid is perpendicular to the base of the solid, the edge is perpendicular to any line passing through its foot. (This follows from the definition of a line being perpendicular to a plane.) Therefore, $\overline{GC} \perp \overline{CA}$, and $\triangle GCA$ is a right triangle in which $\angle GCA$ is a right angle.

We want to find the length of $\overline{GA}$, the hypotenuse of $\triangle GCA$, knowing the lengths of the other two legs. Once again, the Pythagorean Theorem is suggested.

In right $\triangle GCA$, $(GA)^2 = (CA)^2 + (GC)^2$.

By substitution, $(GA)^2 = (5)^2 + (12)^2 = 25 + 144 = 169$,

$$GA = \sqrt{169} = 13.$$

Therefore, $\overline{GA}$, the diagonal of the solid, measures 13.

(c) In this part we must follow the same logic and reasoning as above. However, instead of substituting in numerical measurements, we are asked to be more general and substitute letters as variables for actual lengths.

To find GA, given DA = $\ell$, DC = w, and GC = h, we must first calculate CA.

As in part (a), $(CA)^2 = (DA)^2 + (DC)^2$.

Again, by substitution, $(CA)^2 = \ell^2 + w^2$. $CA = \sqrt{\ell^2 + w^2}$.

Now that we have represented $\overline{CA}$, we can proceed as in (b). Therefore, $(GA)^2 = (CA)^2 + (GC)^2$. Substitute to obtain

$$(GA)^2 = \left[\sqrt{\ell^2 + w^2}\right]^2 + h^2$$
$$(GA)^2 = \ell^2 + w^2 + h^2$$
$$GA = \sqrt{\ell^2 + w^2 + h^2}$$

Therefore, $GA = \sqrt{\ell^2 + w^2 + h^2}$.

Note: Given the length, $\ell$, and width, w, of the base and the height, h, of the rectangular solid, the length of the diagonal of the solid, d, is given by $d = \sqrt{\ell^2 + w^2 + h^2}$.

● **PROBLEM 11-19**

How many cubic feet are contained in a packing case which is a rectangular solid 4 ft. long, 3 ft. wide and $3\frac{1}{2}$ ft. high?

Solution: The volume of a rectangular prism having a base
area B and an altitude h is V = Bh. Since the base of the
rectangular solid is a rectangle, the area of the base (of
length ℓ and width w) is B = ℓw. By substitution, B = 3 × 4
= 12. Since h = $3\frac{1}{2}$:

Volume of the solid = Bh = 12 × $3\frac{1}{2}$ = 42.

Therefore, the packing case contains 42 cu. ft.

● **PROBLEM** 11-20

Find the volume of a cube whose total area is 54 sq. in.

Solution: The volume, V, of a cube, whose edge is length e,
is given by the product of the area of the base, $e^2$, and the
height of the cube, e. Therefore, $V = e^3$.

The area of any face is $e^2$. Therefore, the total area
of the 6 faces is $6e^2$. This fact will enable us to calculate
the length of the edge, given the total area

$$54 \text{ in.}^2 = 6e^2$$
$$9 \text{ in.}^2 = e^2$$
$$3 \text{ in.} = e.$$

Since $V = e^3$, by substitution,

$$V = (3 \text{ in.})^3 = 27 \text{ in.}^3$$

Therefore, the Volume of the cube is 27 in.$^3$

# PRISMS

The lateral edges of a prism are congruent and parallel.
Prove this.

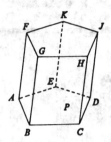

__Solution__:  A prism is a polyhedron whose faces consist of two
parallel and congruent polygons, called bases, and the parallelograms, called lateral faces, formed by connecting pairs
of corresponding vertices of the parallel polygons.  Since
the lateral edges are opposite sides of parallelograms, by
transitivity, we can show they are all congruent.

Given:  Prism P with lateral edges $\overline{AF}$, $\overline{BG}$, $\overline{CH}$, $\overline{DJ}$, $\overline{EK}$.

Prove:  $\overline{AF} \cong \overline{BG} \cong \overline{CH} \cong \overline{DJ} \cong \overline{EK}$

$\overline{AF} \parallel \overline{BG} \parallel \overline{CH} \parallel \overline{DJ} \parallel \overline{EK}$

| Statements | Reasons |
|---|---|
| 1.  Prism P with lateral edges $\overline{AF}$, $\overline{BG}$, $\overline{CH}$, $\overline{DJ}$, $\overline{EK}$... | 1.  Given. |
| 2.  Quadrilateral FGBA, GHCB, HCDJ... are parallelograms. | 2.  The lateral faces of a prism are parallelograms. |
| 3.  $\overline{AF} \parallel \overline{BG}$, $\overline{BG} \parallel \overline{CH}$,... | 3.  Opposite sides of a parallelogram are parallel. |
| 4.  $\overline{AF} \parallel \overline{BG} \parallel \overline{CH}$... | 4.  If a line is parallel to a given line, then it is parallel to all lines parallel to the given line. |
| 5.  AF $\cong$ BG, BG $\cong$ CH,... | 5.  Opposite sides of a parallelogram are congruent. |

281

6. $\overline{AF} \cong \overline{BG} \cong \overline{CH}$...

6. Segments congruent to a given segment are congruent (Transitive Property).

● **PROBLEM 11-22**

Show that every section of a prism made by a plane parallel to the bases is congruent to the bases.

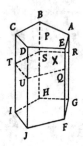

Solution: By inspection, we see that the plane cuts the prism into two prisms and, therefore, the section cut by the plane is a base of both prisms and congruent to both. To prove this we must show the polygon formed by the plane and the prism must have sides and angles congruent to the corresponding sides and angles of the base. We prove the sides congruent by showing that the faces of the "new prism" are parallelograms and, since the opposite sides of a parallelogram are congruent, corresponding sides of the polygons are congruent. To show the angles are congruent, we prove that all triangles in the new polygon formed by three consecutive vertices are congruent to the triangles formed by the corresponding three vertices in the base. Thus, the interior angles are congruent by definition of triangle congruency.

Given: Prism P intersects plane X in polygon QRSTU...; Plane X ∥ bases of P.

Prove: Polygon QRSTU... ≅ base of P.

| Statements | Reasons |
|---|---|
| 1. Prism P intersects plane X in polygon QRSTU...; plane X ∥ bases of P. | 1. Given. |
| 2. $\overline{UJ} \parallel \overline{QF} \parallel \overline{RG}$... | 2. The lateral edges of a prism are parallel. |
| 3. $\overline{UQ} \parallel \overline{JF}$, $\overline{QR} \parallel \overline{FG}$... | 3. If a plane intersects two parallel planes, then they intersect in two parallel lines. |

282

<table>
<tr>
<td>

4. Quadrilaterals UQFJ, QRGF, TUJI... are parallelograms.

</td>
<td>

4. If both pairs of opposite sides of a quadrilateral are parallel, then the quadrilateral is a parallelogram.

</td>
</tr>
<tr>
<td>

5. $\overline{UQ} \cong \overline{JF}$, $\overline{QR} \cong \overline{FG}$, TU $\cong$ IJ...

</td>
<td>

5. Opposite sides of a parallelogram are congruent.

</td>
</tr>
<tr>
<td>

6. $\overline{TQ} \parallel \overline{IF}$, $\overline{UR} \parallel \overline{JG}$...

</td>
<td>

6. If a plane intersects two parallel planes, then they intersect in two parallel lines.

</td>
</tr>
<tr>
<td>

7. Quadrilaterals TIFQ, UJGR,... are parallel.

</td>
<td>

7. If both pairs of opposite sides of a quadrilateral are parallel, then the quadrilateral is a parallelogram.

</td>
</tr>
<tr>
<td>

8. $\overline{TQ} \cong \overline{IF}$, $\overline{UR} \cong \overline{JG}$.

</td>
<td>

8. Opposite sides of a parallelogram are congruent.

</td>
</tr>
<tr>
<td>

9. $\triangle TUQ \cong \triangle IJF$, $\triangle UQR \cong \triangle JFG$...

</td>
<td>

9. The SSS Postulate.

</td>
</tr>
<tr>
<td>

10. $\sphericalangle TUQ \cong \sphericalangle IJF$, $\sphericalangle UQR \cong \sphericalangle JFG$...

</td>
<td>

10. Corresponding angles of congruent triangles are congruent.

</td>
</tr>
<tr>
<td>

11. Polygon QRSTU... $\cong$ base of P.

</td>
<td>

11. If the corresponding angles and the corresponding sides of two polygons are congruent, then the two polygons are congruent.

</td>
</tr>
</table>

● **PROBLEM** 11-23

The base of a right prism is a regular hexagon with area 24 $\sqrt{3}$. If the lateral faces of the prism are squares, what is the lateral area?

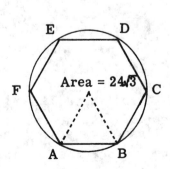

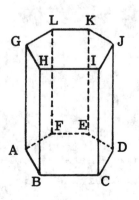

<u>Solution</u>: The area of a prism = $e \cdot p$ where e is the length of the edge and p is the perimeter of a right section. Since this is a right prism, the bases themselves are right sections. Thus p = perimeter of hexagon = 6s (where s is the length of the side of the hexagon). Also, because each lateral face is a square, the edge e must equal the length of the side of the base s. Thus, area = $e \cdot p = s \cdot (6s) = 6s^2$.

We use the given area of the hexagon to solve for s. The area of a regular polygon is $\frac{1}{2}a \cdot p$ where a is the length of the apothem and p is perimeter. To solve for a and p would be lengthy and unnecessary. We note, instead, that the area of a regular hexagon is the sum of the areas of six equilateral triangles, each of side s. (In fact, this division of a regular polygon into congruent triangles is how the formula $\frac{1}{2}ap$ is usually proved.) Therefore,

Area of base = $24\sqrt{3}$ = 6 · (Area of equilateral triangle of

$$\text{side s}) = 6 \cdot \left(\frac{s^2\sqrt{3}}{4}\right) = \frac{3}{2}\sqrt{3}\ s^2$$

$$24\sqrt{3} = \frac{3}{2}\sqrt{3}\ s^2$$

$$s^2 = \frac{24\sqrt{3}}{3/2\sqrt{3}} = \frac{2 \cdot 24}{3} = 16$$

$$s = \sqrt{16} = 4.$$

From above, we showed that the lateral area of the prism $= e \cdot p = s \cdot (6s) = 6s^2 = 6(4)^2 = 96$.

● **PROBLEM** 11-24

Show that the lateral area of a prism is equal to the product of the perimeter of a right section and the length of a lateral edge.

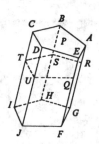

<u>Solution</u>: The lateral area of a prism equals the sum of the areas of the lateral faces, which, by definition, are parallelograms. The area of the nth parallelogram is $a_n b_n$ where $a_n$ is the altitude and $b_n$ is the lateral edge that forms the

base. The lateral area of the entire prism equals $a_1b_1 + a_2b_2 + \ldots + a_nb_n$. The lateral edges of a prism are congruent, $b_1 = b_2 = \ldots b_n$. Therefore, the expression for lateral area can be expressed as $b_1(a_1 + a_2 + \ldots a_n)$. We show that the altitudes form the sides of a right section of the prism.

Therefore, $a_1 + a_2 + \ldots + a_n$ is the perimeter of the right section and the proof is complete.

Given: Prism P with right section QRSTU...; e the length of the lateral edge; Z the lateral area; w the perimeter of the right section.

Prove: $Z = e \cdot w$.

| Statements | Reasons |
|---|---|
| 1. Prism P with right section QRSTU...; e the length of the lateral edge; Z the lateral area; w the perimeter of the right section. | 1. Given |
| 2. $\overline{DJ}$, $\overline{EF}$, $\overline{AG}$... $\perp$ QRSTU. | 2. The right section of a prism is perpendicular to each lateral edge. |
| 3. $\overline{DJ} \perp \overline{UQ}$, $\overline{EF} \perp \overline{QR}$... | 3. A line that is perpendicular to a plane is perpendicular to each line in the plane that passes through the point of intersection. |
| 4. $\overline{UQ}$, $\overline{QR}$, $\overline{RS}$...are altitudes of parallelograms DJFE, EFGA, BAGH, etc. | 4. An altitude of a parallelogram is a line segment whose endpoints lie on opposite sides of the parallelogram and which is perpendicular to those sides. |
| 5. Area of DJFE = $UQ \cdot EF$. Area of EFGA = $QR \cdot AG$. | 5. The area of a parallelogram equals the length of the base times the length of the altitude drawn to the base. |
| 6. Lateral Area of P = $UQ \cdot EF + QR \cdot AG + RS \cdot BH$... | 6. The lateral area of a prism is the sum of the areas of the lateral faces. |
| 7. $EF = AG = BH$... | 7. The lateral edges of a prism are congruent. |
| 8. Lateral Area of P = $EF \cdot (UQ + QR + RS...)$. | 8. Substitution Postulate and Distributive Property. |

| 9. $e = EF$. | 9. Given. |
|---|---|
| 10. $w = UQ + QR + RS...$ | 10. The perimeter of a polygon is the sum of the lengths of its sides. |
| 11. Lateral Area of $P = Z = e \cdot w$. | 11. Substitution Postulate. |

● **PROBLEM 11-25**

The base of a right prism, as shown in the figure, is an equilateral triangle, each of whose sides measures 4 units. The altitude of the prism measures 5 units. Find the volume of the prism. [Leave answer in radical form.]

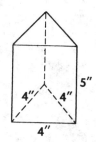

**Solution:** We imagine the prism as a stack of equilateral triangles, congruent to the base of the prism. Let each of these triangles be one unit of measure thick. We can then calculate the area of the base, B, and multiply it by the number of bases needed to complete the height of the prism, h, to obtain the volume of the prism. Therefore, $V = Bh$. All prism volumes can be thought of in this way.

In this particular problem, the base is an equilateral triangle. Therefore $B = \frac{s^2\sqrt{3}}{4}$, where s is the length of a side of the base. By substitution, $B = \frac{(4)^2\sqrt{3}}{4} = 4\sqrt{3}$. Since the prism is 5 units high,

$$V = Bh = (4\sqrt{3})5 = 20\sqrt{3}.$$

Therefore, the volume of the prism is $20\sqrt{3}$ cu. units.

● **PROBLEM 11-26**

Show that two prisms have equal volumes if their bases have equal areas and their altitudes are equal.

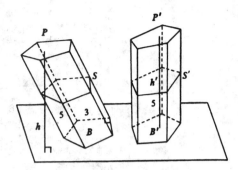

Solution: In defining the volumes of polyhedral regions,
three postulates are needed: (1) to each polyhedral region,
there corresponds a unique positive number - in other words,
every polyhedral region has one and only one volume; (2) the
volume of a rectangular solid equals the product of its length,
width, and height - this defines a standard from which other
volume formulas can be derived; and (3) (Cavalieri's Principle) if two solid regions have equal altitudes, and if the
sections, made by planes parallel to the base of each solid
and at the same distance from each base, are always equal in
area, then the volumes of the solid regions are equal - this
provides a means of relating the volumes of all figures from
the second postulate.

For this problem, we show that all sections cut by planes
parallel to the bases of a prism are congruent to the bases,
and thus, for prisms, Cavalieri's Postulate can be reduced to
two requirements. For two prisms to have equal volumes, they
must have (1) equal base areas, and (2) equal altitudes.

Given: Prisms P and P' with bases B and B' such that
area of B equals area of B'; and altitudes h
and h' such that h = h'.

Prove: Volume of P = Volume of P'.

| Statements | Reasons |
|---|---|
| 1. Prisms P and P' with bases B and B' such that area of B = area of B'; and altitudes h and h' such that h = h'. | 1. Given. |
| 2. Construct two planes parallel to the bases of P and P' making sections S and S' at equal distances d and d' from the bases B and B'. | 2. In a given space, only one plane can be drawn a given distance from the given plane. |
| 3. S ≅ B.  S' ≅ B'. | 3. Every section of a prism made by a plane parallel to the bases is congruent to the bases. |

287

4.  Area of S = Area of B
    Area of S' = Area of
    B'.

5.  Area of S = Area of S'.

6.  Volume of P = Volume
    of P'.

4.  If two figures are congru-
    ent, then their areas are
    equal.

5.  Transitivity Postulate.

6.  If two solid regions have
    equal altitudes and if the
    sections made by planes
    parallel to the base of
    each solid and at the same
    distance from each base are
    always equal in area, then
    the volumes are equal.
    (Cavalieri's Principle.)

## PYRAMIDS AND TETRAHEDRONS

● PROBLEM 11-27

In a regular square pyramid, the length of each side of the
square base is 12 in., and the length of the altitude is
8 in.

(a)  Find the length of the slant height of the pyramid.

(b)  Find, in radical form, the length of the lateral
     edge of the pyramid.

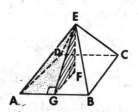

Solution: Both parts of this example will involve an application of the Pythagorean Theorem in solid geometry. If h is
the length of the hypotenuse, and a and b the lengths of the
other legs of a right triangle, then, $h^2 = a^2 + b^2$.

(a)  The slant height is the perpendicular from the vertex of the pyramid to any side of the base. Since each face
of a regular pyramid is an isosceles triangle, the slant
height bisects the base. To find the slant height, note that
slant height $\overline{EG}$ is the hypotenuse of ΔEFG. The altitude of
the pyramid, $\overline{EF}$, as shown in the figure, is perpendicular to
the plane of the base ABCD, by definition. As such, $\overline{EF} \perp \overline{FG}$,
because $\overline{FG}$ lies in the plane of the base and intersects $\overline{EF}$
at the latter's point of intersection with the base. The al-
titude must be drawn to the center of the base. Therefore,
FG equals one-half the length of a side of the base.

$$FG = \frac{1}{2}(12)\text{in.} = 6\text{ in.}$$

Since $\triangle EFG$ contains a right angle, it is a right triangle. $\overline{EG}$ is the hypotenuse, or slant height. Therefore,

$$(EG)^2 = (EF)^2 + (FG)^2.$$

By substitution, $(EG)^2 = (8\text{ in.})^2 + (6\text{ in.})^2 = (64 + 36)\text{in.}^2$

$$= 100\text{ in.}^2$$

$$EG = \sqrt{100}\text{ in.} = 10\text{ in.}$$

Therefore, the slant height is 10 in.

(b)  The lateral edge of a pyramid is the intersection of any two adjacent lateral faces. It is given, in this problem, by the hypotenuse of the right triangle formed when the slant height is drawn, namely hypotenuse $\overline{EA}$ of right triangle EAG. Since the slant height $\overline{EG}$ is the altitude to the base of isosceles triangle AEB, G is the midpoint of $\overline{AB}$. Therefore, AG equals one-half the length of the side of the base, i.e. AG = $\frac{1}{2}(12)$in. = 6 in.

In rt. $\triangle EGA$, $(EA)^2 = (EG)^2 + (AG)^2.$

By substitution, $(EA)^2 = (10\text{ in.})^2 + (6\text{ in.})^2 = (100 + 36)\text{in.}^2$

$$= 136\text{ in.}^2$$

$$EA = \sqrt{136}\text{ in.} = \sqrt{4}\cdot\sqrt{34}\text{ in.} = 2\sqrt{34}\text{ in.}$$

Therefore, the length of the lateral edge is $2\sqrt{34}$ in.

● **PROBLEM** 11-28

If two pyramids have congruent altitudes and bases with equal areas, show that sections parallel to the bases at equal distances from the vertices have equal area.

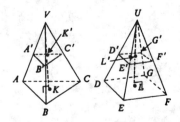

Solution:  Planes parallel to the base intersect a pyramid in a polygon similar to the base, with the ratio of similitude

289

dependent on the height of the pyramid and the distance between the polygon and the base. From an earlier theorem, we know that the ratio of the areas of similar polygons is proportional to the square of the ratio of similitude.

Given two sections parallel to the bases at equal distances and two pyramids with congruent altitudes, the ratio of similitudes is equal if the ratio of areas is equal. If we are further told that the bases of the pyramids have equal areas, then the area of the sections must also be equal.

Given: Pyramids V-ABC and U-DEFG, where $\overline{VK}$ is an altitude of V-ABC and $\overline{UL}$ an altitude of U-DEFG; $\overline{VK} \cong \overline{UL}$ . Area of $\triangle ABC$ = Area of DEFG; plane A'B'C' $\parallel$ plane ABC and meets $\overline{VK}$ at K'; plane D'E'F'G' $\parallel$ plane DEFG and meets $\overline{UL}$ in L'; $\overline{VK'} \cong \overline{UL'}$ .

Prove: Area of $\triangle A'B'C'$ = Area of quadrilateral D'E'F'G'.

| Statements | Reasons |
|---|---|
| 1. (See above). | 1. Given. |
| 2. $\triangle A'B'C' \sim \triangle ABC$ quadrilateral DEFG $\sim$ D'E'F'G'. | 2. If a pyramid is cut by a plane parallel to its base, then the section is a polygon similar to the base. |
| 3. The ratio of similitude of $\triangle A'B'C'$ and $\triangle ABC = \dfrac{A'B'}{AB}$. The ratio of similitude of quad D'E'F'G' and DEFG $= \dfrac{D'E'}{DE}$. | 3. The ratio of similitude of two similar polygons is the proportion of the lengths of corresponding sides. |
| 4. The ratio of similitude of $\triangle A'B'C'$ and $\triangle ABC = \dfrac{VK'}{VK}$. The ratio of similitude of quad D'E'F'G' and DEFG $= \dfrac{UG'}{UG}$. | 4. If a pyramid is cut by a plane parallel to its base, then the ratio of the lengths of the altitudes is equal the ratio of similitude of the base and the section. |
| 5. $\dfrac{\text{Area of } A'B'C'}{\text{Area of } ABC} = \left(\dfrac{VK'}{VK}\right)^2$. $\dfrac{\text{Area of quad D'E'F'G'}}{\text{Area of quad DEFG}} = \left(\dfrac{UG'}{UG}\right)^2$. | 5. The ratio of the area of two similar polygons is the square of the ratio of similitude. |
| 6. $\dfrac{VK'}{VK} = \dfrac{UG'}{UG}$ | 6. Division Property of Equality. |

7. $\dfrac{\text{Area of } \Delta A'B'C'}{\text{Area of } \Delta ABC} =$      7.   Transitivity Postulate.
    $\dfrac{\text{Area of quad } D'E'F'G'}{\text{Area of quad } DEFG}$.

8.   Area of $\Delta ABC =$          8.   Given.
    Area of quad $DEFG$.

9.   Area of $\Delta A'B'C' =$       9.   Multiplication Property
    Area of quad $D'E'F'G'$.         of Equality.

● **PROBLEM** 11-29

---

Find the surface area of a regular tetrahedron when each edge
is of length a) 1; b) 2.

---

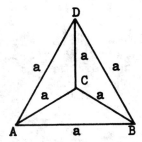

Solution: The illustration shows a regular tetrahedron. A
tetrahedron is a closed space figure with 4 triangular faces,
and a regular tetrahedron is one in which the 4 triangular
faces are congruent.

     The surface area, S, of this polyhedron is equal to the
sum of the areas of its 4 faces. That is,

$$S = \text{Area}(\Delta ADB) + \text{Area}(\Delta BCD) + \text{Area}(\Delta ACD) + \text{Area}(\Delta ACB). \qquad (1)$$

But,

$$\Delta ADB \cong \Delta BCD \cong \Delta ACD \cong \Delta ACB.$$

Therefore, we may rewrite (1) as

$$S = 4 \ \text{Area}(\Delta ADB). \qquad (2)$$

Note that $\Delta ADB$ is an equilateral triangle of edge length a.
The area of an equilateral triangle is equal to $\sqrt{3}/4$ times
the square of its edge length. Hence,

$$\text{Area}(\Delta ADB) = \sqrt{3}/4\left(a^2\right)$$

and, using this in (2),

$$S = a^2\sqrt{3}.$$

a)  If a = 1,  s = $\sqrt{3}$.

b)  If a = 2,  s = $4\sqrt{3}$.

Find the lateral area and the total surface area of a regular triangular pyramid if each edge of the base measures 6 in. and each lateral edge of the pyramid measures 5 in.  (Answer may be left in radical form.  See figure.)

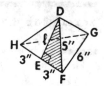

<u>Solution</u>:  The lateral area is the sum of the areas of the lateral faces of the pyramid.  The total surface area is the lateral area plus the area of the base.

Since the pyramid is regular, all the faces are congruent isosceles triangles, each of whose area is given by $\frac{1}{2}$bh, where b is the length of the base  of the Δ, and h is the height. There are three such faces.  We shall examine ΔDHF, shown in the figure.

The altitude, $\overline{DE}$, of ΔDHF, is perpendicular to $\overline{HF}$.  Also, $\overline{DE}$ bisects $\overline{HF}$ because  DHF is isosceles.  Since HF = 6, EF = HE = 3.  We need $\overline{DE}$ to find the area.  By the Pythagorean Theorem, since ΔDEF is a right triangle,

$$(FD)^2 = (DE)^2 + (EF)^2$$

By substitution,  $(5 \text{ in.})^2 = (DE)^2 + (3 \text{ in.})^2$

$$(DE)^2 = 25 \text{ in.}^2 - 9 \text{ in.}^2 = 16 \text{ in.}^2$$

$$DE = 4 \text{ in.}$$

Area of ΔDEF = $\frac{1}{2}$(DE)(HF)

By substitution, Area of ΔDEF = $\frac{1}{2}$(4)(6)in.$^2$ = $\frac{1}{2}$(24) in.$^2$

$$= 12 \text{ in.}^2$$

Lateral Area = 3(Area of ΔDEF) = 3(12)in.$^2$ = 36 in.$^2$

The base is an equilateral triangle, since each edge of the base measures 6 in.  Therefore,

Base Area = $\frac{s^2\sqrt{3}}{4}$

(the area of an equilateral triangle), where s is the length of an edge of the triangle. By substitution,

$$\text{Base Area} = \frac{(6)^2 \sqrt{3} \text{ in.}^2}{4} = 9\sqrt{3} \text{ in.}^2$$

Total Surface Area = Lateral Area + Base Area = $(36 + 9\sqrt{3}) \text{ in.}^2$

Therefore, Lateral Area = 36 sq. in.; Total Surface Area = $(36 + 9\sqrt{3})$ sq. in.

● **PROBLEM 11-31**

Let $\underline{ABCD}$ be a regular tetrahedron with each edge of length 2. Let $\overline{AE}$ be perpendicular to the base, and assume that CE = $\frac{2}{3}$CF. (See figure). In $\triangle BCD$, $\overline{CF} \perp \overline{BD}$. a) What is the length of CF? b) What is the length of CE? c) What is the length of AE? d) What is the base area of $\triangle BCD$? e) What is the volume of the tetrahedron?

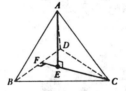

Solution:

a) We can prove that $\triangle CFB \cong \triangle CFD$ by the A.A.S. (angle angle side) Postulate in order to show DF = BF. Since we know DB, we can find DF. By using the Pythagorean Theorem we can determine CF. $\sphericalangle CFB \cong \sphericalangle CFD$ because $\overline{CF} \perp \overline{BD}$ and all right angles are congruent. Since all the edges of ABCD are of length 2, $\triangle DBC$ is equilateral. By definition, then, $\sphericalangle FBC \cong \sphericalangle FDC$, and $\overline{DC} \cong \overline{BC}$. By the A.A.S. Postulate, $\triangle CFB \cong \triangle CFD$, hence DF = BF. But DF + BF = DB. Thus,

$$DF = \frac{1}{2}DB.$$

Since DB = 2,

$$DF = 1.$$

Applying the Pythagorean Theorem to $\triangle DFC$ gives

$$(DF)^2 + (FC)^2 = (DC)^2$$

or

$$FC = \sqrt{(DC)^2 - (DF)^2}.$$

Noting that DC = 2 and DF = 1

293

$$FC = \sqrt{4 - 1} = \sqrt{3}$$

b) By the statement of the problem,

$$CE = \frac{2}{3}CF.$$

From part (a), CF = $\sqrt{3}$. Hence,

$$CE = \frac{2}{3}\sqrt{3} = \frac{2\sqrt{3}}{3}.$$

c) Using the Pythagorean Theorem, for △AEC,

$$(AE)^2 + (EC)^2 = (AC)^2$$

or
$$AE = \sqrt{(AC)^2 - (EC)^2}.$$

By realizing that AC is an edge of ABCD, we note that AC = 2. From part (b), EC = $\frac{2}{\sqrt{3}}$. Therefore,

$$AE = \sqrt{4 - 4/3}$$

$$AE = \sqrt{8/3}.$$

d) The area of △BCD is $\frac{1}{2}$ the product of its altitude (FC) and its base (DB). Hence,

$$Area = \frac{1}{2}(FC)(DB).$$

Noting that FC = $\sqrt{3}$ from part (a), and that DB = 2,

$$Area = (\frac{1}{2})(\sqrt{3})(2) = \sqrt{3}.$$

e) The volume of a tetrahedron of base area A and altitude h is

$$V = \frac{1}{3}Ah.$$

In our case h = AE = $\sqrt{8/3}$ from part (c). Hence,

$$V = (\frac{1}{3})(\sqrt{3})\left[\frac{\sqrt{8}}{\sqrt{3}}\right]$$

$$V = \frac{2\sqrt{2}}{3}.$$

● PROBLEM 11-32

The slant height of a regular pyramid A-BCD is 2. If the altitude is of length 1, find the volume.

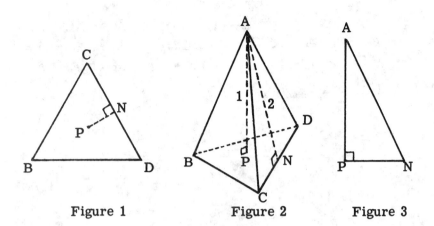

| Figure 1 | Figure 2 | Figure 3 |

Solution: The volume of pyramid A-BCD equals one third the base area times the altitude. The altitude equals 1. Since this is a regular pyramid and only three points of its base are specified, the base must be a regular or equilateral tri-angle. The area of the base, therefore, equals $\frac{S^2\sqrt{3}}{4}$, where S is the length of a side. To find S, we show:

(1)  NC $= \frac{1}{2}$CD $= \frac{1}{2}$S;  (2)  BN $= 3 \cdot$ PN;  (3)  S $=$ BC $= \sqrt{BN^2 + NC^2}$;

(1)  Since A-BCD is a regular pyramid, its lateral edges are all congruent; therefore, face ADC is an isosceles tri-angle and, since the altitude drawn from the vertex angle of an isosceles triangle  bisects the base, CN $= \frac{1}{2}$CD $= \frac{1}{2}$S.

(2)  Since A-BCD is a regular pyramid, the altitude $\overline{AP}$ must intersect the base at the center of the base, or the point equidistant from all sides.  But, by an earlier theorem, this point is also the point of concurrency of all angle bisectors of the triangle.  Therefore, BP bisects ∢B.  Consider equi-lateral triangle △BCD as an isosceles triangle of vertex B. Then, the angle bisector of the vertex angle bisects the base and therefore, angle bisector $\overline{BP}$ is also the median drawn to side $\overline{CD}$.  By similar reasoning, considering △BCD as an isos-celes triangle with C and D as vertex angles, we show that the angle bisectors of an equilateral triangle are the same as the medians of the triangle.  Therefore, P, the point of concurrency of the angle bisectors, is the point of concur-rency of the medians as well.  Since the distance of the point of concurrency of medians from a given side is one third the length of the median, PN $= \frac{1}{3} \cdot$ BN.

To find PN, note that PN is a leg in right triangle APN. By Pythagorean Theorem, $PN^2 = AN^2 - AP^2 = 2^2 - 1^2 = 3$.  PN $= \sqrt{3}$.

(3)  The median drawn to the base of an isosceles triangle is the perpendicular bisector of the base.  Therefore, ∢BNC is a right angle and △BNC is a right triangle.  We wish to find the length of a side $\overline{BC}$.  By Pythagorean Theorem,

$BC^2 = BN^2 + NC^2$. $BC = S$. From (1), we have $NC = \frac{1}{2}S$. From (2), we have $BN = 3 \cdot PN = 3\sqrt{3}$. Substituting in values, we obtain $S^2 = (3\sqrt{3})^2 + (\frac{1}{2}S)^2$ or $S^2 = 27 + \frac{1}{4}S^2$, or $\frac{3}{4}S^2 = 27$. Multiplying both sides by $\frac{4}{3}$, we obtain $S^2 = 36$ or $S = 6$.

$$\text{Area of base} = \frac{S^2\sqrt{3}}{4} = \frac{6^2\sqrt{3}}{4} = 9\sqrt{3}.$$

$$\text{Volume of A–BCD} = \frac{1}{3}a \cdot b = \frac{1}{3}(1)(9\sqrt{3}) = 3\sqrt{3}.$$

● **PROBLEM 11-33**

Find the volume of a frustum of a pyramid if the area of the bases are b and b' and the altitude is h.

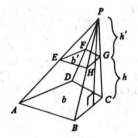

**Solution**: The frustum of a pyramid is the figure formed by the base of the pyramid, a section of the pyramid parallel to the base and the surface of the pyramid between the base and the section. Another way of viewing this is to consider the section of the pyramid parallel to the base. The part "above" the section forms a little pyramid with the section as its base. The part of the pyramid below the section forms a frustum. Therefore, the volume of the frustum equals the volume of the larger pyramid minus the smaller pyramid. (See figure. Note: b is the area of quadrilateral ABCD, b' is the area of EFGH, h is the altitude of the frustum, and h' is the altitude of the smaller pyramid.)

Volume of P–EFGH = $\frac{1}{3}$(base area)(height) = $\frac{1}{3}b'h'$

Volume of P–ABCD = $\frac{1}{3}$(base area)(height) = $\frac{1}{3}b(h + h')$

Volume of frustum = $\frac{1}{3}b(h + h') - \frac{1}{3}b'h'$

$$= \frac{1}{3}[bh + h'(b-b')].$$

We are not finished yet, because our formula contains an h'. The formula that is the answer must only be in terms of b, b' - the area of the bases - and h, the altitude. We solve for h' in terms of these three terms and then eliminate h' from the equation.

To solve for h', we take advantage of the similarities between the little pyramid P-EFGH and the larger one P-ABCD. From an earlier theorem, we know that when a plane parallel to the base cuts a pyramid, the polygon formed is similar to the base with its ratio of similitude equal to the ratio of the altitudes. Therefore,

$$\frac{\text{altitude of P-EFGH}}{\text{altitude of P-ABCD}} = \frac{\text{side of EFGH}}{\text{corresponding side of ABCD}} \qquad \text{or}$$

$$\frac{h'}{h + h'} = \frac{EH}{AB} = \text{ratio of similitude.}$$

We wish to find h' in terms of h, b, and b' and therefore we must get rid of $\frac{EH}{AB}$, the ratio of similitude. By earlier theorem, the ratio of the areas of similar polygons equals the square of the ratio of similitude. Therefore, $\frac{\text{area of EFGH}}{\text{area of ABCD}} = \left(\frac{EH}{AB}\right)^2$. But area of EFGH = b' and area of ABCD = b. Therefore, $\frac{b'}{b} = \left(\frac{EH}{AB}\right)^2$ or $\frac{EH}{AB} = \frac{\sqrt{b'}}{\sqrt{b}}$. We can substitute this result in the equation above to obtain a relation solely in terms of h', h, b', and b.

$$\frac{h'}{h + h'} = \frac{\sqrt{b'}}{\sqrt{b}} .$$

By crossmultiplication, $h'\sqrt{b} = (h + h')\sqrt{b'} = h\sqrt{b'} + h'\sqrt{b'}$

$$h'\sqrt{b} - h'\sqrt{b'} = h\sqrt{b'}$$

$$h'(\sqrt{b} - \sqrt{b'}) = h\sqrt{b'}$$

$$h' = \frac{h\sqrt{b'}}{\sqrt{b} - \sqrt{b'}} .$$

By substituting in the volume expression, we obtain:

$$\text{Volume} = \frac{1}{3}[bh + h'(b - b')]$$

$$= \frac{1}{3}\left[bh + \frac{\sqrt{b'}}{\sqrt{b} - \sqrt{b'}} \cdot h \cdot (b - b')\right].$$

Factoring out an h and rationalizing the denominator, we have the final result:

$$\text{Volume} = \frac{1}{3}h\left[b + \frac{\sqrt{b'}}{\sqrt{b} - \sqrt{b'}}(b - b')\right]$$

$$= \tfrac{1}{3}h\left[\, b + \frac{\sqrt{b'}}{\sqrt{b} - \sqrt{b'}} \cdot \frac{(\sqrt{b})^2 - (\sqrt{b'})^2}{1}\,\right]$$

$$= \tfrac{1}{3}h\left[\, b + \frac{\sqrt{b'}}{\sqrt{b} - \sqrt{b'}} \; \frac{(\sqrt{b} + \sqrt{b'})(\sqrt{b} - \sqrt{b'})}{1}\,\right]$$

$$= \tfrac{1}{3}h[\, b + \sqrt{b'}(\sqrt{b} + \sqrt{b'})\,]$$

$$= \tfrac{1}{3}h[\, b + b' + \sqrt{bb'}\,].$$

● **PROBLEM 11-34**

A regular pyramid has a pentagon for its base.

(a) Show that the area of the base is given by the formula $\beta = \tfrac{5}{4}e^2 \tan 54°$ where e = an edge of the base.

(b) If the slant height of the pyramid makes an angle of 54° with the altitude of the pyramid, show that the altitude is given by the formula $h = \tfrac{e}{2}$.

(c) Using the formulas of part a and b, write a formula for the volume of the pyramid in terms of the base edge e.

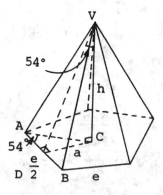

<u>Solution</u>:

(a)  The area of a regular polygon A, whose perimeter is p and whose apothem is a, is given by the formula $A = \tfrac{1}{2}ap$. The perimeter of a regular n-gon equals n times the length of any one side. For this pentagon, p = 5e.

To find the length of the apothem a, draw the perpendicular from the center of the pentagon, C, to any side $\overline{AB}$, intersecting $\overline{AB}$ at point D.  D is the midpoint of $\overline{AB}$.  (To see this, remember that the center of a regular polygon is also the center of the circumscribing circle.  Thus, $\overline{AC}$ and $\overline{BC}$ are

298

radii of that circle. $\overline{AC} = \overline{BC}$ and $\triangle ABC$ is isosceles. $\overline{CD}$ is then the altitude drawn from the vertex angle of an isosceles triangle and therefore bisects the base.) Thus, $AD = \frac{1}{2}AB = \frac{e}{2}$. Furthermore, m∢CAD = 54°. (To see this, note that all five central angles of the pentagon are congruent. Therefore, m∢ACB = $\frac{360°}{5}$ = 72°. Since $\triangle ABC$ is isosceles, ∢CAD ≅ ∢CBA. By using the fact that the angle sum of a triangle is 180°, we have m∢CAD + m∢CBA + m∢ACB = 180°, or 2m∢CAD = 180° − 72° or m∢CAD = 54°.)

In right $\triangle ACD$, then, a is the length of the leg opposite known ∢CAD. Leg AD is also known. The relationship between these three quantities is tan ∢CAD = $\dfrac{\text{length of opposite leg}}{\text{length of adjacent leg}}$ = $\frac{CD}{AD}$ or tan 54° = $\frac{a}{e/2}$. Solving for a, we obtain a = $\frac{e}{2}$ tan 54°.

We have a and p. Thus, the base area equals $\frac{1}{2}ap$ = $\frac{1}{2}(\frac{e}{2}$ tan 54°)(5e) = $\frac{5}{4}e^2$ tan 54°.

(b) To find h, we construct another triangle, $\triangle VDC$. To show that $\triangle VDC$ is indeed a right triangle, we remember that the pyramid is regular. The perpendicular to the base of a regular pyramid passes through the center of the base. Since $\overline{VC}$ is the segment connecting the vertex to the center of the base, it is perpendicular to the base and ∢VCD is a right angle. In $\triangle VDC$, we are given leg $\overline{DC}$ = a = $\frac{e}{2}$ tan 54°. Furthermore, ∢DVC is given to be 54°. Relating height $\overline{VC}$ to these quantities, we have

tan 54° = $\dfrac{\text{length of opposite leg}}{\text{length of adjacent leg}}$ = $\dfrac{DC}{VC}$ = $\dfrac{\frac{e}{2}\ \text{tan } 54°}{\overline{VC}}$ . Thus,

$$h = VC = \dfrac{\frac{e}{2}\ \text{tan } 54°}{\text{tan } 54°} = \frac{e}{2}.$$

(c) The volume of any pyramid is given by the formula $\frac{1}{3}bh$ where b = base area and h = height of the pyramid. From part (a), we know the base area to be $\frac{5}{4}e^2$ tan 54°. From part (b), the height is $\frac{e}{2}$. Thus,

$$V = \frac{1}{3}bh = \frac{1}{3}(\frac{5}{4}e^2 \text{ tan } 54°)(\frac{e}{2}) = \frac{5}{24}e^3 \text{ tan } 54°.$$

# SPHERES

On a sphere of radius 9 inches, the perimeter of a spherical triangle is 12π inches. The sides of the triangle are in the ratio 3:4:5.

   a) Find the sides of the triangle in degrees.
   b) Find the angles of its polar triangle.
   c) Find the area of the polar triangle in square inches. (answer may be left in terms of π.)
   d) A zone on this sphere is equal in area to the polar triangle. Find the number of inches in the altitude of the zone.

Solution:

(a) The perimeter is given in inches; we wish to find the lengths of the sides of the triangle in degrees. Therefore, we first convert the perimeter into degrees, p°, and then use the ratio 3:4:5 to find the number of degrees in each side.

If the radius is 9, then the circumference of a great circle is $2\pi r = 2\pi(9) = 18\pi$. Thus, a length of 18π would span 360°. Since the length is proportional to the number of degrees spanned, we have the ratio:

$$\frac{p°}{360} = \frac{\text{length}}{\text{circumference}} = \frac{12\pi}{18\pi}$$

$$p° = \frac{12\pi}{18\pi}\ 360° = \frac{2}{3} \cdot 360° = 240°.$$

Suppose the three sides are a, b, and c. Because they are in a 3:4:5 ratio, then there is some number x such that a = 3x, b = 4x, and c = 5x. The perimeter equals the sum of the sides. Therefore, p° = a + b + c. 240° = 3x + 4x + 5x = 12x or x = $\frac{240°}{12}$ = 20°. Then, a = 3(20°) = 60°; b = 4(20°) = 80°; and c = 5(20°) = 100°. The measure of the sides are 60°, 80°, and 100°.

(b) By an earlier theorem, we know that the angles of the polar triangle are supplementary to the sides of the spherical triangles opposite them. Therefore, if the sides of the triangle are 60°, 80°, and 100°, the angles of the polar triangles are (180 -60°), (180 -80°), and (180°-100°) or 120°, 100°, and 80°.

(c) The area of a spherical triangle of angles a, b, and

c is  is given by the formula $\frac{a+b+c-180}{720}$ s.  s, the surface

area of the sphere is $4\pi r^2 = 4\pi(9)^2$. Thus, the area of the triangle is $\frac{120+80+100-180}{720}(4\pi(9)^2) = \frac{120}{720}4\pi(9)^2 = \frac{2}{3}\pi(9)^2 = 54\pi$.

(d)  The zone of a sphere is the region formed when two parallel planes intersect a sphere.  That part of the sphere between the planes is called a zone and the distance between the planes is the altitude of the zone.  The surface area of the zone is always equal to the lateral surface area of a cylinder of height equal to the altitude of the zone and base congruent to a great circle of the intercepted sphere.  We are given that the surface area of the zone equals the area of the triangle.  Thus,

$$(2\pi r)h = 54\pi.$$

Since $r = 9$, $h = \frac{54\pi}{2\pi(9)} = 3$ inches.

● **PROBLEM** 11-36

Show that if a point on a sphere is at a distance of a quadrant from each of two other points on the sphere, not the extremities of a diameter, then the point is a pole of the great circle passing through these points.

**Solution:**  Let's begin by defining our terms.  In a sphere of radius r, the great circle is a circle, all of whose points lie on the sphere, and which has a radius equal to the radius of the sphere.  All great circles have a common center and that center is the center of the sphere.  Most planar and linear measurements of the sphere involve the great circles in some way.  The circumference of a sphere, for example, is the circumference of any great circle.  In addition, the shortest distance between any two points of a sphere is found by drawing the great circle determined by the two points. The part of the circumference between the two points is the geodesic - or path of shortest distance.  Examples of great circles are the equator of the earth and the prime meridian.

A quadrant of a sphere is defined to be one-fourth the great circle.  It is a sector of a circle of radius r, and the measure of its central angle is $\frac{360}{4} = 90°$.  The distance of a quadrant is the arc of the quadrant.  The North Pole and any point on the equator are a distance of a quadrant away from each other.

301

For every great circle, there are two points on the sphere, one on each side of the great circle, that are a quadrant away from the circumference of the great circle. These are the poles of the great circle. The segment with the two poles as endpoints is called the axis and is a diameter of the sphere. Thus, the axis intersects the great circle at the center of the sphere. In addition, this diameter is perpendicular to the plane of the great sphere.

In the accompanying figure, sphere O has great circle ABC as a great circle. $\overset{\frown}{PA}$ and $\overset{\frown}{PB}$ are quadrants.

We must show that P is a pole of ⊙ABC. To show that a point of a sphere is a pole a great circle, it is sufficient to show that the axis of the point $\overline{POP'}$ is perpendicular to the plane of the great circle. We show $\overleftrightarrow{PO} \perp \overleftrightarrow{AO}$ and $\overleftrightarrow{PO} \perp \overleftrightarrow{OB}$. Since $\overleftrightarrow{PO}$ is perpendicular to two lines in plane AOB, $\overleftrightarrow{PO} \perp$ plane of the great circle.

Given: Points P, A, and B on the sphere O; $\overset{\frown}{AB}$ of a great circle ABC; and the quadrants $\overset{\frown}{PA}$ and $\overset{\frown}{PB}$.

To Prove: P is a pole of ⊙ABC.

| Statements | Reasons |
|---|---|
| 1. Draw $\overline{AO}$, $\overline{BO}$ and diameter $\overline{POP'}$. | 1. Two points determine a line; a diameter is a line segment passing through the center and having its endpoints on the sphere. |
| 2. $\overset{\frown}{PA}$ and $\overset{\frown}{PB}$ are quadrants. | 2. Given. |
| 3. ⊄POA and ⊄POB are right angles; or $\overline{PO} \perp \overline{OA}$, $\overline{PO} \perp \overline{OB}$. | 3. The central angle of a quadrant is a right angle. |
| 4. $\overline{PO} \perp$ plane ABC (or $\overline{PP'} \perp$ ABC). | 4. If a line is perpendicular to each of two intersecting lines at their point of intersection, then it is perpendicular to the plane of the lines. |
| 5. PP' is the axis of ⊙ABC. | 5. The axis of a circle of a sphere is the diameter of the sphere which is perpendicular to the plane of the circle. |
| 6. P is a pole of ⊙ABC. | 6. The extremities of the axis are the poles of the circle. |

The most remote spot of ocean, the point at 48°30' S and 125°30' W in the Pacific, is 1660 miles from the nearest land Pitcairn Island. Approximate the area of this oceanic expanse as (1) a circle; (2) a zone of a sphere. Compare the two. (The radius of the earth is 3960 mi.)

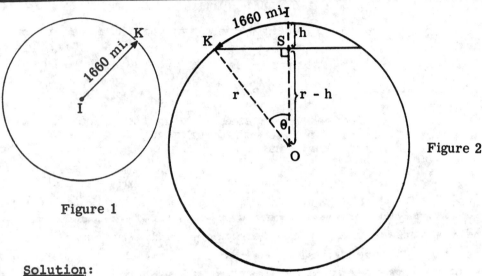

Figure 1

Figure 2

**Solution:**

(1)   The area of a circle with radius r equals $\pi r^2$. Therefore, the area of the watery expanse is $\pi(1660 \text{ mi.})^2 = 2.76 \times 10^6 \pi \text{ mi.}^2$

(2)   The area of a zone is given by the formula $2\pi rh$. To find h, we first find $\theta$. With $\theta$, we can find $\overline{OS}$. Since h is the radius minus $\overline{OS}$, we can find h if we know $\theta$.

To find $\theta$, remember that the arc length and central angle measure are proportional

(i)   $\dfrac{\theta}{360} = \dfrac{m\overset{\frown}{IK}}{\text{circum. of earth}}.$

The circumference of the earth (of radius 3960 miles) is $2\pi r = 2\pi(3,960 \text{ mi.})$.   IK is given to be 1660 mi.

(ii)   $\dfrac{\theta}{360} = \dfrac{1660 \text{ mi.}}{2\pi(3960 \text{ mi.})}$

(iii)   $\theta = 360 \dfrac{1660}{2\pi \cdot 3,960} = \dfrac{830}{11\pi} = 24°.$

To find $\overline{OS}$, note that in right $\triangle KSO$:

(iv)   $\cos \theta = \dfrac{OS}{KO} = \dfrac{r-h}{r} = \dfrac{3,960 \text{ mi} - h}{3960}.$

Consulting the trigonometric tables, we find cos 24° = .914.  Substituting this value in and multiplying both sides by 3,960, we obtain:

(v)   (.914)(3,960) = 3,960 - h

(vi)   h = 3,960 - (.914)(3,960) = 3,960(1-.914)

= 3,960(.086) = 341 mi.

With a value for h, we can now solve for the area of the zone:

(vii) Area = $2\pi rh$ = $2\pi$(3960 mi.)(341 mi.) =

$2.7 \times 10^6$ mi.$^2$

The zone approximation is smaller than the planar approximation by 2%. In either case, the area covered by the water is greater than any single nation.

● **PROBLEM** 11-38

Find the surface area of a sphere whose radius measures 14 in. [Use   $\pi = \frac{22}{7}$] (See figure.)

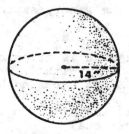

Solution:  The surface area of a sphere is, by postulate, equal to four times the area of one of its great circles.

Therefore, S = $4\pi r^2$, where r is the radius of a great circle of the sphere.  Since the radius of a great circle of a sphere is equal to the radius of the sphere itself, r = 14 in.  By substitution,

$$S = 4(\tfrac{22}{7})(14)^2 \text{ in.}^2$$

$$S = 2464 \text{ in.}^2$$

Therefore, area of the sphere = 2464 sq. in.

The ratio of the altitude of a zone to the diameter of the sphere on which it is drawn is 1:5. The area of the zone is 80π.

    a)   Find the area of the sphere.
    b)   If one of the bases of the zone is a great circle, find the area of the other base.

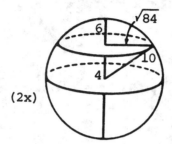

(2x)

Solution:

    (a)  To find the area of the sphere we use the formula $S = 4\pi r^2$. To use the formula, though, we must solve for r. We solve for r using the given zone area. We know that the zone area and r are related by the formula,

$A_{zone}$ = (circumference of the great circle) • (zone height)

    $80\pi = 2\pi r \cdot h$.

    This equation can be solved for r if we can eliminate the second variable h. From the given, though, we know that $h:d = 1:5$ or $h = \frac{1}{5}d$. Since the diameter d is twice the radius, we have $h = \frac{1}{5}(2r) = \frac{2}{5}r$. Substituting this result in the zone area formula, we have

$$80\pi = 2\pi r \cdot (\tfrac{2}{5}r) = \tfrac{4}{5}\pi r^2$$

$$r^2 = 80\pi \cdot (\tfrac{5}{4\pi}) = 100$$

$$r = 10.$$

    Thus the radius of the sphere is 10 and its area equals $4\pi r^2 = 4\pi(10)^2 = 400\pi$.

    (b)  To find the area of the smaller base, we use the formula $\pi r_1^2$, where $r_1$ is the radius of the smaller base, To find $r_1$, consider the line drawn from the center of the sphere perpendicular to the plane of the circle. By an earlier theorem, we know that this line intersects the circle at its

305

center. Thus, a right triangle is formed with hypotenuse equal to the radius of the sphere, one leg equal to the altitude of the zone and one leg equal to the radius of the smaller base. The radius of the sphere equals 10 (see Part a). The altitude of the zone can be found by the relationship used in Part a, namely $h = \frac{2}{5}r$, where r is the radius of the sphere.

So $h = \frac{2}{5}(10) = 4$. Then, by the Pythagorean Theorem, we have

$$(\text{radius of circle})^2 = (\text{radius of sphere})^2 - (\text{altitude of zone})^2$$

$$= 10^2 \qquad\qquad - 4^2$$

$$= 84.$$

Since the area of the circle = $\pi(\text{radius of circle})^2$, we have $\pi(84) = 84\pi$.

● **PROBLEM 11-40**

Find the volume of sphere of radius 2.

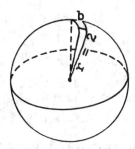

Solution: The volume of a sphere equals $\frac{4}{3}\pi r^3$. To see this, consider any polygon on the surface of the sphere. Draw the radii of the sphere to the vertices. The resulting solid resembles a pyramid with altitude roughly equal to the radius and a base that is not a plane surface but slightly spherical. By choosing polygons of smaller and smaller areas, the base becomes less curved and more like a plane figure; and, thus, the volume of the pyramidlike figure approaches $\frac{1}{3}r \cdot b$ where b is the area of the base polygon and r, the radius of the circle, is approximately the altitude. Suppose we divide the sphere into n pyramidlike figures. Then, if $b_1, b_2, \ldots, b_n$ are the areas of each base, the volume of the sphere equals the sum of the volumes of the n pyramids:

$$V = \frac{1}{3}rb_1 + \frac{1}{3}rb_2 + \ldots + \frac{1}{3}rb_n.$$

Factoring out $\frac{1}{3}r$, we obtain

$$V = \tfrac{1}{3}r(b_1 + b_2 + \ldots b_n).$$

Since the n pyramids comprise the entire volume, the n bases must sum to the total surface area; that is,

$(b_1 + b_2 \ldots + b_n) = 4\pi r^2.$  Thus,

$$V = \tfrac{1}{3}r(4\pi r^2) = \tfrac{4}{3}\pi r^3.$$

Getting back to the problem, the sphere of radius 2 has volume $\tfrac{4}{3}\pi(2)^3$ or $\tfrac{32}{3}\pi$.

● **PROBLEM** 11-41

Given a sphere of radius r, find the volume of the regular tetrahedron that circumscribes the sphere.

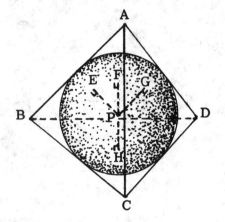

Figure 1

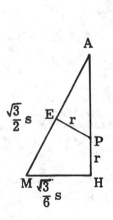

Figure 3

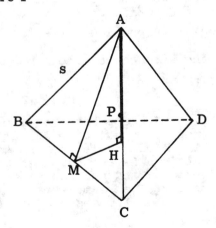

Figure 2

307

**Solution:** In Figure 1, sphere P of radius r is circumscribed by regular tetrahedron ABCD. Sphere P is tangent with face ABC at point E; face ABD at F; face ACD at G; and face BCD at H. s is the length of the edge of tetrahedron ABCD. We wish to find the volume V of ABCD in terms of the radius r. From an earlier proof, we know that the volume of a tetrahedron is $\frac{\sqrt{2}}{12}s^3$ where s is the length of the edge. Therefore, we find s in terms of r; substitute in the tetrahedron volume formula; and the problem is solved.

We will find the relationship of the edge AB = s and the sphere radius PE = r. We do this by considering triangle AMH in Figure 2, formed by the slant height $\overline{AM}$ and the perpendicular from the vertex A to the base $\overline{AH}$. We can find AM and MH. Furthermore, from an earlier proof, we know that (1) since P, the sphere center, is equidistant from the faces of the regular pyramid (the distances to the faces from an inscribed sphere are radii. Since all radii are congruent, the center is equidistant), and since all points equidistant from the faces of a regular pyramid lie on the perpendicular from the vertex, then P must lie on the perpendicular $\overline{AH}$, or $\overrightarrow{APH}$; and (2) the perpendicular $(\overline{PE})$ to the face of a regular pyramid (A-BCD...) from a point (P) on the vertex perpendicular $(\overrightarrow{AH})$ intersects the face (ABC) on its slant height $(\overrightarrow{AM})$. Therefore, $\overrightarrow{AEM}$.

Combining all these facts, we construct Figure 3. Note that ∡AEP and ∡AHM are right angles (thus, ∡AEP ≅ ∡AHM) and ∡A ≅ ∡A. Therefore, ΔAEP ∼ ΔAHM by the A-A Similarity Theorem. Because the sides of similar triangles are proportional, we have

(i)     $\dfrac{EP}{AP} = \dfrac{HM}{AM}.$

Because EP is a radius, EP = r. To find AM, note that $\overline{AM}$ is a leg of right ΔABM. (ΔABM is a right triangle because a slant height of a face is always ⊥ to the base.) We know that AB = s. Furthermore, because face ΔABC is an equilateral triangle (every face of a regular tetrahedron is an equilateral triangle) perpendicular $\overline{AM}$ bisects base $\overline{BC}$, and BM = $\frac{1}{2}$BC = $\frac{1}{2}$s. By the Pythagorean Theorem, $AM^2 = BA^2 - BM^2 = s^2 - \left(\frac{1}{2}s\right)^2 = \frac{3}{4}s^2$, or AM = $\frac{\sqrt{3}}{2}$s.

To find MH, remember that the perpendicular from the vertex of a regular pyramid intersects the base polygon at its center. Therefore, H is the center of the base equilateral ΔBCD — that is H is the point of concurrency of the altitudes, angle bisectors, and medians. (Note in an equilateral triangle, these are the same three lines.) Because H is the concurrency point of the medians, it divides the median DM such that HD = $\frac{2}{3}$DM or HM = $\frac{1}{3}$DM. By considering right ΔBDM, we show by the Pythagorean Theorem that $DM^2 = BD^2 - BM^2 = s^2 - \left(\frac{1}{2}s\right)^2$

308

$= \frac{3}{4}s^2$ or DM $= \frac{\sqrt{3}}{2}s$. Since HM $= \frac{1}{3}$DM, then HM $= \frac{1}{3}\left(\frac{\sqrt{3}}{2}s\right) = \frac{\sqrt{3}}{6}s$.

Returning to the equation (i) and substituting in our values, we obtain:

(ii) $\quad \frac{r}{AP} = \frac{\frac{\sqrt{3}}{6}s}{\frac{\sqrt{3}}{2}s}$ or r $= \frac{\frac{\sqrt{3}}{6}s}{\frac{\sqrt{3}}{2}s}AP = \frac{1}{3}AP$.

Refer back to Figure 3. We have discovered that r $= \frac{1}{3}AP$ or AP $= 3r$. Since $\overline{PH}$ is a radius of the sphere, PH $= r$, and thus AH $=$ AP $+$ PH $= 3r + r = 4r$. In right $\triangle$AMH, we have hypotenuse AM expressible in terms of s, leg MH expressible in terms of s, and leg AH expressible in terms of r. By using Pythagorean Theorem, we can relate s to r.

(iii) $\quad AM^2 = MH^2 + AH^2$

(iv) $\quad \left(\frac{\sqrt{3}}{2}s\right)^2 = \left(\frac{\sqrt{3}}{6}s\right)^2 + (4r)^2$

(v) $\quad \frac{3}{4}s^2 = \frac{1}{12}s^2 + 16r^2$.

(vi) $\quad 16r^2 = \frac{3}{4}s^2 - \frac{1}{12}s^2 = \left(\frac{9}{12} - \frac{1}{12}\right)s^2 = \frac{2}{3}s^2$

(vii) $\quad \frac{3}{2} \cdot 16r^2 = s^2$

(viii) $\quad 24r^2 = s^2$

(ix) $\quad s = \sqrt{24}r = 2\sqrt{6}r$.

Now, we can use the volume formula.

(x) $\quad V = \frac{\sqrt{2}}{12}s^3 = \frac{\sqrt{2}}{12}(2\sqrt{6}r)^3 = 8\sqrt{3}r^3$.

# CYLINDERS

● **PROBLEM 11-42**

A right circular cylinder has a base whose diameter is 7 and height is 10. What is the surface area of the cylinder, not including the bases?

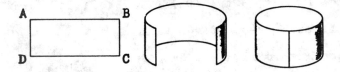

309

<u>Solution</u>:  From the figure, we see that calculating the re-
quired surface area is equivalent to calculating the area of
the rectangle shown.  The area of the rectangle, K, is

$$K = (AB)(BC).$$

But BC is the height of the cylinder, and BC = 10.  AB is
equivalent to the circumference of the base of the cylinder.
If the base has diameter d, the circumference of the base
is πd, which equals 7π in our case.  Hence, AB = 7π.  Therefore,

$$K = (7\pi)(10) = 70\pi$$

is the required surface area.

● **PROBLEM 11-43**

Find, in terms of π, the lateral area and the total surface
area of a right circular cylinder if the radius of its base
measures 5 in. and its altitude measures 8 in.  (See figure).

<u>Solution</u>:  The lateral face of a right circular cylinder is
actually a rectangle, whose base length (b) is the circumference of the base of the cylinder, and whose height (h) is
the height of the cylinder.  Therefore, the lateral area is
equal to bh.  In the case of a right circular cylinder, b =
2πr, the circumference of the base, where r is the base
radius.

Lateral Area = 2πrh.

By substitution, Lateral Area = $2\pi(5 \text{ in.})(8 \text{ in.}) = 80\pi \text{ in.}^2$
The total surface area equals the lateral area plus the sum
of the area of the two bases.

Area of one Base = Area of a circle = $\pi r^2$

$$= \pi(5)^2 \text{ in.}^2 = 25\pi \text{ in.}^2$$

Area of the two Bases = $2(25\pi \text{ in.}^2) = 50\pi \text{ in.}^2$

Total Surface Area = $(80\pi + 50\pi) \text{ in.}^2 = 130\pi \text{ in.}^2$

Therefore, Lateral area = 80π sq. in.

Total Surface area = 130π sq. in.

Find, in terms of π, the volume of a right circular cylinder
if the radius of its base measures 4 in. and its altitude
measures 5 in.

Solution: If we picture the base of the cylinder as having
a depth of one unit of measure, we can then calculate the
volume by determining the area of the base and multiplying
it by the height of the cylinder. In effect, this multiplication amounts to stacking the bases up to the height of the
cylinder.

Area of the base = $\pi r^2$, where r is the radius of the
circular base. Therefore, the volume is given by

$$V = \pi r^2 h.$$

By substitution, $V = \pi(4)^2 5 \text{ in.}^3 = 80\pi \text{ in.}^3$.

Therefore, volume of the cylinder = $80\pi \text{ in.}^3$.

Find the volume of a right circular cylinder of height 6 if
it has the same lateral surface area as a cube of edge 3.

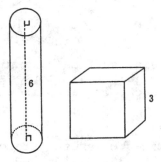

Solution: The volume of a cylinder equals $\pi r^2 h$. The height,
h, equals 6. The radius can be found by relating the lateral
surface area of the cube and the cylinder. The lateral surface area of the cylinder equals (base perimeter) · (height)
= $2\pi rh$. The lateral surface area of the cube which has no

bases equals $4s^2$.  By equating these two expressions, we obtain

$$2\pi rh = 4s^2.$$

By substitution,  $\qquad 2\pi r(6) = 4(3)^2$

$$r = \frac{4(3)^2}{2\pi(6)} = \frac{36}{2\pi(6)} = \frac{3}{\pi}.$$

Therefore,

$$\text{Volume of cylinder} = (\text{Area of base}) \cdot (\text{height})$$

$$= \pi r^2 \qquad\qquad \cdot h$$

$$= \pi\left(\frac{3}{\pi}\right)^2 \qquad \cdot 6$$

$$= \frac{54}{\pi}.$$

# CONES

● **PROBLEM** 11-46

Find the lateral area and the total area of a right circular cone in which the radius measures 14 in. and the slant height measures 20 in.  [Use $\pi = \frac{22}{7}$].

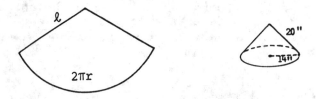

Solution:  The lateral surface of a right circular cone, with base radius r, when laid flat, appears to be a sector of a large circle.  As such, its area is equal to the area of that sector.

The radius of the sector is equal to the slant height, $\ell$, of the cone.  The arc length intercepted is equal to the circumference of the base of the cone, $2\pi r$.
Area of the Sector

$$= (\text{Area of entire circle})\left(\frac{\text{Central Angle measure}}{\text{Measure of full circle}}\right).$$

Let $\theta$ = Central angle measure.

$$\text{Area of the Sector} = \pi\ell^2\left(\frac{\theta}{2\pi}\right) = \ell^2\,\frac{\theta}{2}.$$

All arcs and angles are measured in radians. In radians,

$$\theta = \frac{\text{arc length}}{\text{radius}} = \frac{2\pi r}{\ell}.$$

Therefore, area of the sector $= \ell^2 (\frac{1}{2}) (\frac{2\pi r}{\ell})$.

Area of the sector $= \pi r \ell =$ Lateral area of the cone.

Hence, by substitution,

Lateral Area of the cone $= \pi (14)(20) \text{in.}^2 = (\frac{22}{7})(14)(20) \text{in.}^2$

$$= 880 \text{ in.}^2$$

Total Area = Lateral area + Base area

$$= \pi r \ell + \pi r^2$$

$$= 880 \text{ in.}^2 + \frac{22}{7}(14)^2 \text{ in.}^2$$

$$= (880 + 616) \text{in.}^2 = 1496 \text{ in.}^2$$

Therefore, Lateral Area = 880 sq. in.

Total Area = 1496 sq. in.

● PROBLEM 11-47

The flat pattern in the accompanying diagram is used to make a lampshade. It is the lateral surface of the frustum of a right circular cone.

The two concentric circles have radii of 12 and 4 inches and m∢AOB = 60°. The minor sector AOB and the remainder of the interior of the circle are removed and discarded. $\overline{AC}$ is fastened to $\overline{BD}$ with no space or overlap.

(a) Find the radius of each of the two bases of the lampshade.

(b) Find the area of the outer surface of the lampshade. [Leave answer in terms of $\pi$.]

(c) Find the altitude of the lampshade. [Leave in radical form.]

Solution:

(a) The smaller base of the lampshade will be formed out of the portion of the smaller circle remaining after the 60° sector has been removed. Since 60° is $\frac{1}{6}$ of the total measure of the circle, the smaller base of the lampshade will be a circle whose circumference will be $\frac{5}{6}$ of the original small circle.

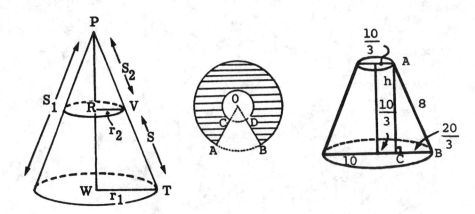

Since the circumference is a linear function of the radius, the ratio of the circumferences of any two circles will be equal to the ratio of the radii. Thus, the radius $\overline{OC}$ of the smaller circle will be $\frac{5}{6}$ of the original smaller radius of 4. Therefore, the radius of the smaller base of the lampshade is $\frac{5}{6}(4)$ or $\frac{10}{3}$ inches.

By similar logic, the radius of the larger base is $\frac{5}{6}$ of the original large radius of 12. The larger base has a radius of $\frac{5}{6}(12)$ or 10 inches.

Therefore, the radii of the bases of the lampshade are $\frac{10}{3}$ in. and 10 in.

(b)  The area of the outer surface of the lampshade has the form of the surface area of a frustum of a cone. Therefore, its area can be found by first looking at a frustum in general.

Assume that a frustum of a cone is formed with base radii $r_1$ and $r_2$ and slant height s. The entire cone has slant height $s_1$ and the upper cone is left with slant height $s_2$.

The lateral area of the entire cone is, in general, $\pi$(base radius)(slant height). In this case, $L_1 = \pi r_1 s_1$.

The lateral area of the upper cone is $L_2 = \pi r_2 s_2$. Hence, the lateral area of the frustum is $L = L_1 - L_2 = \pi(r_1 s_1 - r_2 s_2)$. Since we are only given data about the frustum, we don't know $s_1$ and $s_2$ and, as such, must try to eliminate them.

We note that $\triangle PWT$ is a right triangle and since $r_2 \parallel r_1$

314

(this is the case in all frustums of right circular cones).
$\triangle PRV \sim \triangle PWT$, by the AA Similarity Theorem. Therefore,

$$\frac{s_2}{s_1} = \frac{r_2}{r_1} \quad \text{and} \quad s_2 = \frac{s_1 r_2}{r_1}.$$

Now, by substituting into the equation for L, we obtain

$$L = \pi \left( r_1 s_1 - \frac{s_1 r_2^2}{r_1} \right) = \frac{\pi}{r_1}(r_1^2 s_1 - s_1 r_2^2) = \frac{\pi s_1}{r_1}(r_1^2 - r_2^2)$$

$$= \frac{\pi s_1}{r_1}(r_1^2 - r_2^2) = \frac{\pi s_1}{r_1}(r_1 - r_2)(r_1 + r_2)$$

$$= \left( \pi s_1 - \frac{\pi s_1 r_2}{r_1} \right)(r_1 + r_2).$$

Substituting $s_2 = \frac{s_1 r_2}{r_1}$ into the last equation,

$$L = \pi(s_1 - s_2)(r_1 + r_2).$$

We see that $s = s_1 - s_2$. Therefore,

$$L = \pi s(r_1 + r_2).$$

In our lampshade problem we know $r_1 = 10$, $r_2 = \frac{10}{3}$ and $s = CA$ = DB = the difference between the original two radii, 12 - 4, or 8.

By substitution,

$$L = \pi(8)(10 + \frac{10}{3}) = \pi(8)(\frac{40}{3}) = \frac{320}{3}\pi.$$

Therefore, the area of the outer surface is $\frac{320\pi}{3}$ sq. in.

(c) We can find the altitude, AC, by recongizing that $\triangle ABC$ is a right triangle and then applying the Pythagorean Theorem. The hypotenuse of $\triangle ABC$ is 8 in., since it corresponds to the slant height of the frustum.

The top radius is $\frac{10}{3}$ in and the bottom radius is 10 in. By projecting the top radius onto the bottom we see that CB = $10 - \frac{10}{3} = \frac{20}{3}$.

Let h = the length of the altitude. Then,

$$h^2 = 8^2 - (\frac{20}{3})^2 = 64 - \frac{400}{9} = \frac{576 - 400}{9} = \frac{176}{9}$$

315

$$h = \sqrt{\frac{176}{9}} = \frac{\sqrt{16}\sqrt{11}}{3} = \frac{4}{3}\sqrt{11}.$$

Therefore, the altitude of the frustum is $\frac{4}{3}\sqrt{11}$ in.

● **PROBLEM 11-48**

a) Find the volume of a solid right circular cone whose height is 4 ft. and whose base has radius 3 ft.

b) What is the slant height of this cone?

c) Find the surface area of this cone.

**Solution:** Figure (A) shows the cone. s is the measure of the slant height, h is the measure of the height, and r is the measure of the radius of the base.

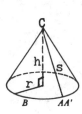

Figure A

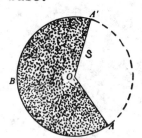

Figure B

a). The volume of a solid right circular cone whose height is h, and whose base has radius r, is

$$V = \frac{1}{3}\pi r^2 h.$$

In our case, r = 3 ft., h = 4 ft., and

$$V = (\frac{1}{3})(\pi)(9 \text{ ft.}^2)(4 \text{ ft.})$$

$$V = 37.70 \text{ ft.}^3.$$

b). The slant height of a right circular cone can be calculated by the Pythagorean Theorem. Look at the right triangle with sides h, r, and s, in figure (A). Applying the Pythagorean Theorem to this triangle,

$$s^2 = h^2 + r^2$$

or

$$s = \sqrt{h^2 + r^2}$$

$$s = \sqrt{16 \text{ ft.}^2 + 9 \text{ ft.}^2} = 5 \text{ ft.}$$

316

c). Figure (B) shows the region obtained by cutting the cone of figure (A) along $\overline{AC}$. This region has the same area as the surface area of the cone. The area of the region can be calculated from the following proportion

$$\frac{\text{Area(region)}}{\text{Area(circle O)}} = \frac{\text{length } \overparen{ABA'}}{\text{length of circle O}}$$

$$\text{Area(region)} = \frac{(\pi s^2)(2\pi r)}{(2\pi s)}.$$

Here we have used the fact that the length of $\overparen{ABA'}$ is $2\pi r$, since $\overparen{ABA'}$ is the boundary of the circular base of the cone. Hence,

$$\text{Area(region)} = \pi r s.$$

In our case, s = 5 ft. and r = 3 ft. Then

$$\text{Area(region)} = 15\pi \text{ ft.}^2 = 47.12 \text{ ft.}^2.$$

The surface area of the cone is therefore 47.12 ft.$^2$.

● **PROBLEM 11-49**

A frustum of a solid cone is the portion of solid cone remaining when the solid cone above a given section is removed. (See figure.) (a). Using the properties of similar triangles, what can we say about x/3 and (x + 4)/5? (b). Find the height, x + 4, of the large cone. (c) Find the volume of the small solid cone. (d) Find the volume of the large solid cone. (e) Find the volume of the frustum. (f) Taking $r_1 = 3$, $r_2 = 5$, and h = 4, compute

$V = \frac{1}{3}\pi h(r_1^2 + r_1 r_2 + r_2^2)$. Compare this with part (e).

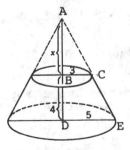

**Solution:**

(a) We will prove that $\triangle ABC \sim \triangle ADE$, by the A.A. (angle-angle) Similarity Theorem. We will then be able to set up a proportion between $\overline{AB}$, $\overline{AD}$, $\overline{BC}$, and $\overline{DE}$, thereby finding a relationship between x/3 and (x + 4)/5.

317

First, ∢A is common to both ΔABC and ΔADE. Therefore, ∢BAC ≅ ∢DAE. Furthermore, the plane containing $\overline{BC}$ is parallel to the base of the cone. Hence, ∢ACB ≅ ∢AED, since they are corresponding angles of the parallel segments $\overline{BC}$ and $\overline{DE}$. In conclusion, ΔABC ∿ ΔADE, and we may write

$$\frac{AB}{AD} = \frac{BC}{DE}.$$

Since AB = x, AD = x + 4, BC = 3 and DE = 5, the last equation may be rewritten as

$$\frac{x}{x+4} = \frac{3}{5}$$

or                                     5x = 3x + 12

or                                      x = 6.

Hence, $\frac{x+4}{5} = 2$ and $\frac{x}{3} = 2$ (i.e., $\frac{x+4}{5} = \frac{x}{3}$).

(b)   The height of the large cone, x + 4, is, from part (a), 10.

(c)   The volume of the small cone is equal to $\frac{\pi}{3}$ times the product of its height (x) and the square of the length of the radius of its base ($3^2$).  Hence,

$$V_S = (\tfrac{\pi}{3})(x)(3^2)$$

$$V_S = (\tfrac{\pi}{3})(6)(9) = 56.52.$$

(d)   The volume of the large solid cone is equal to $\frac{\pi}{3}$ times the product of its height (x + 4) and the square of the length of the radius of its base ($5^2$).  Hence,

$$V_L = (\tfrac{\pi}{3})(x+4)(5^2)$$

$$V_L = (\tfrac{\pi}{3})(10)(25) = 261.67.$$

(e)   The volume of the large cone, minus the volume of the small cone, equals the volume of the frustum, ($V_F$). Therefore,

$$V_F = V_L - V_S = 261.67 - 56.52$$

$$V_F = 205.15.$$

(f)   If $r_1 = 3$, $r_2 = 5$, and h = 4,

$$V = \frac{1}{3}\pi h(r_1^2 + r_1 r_2 + r_2^2)$$

$$V = (\frac{\pi}{3})(4)((3)^2 + (3)(5) + (5)^2)$$

$$V = (\frac{\pi}{3})(4)(9 + 15 + 25)$$

$$V = (\frac{4\pi}{3})(49)$$

$$V = 205.15.$$

Note that this conforms to the volume of the frustum as calculated in part (e).

● **PROBLEM 11-50**

In the accompanying figure, a right circular cone is constructed on the base of a hemisphere. The surface of the
hemisphere is equal to the lateral surface of the cone. Show
that the volume V of the solid formed can be found by the
formula $V = \frac{1}{3}\pi r^3(2 + \sqrt{3})$.

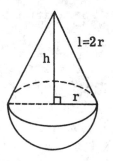

**Solution:** The volume of the solid formed equals the volume
of the hemisphere plus the volume of the right circular cone.
The volume of a hemisphere is half the volume of a sphere.
Thus, $V_{hemi.} = \frac{1}{2}(\frac{4}{3}\pi r^3) = \frac{2}{3}\pi r^3$. The volume of a cone of base
radius r and height h equals $\frac{1}{3}\pi r^2 h$. (Note in this case that
the base of the cone is the great circle of the hemisphere.
Thus, r, the base radius of the cone, equals r, the radius of
the hemisphere.) The desired volume, V, of the solid is,
therefore, $V = \frac{2}{3}\pi r^3 + \frac{1}{3}\pi r^2 h = \frac{\pi}{3}r^2(2r + h)$.

The problem, though, asks us to express the volume
totally in terms of r, not r and h.

Consider the right triangle formed by altitude h, base radius r and slant height ℓ. By the Pythagorean Theorem, $h^2 = ℓ^2 - r^2$. r is known; and ℓ and r are related by the surface area formulas. Thus, ℓ can be expressed in terms of r and the results substituted in the Pythagorean equation above to express h in terms of r.

Surface Area of hemisphere = $2\pi r^2$.

Lateral Area of cone = $\pi r ℓ$.

By the given, the two surface areas are equal. Then, $2\pi r^2 = \pi r ℓ$ or ℓ = 2r.

Using the Pythagorean equation, we have $h^2 = (2r)^2 - r^2 = 4r^2 - r^2 = 3r^2$. Thus, $h = \sqrt{3}r$.

We substitute this in our expression for V and obtain $V = \frac{\pi}{3}r^2(2r + \sqrt{3}r) = \frac{\pi}{3}r^3(2 + \sqrt{3})$.

● **PROBLEM** 11-51

An isosceles triangle, each of whose base angles is θ and whose legs are a, is rotated through 180°, using as an axis its altitude to the base.

(a) Find the volume V of the resulting solid, in terms of θ and a.

(b) Using the formula found in part a, find V, to the nearest integer if a = 5.2 and θ = 27°. (Use π = 3.14 )

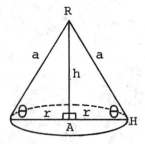

Solution:

(a) The resulting figure is a right circular cone. Its volume, V, is given by $V = \frac{1}{3}\pi r^2 h$ where h is the altitude of the cone and r is the radius of the base. First, we express r and h in terms of the given angle, θ, and the given length, a.

In the figure, we see that when the altitude to the base of an isosceles triangle is drawn, a right triangle, $\triangle ARH$, is formed. Since we know one acute angle and the length of the hypotenuse, we can express the length of the other legs by applying several trigonometric ratios.

We can calculate the length of the leg opposite $\theta$, the altitude, with the help of the sine ratio. $\sin \theta = \dfrac{\text{opposite}}{\text{hypotenuse}}$. By substitution, $\sin \theta = \dfrac{h}{a}$.

Therefore, $h = a \sin \theta$.

The length of the leg adjacent angle $\theta$, the radius, can be found using the cosine ratio. $\cos \theta = \dfrac{\text{adjacent}}{\text{hypotenuse}}$. By substitution, $\cos \theta = \dfrac{r}{a}$. Therefore, $r = a \cos \theta$.

We have now expressed $r$ and $h$ in terms of $\theta$ and $a$. By substituting these expressions in the volume formula, $V = \frac{1}{3}\pi r^2 h$, we can find the volume in terms of $a$ and $\theta$.

$$V = \frac{1}{3}\pi r^2 h.$$

By substitution, $V = \frac{1}{3}\pi (a \cos \theta)^2 (a \sin \theta)$

$$= \frac{1}{3}\pi a^2 \cos^2 \theta \, a \sin \theta.$$

Therefore, $V = \frac{1}{3}\pi a^3 \cos^2 \theta \sin \theta$.

(b)  In this part we substitute $a = 5.2$ and $\theta = 27$  into the formula found in part (a) and proceed with the calculation. We use $\pi = 3.14$.

$$V = \frac{1}{3}(3.14)(5.2)^3 (\cos 27°)^2 (\sin 27°).$$

According to a standard table of trigonometric functions $\cos 27° = .8910$ and $\sin 27° = .4540$. Hence, by substitution,

$$V = \frac{1}{3}(3.14)(5.2)^3 (.8910)^2 (.4540)$$

$$V = 53.04.$$

Therefore, $V = 53$ to the nearest integer.

# INDEX

Numbers on this page refer to <u>PROBLEM NUMBERS</u>, not page numbers

A-A Similarity theorem, 6-2,
    6-8, 6-25, 7-12, 7-25, 7-28,
    7-31, 7-44, 11-49
Addition postulate, 3-17, 3-46,
    7-9, 7-37
Addition property of equality,
    1-6, 11-14
Altitude, 3-37, 5-13, 5-17,
    5-19, 6-8, 6-12, 6-13, 6-18
Angles, 2-3
    addition postulate, 1-6,
    7-35, 7-44, 8-21
    bisector, 6-10, 6-11, 6-13,
    7-30
    complementary, 5-11, 7-34
    congruent, 3-21
    corresponding, 3-7
    exterior, 3-14, 6-32, 6-35
    inscribed, 7-6, 7-33, 7-36
    interior, 3-10, 5-3, 5-14,
    6-33, 6-35
    polyhedral, 11-12
    reflexive property, 3-21
    right, 3-44, 5-6, 5-10 to
    5-12, 6-11, 7-34, 7-38,
    10-30
    sum theorem, 3-11
    supplementary, 2-4, 2-5,
    4-3, 5-3, 7-34, 7-36
    vertical, 2-5

Angle-angle-side postulate,
    5-4, 5-13
Angle-side-angle postulate,
    3-33 to 3-35, 8-13, 8-16
Angle-side postulate, 3-25
Arc length, 7-45
Arcs, 7-4
Area:
    by the pythagorean theorem,
    6-2, 8-23, 8-27, 10-28
    by the trigonometric func-
    tions, 8-32 to 8-34
    lateral, 11-40, 11-43, 11-46,
    11-47
    of a circle, 8-17 to 8-22
    of a cone, 11-48, 11-50
    of a cylinder, 11-42, 11-43
    of an equilateral triangle,
    8-6
    of an inscribed polygon,
    8-24 to 8-29
    of an isosceles triangle,
    8-11
    of a parallelogram, 8-12,
    9-12
    of a pentagon, 8-28, 8-30
    of a polygon, 10-21
    of a rectangle, 8-2, 8-3,
    9-12
    of similar triangles, 8-9,

322

HANDBOOK of
**MATHEMATICAL,
SCIENTIFIC, &
ENGINEERING**
FORMULAS, FUNCTIONS,
GRAPHS, TABLES,
& TRANSFORMS

**REA** RESEARCH & EDUCATION ASSOCIATION

A particularly useful reference for those in math, science, engineering and other technical fields. Includes the most-often used formulas, tables, transforms, functions, and graphs which are needed as tools in solving problems. The entire field of special functions is also covered. A large amount of scientific data which is often of interest to scientists and engineers has been included.

*Available at your local bookstore or order directly from us by sending in coupon below.*

**RESEARCH & EDUCATION ASSOCIATION**
61 Ethel Road W., Piscataway, New Jersey 08854
Phone: (732) 819-8880     website: www.rea.com

**VISA**     **MasterCard.**

Charge Card Number

☐ Payment enclosed
☐ Visa  ☐ MasterCard

| | | | | | | | | | | | | | | |
|--|--|--|--|--|--|--|--|--|--|--|--|--|--|--|

Expiration Date: _____ / _____
                    Mo          Yr

Please ship the **"Math Handbook"** @ $34.95 plus $4.00 for shipping.

Name _____

Address _____

City _____ State _____ Zip _____

# Super Review® Language Books

☑ **French**

☑ **Greek** (Classical/Ancient)

☑ **Italian**

☑ **Japanese**

☑ **Latin**

☑ **Russian**

☑ **Spanish**

- The material is presented in student-friendly form that makes it easy to follow and understand

- Individual topics can be easily located

- Provide excellent preparation for midterms, finals and in-between quizzes

---

**RESEARCH & EDUCATION ASSOCIATION**
61 Ethel Road W. • Piscataway, New Jersey 08854
Phone: (732) 819-8880     **website: www.rea.com**

**Please send me more information about your Super Review Languge Books**

Name _____

Address _____

City _____ State _____ Zip _____

## Research & Education Association

# MATH BUILDER:
## An Excellent Review
### *for* Standardized Tests

**Specifically designed to prepare you for all tests requiring math ability, including**

**SAT • ACT • GRE • GMAT
CBEST • CLEP • ELM • GED
PPST • PRAXIS • PSAT**

*Available at your local bookstore or order directly from us by sending in coupon below.*

**RESEARCH & EDUCATION ASSOCIATION**
61 Ethel Road W., Piscataway, New Jersey 08854
Phone: (732) 819-8880        **website: www.rea.com**

**VISA®**   **MasterCard**

☐ Payment enclosed
☐ Visa   ☐ MasterCard

Charge Card Number

| | | | | | | | | | | | | | | |
|--|--|--|--|--|--|--|--|--|--|--|--|--|--|--|

Expiration Date: _____ / _____
                          Mo              Yr

Please ship **REA's MATH BUILDER** @ $16.95 plus $4.00 for shipping.

Name _____

Address _____

City _____ State _____ Zip _____

**THE BEST TEST PREPARATION FOR THE**

# SAT* II:
# Subject Test

# MATH
# LEVEL IC

**6 Full-Length Practice Exams**

Based on official exam questions released by the College Board

**Detailed explanations to every exam question**

**Far more comprehensive than any other test preparation book**

Includes a **COMPREHENSIVE REVIEW COURSE** of Math covering all major topics found on the exam

**REA** *Research & Education Association*

* SAT is a registered trademark of the College Entrance Examination Board, which does not endorse this book.

---

*Available at your local bookstore or order directly from us by sending in coupon below.*

**RESEARCH & EDUCATION ASSOCIATION**
61 Ethel Road W., Piscataway, New Jersey 08854
Phone: (732) 819-8880        **website: www.rea.com**

**VISA**    **MasterCard**

Charge Card Number

☐ Payment enclosed
☐ Visa   ☐ MasterCard

Expiration Date: _____ / _____
                    Mo          Yr

Please ship REA's **"SAT II: Math Level IC"** @ $16.95 plus $4.00 for shipping.

Name _____

Address _____

City _____ State _____ Zip _____

*Available at your local bookstore or order directly from us by sending in coupon below.*

---

**RESEARCH & EDUCATION ASSOCIATION**
61 Ethel Road W., Piscataway, New Jersey 08854
Phone: (732) 819-8880          website: www.rea.com

*VISA®*   *MasterCard*

☐ Payment enclosed
☐ Visa   ☐ MasterCard

Charge Card Number

Expiration Date: _____ / _____
Mo          Yr

Please ship REA's **"SAT II: Math Level IIC"** @ $17.95 plus $4.00 for shipping.

Name _____

Address _____

City _____ State _____ Zip _____

# "The ESSENTIALS"
# of Math & Science

Each book in the ESSENTIALS series offers all essential information of the field it covers. It summarizes what every textbook in the particular field must include, and is designed to help students in preparing for exams and doing homework. The ESSENTIALS are excellent supplements to any class text.

The ESSENTIALS are complete and concise with quick access to needed information. They serve as a handy reference source at all times. The ESSENTIALS are prepared with REA's customary concern for high professional quality and student needs.

## Available in the following titles:

Advanced Calculus I & II
Algebra & Trigonometry I & II
Anatomy & Physiology
Anthropology
Astronomy
Automatic Control Systems /
　Robotics I & II
Biology I & II
Boolean Algebra
Calculus I, II, & III
Chemistry
Complex Variables I & II
Computer Science I & II
Data Structures I & II
Differential Equations I & II
Electric Circuits I & II
Electromagnetics I & II

Electronics I & II
Electronic Communications I & II
Fluid Mechanics /
　Dynamics I & II
Fourier Analysis
Geometry I & II
Group Theory I & II
Heat Transfer I & II
LaPlace Transforms
Linear Algebra
Math for Computer Applications
Math for Engineers I & II
Math Made Nice-n-Easy I to XII
Mechanics I, II, & III
Microbiology
Modern Algebra
Molecular Structures of Life

Numerical Analysis I & II
Organic Chemistry I & II
Physical Chemistry I & II
Physics I & II
Pre-Calculus
Probability
Psychology I & II
Real Variables
Set Theory
Sociology
Statistics I & II
Strength of Materials &
　Mechanics of Solids I & II
Thermodynamics I & II
Topology
Transport Phenomena I & II
Vector Analysis

*If you would like more information about any of these books,*
*complete the coupon below and return it to us or visit your local bookstore.*

---

**RESEARCH & EDUCATION ASSOCIATION**
61 Ethel Road W. • Piscataway, New Jersey 08854
Phone: (732) 819-8880　　**website: www.rea.com**

**Please send me more information about your Math & Science Essentials books**

Name _____

Address _____

City _____ State _____ Zip _____